Assessment of Individuals with Severe Disabilities

Assessment of Individuals with Severe Disabilities

An Applied Behavior Approach to Life Skills Assessment

Second Edition

by

Diane M. Browder, Ph.D.
Professor of Special Education
Lehigh University
Bethlehem, Pennsylvania

with invited contributors

Baltimore • London • Toronto • Sydney

Paul H. Brookes Publishing Co.
P.O. Box 10624
Baltimore, Maryland 21285-0624

Typeset by Brushwood Graphics, Inc., Baltimore, Maryland.
Manufactured in the United States of America by
The Maple Press Company, York, Pennsylvania.

Photographs courtesy of Kenneth Friedman and Barbara West.

Library of Congress Cataloging-in-Publication Data
Browder, Diane M.
    Assessment of individuals with severe disabilities : an applied
behavior approach to life skills assessment / by Diane M. Browder. —
2nd ed.
        p.   cm.
    Rev. ed. of: Assessment of individuals with severe handicaps.
    Includes bibliographical references (p.   ).
    Includes index.
    ISBN 1-55766-067-0
    1. Handicapped children—Education.   2. Educational evaluation.   3. Handicapped
children—Psychological testing.   4. Handicapped children—Life skills guides.
I. Browder, Diane M. Assessment of individuals with severe handicaps.   II. Title.
LC4015.B747   1991
371.9—dc20
                                                                        90-15052
                                                                        CIP

CONTENTS

ABOUT THE AUTHORS

DIANE M. BROWDER, PH.D., is Professor and Coordinator of Special Education in the Department of Counseling Psychology, School Psychology, and Special Education at Lehigh University, Bethlehem, Pennsylvania. She received her Ph.D. in special education from the University of Virginia in 1981. Her research and publications include work on sight word instruction, daily living skills, extended school year, problem behavior, staff development, data-based decisions, and assessment of individuals with severe disabilities. Diane is Executive Director of Lehigh Continuing Education for Adults with Severe Disabilities and a consultant to Centennial School for children with serious emotional disturbance. She has conducted numerous workshops for instructors from schools and adult agencies and been a consultant to schools developing integration programs. With Dr. Ed Shapiro and Christina Ager, she is conducting a 3-year study on the integration of Lehigh's Centennial School classrooms into area public schools. Recently, she consulted with Pennsylvania's Statewide Systems Change Project to encourage dissemination to teacher training programs.

CHRISTINA L. AGER, M.ED., is a doctoral student in special education at Lehigh University, Bethlehem, Pennsylvania. She is also an associate research scientist on a project investigating the effects of integrating students with serious emotional disturbances from a private school into a public school setting. Other areas of research include self-management, social skills, and preschool behavioral assessment.

LINDA M. BAMBARA, ED.D., is an Assistant Professor of Special Education and Director of the Lehigh Project on Developmental Disabilities, a university affiliated program that provides residential living support to adults with moderate to severe developmental disabilities, at Lehigh University, Bethlehem, Pennsylvania. She received her doctor of education degree in special education from George Peabody College for Teachers of Vanderbilt University in 1985. She is an active advocate for positive approaches to behavior management in her state and in the nation. Dr. Bambara's current research interests include independence training for home and community living, self-management, and choice-making skills development for adults.

PHILLIP J. BELFIORE, M.ED., is currently a research scientist completing his last year in the Ph.D. program at Lehigh University, Bethlehem, Pennsylvania. Mr. Belfiore is also the director of Project LCEASD (Lehigh Continuing Education for Adults with Severe Disabilities). He received his bachelor of science in education degree from Duquesne University in 1982, and his master of education degree from Kent State University in 1984. He has been published in such journals as *Research in Developmental Disabilities,* the *Journal of Applied Behavior Analysis,* and *Behavior Disorders.*

MARYANN DEMCHAK, PH.D., is an Assistant Professor of Special Education in the Department of Curriculum and Instruction at the University of Nevada, Reno. She has worked in public schools, group homes, and adult programs with individuals with severe disabilities. She has authored several articles related to prompt hierarchies and data-based instruction as well as training of professional and paraprofessional staff. Her current research focuses on effective integration programs for students with severe disabilities. MaryAnn received her doctor of philosophy degree in special education from The Pennsylvania State University in 1987.

BARBARA J. WEST, M.ED., earned her master of education in school psychology degree from Lehigh University, Bethlehem, Pennsylvania. She is currently a doctoral candidate at the same university. Ms. West has worked with both adults and children with severe disabilities in the areas of assessment and instruction. She now serves as a psychologist with the Pediatric Feeding Program at Children's Seashore House in Philadelphia. Her research interests include behavioral momentum, self-management, and skill acquisition.

FOREWORD

MEANINGFUL ASSESSMENT IS essential to good educational programs, a point not argued by many experts. Still, I think of assessment or testing as being an evil necessity: necessary for educators, but not instructional for learners. People who are being tested typically do not learn during test time, nor is testing enjoyed by many. But when assessment is used properly, its findings provide valuable guides for instructors, parents, and others who work with persons having disabilities. However, assessment findings are only valuable if they are accurate, if they are meaningful to the individual's current and future life, and if they are actually used.

When used *improperly,* assessment or testing results can do real damage or can simply waste valuable learning time. For example, inaccurate or nonrelevant assessment findings can misguide the selection of teaching goals, can lead to cessation of teaching prematurely or prolongation of instruction beyond what is needed, or can contribute to erroneous placement or program decisions.

While educational assessment encompasses many things, for the purposes of this text I limit the definition of assessment to the following: procedures used by teaching staff, related services personnel, and parents to obtain data relevant to planning or improving the educational program for a given individual. This definition excludes intelligence tests and other psychological assessments administered by school psychologists, but may include standardized, norm-referenced tests used by instructors to determine levels of general achievement, reading ability, math skills, vocational abilities, and so forth, as well as interviews to estimate a learner's adaptive behavior. Assessment also includes informal collection of performance data through direct observation of the learner under training or criterion conditions. Assessment, defined in this way, remains unchanged whether one is concerned with individuals who have identified disabilities or those who do not.

When the disability is such that an individual's curriculum needs to focus on the practical everyday skills involved in life, assessment procedures typically shift away from norm-referenced tests to informal tests involving observation and interview. Examples of assessment procedures that are pertinent to program planning and improvement for learners with more significant disabilities include:

1. *Ecological inventory*   Interviews and observations to assess current and future skills needed by a particular learner in the home, at school, in the community, during leisure, and at work
2. *Task analytic assessment*   Direct observations of a learner performing skills or tasks identified as being important for that person now and/or later in life (personal management, domestic, leisure time, community use, vocational)

3. *Direct observation of discrete behaviors* Measurement by counting or timing while directly observing learner's communication or social interaction with peers, the range and limits of their functional movement ability, use of academic skills, or their problem behavior and any functions it serves for them

4. *Assessment of learner's preferences and choices* Measurement through interview or direct observation of a learner and his or her friends and care providers to determine what activities, people, objects, or events the learner prefers or finds enjoyable

5. *Selecting teaching sites in the school and community* Identification of locations to teach targeted skills that are tolerant of instruction, are appropriate for the learner's needs and chronological age, match family and learner preferences, and are accessible

Ironically, the literature on data collection shows that most instructors fail to collect these and other types of learner performance data on targeted skills. Some instructors lack the ability to collect and use such data, while others are not convinced of the value of collecting these assessment data. Most teacher-training programs report that assessment methods are covered during college coursework, but it appears that few programs prepare instructors to:

Regularly collect meaningful, informal learner performance data relevant to targeted skills

Use those data to monitor progress and improve programs

Educators who have not been trained to collect or use learner performance data to evaluate progress rely on their subjective opinion of gains or losses in learner performance. While the opinions of experienced instructors are valuable, opinion is not a substitute for accurate data. Even those who know the mechanics of data collection may find that data-based instruction is quite tedious, that use of these procedures is not required (or admired) by their supervisors, or that they really do not know how to use the data that were so time-consuming to collect and organize.

No one ever said that operating a quality educational program was easy. For individuals with more significant disabilities, the definition of an "appropriate educational program" is no less complex than for other students, and may be more so. Good educational programs require the following:

1. Instructors must work with parents and learners to plan for each learner's future in an individualized, optimistic, and sensitive manner.

2. Functional and age-appropriate skills must be identified through ecological inventory.

3. A school and community-based instructional program suited to students' chronological ages and needs must be arranged and maintained to promote skill generalization and integration.

4. School programs must be restructured so that interactions with nondisabled peers occur naturally across the day and school years.

5. Systematic teaching methods must be applied so learning occurs.

6. Data-based decisions must be made to guarantee that learning results from teaching.

Meaningful assessment is a part of each of these steps, and thus influences every aspect of teaching.

This book provides the detailed guidance needed to design and use meaningful assessment procedures at each step of the way, from program planning to ongoing evaluation and improvement. Its relevance extends beyond school age, and addresses assessment methods useful in programs for adults with disabilities. Further, this second edition keeps current with the important themes of integration, personal futures planning, and choice. Diane Browder and her co-authors have written a valuable guide to assessment and data-based decision making for all instructors.

Martha E. Snell, Ph.D.
University of Virginia

PREFACE

THIS TEXT CONTINUES in the tradition of the first edition: to provide a resource for professionals who work with individuals with severe disabilities to develop educational programs based on a life skills assessment. The positive response to the first edition was a pleasant surprise. My work with teachers and other professionals led me to identify the need for a resource on assessment. I have been gratified to discover that this approach has such broad appeal. In response to the growing popularity of this approach, I felt obligated to update the book to include new information and critical omissions from the first edition.

The most critical information lacking in the first edition was a focus on integrated services. Since the original field testing of the assessment work in 1986, Lehigh University's field-based programs, like many services in the United States, have experienced increasing integration. Centennial School now provides some classes for students with autism and severe behavior disorders in area public schools, with integration increasing each year. Lehigh Continuing Education for Adults with Severe Disabilities has increasingly become a part of the community of Bethlehem, Pennsylvania. For example, participating adults take classes at the area YMCA or provide custodial services to agencies and churches.

Assessment must be guided not only by technical skills, such as construction of a task analysis, but also by a value system. The ideal of integration—full participation in services available to others of the same age group—will influence priorities for educational planning. Because I value integration, I highlighted this topic, along with generalization, in a chapter written with Chris Ager, and made revisions throughout the book to reflect this priority. In Chapter 6, for example, Phil Belfiore and I describe assessment for integrated leisure activities (e.g., for senior citizens) and for supported employment.

I also value procedures that respect the preferences and lifestyles of the individuals receiving services and that are usable in the settings and schedules of their daily lives. While the first edition provided information on assessment of preference and functional skills, this edition advances these ideas. New resources on personal futures planning (lifestyle planning) provide an invaluable framework for deciding first, and foremost, what a person values, before conducting assessment to select educational goals. I am especially grateful to Linda Bambara for introducing me to the concept of personal futures planning and working with me to develop applications for home assessment, as found in Chapter 5. Also, because of the influence of personal futures planning approaches, the case study descriptions in Appendix A now include abilities, as well as disabilities.

During consultations with instructors, I have struggled with the issue of making skills more usable and durable. The information on generalization assessment in Chapter 9 reflects some of the ideas from research we have found useful in this effort. However, the most substantial change toward this goal of increasingly functional assessment is the use in this edition of routine assessment. For the last 12 years, I have relied primarily on task analytic assessment of specific skills to track ongoing progress. Through this approach, it has been rewarding to observe many individuals learn a variety of functional skills. However, these task analytic assessments have often failed to determine whether the individual knows when and why to perform the skill. When I first read the routine assessment described by Richard Neel and Felix Billingsley (1989), I realized with excitement that they had defined what many have discussed—teaching the why and when for skill use. I have built upon their work to offer a detailed approach for routine assessment. In our model programs at Lehigh, routine assessment is rapidly replacing the old task analyses for ongoing assessment. However, some task analytic assessment is retained to monitor acquisition of specific, high-priority skills.

Chapter 8 continues to provide assessment strategies for a positive, educative approach to problem behavior. I have been disappointed by the division among professionals over the issue of managing problem behavior, but have found through working with the professionals at Centennial School that a positive approach is often more effective, as well as more humane. To develop this chapter, I worked with Barbara West, a psychologist with a behavior analytic perspective who accepted the positive focus of the chapter, but could share insights from a more radical behaviorist stance. She and I found through our work together at Centennial School and in writing Chapter 8 that we had similar priorities and could effect compromises with which we were both satisfied.

As did the first edition, this book provides examples from case studies of real individuals. While the information has sometimes been embellished or changed to make a point in the chapter, these examples are field tested, not "armchair" examples. Since it was not possible to update most of the first edition's case studies (most of these individuals and their instructors have moved), I simply retained the cases with no change in age. These case studies continue to offer examples of individuals challenged by severe behavior problems and autism, spastic quadriplegia, profound mental retardation, and deaf/blindness.

I added new case studies to illustrate approaches to assessment challenges not covered by the previous cases. Eva is actually a composite of two individuals and was chosen to illustrate assessment in a new, integrated school placement. She also enriches the examples by adding a new age level (middle school) and cultural diversity. Lester's case provides a senior citizen focus. Lester's large amount of leisure time and his physical changes related to aging raise different assessment issues than did Ann's case, a younger adult in the first edition. In Liz's case, I had the opportunity to coordinate and write the assessment report myself (in the others, I consulted with instructors). By working with a group of professionals, I was able to provide an illustration for a multidisciplinary team providing a joint comprehensive assessment. While each member of the team also wrote an individual report, the meetings to coordinate our efforts and the final, synthesized single report helped foster ongoing collaboration.

Finally, in this book, I have struggled with language to reflect my desire to be inclusive. The title change from "severe handicaps" to "severe disabilities" is more than semantics. A disability is not necessarily a handicap. Whether or not a person has a handicap depends on the extent to which society values the person's contribution and offers accommodation. Also, I was no longer satisfied with using the terms "teachers" and "students" when referring to other professionals and to adults with disabilities, respectively. "Instructor" and "educator" seemed to have more applicability across professionals. "Person with severe disabilities" and "learner" seemed more age inclusive.

ACKNOWLEDGMENTS

I AM GRATEFUL to those who supported the development and refinement of this edition. I especially appreciate Kenneth Friedman and Barbara West, for their donation of the photographs in this volume. Meredith Heller, supervisor of the Life Skills, has been my ongoing mentor on how to stay practical. I am thankful for her critique of the entire manuscript. Also helping me to refine the manuscript to keep it "user friendly" for practitioners were Tony Rogerson and Sue Gormley. Felix Billingsley provided an important review of my work on routine assessment and generalization. I appreciate Felix's moral support and flexibility in allowing his work to be used and revised. I also appreciate the insights I gained from the reviews of the first edition that were published in several journals.

I am especially grateful to the professionals who shared their work so graciously with me for the examples in this book. Ed Nientemp and Theresa Katzer provided the work for Eva and Lester. Retained from the first edition are the contributions by Tom Albright, Natalie Sadofsky, Debra Kopp, JoAnn Prekel, and Janet McGowen. I am especially grateful to Robert Richardson and the Hampton School District for Liz's case study, and to the professionals who participated on the assessment team: Renee Barnes, speech/language pathologist; Alice Enault, occupational therapist; Bertina Giles, special education teacher; Lisa Sawyer, physical therapist; and Susan Browder, parent. I believe one of the reasons these case studies are so rich with examples is because of the diversity of people who contributed them. I encourage others to consider the benefits of inclusiveness among professionals (e.g., cultural diversity, professionals with disabilities.)

Melissa Behm and the professionals at Paul H. Brookes Publishing Co. deserve special credit for working with me around a summer hiatus and sabbatical travel, and I offer special thanks to the copyeditor, Susan Hughes Gray. I also appreciate that Brookes Publishing Co. took the extra steps to increase the textbook usability of this edition. I look forward to the response to the new hardcover format and the study questions. Educators in the field may also appreciate this more durable edition since it is a resource for frequent reference.

Finally, I wish to acknowledge the contributors most important to this edition—the individuals with severe disabilities whose case studies are contained here, and the many others who have taught me so much about the enduring qualities of life. While I like to think of the skills I teach as "functional," the skills I learn from people with severe disabilities are probably far more functional for us all. I thank God to have had these opportunities to learn, and for people like Beth, Irmgart, and my friends from Centennial and LCEASD.

To my niece,
Marjorie Elizabeth Browder

chapter 1

OVERVIEW OF
EDUCATIONAL ASSESSMENT

IN THE 1980s, practitioners became increasingly adept at teaching people with severe disabilities within community settings. Many programs for people with severe disabilities extended beyond the classroom—to shopping malls, restaurants, factories, buses, and other public settings. For many people with disabilities, the 1980s was a decade of firsts—first jobs, first apartments, first classes in public schools. The priority for service delivery, including assessment services, was preparing people with severe disabilities for new community settings. Adults who had spent 40 years in institutions needed to adjust to the new culture of a community in much the same way an immigrant would need to adjust to a new country. Perhaps the most important assessment tool of this decade was the *ecological inventory*. The ecological inventory enabled professionals to help people with disabilities adjust to the myriad of new experiences in new settings. Similarly, "going public" with programming (i.e., out of segregated facilities) meant that a lot of the "accessories" (e.g., clipboards, stopwatches) and technologies of behavioral assessment needed to be modified if goals of normalization were to be achieved.

As we enter the 1990s, learning to maintain a home, hold a job, and use public facilities are still key components of curricula for people with severe disabilities. Professionals still need to conduct ecological inventories to help people with disabilities adjust to new settings. In addition, a decade of experience has suggested two other areas on which professionals need to focus. First, professionals are becoming increasingly aware that "temporal" integration—that is, simply being with people who do not have disabilities—is not always adequate for achieving social integration. While holding a job, having an apartment, attending a public school, and using public facilities increase contact with people without disabilities, they do not ensure that friendships will be formed, opportunities will be fully realized, or learning from role models without disabilities will occur. Once true integration has taken place, assessment needs to be done to identify the skills that will help persons with severe disabilities reap the benefits of being in the mainstream.

A second lesson that emerged from a decade of work in community settings is the importance of respecting the right of people with disabilities to control their own lives. People with severe disabilities first taught us how much they can learn when given meaningful opportunities and systematic instruction. Now people with severe disabilities are showing that they can and should make choices and control their own lives. This increasing respect for autonomy changes the focus of assessment. For example, in the 1980s, "partial participation" meant selecting a response for an activity of daily living based on an ecological inventory of the responses of people without disabilities. However, partial participation does not necessarily make an activity meaningful or functional. By contrast, if a response enables a person to influence an activity (e.g., by making a choice, by setting the pace), it may be meaningful. Similarly, the perception of "functional activities" is becoming increasingly rigorous. Responses that are required for daily living are not necessarily functional if performed out of context and if they fail to achieve the point of the activity (or critical effect). Consideration of context and effect has led to conceptualization of "routines" of daily living that combine categories of skills that traditionally had been separated (e.g., communication, motor, domestic) to achieve a particular effect (e.g., getting from the bus to a classroom). Thus, the definition of "functional" is shifting from activities embraced by an identified norm group to what is meaningful for the individual.

GOALS OF EDUCATIONAL ASSESSMENT

Assessment, in general, is the process of gathering information in order to make a decision. Special education teachers, support staff, job specialists, and other professionals must gather information on the learner's needs in order to decide what to teach. These professionals also need information to decide when to change instructional strategies to improve student performance. If the view is taken that all people can learn and that learning is facilitated by good teaching, then instructors should be especially concerned when the learner is not acquiring target skills.

Educational assessment usually falls within the purview of a teacher or a specialist with a background in teaching. Information gathered by the teacher or other professional is then shared with other members of an assessment team, such as the school psychologist, physical therapist, and speech-language pathologist, who also make recommendations on the type and content of educational services. (This book focuses on the contributions of teachers and other direct service professionals [e.g., support staff, job specialists] to this interdisciplinary effort. While most of the book concerns the professionals' efforts per se, Chapter 5 suggests ways parents and supported living staff can collaborate with professionals in this process. Chapter 7 addresses the importance of teachers and other professionals coordinating assessment with therapists and other specialists, and Chapter 10 provides guidelines for supervisors to encourage teachers' success.)

The general goals of educational assessment for people with severe disabilities may be clarified by considering the following questions:

1. What is the purpose of educational assessment?
2. What type of educational assessment will best identify individual learner needs?
3. What approaches have been taken to educational assessment of people with severe disabilities?
4. What criteria should be used to evaluate whether or not specific assessment procedures are appropriate and adequate?
5. How can learners' human rights be protected during the assessment process?

PURPOSES OF EDUCATIONAL ASSESSMENT

Educational assessment is conducted to screen individuals to identify those in need of special services, to determine eligibility for services, to identify specific skills to be taught, to evaluate individual progress, and to evaluate a program.

Identifying the Cause of Learning Problems

Sometimes educators follow a medical model by conducting assessment to "diagnose" the cause of learning problems. In the medical model, symptoms are attributed to some underlying cause (e.g., a rash is diagnosed as chicken pox and treatment follows the prescribed course). When educators have attempted to identify the underlying cause for learning problems, they have sometimes lost sight of identifying the specific skills to be taught. In the late 1960s and early 1970s, educators began focusing on the cognitive processes that were believed to be responsible for learners' difficulties. Assessment tools such as the Illinois Test of Psycholinguistic Abilities (ITPA) (Kirk, McCarthy, & Kirk, 1968) were designed to identify these processes. Unfortunately, as instructors focused on these processes, they sometimes neglected instruction. By the mid-1970s, critics began questioning the validity of tests such as the ITPA, and began promoting a return to direct academic assessment and instruction (Hammill & Larsen, 1974). The critics noted that individuals need to be taught directly the skills they need to learn. Generalization from "process training" to improving reading skills, for example, could not be assumed.

A parallel example can be found in the developmental approach to education for people with severe disabilities. The developmental approach, which was prevalent in the early 1970s, used infant psychology to design assessment and instruction for people with severe disabilities, regardless of their age. The theory behind this approach was that people with severe disabilities could be educated at a level appropriate to their mental age (MA) by following the sequence of normal child development. To remediate the cause of learning problems, the developmental approach also focused on cognitive remediation.

Piaget's theory of cognitive development was used to design assessment and instruction. For example, Dunst (1980) adapted Uzgiris and Hunt's (1978) assessment for infants for use with learners of all ages with severe disabilities. Application of the Piagetian stages of sensorimotor development to older people with severe disabilities met with mixed results (Kahn, 1978). In the late 1970s, critics began to appeal to educators to teach people with severe disabilities the life skills they need using real, age-appropriate activities and environments (L. Brown, Nietupski, & Hamre-Nietupski, 1976).

While the goal of remediating underlying cognitive deficits can derail the educator from the critical task of teaching, assessment to identify the cause of symptoms is critical in medical evaluations of people with severe disabilities. For example, poor educational progress or maladaptive behaviors may be due to ear infections, unrecognized seizures, or allergies. Parents often want to know the etiology of the individual's disability when the diagnosis is first made. However, issues related to etiology are best handled by the physician, not the educator.

Screening and Selecting Services

A second purpose of educational assessment is to determine eligibility for specific services. Screening may be conducted to determine if assessment for eligibility should be performed. Assessment is then conducted, where indicated, to determine if a learner meets the eligibility criteria for a given service. People with severe disabilities often have skill deficiencies that make the need for special services obvious. Assessment is conducted to match a learner with the appropriate services. Screening, which is often a broad assessment of skills to see if learners meet age expectations, may help determine whether referral for evaluation for related services (e.g., speech therapy, physical therapy, occupational therapy) is warranted. The instructor's role in screening and eligibility assessment is to collect information on the individual's skill needs (i.e., the need for life skills versus academic skills). Sometimes a vocational or supported living program may have specific entry skill requirements. Such requirements, when appropriate to the demands of the setting, focus the instructor's initial assessments. When a learner fails to meet the requirements of a particular program, the instructor should identify an alternative service that better matches the individual's current skills.

Meeting State Program Requirements State definitions of a disability often must be met before a service can be received. Geiger and Justen (1983) reviewed state definitions for public school services and found that 35 states had definitions pertaining to people with severe disabilities. Of these 35 states, 19 had *categorical* definitions, and 16 had *generic* definitions. Categorical definitions refer explicitly to a particular disability (e.g., autism, severe mental retardation). Generic definitions refer to commonalities of educational need for a diverse population. Some states define IQ ranges or psychiatric classifications that must be met to qualify for services. Because it is difficult to test people with severe disabilities, such data are often difficult to obtain. Another problem with categorical definitions is that they often focus only on individuals with severe and profound mental retardation, often leaving out other individuals with similar curriculum needs (e.g., severe multiple disabilities, autism).

Working with Psychologists Psychologists may turn to educators for advice on evaluating learners with severe and multiple disabilities. Because the psychologist's evaluation often has considerable influence in determining placement, the instructor should consider potential solutions to the problems that complicate this evaluation. First, the instructor can point out the limitations of intelligence testing for this population. Then, he or she may offer ideas for curriculum-based assessment.

When confronted with the challenge of giving a traditional IQ test to blind learners or those with epilepsy or severe physical or mental disabilities, psychologists may conclude that the learner is "untestable." In fact, making evaluations based on tests individuals cannot complete because of such differences is discriminatory (Duncan, Sbardellati, Maheady, & Sainato, 1981).

The testing situation is also complicated by the limitations of the tests. Many IQ tests have too few items to establish a basal level for learners with limited skills. Although infant developmental assessments are sometimes used, these tests and checklists fail to provide opportunities for such individuals to demonstrate skills appropriate to their chronological ages, instead determining a stigmatizing assessment of mental age. Psychologists often use these tests in order to obtain a normative score with which to justify the extra expenditure of more intensive special services. Perhaps because of the pressure to meet criteria for services, inappropriate testing for people with severe disabilities continues to be widespread (Sigafoos, Cole, & McQuarter, 1987).

Once these limitations of IQ testing are clear, the instructor can offer assistance to plan an alternative such as curriculum-based assessment. Many psychologists have begun using curriculum-based assessments to make placement decisions and to help educators solve instructional problems (Shapiro & Lentz, 1986). That is, psychologists assess learners to determine their placement in school curricula by using criterion-referenced testing matched to the curriculum. This practice need only be extended to the curriculum appropriate for learners with severe disabilities. Some of the newer *adaptive behavior scales* include many items that are relevant to life skills curriculum planning. Adaptive behavior scales are assessment instruments that are used to evaluate a learner's overall skills in meeting the demands of daily living. Because adaptive behavior scales focus on daily living, they provide more relevant information than IQ tests for educational planning. Some of these scales also provide normative scores that may help support recommended placements (see Chapter 2). These adaptive behavior scales are usually completed by interviewing the instructor or parent. Some of the adaptive behavior scales (e.g., Cone, 1984) provide data on the correlation between such reports and direct observations derived from field testing. If time permits, psychologists may make some classroom, workshop, or home observations to verify some of the verbal reports for the individuals evaluated. (Guidelines for such observations are given in Chapter 2.) These observations may be preferable to a test in a novel environment because they provide evidence of how learners typically behave in familiar surroundings; further, they minimize the need for psychologists to learn to manage the complicated medical and behavioral problems that testing requires.

Selecting Skills and Evaluating Progress

The two most critical decisions instructors and other professionals must make are what skills to teach and when to change instruction to improve performance. Skill selection requires assessing not only the learner, but also his or her environment to determine which skills are most critical for functioning. Since many skills may be identified, educators need a system by which skills for instruction can be prioritized. Chapter 2 provides a detailed look at this skill selection and prioritization process. Instructors also need to decide if instruction is effective, and if not, how to change it. Chapters 3 and 4 provide guidelines for the ongoing assessment of progress and the evaluation of progress to make instructional decisions.

Evaluating Program Quality

The final purpose for assessment to be considered here is evaluation of program quality. Often, decisions regarding progress, or even educability (i.e., ability to learn), are made without giving consideration to the quantity and quality of services received. Older people with severe disabilities may have spent years in institutions that provided them with limited education or other opportunities to learn about their communities. Such individuals may need time to "learn to learn" in new community-based programs. Slow progress can be due to poor teaching, lack of time invested in teaching (e.g., due to numerous daily interruptions), or poor management of interfering behaviors. Thus, evaluation of service quality is related to assessment of learner progress. Guidelines for program evaluation are provided in Chapter 10.

Planning Assessment Appropriate to Purpose

Instructors must plan assessment that will provide information relevant to the educational decision to be made. For eligibility considerations, instructors often must compare a learner's overall skill performance with the expectations associated with his or her chronological age. For skill selection, more information is needed on each learner's overall skill performance. Information is also needed on environmental demands. If educators want to evaluate progress to make instructional decisions that will improve learner performance, assessment must be matched to specific objectives. Instructors also need guidelines for determining whether or not learners are progressing toward mastery of the objective. Further, supervisors need guidelines for the assessment and evaluation of educators.

UNDERLYING PRINCIPLES OF ASSESSMENT

The principles that may best guide assessment are those of *applied behavior analysis* and *normalization*. Applied behavior analysis focuses on a person's measurable, observable responses. Target responses are encouraged or discouraged through arrangement of stimuli in the learner's environment that occur immediately before the response (antecedents) and after the response (consequences). The methodology of applied behavior analysis has been described in detail in several resources (e.g., Bijou & Baer, 1961; Repp, 1983; Sulzer-Azaroff & Mayer, 1977). Normalization focuses on making opportunities that are available to people without disabilities available to people with disabilities. In his book on normalization, Wolfensberger (1972) described the attitudes of professionals who work with people with disabilities and of society in general that block this equality of opportunity (e.g., the "mental age" approach to service delivery).

The theories of applied behavior analysis and normalization have directly and indirectly influenced recent theory and practice (e.g., Falvey, 1989; Gaylord-Ross & Holvoet, 1985; Neel & Billingsley, 1989; Sailor & Guess, 1983; Snell, 1987; Wilcox & Bellamy, 1987a, 1987b). To understand how these approaches have emerged, it is helpful to review briefly the history of individualized instruction for people with disabilities.

History of Individualization in Education

Assessment has relevance when the educational system is designed to be responsive to individual learners. To be responsive, tools are needed to determine the entry level and progress of each learner. Sometimes instruction is designed to meet the needs of the majority of the learners in a given classroom, with some accommodation made for "slow" or "fast" groups. The first phase in the evolution of educational systems toward greater responsiveness to individual needs was the practice of individualization by homogeneous grouping. White (1981) described how the educational system was modified for such groupings:

> If a child was blind, he needed "mobility" training. If a child were deaf, certain adaptations were required in the communication curricula. If a child were crippled, various occupational therapy or physical therapy approaches would be advised. If a child were mentally retarded, the curriculum would be watered down, a ceiling on expected development would be imposed, and basic skills would be drilled in endless repetition. Each approach was, in retrospect, still likely to be somewhat inflexible, but at least it represented some attempt to meet the special needs of the pupil. It was a start. (p. 1)

The practice of making educational accommodations based on stereotypes and homogeneous groupings is, unfortunately, still apparent in some programs.

For example, some school systems place all students with severe disabilities in separate schools or in one wing of a school. All students may receive instruction in the use of infantile and preschool materials regardless of their chronological age. In extreme cases, such programming might include little or no assessment.

The diagnostic/prescriptive approach emerged in the 1960s and represented a further refinement of assessment to identify and meet the needs of individual learners. In this approach, instructors or "diagnosticians" assessed individuals using a battery of tests. For individuals with academic skills, these tests often included diagnostic assessments of reading, math, and language skills. This information was used by educators to design an individualized plan. Problems of inflexibility and overlooking individual needs also emerged with this model. Educators often made this assessment a comprehensive, but episodic, event. That is, once the individualized plan was written, instruction continued without systematic review of learner progress and adaptations based on this review. If such a review were scheduled, it often occurred only a few times per year, allowing learners to waste months in ineffective instructional lessons. Further, assessment was not always matched to objectives. For example, an adaptive behavior scale might be used to assess progress, but the scale items would be too global to correspond directly to the learner's objectives. Another problem that emerged was the attempt to diagnose the cause of the learning problem (i.e., the medical model discussed earlier). Diagnostic/prescriptive teaching at its best used *criterion-referenced testing* that was matched directly to learner objectives. Criterion-referenced testing compares learner performance to preset criteria (e.g., criteria for mastery of an instructional objective). The items used on such tests are the same as or similar to those used in instruction. Even when criterion-referenced testing was used, the episodic nature of assessment often rendered it inefficient for making decisions about learner progress.

The influence of the diagnostic/prescriptive era is still strong in special education, with current emphasis given to academic remediation. This influence has had positive and negative effects on services for people with severe disabilities. Following the "mental age" logic, tests have been developed to determine an individual's developmental level. Instruction is then designed to match this level. Applications of the diagnostic/prescriptive approach are not limited to the developmental model. Some instructors who focus on chronological age–appropriate skills conduct assessment only episodically. The value of this episodic assessment is further weakened if the assessment does not correspond directly to learners' specific objectives (e.g., repeated use of adaptive behavior scales).

A third approach to meeting individual learner needs emerged in the 1960s and 1970s, as Lindsley (1964) began suggesting ways educators could use applied behavior analysis to improve teaching. Lindsley's work became the basis for the *precision teaching model* (White & Haring, 1980), which is discussed further later in this chapter. In the precision teaching approach, criterion-referenced testing is used to assess progress on defined objectives. Assessment is direct (i.e., the instructor tests or observes the learner and counts responses) and frequent (e.g., daily). Through systematic review of these data, educators make ongoing instructional changes to improve learner progress.

The precision teaching approach is still evident in special education in programs for people with mild or severe disabilities. The advantages of this approach are that it relates assessment directly to instructional objectives, and it provides guidelines for using data to make decisions about learner progress. The disadvantage is that the model itself does not specify how skills should be selected—unfortunately, some educators use precise, ongoing assessment and charting of objectives related to skills that are neither age-appropriate nor relevant to a learner's environments. To remedy this, the precision teaching approach can be used, for example, after selecting skills from a developmental assessment.

Current Trends in Individualization

Current trends in assessment for the purpose of individualizing instruction follow Lindsley's (1964) direction of frequent, direct assessment matched to specific objectives. Textbooks on educating people with severe disabilities have described ways to design a criterion-referenced assessment and suggest frequent schedules for data collection and review (e.g., Sailor & Guess, 1983; Snell, 1987). In special education in general, researchers have been encouraging educators to use this curriculum-based assessment for both eligibility decisions and evaluation of student progress (Blankenship, 1985; Deno, 1985; Tucker, 1985). Because ongoing assessment arose in the applied behavior analysis tradition, some researchers have encouraged educators to use single-subject designs to evaluate data. Voeltz and Evans (1983) noted that such designs have limitations that make them particularly unsuitable for instructional decision making (e.g., prolonged baselines or replications of baseline). N. Haring, Liberty, and White (1980, 1981) suggested an alternative approach that uses empirically derived rules to make instructional decisions based on trend. They offered an assessment approach based on applied behavior analysis in which criterion-referenced assessment is designed to assess specific objectives, and learner progress is evaluated based on empirically derived guidelines for data review.

Two other trends are also important. First, in response to the "bottom up" approach of developmental models, in which learners are limited to the sequence of skills of normal infant and child development, L. Brown, Branston, et al. (1979) advocated a "top down" approach to skill selection, in which skills are matched to learners' chronological age–peers. L. Brown, Branston-McLean, et al. (1979) provided guidelines for developing this curriculum based on ecological inventories, which are assessments of the activities and skills required in given environments (see later section in this chapter and Chapter 2).

Thus, L. Brown and colleagues (L. Brown, Branston, et al., 1979; L. Brown, Branston-McLean, et al., 1979) provided an important new component to assessment for people with severe disabilities: assessment of the environment as well as of the individual. An analogy of this approach was evident in applied behavior analysis in the 1970s, when behavior analysts began to discuss the need to obtain social validation of behaviors selected for treatment (Kazdin, 1977; Wolf, 1978).

Second, L. Brown and colleagues (L. Brown, Branston, et al., 1979; L. Brown, Branston-McLean, et al., 1979) advocated that no one be excluded from curriculum planning based on selecting skills that will be useful in community environments and are appropriate to a learner's chronological age. They suggested that educators select skills for "partial participation" in community-referenced activities if learners could not master independent performance. F. Brown, Evans, Weed, and Owen (1987) further developed the idea of partial participation by describing the importance of "meaningful participation." Responses that increase the person's choice or control of the activity, for example, may result in more meaningful participation than those that do not.

The influence of these various trends has led to differing approaches to assessment and program planning based on applications of the principles of applied behavior analysis and normalization. The pros and cons of these various approaches are examined in the following section, and serve as an introduction to the approach taken in this text.

APPROACHES TO BEHAVIORAL ASSESSMENT OF LIFE SKILLS

In the 1980s, when services for people with severe disabilities expanded rapidly, several service models emerged that provide data-based instruction of life skills. These models differ in: 1) the way in which skills are chosen, 2) the selection of discrete versus chained target behaviors, 3) the assessment of massed versus interspersed opportunities to respond, 4) the inclusion of noninstructional tests or observations, 5) the use of time-based data, 6) methods of data display, and 7) procedures for systematic data review. Each of these models has its strengths and weaknesses. By becoming more familiar with each, educators may learn new methods for assessment that can complement current practice.

Applied Behavioral Psychology

The fields of special education and applied behavioral psychology have both contributed in providing service and research for people with severe disabilities. Often, professionals in these fields have collaborated to develop service models. One approach, which is more closely aligned with applied behavioral psychology than with special education, views the selection of skills as the identification of target behaviors. One of the strengths of this model is that these behaviors are carefully defined to be observable and measurable. Often, emphasis is placed on defining interfering behaviors. Because of the way a single behavior is selected and defined, assessment is often focused on discrete behaviors rather than chains of behavior. Time sampling is then employed to record accurately the occurrence of one or more behaviors. Data are typically displayed in a grid graph typical of behavioral journals. Data evaluation is based on the use of single-subject research designs that replicate treatment results across behaviors, settings, or individuals. The application of this behavioral assessment model has been described by Powers and Handleman (1984). The strengths of this model are its exemplary definitions of target behaviors and its precise data collection methods. Its disadvantages are that skill selection does not always take into consideration individuals' priority life skill needs and that task analytic assessment is deemphasized. The data collection and evaluation methods are also difficult to implement. Such designs also do not provide the best empirical orientation for instructors, who must judge the effectiveness of instruction and make changes on an ongoing basis (Voeltz & Evans, 1983).

Task Analytic Model

A second model to consider can be called a *task analytic* model, because of its strong reliance on the use of task analyses for assessment and instruction. This model also grew out of applied behavioral psychology and was exemplified in research that focused on daily living skills (e.g., Cuvo, Leaf, & Borakove, 1978; Tucker & Berry, 1980). While the choice of skill in this model may be subjective, the task analysis developed for instruction may be carefully validated throughout observations of peers without disabilities and consultation with experts (Cuvo, 1978). Thus, the defined target behaviors are typically chains of behavior with some demonstrated validity for these chains. Assessment usually involves setting up the task and observing learners performing it. Often there are "test" observations that are distinct from teaching observations in that no prompts or reinforcements are given. These test observations are then graphed using a grid graph (e.g., the graph may display number of steps performed independently on the task analytic assessment). The observation is typically not timed. Evaluation of the data is based on review of the graph after a period of teaching. Single-subject designs may be used to provide further evidence of effectiveness. Snell and Grigg (1987) and Wehman, Renzaglia, and Bates (1985) described task analytic assessment in detail. These authors also presented a blending of this approach with other applied behavioral analysis procedures (e.g., time sampling) and with ecological inventories, described in the next section.

The advantages of task analytic assessment are that it can be implemented by classroom teachers for a wide variety of skills, it typically focuses on life skills, and it provides a method to measure performance of a chain of behaviors. A disadvantage is that the different "steps" or behaviors in the chain may have quite different topographies and levels of difficulty. Collapsing such divergent skills into a graph of the "number of steps correct" sometimes masks the source of learning difficulties (e.g., a learner has difficulty with steps that require small finger movements). Sailor and Guess (1983) noted that individuals with severe disabilities may need to learn one step of the chain at a time. When such serial chaining is used, a graph of "number of steps correct" will show minimal progress. Task analytic assessment as traditionally used also provides no time-based measure. Often, instruction is terminated when all or most steps are performed correctly. However, a chain of behaviors, such as pulling up one's pants, which is performed extremely slowly, may have limited functional utility. Criteria are needed for the duration of responding as well as for accuracy. Finally, as the chain of behaviors in a task analysis is arbitrarily defined by whatever is conceptualized as a task, this chain may not produce a critical effect for the learner or enhance a daily routine. Without the chain's being part of a daily routine and leading to a critical effect, maintenance and motivation may be ongoing problems.

Ecological Inventories

Ecological inventories are assessments of the activities performed in and skills required by a given environment. For example, an ecological inventory of a restaurant may reveal that skills needed to use this facility are ordering from a menu, paying for an order, conversing with companions, and so on. They have had a major influence on assessment of individuals with severe disabilities, and are important as well in the guidelines they provide for skill selection. L. Brown, Branston-McLean, et al. (1979) first used "ecological inventory" to describe an approach in which the characteristics of learners' current and future least restrictive environments are identified to determine the skills needed to achieve community integration. The life domains of community, recreation, vocational, and domestic skills provide a framework for this planning. For example, in considering domestic needs, an instructor observes or interviews caregivers in a person's current home and potential next home (e.g., supported living). By considering each subenvironment in these settings (e.g., kitchen, bathroom, bedroom), the instructor generates a list of activities and skills. The advantage of this approach is that it helps professionals generate or adapt curricula that meet each learner's needs. The disadvantage is that it can lead to an unmanageable list of skill needs. Setting priorities can be the most difficult part of the process. With this approach, some related skills that are useful across domains (e.g., language, motor) may be omitted from the skill selection process. Obviously, this approach is relevant only to skill selection; other procedures would be needed to assess performance of selected skills.

Massed Trial Assessment

Another approach that grew out of the behavior analysis tradition, the *massed trial assessment,* involves the presentation of repeated opportunities to respond in a test or teaching session. In this model, a discrete skill is chosen (e.g., a manual sign). Instructors usually provide a verbal cue (e.g., "What is this?").

Learners' responses are scored and the instructor immediately presents the next trial (e.g., a new item is presented and the learner is asked "What is this?"). These data are usually graphed on a grid. Evaluation is similar to that used in the task analytic model. This assessment model was traditionally used in research in language (e.g., Browder, Morris, & Snell, 1981; Striefel, Wetherby, & Karlan, 1976). The advantage of this model is that it provides multiple opportunities for the learner to respond correctly. The disadvantage is that these responses may not generalize from the massed trial format to natural opportunities for their use. This model also has limited value for evaluation and skill selection.

Precision Teaching Model

The *precision teaching* model is an improvement over the massed trial assessment format. In this model, learners are given the opportunity to perform a response repetitively or to perform a chain of responses without being interrupted by the instructor, while the instructor counts correct responses and errors and times responding. Correct responses and errors per minute are then plotted using a standard 2½ cycle semilogarithmic graph. N. Haring, Liberty, and White (1979) described how this data collection system can be used with people with severe disabilities, and also provided empirically derived rules for reviewing the data obtained to make instructional decisions. This model offers the most systematic data evaluation procedures, and thus makes optimal use of the data obtained. The use of standard graphs simplifies the data evaluation process. The consideration of time-based data can reveal subtle improvements when learners become more proficient at a task. The disadvantage of this approach is that it is difficult to use with varied response chains such as those typical of task analytic assessment or the individualized curriculum sequencing (ICS) model, described next. The semilogarithmic graph and collection of time-based data also make the system difficult to implement for instructors who have not been trained in this model.

Individualized Curriculum Sequencing Model

One approach that provides repeated opportunities to respond, but builds in generalization, is the individualized curriculum sequencing (ICS) model. This model, developed by Guess and colleagues (Guess et al., 1978; Holvoet, Guess, Mulligan, & Brown, 1980), provides a series of trials in which one response logically sets the occasion for the next. Skill clusters are developed from traditional areas such as language, motor, self-care, and socialization skills. In instruction, learners are given the opportunity to make a chain of responses. However, this chain is usually different from those in task analyses, which typically present only one skill domain. Instead, learners might communicate the need for an item, use the item, and pass the item to a peer (i.e., language, self-care, socialization). Opportunities to use this chain (e.g., communicate, use, pass) are then presented across people, materials, and tasks through-out the day. Data are recorded and graphed in a manner similar to the task ana-lytic graph. However, instructors can also note the percentage correct for each type of response (e.g., communication of "I want _____"). This model typ-ically does not provide test observations, but rather bases data evaluation on the data collected during teaching. Data evaluation is similar to that described for task analytic assessment, but has the added advantage that individual responses can be monitored more easily. The advantages of the ICS model are that ac-quisition and generalization of skills are assessed concurrently. This model also provides an excellent method for assessing language and motor skills in the context of varied response chains that are typical of daily living. The disadvan-tage of this model is that the response chains selected may not be comprehen-sive enough to teach learners to perform activities independently.

Routines and Critical Effect

Similar to the ICS model, assessment of routines incorporates responses across traditional areas such as communication, motor, and domestic skills for assess-ment purposes (Neel & Billingsley, 1989). In this way, routines are a type of individualized curriculum sequencing. However, when attention is focused on assessing and teaching a routine to achieve a critical effect for an activity, a chain of responding is often generated. Thus, a routine may be viewed as a type of task analysis. However, unlike the task analysis, the chain of responding is not specific to one skill (e.g., opening a door), but rather includes multiple skills across an activity (e.g., getting from the bus to the classroom) to achieve a defined critical effect (e.g., arrival in class). Also, unlike the specific skill task analysis, which usually defines that single responses be counted as correct or assisted, the routine task analytic assessment may have varying methods of measurement within it. For example, the routine of walking to the classroom may include noting the occurrence of a greeting response, recording the dura-tion of walking time, and recording skills that could be further task analyzed (e.g., removing coat). What determines the final response of this chain of re-sponding is the defined effect for which the routine is written (e.g., getting food, arrival at a destination). This approach to assessment can be especially beneficial for incorporating language skills within a functional context.

Curriculum-Based Assessment

In special education and related fields, attention has focused on the benefits of curriculum-based assessment (Tucker, 1985). An individual's curriculum can be used for identification and placement, for development of an individualized plan, or for ongoing assessment of progress. The field of severe disabilities has traditionally been strong in ongoing curriculum-based assessment. Data collec-tion to make ongoing decisions about progress was a component of early tests in the field (e.g., Snell, 1978) and has been refined in the last decade (see Chapter 4). Curriculum-based assessment for planning an individualized education program (IEP) or individualized habilitation plan (IHP) has been less well focused. Because written curricula in programs for people with severe disabilities were historically an adaptation of early childhood curricula and lacked a functional community focus, many professionals abandoned the use of published curricula. For an interim, the ecological inventory was the primary method of generating a curriculum. Classwide or programwide curricula were often viewed as nonfunctional because they were not individualized. Clearly, the task of conducting ecological inventories of every relevant setting for every person every time a plan is developed is arduous and inefficient. What educators have been trying to do is both to write a curriculum and to assess a learner every time an IEP/IHP is due.

In the 1980s, four approaches emerged with regard to this issue of curriculum-based assessment for IEP/IHP planning. One approach is to continue to rely on ecological inventories, but to give instructors more guidance for this process. The first edition of this book (Browder, 1987) followed this tactic and gave examples for writing individual curricula to use across years of IEP/IHP development. Similarly, the IMPACT curriculum (Neel & Billingsley, 1989) was developed as a handbook for this process of skill selection. While these resources guide educators through the process of skill selection, they offer no curricula. A second approach is to make the ecological inventory process more efficient by developing "catalogs" of activities based on these inventories to use in skill selection (Wilcox & Bellamy, 1987a, 1987b). This second approach comes closer to offering instructors a written curriculum from which to work. A third approach, adopted by many school districts with state mandates for curriculum guides, is to translate L. Brown, Branston, et al. and L. Brown, Branston-McLean, et al.'s (1979) "top down" curriculum domains into curriculum guides that list skills for the domestic, recreation, vocational, and community domains (e.g., Philadelphia School District Urban Training Model Curriculum). This approach is appealing to instructors because it offers specific skills to consider—but it also has the potential disadvantage of not being relevant to an individual learner's current and future environments if not supplemented with ecological inventories. A fourth approach offers an innovation to curriculum by providing both skill sequences and methods for individualized skill selection. The Syracuse curriculum (Ford et al., 1989b) is developed to be incorporated into the curriculum of a regular school, and includes scope and sequence charts for academic, as well as daily living skills, planning. This curriculum resource also guides the instructor through the process of selecting goals for instruction considering the individual needs of a learner. Through all of these approaches, curriculum-based assessment for skill selection is emerging as a new strength of programs for people with severe disabilities.

Generalization

Some assessment models address the specific issue of generalization. Horner and colleagues (e.g., Horner, Sprague, & Wilcox, 1982) have demonstrated a method known as *general case instruction*, which identifies the specific stimulus and response variation required for a defined generalization goal. For example, to be able to go into any convenience store and purchase a soda requires discriminating critical features within the wide variation of stores in a community and using differing responses as necessitated by this variation (e.g., opening a pull door or using an automatic door). This methodology frequently builds on task analytic assessment by analyzing the discriminative stimuli and responses for each step of the task analysis across a set of generalization environments and/or materials.

A second model of generalization assessment to emerge is a decision-making process developed by Liberty and Billingsley (1988) and evaluated by Liberty, Haring, White, and Billingsley (1988). When generalization deficits occur, instructors can conduct direct observations of attempts to generalize and then review a series of questions to determine the type of generalization problem provided and remedial procedures.

Functional Analysis

Most recently, behavioral psychology for assessing people with severe disabilities has focused on identifying the "function" of a problem behavior (Durand, 1990; Mace, Lalli, & Pinter-Lalli, in press). The function of the behavior is the critical effect or consequence it achieves for the person in his or her environment. For example, the function of crying for an infant may be to obtain food, comfort, or rest. Later, the infant learns to use language to obtain these functions. Because of a lack of communication skills, people with severe disabilities may have socially unacceptable behavior that functions to communicate the need for food, attention, or rest, for example. Special educators have also developed assessment models that take this function into consideration in selecting alternative, appropriate responses (Donnellan, Mirenda, Mesaros, & Fassbender, 1984). Functional analysis helps the professional shift the focus of intervention away from eliminating behavior to replacing behavior that achieves a critical effect with a more socially appropriate form.

Synthesis of the Models

While these models take different approaches to data collection and evaluation, they share the common foundations of applied behavior analysis and life skills curriculum planning. Although researchers tend to specialize in one of these models, instructors and other applied professionals may find that several approaches best meet their needs. Table 1 provides a comparison of these models and their potential for educational use.

This book helps instructors decide which assessment model to use for specific skills and learners. It suggests that instructors begin with a routine task analytic focus. This fairly easy methodology lends itself well to many daily living skills that are important for people with severe disabilities. Instructors of

Table 1. Overview of several assessment models

Model	Characteristics	Utility in educational assessment
Applied behavioral psychology: Discrete response	• Defined target behavior • Time sampling measurement/reliability • Single-subject design (replication) • Linear graphs	• To define behavior for measurement • To conduct functional analysis • To plan reliability measures • To develop data summaries (graphs)
Task analysis (TA)	• Chains of behavior • Graphs of behavior (e.g., percentage steps correct) • Single-subject design	• To develop task analytic assessment for specific skills • To graph TAs
Ecological inventory	• Lists of activities and skills by environment • Overview of expectations of a setting • Social validation of skill selection	• To select skills during comprehensive and annual assessments
Massed trials	• Single response (e.g., eat) or set of responses (e.g., eat, drink, toilet) • Opportunities to respond presented in rapid, repeated format (e.g., 10 trials)	• To test specific skills during initial assessment • To address generalized use of these skills (use routines instead)
Precision teaching	• Single response or cluster of responses • Learners respond at their own rate • Rate data • Standard semilog graph • Decision rules for data review	• To assess IEP/IHP objectives on an ongoing basis • To evaluate ongoing data
Individualized curriculum sequencing (ICS)	• Skill clusters (e.g., sign "eat," grasp cracker, pass plate)	• To assess IEP/IHP objectives for people with profound disabilities

(continued)

Table 1. *(continued)*

Model	Characteristics	Utility in educational assessment
Routines	• Task analyses of several skills related to an activity • Routine ends with "critical effect" (naturally occurring reinforcer)	• To assess IEP/IHP activity objectives (recommended as primary form of ongoing assessment)
Curriculum-based assessment (CBA)	• Utilizes a preexisting curriculum • Provides overview of mastered skills	• To obtain skill overview for comprehensive and annual assessments for IEP/IHP
Generalization	• General case analysis • Decisions regarding performance of skills across settings, people, time, materials	• To assess IEP/IHP objectives related to generalization • To conduct initial assessment
Functional analysis	• Patterns of behavior across consequences/antecedents • Generates hypothesis as to reason for behavior	• To conduct initial assessment on problem behavior

people with profound disabilities may find that they rely primarily on the ICS model, because it lends itself well to partial participation planning. Planning for problem behaviors and generalization will require using models such as functional analysis and general case instruction. Finally, evaluation of ongoing instruction is considered for each assessment model. Whichever model is selected, educators should outline an individualized curriculum to enhance longitudinal planning of IEPs/IHPs.

PLANNING APPROPRIATE ASSESSMENT

This book provides a model for assessment that is in the tradition of applied behavior analysis and normalization. It provides a blending of behavioral and life skills approaches. Given this framework, several criteria can be suggested for planning assessment that will be appropriate for skill selection and ongoing evaluation of learner progress:

The data that instructors collect vary depending on the model of assessment used.

1. Skills should be selected that will enhance learners' integration in community environments and lead to the opportunities (e.g., employment) available to people without disabilities.
2. Reliable, valid assessment strategies must be developed for skill selection and ongoing assessment.
3. Ongoing assessment must be frequent (i.e., daily, semiweekly) and direct.
4. Data must be collected during ongoing assessment.
5. Data must be summarized on a graph or chart.
6. The graph must be periodically reviewed to make and record data-based instructional decisions.
7. Instructional decisions must be implemented.
8. Skills selected should be reviewed annually and comprehensive assessment conducted at least every 3–5 years to prioritize skills for instruction.

Organizing Assessment

To meet the criteria suggested above, instructors will need to organize assessment for skill selection, ongoing assessment, and evaluation. This book provides an organization for instructors to follow and offers examples of its use in case studies.

The content areas for this assessment are divided into skills used in the home and skills used in the community. Related skill areas such as communication, motor skills, academics, and social skills are given additional consideration to ensure that these critical functions are not underrepresented in the curriculum plan. Since many educators must develop curriculum-based assessment without a written life skills curriculum, instructions are given for generating an individualized curriculum as part of this comprehensive assessment. By contrast, suggestions for conducting curriculum-based assessment are suggested for instructors who are working with a written curriculum. Obviously, comprehensive assessment and curriculum development are not needed every year. Rather, these form the basis for initial educational evaluation during placement and updated evaluation that is conducted every 3–5 years. Each year's IEP/IHP can be developed from this longitudinal curriculum chart and review of the previous year's progress. Guidelines are given for annual assessment for IEP/IHP planning. Once the IEP/IHP is developed, ongoing assessment will be frequent (i.e., daily), with systematic (i.e., biweekly) evaluation of these data to make instructional decisions. The phases of educational assessment are shown in Figure 1 and Table 2. The remainder of this book describes specific ways to develop these plans for individual learners.

In Chapter 10, guidelines are also given for supervisors or instructors to evaluate adherence to the assessment plan and to instruction itself. This evaluation can both provide documentation for program evaluation and help instructors identify areas that need improvement.

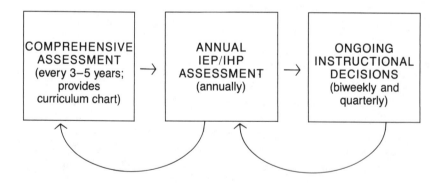

Figure 1.   Schedule for assessment. As the arrows indicate (left to right), the comprehensive assessment generates a curriculum chart of skills for 3–5 years of IEPs/IHPs. Annual assessment is used to update this curriculum for the IEP/IHP. Ongoing assessment provides progress monitoring on these IEP/IHP objectives. Following the arrows right to left, this ongoing assessment can be summarized for the annual assessment for IEP/IHP development. During the next comprehensive assessment, these annual summaries can provide a starting point to select skills for the new assessment.

Table 2. Phases of assessment

Phase	Goal	Steps	Frequency

Comprehensive assessment	To develop a longitudinal educational plan	1. Identify skills for assessment
		  a. Review records
		  b. Assess adaptive behavior
		  c. Conduct ecological inventories
		  d. Establish priorities for current assessment
		2. Conduct current assessment
		3. Write comprehensive assessment report
		4. Outline individualized curriculum chart for next 3–5 years
			3–5 years

Annual assessment for IEP/IHP development	To develop an IEP/IHP based on longitudinal planning of current priorities	1. Summarize annual progress 2. Consult caregiver 3. Inventory new integration priorities 4. Review curriculum chart 5. Complete prioritization chart 6. Write the IEP/IHP	Annually
Ongoing data-based instructional decisions	To enhance student progress by improving effectiveness	1. Develop ongoing assessment for each IEP/IHP objective	Annually
		2. Collect data on each objective taught	Daily
		3. Summarize data and make instructional decisions	Biweekly
		4. Summarize progress and communicate formally with caregivers (e.g., report cards, quarterly reviews)	Quarterly

Developing Reliable and Valid Assessment

As well as following an organized assessment plan, instructors need to consider the quality of each assessment tool they use or develop. The quality of assessment is usually judged by its *reliability* and *validity*. Reliability refers to the consistency of measurement. When measurement is designed to sample some relatively stable trait (e.g., intellectual functioning), testers are concerned with cross-time reliability. For example, a school psychologist would hope to obtain the same score if an IQ test were repeated after a month's time, since intellectual functioning is presumed to be a fairly stable trait. Since such retesting seldom reveals the same score, a standard error of measurement is reported. In educational assessment, instructors are not concerned with stable traits, but rather with evolving skills. Fluctuations in performance across days are often typical. However, instructors still hope to obtain a measure of the learner's performance at the time of the assessment that would be consistent across observations. With such consistency, instructors can consider fluctuations in performance in making instructional decisions (e.g., whether learners are motivated to perform the skill consistently). Without such consistency, fluctuations may be due to inconsistent data collection. In research, consistency of data collection is evaluated by having a second observer collect data concurrently and comparing the results. These reliability checks may be scheduled as frequently as every third observation. (Chapter 3 provides more information on the computation of reliability.) Such checks are not feasible in the classroom. How, then, can classroom teachers be confident of having data that are accurate enough to use to make instructional decisions? By implementing one or more of the following suggestions, instructors may improve and maintain data consistency in applied settings.

1. When instructors first learn to collect data, frequent reliability checks should be scheduled (e.g., by a supervisor) until a criterion for agreement has been demonstrated (e.g., 90% agreement across three lessons and settings). This is often an appropriate goal for student teachers.
2. Instructors should use data collection procedures learned with a co-observer. When a new procedure is implemented, someone should be recruited to co-observe for one or more times to check reliability.
3. To maintain reliability, instructors could ask an aide, supervisor, principal, or other professional who sometimes visits the classroom to co-observe a session to check agreement. Even if infrequent, these co-observations may help maintain consistency.

To be useful, measurement must not only be reliable, it must also be valid. Validity is the degree to which an instrument measures what it purports to measure. For example, a bathroom scale cannot be used to measure height—its only valid measurement is weight. In the construction of standardized tests, validity is often demonstrated by computing correlations with similar tests or correlations between items. Content validity can also be evaluated by examining test items to determine how well they sample the skill or concept to be tested. As instructors review adaptive behavior scales, some test items will have questionable adaptive behavior validity. That is, skills listed will not be those needed for daily living. For example, the fine motor section of the Pyramid Scales (Cone, 1984) contains items related to block stacking and bead stringing, skills that have little to do with daily living. By contrast, other sections of the Pyramid Scales (e.g., washing and grooming, domestic behavior) relate to daily living. Thus, the content validity of this test differs across scales.

When instructors construct their own tests, the issue of validity must also be considered. Instructors need to consider how well an observation or test samples the target behavior. Instructors need to write objectives that relate directly to skills of daily living for learners' chronological age groups. The assessment procedures developed then need to match these objectives.

For example, the following objective is both measurable and functional for Don: "When Don enters the classroom or work setting, he will put away his belongings and sit in his assigned seat by the time the work bell rings (mastery criteria: 4 out of 5 days)." An instructor-made task analysis of this objective is:

1. Walk to teacher.
2. Look at teacher.
3. Say "hello" to teacher.
4. Take off coat.
5. Comply with teacher's request to sit down.

While this task analysis measures Don's interaction with his teacher and his ability to take off his coat, the objective also implies Don's independent performance of a morning routine. Such independence is typical of adult settings. Social greetings would also be appropriate, but they are not specified in this objective. To be appropriate, such social greetings might be targeted for Don's discussion with peers at his work bench prior to the bell, or upon first entering the building. The following task analysis is thus a more valid measure of the stated objective:

1. Walk to coatroom.
2. Put lunchbox on shelf.
3. Take off gloves.
4. Put gloves in pockets.
5. Take off hat.
6. Hang hat on hook.
7. Take off coat.
8. Hang coat on hook.
9. Walk to assigned seat.
10. Be seated by the time the bell rings.

To summarize, to have a valid assessment, educators must first write a functional objective and then design assessment that measures the specific behavior and criteria stated in the objective. When instructors review published instruments to consider validity, they should consider the specific skills sampled by each test item.

PROTECTING HUMAN RIGHTS DURING ASSESSMENT

Besides making sure educational assessment matches its purpose and meets criteria set for quality, instructors must consider the learners' legal and human rights when planning assessment. Due process requires that:

1. Consent of both the learner and the parents or legal guardian must be obtained prior to conducting evaluation to determine if learners qualify for special services.
2. Parents or guardians have the right to inspect all related educational evaluations and placement records.
3. Parents have the right under The Education for All Handicapped Children Act (PL 94-142) to obtain an independent evaluation to be considered in planning their children's educational programs. Professionals in adult programs should also honor clients' or parents' requests to review and consider evaluations by professionals outside the clients' programs.
4. Written notice must be given to parents or guardians prior to an educational placement change. This notice should include descriptions of the evaluation that led to the change and the rationale for the change.
5. Parents or guardians and learners have the right to participate in the development of the individualized plan.

Educators should also respect learners' human rights, including the right to treatment and to confidentiality. PL 93-380 (the Buckley Amendment) gives parents and students the right to review their records, and forbids the release of identifiable information without written consent. Educators should maintain records with assessment information that are confidential and relevant to treatment. The following guidelines should govern the ethical aspects of assessment:

1. Assessment should be conducted to plan instruction. Information that is not relevant to the educational process should not be collected or recorded.
2. All information obtained in the assessment of learners should be kept in strictest confidence. Personally identifiable information or names should not be used when discussing a learner with someone who is not involved in that individual's education. Written parental permission must be obtained to share any information about a learner as part of professional training or for publicity about a program.

3. Assessment reports should be shared with parents, and the results stated tactfully.
4. Learner data or other information with learners' names should not be posted without parent and learner permission. Instructional data should be kept private. For example, data sheets that include information about other students should not be shared with parents. Clipboards with data and learners' names should not be left in teachers' lounges. Data, even without names, that portray learners in a negative manner or violate their rights to confidentiality should not be posted.

SUMMARY

The primary purpose of assessment of individuals with severe disabilities is the identification of skills that will increase opportunities for normalized living in community settings. The methodology of applied behavior analysis provides a basis for designing this assessment. By drawing from several of the various models of behavioral assessment of people with severe disabilities, educators can develop assessment plans that include initial assessment for skill selection and ongoing assessment for evaluation of progress. In developing this plan, instructors should be careful to develop valid, reliable measurement, and to respect each individual's legal and human rights.

STUDY QUESTIONS

1. What are the purposes of educational assessment and what are the issues related to each purpose in planning assessment for individuals with severe disabilities?
2. What are some of the past and current practices for responding to individual needs in education?
3. Contrast the differing approaches to behavioral assessment of life skills.
4. How can the issues of reliability and validity be addressed in planning assessment for individuals with severe disabilities?
5. What legal and human rights must be guarded in conducting assessment?

FOR FURTHER THOUGHT

1. What approaches to behavioral assessment have most influenced your work to date?
2. What new approaches would you like to learn through studying this book?

chapter 2

INITIAL ASSESSMENT

COMPREHENSIVE
AND ANNUAL ASSESSMENT

IN THE TWO initial phases of assessment, the comprehensive assessment and the annual assessment for IEP/IHP planning, the instructor identifies priority skills for instruction. In the third phase, ongoing assessment is conducted to evaluate and improve instructional effectiveness (see Chapters 3 and 4). While most professionals are familiar with annual assessment for IEP/IHP planning, the importance of linking IEPs/IHPs across years is not always considered. A comprehensive assessment report and individualized curriculum can focus instructional planning on skills that will enhance participation in both current and future environments.

The comprehensive assessment is conducted when a person first enters a school district or community agency. Reevaluation should be performed every 3–5 years, when the person moves to new levels of service (e.g., from elementary school to junior high). The assessment can be conducted by the classroom teacher or by an educational or curriculum specialist. Whoever assumes this responsibility will find that the time required for both planning and implementing the comprehensive assessment make it unfeasible for annual reevaluation. However, the time investment is both feasible and worthwhile if it is conducted every 3 to 5 years. In the latter part of this chapter, guidelines are given for conducting an annual assessment for IEP/IHP planning that builds on this comprehensive assessment. The annual assessment is feasible for instructors to complete in the planning time devoted to IEP/IHP development.

COMPREHENSIVE ASSESSMENT

The need for long-range planning is especially important when learners have multiple deficiencies and learn slowly. Certo (1983) noted that services for people with severe disabilities need to be longitudinal (i.e., planned across years) and not episodic. If a learner with severe disabilities is to achieve community integration and maximum independence, careful planning must be conducted to ensure that each year's instruction follows the route to these goals.

When conducting a comprehensive assessment, the instructor provides opportunities for the learner to try new tasks. The assessment is scheduled during regular instruction.

To conduct comprehensive educational assessment to develop an individualized and longitudinal curriculum, the instructor must follow several steps:

1. Identify skills to be assessed.
2. Select priorities for assessment.
3. Plan and conduct assessment.
4. Make the curriculum chart and write the IEP/IHP.

Each of these steps is described in the following sections. An overview of and timeline for this comprehensive assessment is also shown in Table 1.

STEP 1: IDENTIFY SKILLS TO BE ASSESSED

With individuals in integrated home and school or job settings, the goal of comprehensive assessment is to identify skills for instruction that will enhance competence in, or enjoyment of, these opportunities. If the individual's current settings are unsatisfactory to parents, to the professional conducting the assessment, or to the individual, *personal futures planning* should be done (Mount & Zwernik, 1988; Vandercook, York, & Forest, 1989). In personal futures planning, the individual being assessed and a group comprising professionals and family members, plan the individual's future based on individualized goals. (Personal futures planning is described more fully in Chapter 5.)

Table 1. Comprehensive educational assessment to develop a 3–5 year plan

Assessment task	Resources within this text	Suggested time frame for a 3-month assessment[a]
Prerequisite: **Develop a personal futures plan (if current environments/ opportunities are unsatisfactory)**	Chaps. 5 and 9	3–12 months prior to assessment
1. Identify skills for assessment	Chap. 2	1st week
• Review prior records —IEP/IHP summary —Other records	Chap. 2, Table 2	
• Conduct ecological inventories	Chap. 2	
—Home visit	Chap. 2, Figure 3, and Chap. 5	2nd week
—Other inventories	Chap. 2, Figure 4	1st month
• Use an adaptive behavior scale (optional)	Chap. 2, Figures 5, 6, and 7	2nd week—on home visit
• Conduct curriculum-based assessment	Chap. 2, Figure 8	1st month
2. Prioritize skills	Chap. 2	End of 1st month
• Draft a chart	Chap. 2, Figure 2	
• Select areas for further assessment	Chap. 2, Figure 11	
3. Plan and conduct assessment		
• Home skills	Chap. 5	2nd month, week 1
• Community and job skills	Chap. 6	2nd month, week 2 (job assessment may continue)
• Related skills —Communication —Motor —Academics	Chap. 7	2nd month, week 3
• Social skills —Problem behavior (functional analyses)	Chap. 8	2nd month, week 4 3rd month, week 1 (functional analysis may continue)
• Generalization/ integration	Chap. 9	3rd month, week 1
4. Make curriculum chart and write first IEP/IHP	Appendix A Chaps. 2 and 10	3rd month, week 3 3rd month, week 4

[a]Schedule assessment tasks with ongoing instruction. See Chapter 2, Figure 12 as an example.

Classification of Skills for Assessment

Educational assessment of people with mild disabilities often focuses on traditional school subjects such as reading and math. In the outmoded developmental approach to the education of people with severe disabilities, areas of assessment were similar to those selected for preschool evaluations (e.g., motor skills, language, cognitive skills). By contrast, a life skills or domain approach to the education of people with disabilities requires an organization for assessment and instruction that relates to the environments of community living. L. Brown, Branston-McLean, et al. (1979) suggested a curriculum development model for people with severe disabilities that focuses on four life domains: community, domestic, vocational, and leisure. Curriculum development that is organized into these domains has been described in numerous resources on educating people with severe disabilities (e.g., Browder & Stewart, 1982; Falvey, 1986; Sailor & Guess, 1983; Snell, 1983; Wehman et al., 1985).

The advantage of the domain approach is that it focuses assessment and instruction on functional activities rather than isolated skills. The disadvantage of this approach is that it typically leads to the identification of only the core skills involved in performing tasks (e.g., washing the dishes).

F. Brown, Evans, Weed, and Owen (1987) noted that independent living requires many other kinds of skills, such as communicating about core skills, knowing when to perform skills, and making transitions from one activity to the next.

F. Brown et al. (1987) classified these other skills into two categories: enrichment and extension skills. Another approach to looking at more than daily living activities is to consider skills that cross all domains. For example, Sailor and Guess (1983) modified the domain orientation approach by also including motor, self-care, and recreation skills that are needed across domains. Both these domain-approach modifications might be referred to as *cross-planning,* since skills that are used across activities and domains are considered separately for assessment. (Of course, for functional use, these skills would probably be taught in the context of specific domain activities.) Because these skills are related to many activities of daily living, "related skills" is used to refer to them here. Communication, motor, academic, and social skills are the related skills of focus. These areas are emphasized because they are distinct areas of special education.

Assessment should be performed for each area in which the learner functions (i.e., the home, the community). The home environment is subdivided into the core areas of: 1) personal maintenance, 2) housekeeping, 3) recreation/socialization, and 4) preparation for community activities. Community environments outside the home are subdivided using the approach of L. Brown, Branston-McLean, et al. (1979): 1) vocational, 2) recreational, and 3) other (e.g., transportation, shopping). Cross-planning is then conducted for assessment of related skills: 1) communication, 2) motor skills, 3) functional academics (if applicable), and 4) social skills. Skills that can function as alternatives to interfering behaviors are also considered across all core areas. This organization is shown in Figure 1, and is used throughout this book to help the educator plan and summarize assessment.

Procedures for Identifying Skills for Assessment

Once the instructor has selected an organizational framework for the curriculum development and assessment to develop the plan, he or she can identify the specific skills to be assessed. This is done by reviewing the learner's records, using ecological inventories, assessing adaptive behavior, and conducting curriculum-based assessment of skills that are related to several environments.

Review of Records Comprehensive educational assessment should begin with a review of the learner's educational progress and of related information (e.g., medical reports, therapy evaluations, psychological reports). This review of the learner's records begins with a summary of previous IEPs/IHPs (Table 2). Such a review reveals which skills have been mastered, which skills have been maintained, which skills have been lost, and which skills have never been acquired. For example, Table 2 reveals that this person had mastered walking to the restroom alone in 1987–88. Perhaps because of teacher turnover, in 1989–90 this skill was not recognized or required of him and this person was escorted to the restroom. Because she had reviewed previous IHPs, the instructor identified this skill as one that needed to be reevaluated to determine if this person simply needed the opportunity to use his mobility skills or if reinstruction would be necessary.

From this history, a list can be made of:

1. Skills that have not yet been mastered.
2. Skills that need to be maintained.
3. Skills that need to be generalized or developed with related skills.

Skills listed should be verified and prioritized in the comprehensive assessment to be included in the curriculum plan. The instructor should also note any reports from other professionals that imply the need for skill training. This information can be summarized as shown in Figure 2.

Other records that may be relevant to planning assessment are reports from other professionals who have evaluated or worked with the learner in the previous 3–5 years. These may include therapists, psychologists, psychiatrists, and physicians. Information gleaned from these reports should be included in the comprehensive assessment report. Skill deficits suggested by this information should be listed on the planning chart. Only relevant information should be included. For example, the fact that a learner is left-handed is relevant for planning instruction in eating with a spoon or dressing. By contrast, information on birth complications is probably irrelevant in planning for a 7-year-old. Including this information might also offend the child's parents.

32

	Domains and Subdomains						
		Home			Community		
	Personal maintenance	Housekeeping	Recreation/ socialization	Community preparation	Vocational	Recreational	Other
Core skills							
Communi-cation							
Motor							
Academics							
Social							
Interfering behavior							

Related skills

Figure 1. Organization of the comprehensive assessment and curriculum chart.

Table 2. Summary of skills from previous IEPs/IHPs

Routines	Years/comments			
	1986–1987	1987–1988	1988–1989	1989–1990
Arrival/departure routines				
Walk to building or van alone				+
Carry tote bag	+	M	M	M
Put bag in cabinet			+	M
Restroom routine				
Walk to restroom alone		+	−	−
Throw towel in trash	+	M	M	M
Close door				+
Mealtime routine				
Eat with spoon	+	M	M	M
Drink from glass	+	M	M	M
Get own lunch box			+	M
Restaurant routine				
Drink from paper cup	+	M	M	M
Use napkin		+	M	M
Locate own seat				+

+ = mastered, − = mastered but not maintained, M = maintained.

Similarly, results of previous testing should be reported only if they relate to the behavioral, life skills focus of the assessment. Thus, adaptive behavior reports would be relevant, but a developmental screening test or IQ score would not.

Use of Ecological Inventories One of the most useful and important techniques for identifying skills for assessment is the *ecological inventory*, also called an *environmental analysis*. An ecological inventory is a survey, interview, or observation that is used to identify the skills that are needed in the settings in which the individual functions or may function in the future.

Identifying the skills demanded in each of an individual's environments can be difficult. To do so the instructor must first decide what environments are relevant. Parental input can be especially helpful in specifying skills for further assessment, and the parents or caregivers should be the first contacted. The instructor may want to correspond with the parents or caregivers by phone or letter, or arrange a meeting. A home visit is highly recommended because it provides the most information and can encourage communication. In this first contact, the instructor can solicit help in: 1) identifying the relevant community environments to be evaluated with ecological inventories, 2) becoming acquainted with the learner and his or her preferences and skills, 3) beginning to consider priorities, and 4) conducting the home ecological inventory. Figure 3

Teacher: **Ms. P.**   Student: **Ann**

Skill areas	Source used to identify skills listed				
	Current IEP/IHP and previous records	Caregiver inventory	Other ecological inventory	Curriculum-based assessment or adaptive behavior scales	Testing and observations
Home					
Personal maintenance	Eating skills Toilet training	Drinking from glass, dressing, toilet training		Using restroom alone Eating with spoon	Pulling pants up/down Eating finger foods
Housekeeping		Wiping table	Work center: discarding trash		Opening containers
Recreation/socialization		Music	Adult peer: playing piano		Using radio, tape player
Community preparation		Putting on coat Getting lunch	Work center: packing/carrying bag lunch		
Community					
Vocational			Work center: mailings photocopying		Putting on labels, Sealing envelopes
Recreational		Sports events Buying soda	Senior citizen center: drinking soda	Walking up/down steps	Drinking soda from can Using vending machine

Other (e.g., travel, shop)	No awareness of danger	Eating in restaurant	7-11, restaurant, bus station: Selecting choice Grasping/releasing	Pedestrian skills	Communicating basic needs, using wallet
<u>Related skills</u> Communication		Need for help Conversing	Making choices Using I.D. card	Imitating social comments	Yes/no
Motor	Grasp/release Thumb-finger opposition	Walking faster	Walking to restroom Carrying bag	Opening doors	
Academics					
Social			Imitating social		
<u>Interfering behavior</u>	Decreasing swearing	Choking when eating		Inappropriate comments	

Figure 2. Inventory of learner skills. This is the "rough draft" of the curriculum chart that lists all skill needs before prioritization and further assessment.

Student's name: Dennis   Date: 9/3/85

Parents or

Teacher: Ms. K   Caregivers: Ms. T.

This survey was developed to assist the teacher in developing a comprehensive educational assessment. The information you provide can help make this assessment relevant to this student.

1. What are Dennis's favorite activities and leisure materials?

2. What other preferences has Dennis expressed (e.g., preferred and non-preferred food, clothing, temperature)?

3. Where does your family typically go, or where would your family like to go for each of these activities?

> Shopping:
> Clubs, church:
> Medical appointments:
> Visit friends and relatives:
> Family recreation:
> Other:

For each of the above, circle the places that your family frequently goes. Star the places that Dennis has frequently gone.

4. What skills were previously taught to Dennis that you would like to see maintained in his future instruction?

5. What changes need to be made in Dennis's educational program?

6. Who in the home provides most of Dennis's care? Who would be willing and have time to implement some instruction for Dennis at home that would be designed by the teacher? How much time would be realistic for this home instruction (e.g., 30 minutes daily)?

7. Attached please find a survey of adaptive behavior. Please follow the instructions to indicate the skills that Dennis currently has.

8. Please feel free to make any general comments about Dennis's educational needs.

THANK YOU FOR YOUR TIME IN COMPLETING THIS SURVEY.

Figure 3.   Example of a form that can be sent to parents to solicit their input in developing the comprehensive educational plan.

shows an example of a form that could be used with parents. This form was used as a guide for the interview conducted during a home visit. Ecological inventories targeted for parents can also be found in some commercially available materials. For example, the home inventory in the IMPACT curriculum asks parents to describe leisure and personal care skills their child can perform (Neel & Billingsley, 1989). Using either an instructor-made or a commercially prepared resource, the home inventory can be extensive enough to generate a "working" curriculum.

From this parental input, the instructor can organize and develop other necessary inventories. The instructor can use forms similar to Figures 1 and 2 to list the environments identified by the parents for the home and community. Sometimes the instructor will have adequate information to plan for one or more of these environments (e.g., the instructor may use the shopping center identified by the parents). Unfamiliar environments (e.g., the learner's home) and environments that will be considered for activities unfamiliar to the instructor (e.g., custodial skills for the shopping mall) will require additional information. For each unfamiliar environment, the instructor must decide how the information will be obtained. One method is to develop an attitude-and-information survey to be completed by a significant person in each environment. For example, the instructor might send a survey to a potential employer and ask him or her to rank the importance of specific skills. (An example of this type of inventory is provided in Figure 1 in Chapter 8 to determine an employer's attitude toward certain social skills.) A second method is to observe each environment, and interview significant people in each. (An example of this approach is illustrated in Figure 5 in Chapter 5, with an ecological inventory for a home environment.) A third method is to observe each environment to obtain information on both the physical layout of the setting and typical activities of peers without disabilities. An example of an inventory is shown in Figure 4. A fourth method is to interview a peer without disabilities or the peer's parents to obtain information on activities typical for the learner's age group. The instructor may think of other ways of obtaining information on specific environments.

Social Validity Ecological inventories enhance the social validity of the assessment to be designed by identifying societal expectations for self-sufficiency. Social validity is the value of behavior change for an individual as evaluated by important others in that person's life or by the individual. The ultimate goal of self-sufficiency can be seen as allowing an individual to function in society in a manner similar to that of his or her peers without disabilities.

Social validation was first described as a criterion for evaluating research (Kazdin, 1977; Wolf, 1978). Kazdin (1977) described two ways in which behavioral research could become more socially valid. One is to consult "experts" in the environments in which the behavior will be performed (e.g., an employer). The other is to use normative comparisons (e.g., peer group). Ecological inventories build on this social validation approach to skill selection. For example, Voeltz, Wuerch, and Bockhaut (1982) asked direct-care staff to evaluate the leisure-time behavior of adolescents with severe disabilities. Their evaluation provided evidence that improvement in leisure skills would be valued by the people who cared for these individuals during their leisure time. Cuvo, Jacobi, and Sipko (1981) took a slightly different approach to validate the task analysis for laundry skills, by consulting an expert in housekeeping (home economist) to determine the best practice for washing and drying clothes.

Sometimes a normative comparison will reveal a range of acceptable behavior that provides more flexibility and efficiency in planning than experts suggest. For example, the schedule for mopping a floor proposed by a profes-

Life Skills Questionnaire

Site _____	Date _____

Interview Contact Person _____

1. Is the facility barrier-free? Are there areas within the facility that are not accessible to a wheelchair?

2. Is there medical treatment available? How close is the nearest hospital?

3. What activities are typical of 12-year-old boys in this facility? How often are these available?

4. What is the average cost of these activities?

5. What accommodations would the staff make for an individual with Tommy's handicaps?

Figure 4. Example of an ecological inventory. (From Browder, D., & Martin, D. [1986]. A new curriculum for Tommy. *Teaching Exceptional Children*, 18, p. 262; reprinted by permission.)

sional housekeeper would probably be less flexible than the range of schedules actually used by most adults.

Empirical Validity   Voeltz and Evans (1983) noted the need for empirical validity, as well as social validity. Empirical validity can be defined as the extent to which a behavior will contribute to an improvement in an individual's eventual outcome. For example, if the ultimate goal of intervention is self-sufficiency, skills should be evaluated for their efficiency in increasing the individual's self-sufficiency. Thus, ecological inventories address not only skills for current environments, but also skills that will lead to independent performance in future environments (Falvey, Brown, Lyon, Baumgart, & Schroeder, 1980).

Use of Adaptive Behavior Scales   It may be useful to perform a global assessment such as that provided by many adaptive behavior scales. This global assessment can be especially helpful in planning for an individual whom the instructor does not yet know. Adaptive behavior scales vary in the number and kind of life skills they include. The best scale for use in a comprehensive educational assessment is the one with the most items in each life skill area. Figure 5 summarizes the content of several adaptive behavior scales. These scales are compared in Figure 6. (Addresses for obtaining the adaptive behavior scales are found in the appendix at the end of this chapter.)

To illustrate how these figures can be used, the following case study examples are presented. In order to fulfill state requirements for a standardized, normative evaluation of Al (see Appendix A), the school psychologist planned to administer an adaptive behavior scale through a parental interview. The Vineland Adaptive Behavior Scale (Sparrow, Balls, & Cicchetti, 1985), Adaptive Behavior Inventory (ABI) (Brown & Leigh, 1987), and Scales of Independent Behavior (SIBS) (Bruininks, Woodcock, Weatherman, & Hill, 1984) are all good choices for this purpose because they yield standard scores based on comparisons to people without disabilities. Further, the technical quality (e.g., reliability, validity) of these tests is strong, which is especially important in norm-referenced comparisons. Of the three scales, the ABI includes the smallest number of items related to life skills. The instructor might therefore ask the school psychologist to use the Vineland or SIBS so that the results could be used for educational planning. By contrast, normative comparisons would be irrelevant for Lester (see Appendix A) who receives adult services that require no interindividual comparisons. Moreover, because of Lester's age (69), neither the Vineland nor the ABI would be appropriate. Lester's instructor chose the Functional Skills Screening Inventory (FSSI) (Becker, Schur, Pavletti-Schelp, & Hammer, 1986) (see sample in Figure 7) because it included the largest number of life skills items and could be scored by computer.

However, profiles and total scores will not provide specific enough information to be useful for educational planning. The information obtained from the adaptive behavior assessment should thus be reorganized by life skill categories, such as those shown in Figure 1.

Use of Curriculum-Based Assessment One of the new trends in the field of severe disabilities is the development of written curricula. Several approaches to curriculum development were described in Chapter 1. The approaches that are most relevant for initial assessment are the comprehensive program-wide curriculum, the activities catalog, and the individual curriculum.

Because of state guidelines or instructors' needs for assistance in skill selection, some programs have developed comprehensive curriculum guides, such as *The Syracuse Community-Referenced Curriculum Guide* (Ford et al., 1989b), that focus on life skills. This curriculum provides scope and sequence charts for community living domains (domestic, vocational, recreational, general community functioning); functional academic skills; and embedded social, communication, and motor skills. The scope and sequence charts are divided by age groups and are applicable to people without disabilities as well. The curriculum gives guidelines for considering a learner's curricular needs—

Scales and number of responses per skill area

Life skills	AAMD ABS	ABI	Balthazar[1]	CTAB	FSSI	Pyramid	SIBS	Vineland
Domestic								
Toileting	*	*		**	*	**	**	**
Hygiene/grooming	***	*	N	**	**	**	**	***
Dressing	**	*	****	****	**	**	**	***
Eating	**	*	****	***	**	**	**	***
Food preparation	N	*	N	****	**	**	**	**
Housekeeping	N	*	N	***	**	**	*	**
Clothing care	N *	*	N	**	*	*	*	N *
Lawn/vehicle care	N *	N *	N	**	N *	N *	N	*
Health care	*	*	N	**	*	*	*	*
Home leisure	*	*	N	**	*	**	*	**
Community								
Pedestrian	*	N *	N	**	N *	**	*	*
Travel/bus	*	*	N	**	*	*	*	*
Shopping	**	*	N	**	*	*	*	*
Restaurant use	**	*	N	*	*	*	*	*
Self-identification	*	*	N	***	*	*	*	*
Telephone use	**	*	N	**	*	*	**	*
Banking/money	*	*	N	N *	*	N *	*	**
Job-specific skills	**	N *	N	*	**	**	*	N *
Job-related skills	**	***	N	*	***	*	**	*
General skills[2]								
Language—vocal	**	***	N	**	**	****	****	***
Language—nonvocal	*	N	N	N	*	*	*	*
Ambulation—walk, sit	N *	N	N	***	*	**		**
Ambulation—wheelchair		N *	N *	*	*	N *	N *	N
Social interaction	**	N *	***	**	***	N	**	***
Problem behaviors	****	N	N	****	**	****	****	****
Academics	**	***		****	**		**	**

Key
N No responses; * 1–5 responses; ** 6–24 responses; *** 25–50 responses; **** more than 50 responses
[1] Designed for individuals with severe disabilities.
[2] Expressive and receptive communication.

Figure 5. Skills assessed by adaptive behavior scales. Some items had several responses. Each response, rather than each item, was counted. (AAMD ABS = American Association on Mental Deficiency Adaptive Behavior Scales [Lambert, Windmiller, Tharinger, & Cole, 1981]; ABI = Adaptive Behavior Inventory [L. Brown & Leigh, 1987]; Balthazar = Balthazar Scales of Adaptive Behavior [Balthazar, 1976]; CTAB = Comprehensive Test of Adaptive Behavior [Adams, 1984]; FSSI = Functional Skills Screening Inventory [Becker, Schur, Pavletti-Schelp, & Hammer, 1986]; Pyramid = The Pyramid Scales [Cone, 1984]; SIBS = Scales of Independent Behavior, Woodcock-Johnson Psychoeducational Battery: Part Four [Bruininks, Woodcock, Weatherman, & Hill, 1984]; Vineland = Vineland Adaptive Behavior Scales [Sparrow, Balla, & Cicchetti, 1985].)

including needs for alternative responses to compensate for disabilities. One of the resources of this curriculum is a manual for programs to develop their own curricula (Schnorr, Ford, Davern, Park-Lee, & Meyer, 1989). As indicated in this manual, one of the first steps in developing a program-wide curriculum is to evaluate any existing resources. Similarly, the first step in conducting curriculum-based assessment is to ensure that the curriculum to be used will accomplish the desired outcome, namely, an individualized, functional, and community-referenced set of skills for instruction. Figure 8 shows a sample of a checklist that can be used for this review.

To use a curriculum for initial assessment, the instructor must evaluate the learner's current level of performance for each skill in the curriculum. As shown in Figure 9, Mary needs assistance for most community functioning skills appropriate for middle school–age students. However, as the instructor reviewed the goal areas, priorities would begin to emerge. These priorities would then be listed in on a chart similar to that in Figure 2 and considered for direct assessment.

Another approach to be considered in life skills planning is an activities catalog, or list of skills. A commercially available catalog, *The Activities Catalog,* (Wilcox & Bellamy, 1987a) saves instructors the work of generating original ideas for skill instruction through numerous ecological inventories. Rather, the instructor can adapt this resource by validating it for the learner's community. Curriculum-based assessment can then be conducted, as shown in Figure 9.

A second alternative is to generate a curriculum for one individual and use this curriculum for subsequent assessments. This approach may be especially useful when commercially available curricula are not appropriate for a particular individual. Later in this chapter guidelines are provided for generating a curriculum chart based on the comprehensive assessment. If a learner has an existing chart from a previous assessment, this can then be used in the current assessment by reviewing skills and noting level of independence and frequency of use. If no chart exists, a tentative curriculum can be generated by asking parents to name all skills their son or daughter needs to acquire or improve in each area shown in Figure 1. This latter approach was used in developing the multidisciplinary comprehensive assessment for Liz that is described in Chapter 7. First, the parents were asked to help generate a large number of potential skills for a curriculum chart for Liz. The parents' list then became the basis for the remainder of the comprehensive assessment planning (e.g., verifying skill needs, further validating through ecological inventories). A final version of the curriculum chart was generated by a multidisciplinary team that included Liz's mother.

STEP 2: SET PRIORITIES FOR ASSESSMENT AND INSTRUCTION

Once the instructor has identified skills for assessment, he or she will begin to generate a long list of deficiencies. (These will be listed on a "rough draft" of

Scale

	AAMD ABS	ABI	Balthazar	CTAB	FSSI	Pyramid	SIBS	Vineland
I. Interindividual comparison								
Age norms in years	3–17	5–18	NA	0–adult	0–adult	NA	0–adult	0–18
Comparison group	People without disabilities, people with mild to moderate mental retardation	People without disabilities, people with mental retardation	NA	People without disabilities, people with mental retardation	People with disabilities	NA	People without disabilities	People without disabilities
Standard score	No	Yes	No	No	No	No	Yes	Yes
Standardization sample size	6,523	1,076	NA	58	51	374	1,764	3,000
Buros or other review	Elliott (1985)	Evans & Bradley-Johnson (1988)		Evans & Bradley-Johnson (1988)	Browder (1989)	Svinicki (1989)	Ipsen (1986)	Oakland & Houchins (1985)

	AAMD ABS	ABI	Balthazar	CTAB	FSSI	Pyramid	SIBS	Vineland
II. Intraindividual comparisons Profile by subscales	Yes	Yes	Yes	Yes	Yes	Yes	Yes	Yes
Adaptations for sensory/physical disabilities	No	No	No	No	Yes	Yes	No	No
Applicable for individuals with severe to profound mental retardation	No	No	No	No	Yes	Yes	Yes	No
Applicable for individuals with behavior disorders	Yes	No	No	No	Yes	No	Yes	Yes
III. Assessment format administration	First person or interview	First person	Observation	First person or interview	First person	First person or interview	Interview	Interview
Computer scoring	No	Yes	No	No	Yes	No	Yes	No

Figure 6. Comparison of various adaptive behavior scales. References are in the reference list at the end of this book. (AAMD ABS = American Association on Mental Deficiency Adaptive Behavior Scales [Lambert, Windmiller, Tharinger, & Cole, 1981]; ABI = Adaptive Behavior Inventory [L. Brown & Leigh, 1987]; Balthazar = Balthazar Scales of Adaptive Behavior [Balthazar, 1976]; CTAB = Comprehensive Test of Adaptive Behavior [Adams, 1984]; FSSI = Functional Skills Screening Inventory [Becker, Schur, Pavletti-Schelp, & Hammer, 1986]; Pyramid = The Pyramid Scales [Cone, 1984]; SIBS = Scales of Independent Behavior, Woodcock-Johnson Psychoeducational Battery: Part Four [Bruininks, Woodcock, Weatherman, & Hill, 1984]; Vineland = Vineland Adaptive Behavior Scales [Sparrow, Balla, & Cicchetti, 1985]; NA = not applicable if criterion-referenced test.)

43

PRIORITY LEVELS

PRIORITY I SKILLS: PROVIDE THE INDIVIDUAL WITH A MEASURE OF PERSONAL AUTONOMY IN ANY SETTING

PRIORITY II SKILLS: *ARE FREQUENTLY REQUIRED FOR SUCCESSFUL SUPERVISED (GROUP HOME) LIVING AND/OR SUPPORTIVE EMPLOYMENT*

Priority III Skills: facilitate successful independent living and competitive employment

SCORING KEY, PART ONE: FUNCTIONAL SKILLS

4 points: the individual performs the item consistently, completely, correctly, spontaneously, and appropriately, with NO cueing, prompting, or assistance required.

3 points: the individual performs the item frequently and substantially, with minimal cueing, prompting, and/or assistance required.

2 points: the individual performs the item inconsistently and/or partially, with moderate cueing, prompting, and/or assistance required.

1 point: the individual performs the item infrequently and/or minimally, with extensive cueing, prompting, and/or assistance required.

0 points: the individual does not perform any part of the item at all, under any circumstances.

Name: __Ronnie__

		9/84 Date	Date
IV.	HOMEMAKING		
A.	Cleaning		
1.	HELPS WITH CLASSROOM/HOUSEHOLD/DORMITORY TASKS (picks up personal belongings, etc.)	3.5	
2.	KEEPS PERSONAL LIVING AREA TIDY (puts personal items away, makes bed, etc.)	3	
3.	CHANGES BED LINENS (sheets, pillowcases, blankets, spread, etc.)	3	
4.	DUSTS (furniture, window sills, shelves, etc.)	1	
5.	SWEEPS (with broom/dustmop)	1	
6.	EMPTIES WASTEBASKETS, GARBAGE PAILS, ETC.	1	
7.	CLEANS BATHROOM FIXTURES (sinks, mirrors, toilets, etc.)	1	
8.	Vacuums rugs/floors	1	
9.	Mops floors	0	
10.	Performs minor household maintenance/repair (changes lightbulbs, replaces screws/nails, washers, etc.)	1	
11.	Cleans kitchen appliances (stove, refrigerator, etc.) as needed	1	
B.	Food Preparation		
1.	CLEARS DISHES FROM TABLE	4	
2.	WASHES TABLES AND COUNTERS	2	
3.	SETS DINING TABLE (plates, utensils, glasses, cups, etc.)	3	
4.	WASHES AND DRIES DISHES	3	
5.	PUTS AWAY DISHES, UTENSILS, PANS, ETC.	3.5	
6.	PREPARES SIMPLE BEVERAGES AND SNACK FOODS	1	
7.	PEELS, SLICES, CHOPS, AND GRATES FOOD IN PREPARATION FOR COOKING	1	

Figure 7. Sample from the Functional Skills Screening Inventory (FSSI). (From Becker, H.; Schur, S., Pavletti-Schelp, M., & Hammer, E. [1986]. *Functional Skills Screening Inventory*, [p. 11]. Austin, TX: Functional Resources Enterprises; reprinted by permission.)

COMMUNITY-REFERENCED CURRICULUM

Philosophy

Does the guide (or do other curricular materials) have a written philosophy?

✓ yes ___ no

If yes, are the following features emphasized?

	No Evidence	Partially Developed	Fully Developed
Every student can learn.	✓	—	—
Students will not be excluded from an activity because they will not be able to engage in it independently; partial participation or interdependence is also a highly valued outcome.	✓	—	—
Every student, regardless of the severity of disability, can become an active and contributing member of society.	✓	—	—
Educational programs should prepare students for the real world; students should be prepared to work in non-sheltered settings, enjoy the same recreational options as their nondisabled peers, have free access to the community with as much support as necessary, and so forth.	—	✓	—
Students with severe disabilities must have ongoing opportunities to learn in the presence of and develop friendships with nonhandicapped peers.	✓	—	—
Active parental involvement is essential to the success of a school program.	—	✓	—

Community Living

Does the guide (or do other curricular materials) address the following areas?

	yes	no
General Community Functioning	___	✓
Recreation/Leisure	✓ some	___
Self-Management/Home Living	✓	___
Vocational (preparation for nonsheltered work)	___	✓

Complete the following chart for each area scored as "yes."
Score each item "yes," "no," or "partially":

	General Community Functioning	Recreation/ Leisure	Self-Management/ Home Living	Vocational
A rationale for teaching community skills in this section	—	no	partially	—

Figure 8. Checklist for evaluating a community-referenced curriculum. (From Schnorr, R., Ford, A., Davern, L., & Park-Lee, S., & Meyer, L. [1989]. *The Syracuse curriculum revision manual: A group process for developing a community-referenced curriculum guide* [p. 27]. Baltimore: Paul H. Brookes Publishing Co.; reprinted by permission.)

Repertoire chart for: **Middle School (ages 12–14)**   Student: _Mary Z._

Domain: _General Community Functioning_   Age: _14_   Date: _9/18/90_

Goal area	Present activities	Performance level — Check one				Critical features — Check all that apply				Note priority goal areas
		Assistance on most steps	Assistance on some steps	Independent	Has related social skills?	Initiates as needed?	Makes choices?	Uses safety measures?		
Travel	Walk, ride bus, ride bike									
	to and from school	✓								
	Wheel									
	~~Walk~~ to various									
	destinations	✓								
	School to mailbox									
	Cross streets safely									
	Use public bus/subway for									
	general transportation									
Community safety	Problem solve if lost in									
	new places	✓								
	Use caution with strangers		✓							
	Uncomfortable with									
	strangers									
Grocery shopping	Buy items needed for									
	specific planned menu,									
	with help	✓								
	Purchases a									_·Purchase familiar items from grocery store._
	familiar item									

Figure 9.   Example of curriculum-based assessment. (From Ford, A., Schnorr, R., Meyer, L., Davern, L., Black, J., & Dempsey, P. [Eds.]. [1989a]. *The Syracuse community-referenced curriculum guide for students with moderate and severe disabilities* [p. 80]. Baltimore: Paul H. Brookes Publishing Co.; reprinted by permission.)

the curriculum chart, as shown in Figure 2.) Clearly, further assessment of the full list, or use of the full list as a curriculum chart would be unwieldy. Rather, the instructor needs to establish priorities for the learner before planning and conducting further assessment to develop the curriculum plan.

Priorities must be set twice in developing a curriculum plan. First, the instructor must review the learner's records, ecological inventories, adaptive behavior screening, and curriculum-based assessment to decide which skill areas warrant further consideration in the assessment. Once assessment has been completed, the instructor must then set priorities for the curriculum plan itself and for the IEP/IHP for the first year. Establishing these priorities can be one of the most difficult tasks in the assessment process. Some of the variables to be considered are: 1) the learner's own preferences, 2) the preferences of caregivers, 3) societal values, 4) the preferences of significant others in settings targeted for instruction, 5) skill utility and other practical issues, and 6) partial participation.

Consideration of Learner's Preferences

One of the first and most important steps in establishing priorities for assessment and instruction is to consider the learner's preferences. Some skills (e.g., leisure) allow a wide range of choice for specific behaviors to be taught. Before

Assessment of preference for students with severe disabilities may require adapting switches to their current motor skills. In this photo, the teacher demonstrates how to activate a tape recorder.

selecting target behaviors, the instructor should observe the learner's preferences. This can be done by offering several materials or activities and noting the learner's choices across several opportunities. Another method is to expose the learner briefly to various activities and note his or her reaction (e.g., attempts to participate, smiles, tries to terminate activity by pulling away). A checklist to assist this assessment of preference is shown in Figure 10. This evaluation requires introducing materials and activities across several days and noting the learner's reaction to each. For people with profound physical disabilities, Dattilo and Mirenda (1987) demonstrated a method of preference assessment based on the use of adaptive switches connected to a computer that provides sensory activities. Preferences are inferred from the frequency with which an individual selects a particular leisure material.

In assessing preferences, instructors should not use skills that are at least potentially enjoyable and avoid using skills that are taught because of societal expectations (e.g., toilet training). Instructors should also make sure that the learner does not select a particular activity merely out of habit (Shevin & Klein, 1984). Sometimes preference for a novel activity or material requires several exposures. Thus, a skill might be included to encourage a learner to become familiar with a new experience (e.g., skiing) that has value (e.g., family preference, health benefits).

Consideration of Caregivers' Preferences

Parents' preferences are also one of the most important criteria for selecting skills for further assessment. The preliminary interview with the parents (see Figure 3) helps the instructor decide which environments to use for assessment, and identifies some of the parents' preferences. This home inventory guides choices about domestic skills, which vary with family values. The instructor may also contact the parents when all of the ecological inventories and the adaptive behavior assessment are complete, to seek their guidance in including or excluding certain skills from assessment. It is also important to obtain parental permission for any assessment involving risk to the learner (e.g., assessment of street crossing, assessment of being alone in public).

Consideration of Societal Values

Some general societal values can also guide the establishment of priorities. In considering societal values, the instructor may wish to reflect on the principle of normalization, which posits that people with disabilities should have the same opportunities as people without disabilities. The values and opportunities of the larger society are thus considered in planning for people with disabilities. Wolfensberger (1972) noted that a true application of normalization also requires society to adapt to differences among people so that all people can be accommodated. Thus, the instructor must determine whether to try to change a

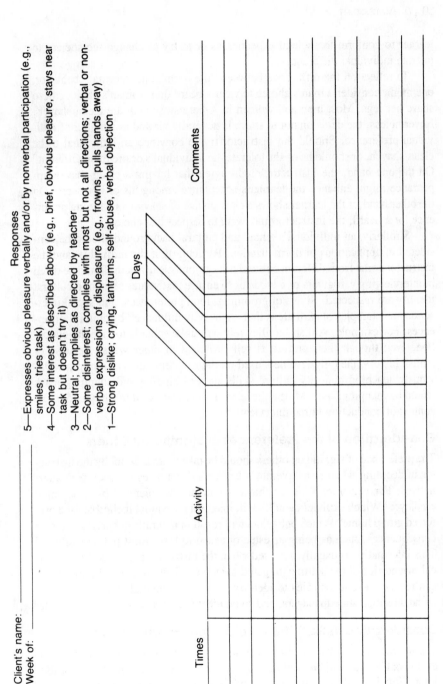

Client's name: _____
Week of: _____

Responses

5—Expresses obvious pleasure verbally and/or by nonverbal participation (e.g., smiles, tries task)
4—Some interest as described above (e.g., brief, obvious pleasure, stays near task but doesn't try it)
3—Neutral; complies as directed by teacher
2—Some disinterest; complies with most but not all directions; verbal or non-verbal expressions of displeasure (e.g., frowns, pulls hands away)
1—Strong dislike; crying, tantrums, self-abuse, verbal objection

Times   Activity   Days   Comments

Figure 10. Preference assessment.

learner to conform to societal expectations or to try to change the society to tolerate individual differences.

To reflect on the difference between "the norm" and "normal" behavior, one might consider a man's choice to wear a beard or a woman's choice not to shave her legs. Most men and women in American society are clean-shaven. Nevertheless, the decision not to shave is generally viewed as a matter of individual preference. Should the instructor try to convince an individual to be clean-shaven, or should he or she tolerate the individual's desire to be different? On the one hand, the instructor might agree that having a clean-shaven appearance might enhance the learner's acceptance among his or her peers. On the other hand, if the learner shows a clear dislike of shaving or a strong preference for a beard, the instructor may wish to respect this choice.

Similarly, an individual's ethnic and cultural background should be considered in applications of normalization. Particularly if the individual and the instructor come from different cultural backgrounds, extra care should be taken in interviewing caregivers or advocates to ensure that values related to cultural identity are respected. Styles of grooming, food preferences, and social interaction are examples of skill areas that are heavily influenced by cultural differences. For example, Amish families rely on public schools for special education, even though their culture is self-sufficient in other ways. Because of Amish history, the only fasteners used on their clothing are straight pins. Obviously, teaching majority culture skills such as zipping and snapping jeans would be inappropriate. (Multicultural issues are discussed in Chapter 5 in the context of conducting home interviews.)

Consideration of the Preferences of Significant Others

The preference of significant others should be taken into account by the instructor in deciding whether to tolerate a learner's differences or teach new alternatives. For example: Which behaviors will not be tolerated by a potential employer? Which skill deficiencies will make an individual ineligible for a preferred group home? Which behaviors will result in naturally occurring aversive consequences, such as being arrested or asked to leave most public facilities? This information is usually obtained when the instructor conducts the ecological inventories of the settings targeted for the curriculum plan. The instructor can review these inventories to identify skills that potential employers, group home directors, store managers, and so on identify as essential, or as intolerable.

Consideration of Skill Utility and Other Practical Issues

The instructor may also consider the issue of the general utility of the skill. For example: Can the skill be used across activities? Does it have long-term or lifelong utility? Is the skill efficient for independent performance of the activity? Does the skill help the individual compensate for physical or sensory deficits? White (1980) noted that it is not the specific responses to perform the activity that matter but the critical effect of making a series of responses (i.e., gaining access to the natural reinforcer of the activity). Many behaviors can achieve the same effect. The instructor will want to find the behaviors that are the most efficient means for the learner to obtain the desired end.

Besides skill utility, the instructor may also want to consider the practical issue of time constraints for assessment and instruction. It sometimes helps an instructor to determine how many skills he or she can feasibly teach per week. This total time figure can then be used to budget time per learner and skill. From this planning, the instructor can decide approximately how many skills are feasible for the annual plan and curriculum chart. In setting these necessary limits, the instructor can consider each learner's priorities, ways to economize instruction (e.g., selecting skills that can be taught to several people simultaneously), and the balance of assessment across areas (e.g., giving equal emphasis to all life domains rather than emphasizing one domain, such as vocational training). The educators whose case studies inspired this book developed annual plans in which 6–14 new skills were taught per individual. Most of the instructors found that it was not feasible to work on more than six new skills per day per learner, but that more skills could be included by identifying some skills that the individual could perform with minimal help and by using rotating schedules of instruction. The curriculum charts in Appendix A reflect the skills these instructors selected from their initial assessment.

Consideration of Partial Participation

L. Brown, Branston, et al. (1979) noted that an individual who cannot wholly achieve independence in an activity might still accomplish mastery of some skills within the activity. Skills that cannot be performed independently might be adapted for partial participation by: 1) providing adult or peer assistance, 2) simplifying the activity to enhance independent performance, or 3) adapting the environment (e.g., using a bar instead of a doorknob on doors).

In assessment, the instructor will want to determine how much of the activity the learner can perform. If sensory and physical deficits do not preclude making the responses required by the activity, full participation should be considered for instruction. If such deficiencies do exist, or if the person is an older adult with few or no responses required by the activity, partial participation may be the goal. Partial participation fits the goal of normalization if one considers that most adults are both independent and interdependent. Most adults depend to some extent on friends, family, and environmental aids to perform their daily routines (e.g., a spouse or roommate prepares dinner, a note is taped to the refrigerator as a reminder of an important errand). People with severe disabilities should also expect to obtain the skills necessary to live in harmony with others in their environment rather than having to do everything alone. Thus, some skills might be identified for the person's companions to perform (e.g., judgment about street crossing at busy intersections), whereas others might be taught to the person (e.g., walking and crossing without guidance). In general, partial participation should be meaningful to the learner. This can be achieved by ensuring that the learner gains increased control over the activity, enjoys the activity, or achieves the critical effect.

Synthesizing Various Considerations to Rank Skills for Assessment and Instruction

Simultaneous consideration of these various factors can be facilitated by the use of some type of prioritization checklist. Examples of rating priorities have been illustrated by Gaylord-Ross and Holvoet (1985) and by Wuerch and Voeltz (1982). An illustration of a rating of priorities is shown in Figure 11.

STEP 3: PLAN AND CONDUCT ASSESSMENT

Through curriculum-based assessment, much useful information can be obtained on the individual's current skills and deficiencies. However, the comprehensive educational assessment will not be complete without direct observation and testing of the learner to develop a relevant and realistic longitudinal educational plan (individualized curriculum chart). From the summary of skills to be assessed, the instructor will have identified areas that require further evaluation to pinpoint specific curriculum goals. For example, curriculum-based assessment might indicate that the individual has few communication skills. The instructor will want to gather more information to identify specific communication goals for the curriculum plan. Not every skill area on the curriculum plan need be derived from direct assessment of the learner. For some skills, such as housekeeping, the parents' survey and the ecological inventory may provide adequate information to set curriculum goals. Direct assessment is used for areas in which indirect assessment has been inadequate because: 1) information obtained is not specific enough, 2) conflicting information is obtained, or 3) the individual has not had the opportunity to perform the activity. To obtain this needed information, the instructor might use checklists, task analytic assessment, frequency counts, or repeated trial assessment.

Scheduling Testing and Observation

Many individuals do not perform well when subjected to prolonged periods of testing and observation. This can be especially true for a person with severe disabilities. The best way to conduct direct, initial assessment of people with severe disabilities is to schedule these tests and observations across several weeks. This scheduling can allow the instructor to use natural opportunities to assess skill performance. The assessment can also be interspersed with instruction to avoid subjecting the learner to prolonged sessions in which he or she is asked to make unfamiliar or difficult responses. However, using this approach to assessment requires that this part of the comprehensive educational assess-

Student's name: _____   Date: _____
Teacher's name: _____

Rate how well each potential skill matches the stated priorities.
Scoring:
  5 All of the time
  4 Most of the time
  3 Frequently
  2 Some of the time
  1 Occasionally
  0 Not applicable

Skills

Priorities								
1. Student preference								
2. Caregiver preference								
3. Societal value								
4. Preference of significant other								
5. Skill utility								
6. Permits partial participation								
Total points								

Figure 11. Sample chart for establishing priorities for assessment and the curriculum.

ment be conducted after the learner has entered the placement, and that the instructor be able to balance a schedule of one person's comprehensive assessment with the entire class's ongoing assessment and instruction. The alternative is for a specialist to conduct the direct assessment in the home and community prior to the individual's placement. Many school districts will not have the resources for this latter option, however.

An example of a schedule of observations and testing is shown in Figure 12. As the figure indicates, the instructor, Ms. N., plans to include Nat in existing instructional groups until his curriculum is complete. Nat's individual instructional time is used for testing. Observations are conducted across the day as opportunities arise. Ms. N. keeps Nat's checklists with her so that skills can be recorded as they are observed.

Student: __Nat__   Teacher: __Ms. N.__

Time	Activity	Assignment Ms. N.	Ms. M.	Independent
8:00	Greetings; find classroom; belongings	D and Nat*	J, K, A	S
8:30	Restroom	Nat**	D, A	S, J, K
9:00	Picture schedule	S, D, A	J, K, Nat	
9:30	Snack preparation[1]	J, K, Nat*	D, A, S	
10:00	Snack	Nat**	J, K, D	A, S
10:30	Dress for PE	S, D, A	J, K, Nat	
11:00	Gymnasium—PE	D, Nat*	A, K, S	J w/Mr. S.
11:30	Restroom	D, A, Nat	(Break)	S, J, K
12:00	Lunch	D, J, Nat*	A, K	S
12:30	Clean up	(Break)	J, A, S, Nat	K, D
1:00	Mainstreaming for recess and recreation	Nat**, D, A	J, K, S	
2:00	Restroom	D, A, Nat	(Group game)	
2:30	Belongings/good-bye/walk to bus	Nat**, J	D, A, K	S
3:00	Student's day ends			

[1]Schedule for 9:30 to 11:30:
    Monday—Classroom and gym as shown
    Tuesday—Purchase snack at convenience store (store varies)
    Wednesday—Classroom and gym as shown
    Thursday—Purchase snack at convenience store
    Friday—Rotate for once per month: visit physician; generalization for classroom activities in a home (e.g., snack prep, chores); shopping mall; fast food restaurant

Figure 12. A schedule for assessing a recently placed student. Assessment is scheduled throughout the day and conducted by the teacher. In this example, Nat is a student being assessed in a young elementary age classroom. (Other students are indicated by the first initials of their names.) Each student is assigned to the teacher (Ms. N.), to the aide (Ms. M.), or to independent work throughout the day. One asterisk indicates when Ms. N. will observe Nat and record his response(s) on a checklist. Two asterisks indicate when Ms. N. will directly test Nat on a scheduled activity. The schedule below the chart provides different activities for the 9:30–11:30 period each day.

Using Skill Checklists

One of the simplest procedures for direct assessment is to develop a checklist of the skills suggested by the ecological inventories and observe performance across time. This can be especially useful if the comprehensive educational assessment is being conducted by the program instructor, who can observe the individual daily. While the format of the checklist may be similar to those found on adaptive behavior scales, the specificity of skills will typically be much greater.

To develop a skill checklist, the instructor must have adequate knowledge of the activity or skill area to be observed. This may be obtained by reviewing the ecological inventories and resources that describe skills in these areas. (Chapters 5 through 8 provide information and references in each domain and related skill area to help the instructor develop these checklists.) The instructor must then determine the format of the checklist. The simplest format is just to list the skills. Alternatively, skills can be listed in order of difficulty. Finally, the instructor must decide how responses will be scored. One approach is for the instructor simply to note whether or not the skill is performed. Another approach to record: 1) the level of assistance needed to perform the response, 2) the frequency of the response, or 3) the consistency of performance.

Using Other Observational Assessments

Throughout this book, skill checklists are recommended to guide observations of skills. Checklists are especially helpful in organizing observations of rarely performed skills. The instructor can keep the checklist nearby and note performance whenever an infrequent opportunity arises during the assessment. The instructor may also be interested in the situations in which the behaviors occur. To organize observations of frequent behaviors, the instructor can use several other procedures. Sometimes the instructor will use verbatim recording of every response (see Chapter 7), or make anecdotal notes on a particular behavior and the situation in which it occurs (e.g., the ABC analysis described in Chapter 8). Alternatively, the instructor may choose simply to make anecdotal notes while observing a person perform a routine that later will be reviewed more systematically. Where a specific behavior to be observed can be defined, a frequency count of its occurrence may also be used.

Testing

When the target skills to be assessed are not observed in daily use, the instructor may want to test the person to see if these skills can be elicited in a highly structured situation. For example, merely by observing, an instructor may be unable to determine if a person fails to use a communication board because he or she does not know *how* to use the board or because he does not know *when* to use the board. By providing repeated opportunities to use the board in a highly structured testing situation, the instructor can identify whether or not the individual needs instruction only in generalization across situations or instruction in use of the board itself as well. To test the learner, the instructor can use repeated opportunities to perform a discrete response that are given together or distributed across the day (repeated trials), or task analytic assessment of a chain of responses. These two test procedures are described in detail in Chapter 3, since they are often used for ongoing assessment. When adapted to initial assessment, a broader list of responses may be targeted for either the repeated opportunities or the task analytic assessment, since at this stage the instructor seeks to pinpoint the learner's current repertoire of skills. In ongoing assessment, these tests will be tailored to the objectives of instruction (i.e., the specific skill the person is to learn).

STEP 4: DEVELOP CURRICULUM CHART AND WRITE IEP/IHP

Case Study Example

The organization of this comprehensive educational assessment and the preparation of the curriculum chart can be illustrated by Al's case study. Mr. A. had taught Al for a year when he conducted this assessment. Mr. A. thought that this reevaluation was critical at this time because Al only had 3 more years of school before he turned 21. The purpose of the assessment was thus to identify skills needed for Al's future adult environments. Mr. A. reviewed Al's records. First, he made a list of all the skills Al had mastered since he entered the high school life skills class by summarizing the previous IEPs. In doing so, he discovered that while Al had mastered an impressive list of skills for the home, his previous IEPs had underemphasized vocational training. In Al's psychological records, Mr. A. found a recent review of Al's ongoing progress that recommended that vocational training and social skills be targeted as Al's highest priorities for his last years of school. Other reports indicated the parents' satisfaction with Al's program. When Al's IEP first reflected a life skills approach in 1982, his parents noted their pleasure that this new focus had been taken. Al also had had a recent physical examination that indicated the need for further evaluation of his potential need for eyeglasses.

Next Mr. A. visited the parents to discuss the need to plan for Al's future. The parents were especially concerned about Al's job options. They had not considered Al's living anywhere except with them, but were interested in knowing more about the expectations of area group homes. Mr. A. also completed the Classroom Version of the Vineland Adaptive Behavior Scales (Sparrow et al., 1985) by using his personal knowledge of Al. Al had most of the skills in the motor and daily living skills domains of the Vineland. His poorest performance was in the area of communication and socialization. This information, along with the specialist's observation, led Mr. A. to make special note of the need for social skills assessment of Al. Mr. A. found the Vineland Scales inadequate for pinpointing Al's vocational needs and thus conducted a curriculum-based assessment, by reviewing the school's life skills curriculum and noting Al's typical level of performance for each skill. This assessment further verified Al's repertoire of domestic skills and provided a list of mastered functional academic skills. A list of job-related skills to be considered for curriculum development was also generated from the vocational section of the curriculum (e.g., time management, time on task, breaktime behavior).

Mr. A. talked with Al about his interests and preferences, especially as they related to his future vocation. Al stated a strong preference to work in a bowling alley. Mr. A. decided that Al's job preference should be pursued in this comprehensive assessment by evaluating job-related skills.

Mr. A. identified 11 environments in which Al currently functioned or might function in the future: 1) his family's home, 2) supported apartment living, 3) the streets in his neighborhood and town, 4) the local public bus, 5) fast-food restaurants, 6) the bowling alley in which he hoped to work, 7) the local shopping center, 8) a video arcade, 9) a park with a fishing stream, 10) the family's church, and 11) the sites cleaned by a mobile work crew on which he might work if he failed to get or lost the job at the bowling alley. Mr. A. then conducted ecological inventories to identify skills for each of these sites. He reviewed a published inventory of skills expected by employers (Rusch, 1983) to identify potential skills. From this published inventory, he designed an interview for the bowling alley manager, which included both job-related skills and a checklist of social behaviors. He conducted ecological inventories related to the community, recreation, and domestic skills through interviews and observations in Al's home and the group home. Mr. A. had taught Al in the shopping center, fast-food restaurant, and video arcade, and thought he had adequate information on the requirements of those sites.

From these inventories and the adaptive behavior assessment, Mr. A. was prepared to plan Al's direct assessment. He listed all of Al's skill needs and the ways in which he planned to assess those skills for which more information was needed (Table 3). Mr. A.'s list of direct assessments would require several weeks to complete. His next step was to schedule times in his day over the next month to test or observe Al in each skill listed. Since Mr. A. already gave each learner some one-on-one instruction, he assigned these times for testing and other times for observations. He then developed a data sheet and instructions for each of the informal tests to be used. These tests would be included with Al's case study to clarify how the information on his current performance had been obtained.

Over the next month, Mr. A. conducted the assessments. Once he had completed them, he again reviewed the guidelines for priorities to set specific goals for the next 3 years. He then wrote the curriculum chart and starred items suggested for the first year. This chart and the case study were shared with the parents. With their recommended revisions, Mr. A. then finalized the chart and wrote Al's IEP. (Al's curriculum chart is shown in Appendix A.)

Table 3. Planning for direct assessment of Al

More information needed for	How to assess
Skills for the home	
Housekeeping	
Meal preparation	Skill checklist
Dishwashing	Task analysis
Laundry skills	Task analysis
Personal maintenance	
Shaving	Task analysis
Laundry skills	Task analysis
Grooming (hair)	Task analysis
Emergencies	Repeated trials ("What if . . . ")
Recreation/socialization	
(information adequate from parent interview)	
Skills for the community	
Vocational	
Duration on task	Time duration
Social skills	Observe—checklist (some simulation needed)
Time management	Observe—checklist
Breaktime behavior	Observe—checklist
Custodial skills	Task analyses
Other community	
Being alone in public	Observe—checklist
City bus, varied routes	Task analysis
Purchase groceries, clothes, and so on from list	Task analysis
Recreational	
(information adequate from parent interview)	
Related skills for cross-planning	
Communication	
Social conversation	Observe—language sample
Motor	
Fitness	Fitness test
Academics	
(information adequate from previous instruction)	
Social	
(include with vocational)	
Interfering behavior	
(information adequate from ongoing assessment)	

ANNUAL ASSESSMENT FOR IEP/IHP PLANNING

The comprehensive educational assessment yields an individualized curriculum chart, or what might be viewed as a longitudinal (3–5-year) IEP/IHP. When such an assessment is available, annual assessment for IEP/IHP planning becomes a simple process of selecting and validating skills from this longitudinal plan. However, instructors will rarely have comprehensive assessments available for all individuals. The time frame for writing IEPs/IHPs also precludes conducting comprehensive assessments on an annual basis. A simplified procedure is needed to conduct an annual assessment for IEP/IHP planning. The following guidelines are intended to help an educator construct an individualized plan efficiently.

Steps for Annual Assessment

The first step in conducting the annual assessment to develop an IEP/IHP is to summarize progress from the preceding year. If data-based evaluation of objectives has been used, this summary can also be data based. For example, if ongoing data summaries are used (see Chapter 4), instructors will have performance means for each 2-week period. By subtracting the mean of the last 2 weeks from the first 2 weeks (or baseline period) of the school year, the instructor obtains the increment of progress for the year. For example, a learner's annual increment of progress for washing dishes can be calculated as follows:

Most recent mean:	89%	
September baseline mean:	−25%	
Increment of progress for year:	64%	(partial mastery)

If regression occurred, the increment would be negative:

Most recent mean:	55%	
September baseline mean:	−75%	
Increment of progress for year:	−20%	(regression)

Mastery might look like this:

Most recent mean:	94%	(mastery achieved)
September baseline mean:	−50%	
Increment of progress for year:	44%	(Mastery)

How this progress is recorded depends on the system used by the school or program. Some instructors use data summaries as report cards. In Lehigh University's field-based programs, data summaries are used as report cards for the school program and as quarterly reviews for adults. Since IEP/IHP development must be done in the last quarter of the programs, the increment of progress is computed at the end of the third quarter and recorded on the report card/quarterly summary. As an alternative, the instructor might write the summaries on the IEP/IHP itself or use a format similar to that shown in Figure 13. Whichever system is used, a form such as that shown in Figure 13 (see also Appendix C) needs to be generated to complete the annual assessment summary. The first step of this summary, then, is to record all current skills and progress to date on the IEP/IHP.

The second step is to identify the caregivers' priorities for the following year's plans. Many programs have a report card/quarterly review conference toward the end of the year. This meeting can be used both to review progress to date and to ask the caregiver to rank priorities. As an alternative, a form such as Figure 13 might be sent to the parents with a cover letter explaining the IEP/IHP development process and requesting their input on priorities.

The third step is to consider the individual's priorities. If the learner understands these priorities, he or she can be asked about preferences for the following year. To ensure that the individual understands what is being asked, the instructor might query him or her about preferences in the context of the activity in question. For example, while Al is playing basketball, Mr. A. might ask him if he likes basketball and wants to learn more ways to play it. For other people, preference must be inferred from ongoing behavior. Appendix C provides a guide to how these priorities might be ranked.

The fourth step is to consider longitudinal planning. If an individualized curriculum chart has been developed through a comprehensive assessment, the priorities of this chart should be considered. If an individualized chart is not available, the instructor might review the school or program curriculum to identify new skills for instruction. These would then be listed as shown in Figure 13.

Finally, the instructor conducts one ecological inventory to consider the highest priority for a new integration opportunity for the learner in the coming year. This might be a potential job training site for an older student or adult, a new site for community-based instruction, a regular class, or extracurricular activities. Obviously, ecological inventories are not needed for ongoing integration activities. Also, inventories of multiple sites are more appropriate for the comprehensive assessment when a learner's entire program is to be redeveloped. For the annual assessment, the inventory is used to help the instructor improve the quality and quantity of integration in each IEP/IHP year by focusing on one new priority, while maintaining previous integration gains. As shown in Figure 13, this instructor's ecological inventory was conducted for the sewing club. Integration opportunities to be maintained are integrated physical education and home economics classes and community-based instruction in a store and restaurant.

After these steps of information gathering have been completed, the instructor must then select those skills most important for the IEP/IHP. First, the instructor should review the entire skill list and note his or her own preferences. In doing so, the instructor has a "vote" in the final selection and has clarified his or her own position. But the instructor's final selection is based on more than his or her own preferences—it also includes looking across each column shown in Figure 13 to consider which skills meet the most priorities. In selecting skills, the instructor should also consider factors not explicitly shown in Figure 13, such as societal values and health and safety.

Case Study: Annual Assessment for Eva

As shown in the far left column of Figure 13, Mr. N. first summarized Eva's annual progress for her current objectives. Next, Mr. N. called Eva's caregiver, Ms. Ortiz, to solicit her priorities for ongoing or new objectives. These priorities were summarized in the "Caregiver preferences" column and the new skill that Ms. Ortiz requested—needlepoint—was recorded under the "New skills" section. Next, Mr. N. considered how Eva had responded to the previous year's lessons and considered any new preferences she had shown. However, Eva's increasing interest in needlepoint, which her mother identified, was the only one he could identify. Next, Mr. N. reviewed each skill on his list based on his ecological inventory of the sewing club that he conducted by interviewing the advisor for this club, and based on his knowledge of Eva's ongoing integration sites (physical education, home economics, store, restaurant). This integration review also revealed new skills to consider—orientation within the school to find the sewing club and age-appropriate dressing. Next, Mr. N. reviewed the life skills curriculum and a recently completed assessment of Eva's adaptive behavior (FSSI, Becker et al., 1986) to consider Eva's longitudinal needs, since she had not yet had a comprehensive assessment with an individualized curriculum chart. From the curriculum and assessment, he identified ordering from a menu and increasing hand strength as potential new skills. Finally, Mr. N. reviewed each skill and rated his own preferences based on the priority considerations shown in Figure 13 and the logistics of planning for his entire class of students.

Once the assessment was completed, Mr. N. was ready to select skills for the IEP/IHP. Some of his decisions for skill selection were easy to make. For example, ordering from a menu and needlepoint were important in all considerations. Eva would use her menu-ordering skills in current community-based integration activities and throughout her lifetime. Eva's parents enjoy eating out and would like Eva to make her own choices. Mr. N. considered this an important skill for Eva and, because other learners have restaurant skills, it also facilitated class planning. Similarly, because the opportunity had arisen for Eva to explore her long-term interest in needlepoint in a school club, teaching needlepoint was a high priority. It was also easy to discontinue Eva's mastered objectives, such as making a signature mark and hanging up her clothes. Some skills needed to be included—but revised to be more applicable to Eva's current and future settings. For example, since Eva had shown skill in learning sight words for grocery shopping, she might benefit from applying this skill in

Instructor _Mr. N._

Placement _____

Date _____

Learner _Eva_

Caregiver _Ms. Ortiz_

New integration priority _Sewing club_

Ongoing integration _Store, restaurant, P.E., Home Ec._

Resources for longitudinal planning _School curriculum and FSSI from 1988_

Annual progress for current objectives	Current objectives/ new skills	Priority source					Selected for IEP/IHP	Comments
		Caregiver preferences	Learner preferences	Integration	Longitudinal planning	Teacher preferences		
Current IEP +72% Mastered	_Signature mark_	MP	HP	HP	HP	X	no	_Mastered and used on a regular basis_
+100% Mastered	_Sight words_	HP	MP	HP	MP	HP	yes	_Select words related to integration activities_
–20% mean = 42% Re-gression	_Personal calendar_	I	X	MP	HP	MP	no	_Discontinue and explore other time management options_

	Skill							
+43% Mastered	Purchase 1 item	MP	HP	HP	HP	HP	yes	Expand to multiple items
+50% mean = 87% Partial mastery	Follow a schedule	HP	MP	HP	HP	HP	yes	Vary schedule for generalization
+18% mean = 67% Partial mastery	Social conversation	HP	I	HP	HP	HP	yes	Change to peer tutoring for motivation
+62% mean = 95% Partial mastery	Group games	MP	HP	HP	HP	MP	yes	General case across new games
+22% Mastery	Hang up clothes	HP	I	I	HP	X	no	Mastered
+0 mean = 0 No Progress	Menstrual care	HP	X	HP	HP	HP	yes	Explore options to improve motivation
New skills	Needlepoint	HP	HP	HP	HP	HP	yes	Join sewing club

Figure 13. Annual assessment for IEP/IHP development skill selection chart. (HP = high priority, MP = medium priority, I = impartial, X = discontinue.) (See Appendix C for explanation of how to rank priorities and for blank assessment form.)

(continued)

Figure 13. (continued)

Annual progress for current objectives	Current objectives/ new skills	Priority source					Selected for IEP/IHP	Comments
		Caregiver preferences	Learner preferences	Integration	Longitudinal planning	Teacher preferences		
	Mobility in school	HP	HP	HP	I	HP	yes	
	Age-appropriate dressing	I	I	HP	HP	HP	yes	Talk with mother privately before IEP conference
	Increase hand strength	MP	MP	MP	MP	I	no	No formal objective— address informally
	Order from menu	HP	HP	HP	HP	HP	yes	Simulate with weekly community outing
	Play basketball	I	HP	HP	MP	MP	yes	P.E. integra- tion or extra- curricular

(Use duplicate pages as needed to list all skills.)

her integrated home economics class. Similarly, while progress had been made in playing games and following a schedule, generalization training was needed for these skills to be useful to Eva longitudinally.

Mr. N. also faced some very difficult decisions. Eva disliked any attention focused on personal hygiene needs during menstruation and would scream and hit when assisted; but she lacked the necessary skills to maintain adequate hygiene (which is taught by Mr. N.'s co-teacher, Ms. P.). Mr. N., Ms. P., and Ms. Ortiz were all keenly aware of the low public or school tolerance for inadequate menstrual hygiene. Thus, while it was vital that the skill be targeted despite Eva's objections, Mr. N. would have to explore ways to improve motivation for self-care.

Another area in which Mr. N. hoped to effect change was in Eva's dress. Eva's mother did not recognize the importance of changing Eva's style of dress, despite the fact that Eva's expensive, but childish clothes solicited negative attention. Mr. N. decided to try to convince Ms. Ortiz of his point of view prior to the official decision making of the IEP conference. Mr. N. then reviewed each skill on the list to choose a subset for Eva's IEP. This list could change in the IEP conference, as a result of further parent or therapist input, but an instructor should always go to the conference with well-developed rationale for the objectives proposed.

Writing Objectives for the First-Year Plan

Once the annual assessment has been completed, the instructor is ready to write the objectives for the IEP/IHP. The quality of these written objectives can influence both ongoing assessment and instructional decisions about mastery. In writing the objectives, the instructor has two primary goals. First, the objective must be stated in observable and measurable terms if ongoing assessment is to be matched to it. Second, the objective must specify conditions and criteria for performance that reflect the normalized, independent performance expected. Many IEPs/IHPs include objectives that are too vague to meet either of these criteria. In a statewide review of IEPs, Browder and Lentz (1985) discovered that most IEP objectives for people with severe disabilities were too vague to interpret what functional skill was being targeted or how assessment would be designed.

To write the objective so that it clearly relates to functional activities of daily living, the instructor must specify the conditions of these settings. If the typical conditions are setting cues (e.g., entering a restaurant), the instructor would not want the objective to be to respond to artificial instructor cues. Criteria should also match normal expectations. The criterion of 90%—suggesting excellent but not perfect performance—is often included as part of an objective. Often such a criterion is inappropriate, however. While some skills (e.g., toileting) must be perfect to meet age expectations, others (e.g., social responses) can have much lower criteria and still fall within normalized performance. Thus, when the instructor gathers information on the need for a skill in a target setting, information should also be obtained on the criteria that should be established.

To write the objective so that assessment can be matched to it requires careful wording. Cole and Cole (1981) recommended using the letters "ABCD" to remember the components of the objective to be included:

A-represents the *audience* that is to perform the objective. More specifically, who will be doing the learning?

B-represents the desired *behavior* that will be exhibited by the child. The behavior should be stated in clear, observable terms.

C-represents the *conditions* under which the audience will perform the desired behavior. This segment is sometimes called the "given," and represents the setting in which the child will perform the learning task. The resources needed are also commonly stated as a condition.

D-represents the *degree of mastery* required to meet an acceptable level of performance on the objective. Mastery statements are frequently stated with one or both of the following components: the number or percentage correct and the specific time limitations required for the completion of the objective by the child. (p. 83)

For example, a well-written ABCD objective for Al would read as follows:

Audience: Al.

Behavior: Cleaning the sink.

Condition: Cue by picture schedule to clean sink of school or bowling alley.

Degree of mastery: No dirt or cleanser residue should be visible on the sink.

Task should be begun and completed within 5 minutes of the times shown on the schedule.

The above objective for Al is well written because it specifies exactly what the individual needs to do. Some poorly written objectives from actual IEPs/IHPs are presented below:

1. John will improve balance. (While doing what? Where? What degree of performance will be accepted as improvement?)
2. Jerry will point to his toothbrush. (Under what conditions? For what purpose? Must he point to it or just pick it up to use it?)
3. Carrie will tie her shoes 90% correct. (What is 90% of shoe tying? Sometimes tied? Partially tied? Under what conditions does she need to be able to perform this skill?)
4. Sally will develop her dressing skills. (What specific behavior is Sally to perform? Under what conditions and to what degree?)

SUMMARY

The two initial phases of assessment are the comprehensive educational assessment and the annual assessment for IEP/IHP planning. A comprehensive assessment can help the instructor chart the course for several years of instruction. Through such assessment, longitudinal services can be developed that lead to community integration. The approach suggested for the comprehensive plan is most appropriate for initial assessment and reevaluation every 3–5 years. The instructor is the person most likely to have the access to the learner and the knowledge required to conduct this assessment. This evaluation will not be conducted in prolonged testing sessions, but rather over the course of several days or weeks as natural opportunities to perform skills arise. Specific skills to be assessed are identified through ecological inventories and prioritization. At the end of this process, the instructor has a curriculum chart that can be used across several years of IEPs/IHPs. In the absence of a comprehensive assessment, or to update one, the instructor can follow the guidelines for the annual assessment. This procedure leads to the development of an IEP/IHP with carefully developed rationale for each objective.

STUDY QUESTIONS

1. What are the steps to identifying skills for a comprehensive assessment?
2. What are some variables to consider in setting priorities for assessment and instruction?
3. What are the steps to follow in conducting annual assessment to develop an IEP or IHP?
4. What are the components of a complete behavioral objective?

FOR FURTHER THOUGHT

1. How do you develop an IEP/IHP?
2. What steps might you add to make this assessment more complete?
3. Have you ever tried a comprehensive assessment?
4. How might you adapt the model provided in this chapter to be beneficial and practical to your setting?
5. Who should receive the comprehensive assessment first (e.g., Who has made the least progress?)?

appendix

Adaptive Behavior Scales

AAMD Adaptive Behavior Scale
Nadine Lambert, Myra Windmiller,
  Deborah Tharinger, and Linda
  Cole (1981)
Publishers Test Service
CTB/McGraw-Hill
Del Monte Research Park
Monterey, California 93940

Adaptive Behavior Inventory
Linda Brown and James E. Leigh
  (1986)
PRO-ED
5341 Industrial Oaks Boulevard
Austin, Texas 78735

Balthazar Scales Adaptive Behavior
Earl E. Balthazar (1976)
Consulting Psychologist Press, Inc.
577 College Avenue
Palo Alto, California 94306

*Comprehensive Test of Adaptive
  Behavior* and *NABC*
Gary L. Adams (1984)
Charles E. Merrill
Columbus, Ohio 43216

*Functional Skills Screening
  Inventory*
Heather Becker, Sally Schur,
Michelle Pavletti-Schelp, and Ed
  Hammer (1986)
Functional Resources Enterprises,
  Inc.
2743 Trail of the Madrons
Austin, Texas 78746

*The Pyramid Scales: Criterion-
  referenced measures of adaptive
  behavior in severely handicapped
  persons*
John D. Cone (1984)
PRO-ED
5341 Industrial Oaks Boulevard
Austin, Texas 78735

*Scales of Independent Behavior,
  Woodcock-Johnson Psychoeduca-
  tional Battery: Part Four*
Robert H. Bruininks, Richard W.
  Woodcock, Richard F. Weather-
  man, and Bradley K. Hill (1984)
Developmental Learning Materials
Allen, Texas 75002

Vineland Adaptive Behavior Scales
Sara S. Sparrow, David A. Balla,
  and Domenic V. Cicchetti (1985)
American Guidance Service
Circle Pines, Minnesota 55014-1796

chapter 3

ONGOING ASSESSMENT

ONCE THE INITIAL assessment has been conducted to identify a 3–5-year curriculum chart and the first year's plan, the instructor needs to design procedures to measure each objective in the annual plan. If this measurement is conducted frequently (e.g., daily, several times per week), the instructor can quickly identify areas of progress or lack of progress. However, collecting data has little utility if it is not used to make decisions to improve instruction. Ongoing assessment is thus conducted for *formative* evaluation; that is, objectives are measured throughout the year to evaluate progress and make necessary changes to achieve the desired outcome. Formative evaluation can be contrasted to *summative* evaluation, which is conducted after a program has been implemented to judge the final results. When an educator measures progress, but does not use this information to modify instruction, he or she is implementing summative evaluation. An educator who only judges results may become discouraged and abandon ongoing data collection because he or she receives no reinforcement from the data to justify the effort required by data collection. The key to making ongoing data collection worthwhile is learning to "read" the data to improve instructional success. Thus, this chapter and Chapter 4 (entitled "Evaluation of Ongoing Assessment") are critically interrelated. To implement formative evaluation, accurate, valid measurement is needed. This chapter provides guidelines for ongoing assessment. The next chapter suggests ways to reap the investment of ongoing assessment by using the data in instructional planning.

TYPES OF ASSESSMENT MODELS

While published instruments are sometimes useful in the two phases of initial assessment, they are rarely useful for ongoing assessment. Ongoing assessment must match the specific skill to be taught and the specific characteristics of the learner (Deno & Mirkin, 1977). Given these requirements, even published task analyses have limited utility unless modified to match the learner. Thus, ongoing assessment is "teacher made" to match the objectives of the individualized plan.

The first chapter of this book described several assessment models used in programs for learners with severe disabilities. The differences between these models are especially evident in the organization of ongoing assessment. In some classrooms, responses during instruction are recorded and graphed. Other instructors use "probes" that are observations or tests of performance without instruction. Some instructors measure chains of responding (e.g., task analytic assessment). Others focus on one or a few specific, distinct responses. As mentioned above, assessment must be matched to the learner and his or her objectives. The instructor would be wise to avoid data collection "fads," and instead use the best measurement to answer the instructional question at hand. For example, is the instructor concerned with performance of a chain of responses or with early performance of a new and complex response (e.g., the first symbolic communication)? These two different questions require different types of measurement.

Whichever data collection techniques are utilized, the instructor must consider the dual goals of applied behavior analysis and normalization (see Chapter 1). The methodology of applied behavior analysis will help the instructor develop accurate and replicable measurement. The principle of normalization will guide the instructor in measuring skills that are needed for the person to participate more fully in the mainstream of society. For example, an instructional objective is written in behavioral terms so that it can be observed and measured. Typically, the frequency of responding is counted, and sometimes the latency, duration, or rate is also noted. Assessment procedures are also designed to measure functional and generalized use of the skill so that the goal of community integration can be realized.

In this chapter, four methods of measurement of objectives related to community living are described: 1) *task analytic assessment*, 2) *repeated trial or opportunity assessment*, 3) *time-based assessment*, and 4) *qualitative assessment*. Task analytic assessment measures the performance of each response in a chain of responses. This chain of responses can be continuous, such as the flow of movement involved in washing hands, or it can be noncontinuous. For example, in partial participation to use the restroom, the person's targeted responses may be discrete—indicating the need to be changed, pressing the tape down on a diaper, indicating readiness for handwashing, and so on. These responses would not occur continuously, but rather would be spaced across time with the instructor's caregiving occurring between responses to be taught and assessed. If the task analysis, whether continuous or noncontinuous, represents an *activity* that begins with a natural cue and ends with some critical effect (e.g., getting outside, obtaining lunch, being able to rest), it is called a *routine,* and the method of measurement is *routine task analytic assessment.*

Sometimes the instructor will want to assess discrete responses that do not form a routine. For example, an instructor might want to evaluate how well a person has learned to use a communication wallet. Or, an instructor might be concerned with specific communication or motor responses to be generalized across tasks. The instructor can use repeated trial or opportunity assessment with regard to one or more target responses. These opportunities may be presented together or distributed across time. The trials may present the stimuli to make one response (e.g., "I want juice"), similar responses (e.g., "I want juice," "I want cookies"), or dissimilar but functionally related responses (e.g., asking for juice, grasping cup, throwing paper cup in trash). Similarly, the instructor may keep a frequency count of a response as it naturally occurs. For example, how often a person spontaneously uses a sign for "I need help" versus how often he or she hits might be measured through a simple frequency count across the day. Sometimes these discrete responses are taught, and assessed, in clusters. For example, a person with profound disabilities might be taught to nod to indicate readiness, grasp his or her hairbrush, and release the brush when finished with hair grooming. This response cluster of nodding, grasping, and releasing might be taught across the day in various activities. (Assessment and instruction in this approach is provided by the individualized curriculum sequencing model [Guess et al., 1978; Holvoet et al., 1980].)

Another option is time-based assessment, which may build on any of the above procedures by measuring rate, latency, or duration of responding. The final option is qualitative assessment, which also builds on the first two models by including judgments regarding qualitative aspects of performance (e.g., meets employer's satisfaction). Table 1 lists the types of ongoing assessment an instructor might select for ongoing measurement of certain IEP/IHP objectives.

Table 1. Options for ongoing assessment of IEP/IHP objectives

Type of assessment	IEP/IHP skill examples
Task analytic assessment	
Task analysis of single skill	Handwashing, vacuuming
Routine task analysis	Arrival, mealtime
General case analysis	Restaurant use
Repeated trial or opportunity assessment	
Repeated, massed trial	Communicating choices
Distributed trial	Reading picture schedule
Individualized curriculum sequencing (ICS)	Nodding "Yes," grasping, releasing
Frequency count of naturally occurring events	Biting; communicating, "Help"
Time-based assessment	
Rate	Vocational assembly, hitting
Latency	Waving to greet peer
Duration	Walking to regular class
Qualitative assessment	
Parental satisfaction	Dressing
Regular teacher appraisal	Communicating "Help"
Comparison to nonhandicapped	Restaurant use

TASK ANALYTIC ASSESSMENT

One of the most useful procedures for the assessment of life skills is task analytic assessment. Most daily routines are performed as chains of behavior. Even when individual responses are targeted for instruction, the ultimate goal is that these responses occur in the context of daily activities. For example, the basic motor skills of grasping and releasing objects would typically be embedded in a chain such as removing clothes from a dryer, washing dishes, brushing teeth, or dressing. The question an instructor may pose is whether to measure reaching and grasping as one step of a task analysis for brushing teeth, to measure these responses across different tasks (e.g., toothbrushing, dishwashing), or to measure these responses in isolation of activities but with real materials. While the last option provides the opportunity to observe repeated attempts to reach and grasp, the first two task analytic options help the instructor know if the person can perform these skills in the context of real activities, and thus may offer better appraisal of functional use of these skills.

Before considering the construction and use of task analyses, it may be helpful to review the conceptualization of this methodology and research in its use. The term task analysis has been used to refer to more than one concept. In one conceptualization, a task analysis is a sequence of skills learned en route to mastery of a competence. For example, addition of single digits, of two digits, and so on constitute a sequence of skills that leads to mastery of computation. A second conceptualization of a task analysis is the chain of responses involved in performing some activity (e.g., tying shoes). All the responses in the chained task analysis are performed in a relatively short period of time. A third type of task analysis, which begins with some specific natural cue and ends with a critical effect, is usually called a routine.

In this book, the term task analysis is used to refer to a chain of responses that are required for one skill (e.g., handwashing, using a vending machine) which may, or may not, be a routine; if for an activity, the term routine task analysis is used. The term *skill sequence* is used to refer to responses, or task analyses, that are arranged in sequence for mastery of a specific competence.

Often *checklists* are used for initial assessment. A checklist does not necessarily reflect a skill sequence, but rather may be a list of related skills with no specification of hierarchy. A checklist of skills without a hierarchy is not typically called a task analysis and will simply be referred to as a checklist throughout this book.

The beginning and end of a task analysis are rather arbitrary. For example, a task analysis could be developed for tying a bow, tying shoes, putting on shoes, dressing, or preparing for school in the morning. The last example, preparing for school in the morning, obviously includes many definable subchains of behavior (e.g., toothbrushing, toileting, dressing). To ensure that instruction is functional, the educator may first want to measure persons participation in an activity that begins with a natural cue and ends with a critical effect (i.e., a routine). For people with limited skills, this does NOT mean performing every response for handwashing, dressing, toothbrushing, and so on. However, it does mean being an active participant in each component of the routine. For example, responses targeted for the routine might include selecting which color shirt will be worn, grasping the toothbrush to indicate readiness for brushing, and putting hands in the sink to request help with washing them. Once the assessment for each routine in a person's day has been identified, the instructor can develop additional assessment that focuses on more independence within a skill. For example, in addition to the morning dressing routine, a specific task analysis might be used for toothbrushing because this is targeted for independent performance. Or, a repeated opportunity assessment (discussed later in this chapter) might be used for grasping and releasing self-care items. Thus, to keep instruction functional, instructors are encouraged to:

1. Define routines for assessment and instruction
2. Define task analyses of skills targeted for increased independence
3. Develop repeated opportunity assessment, where appropriate, for skills that will be addressed both within and across routines
4. Decide if any time-based or qualitative assessments are needed to evaluate skill fluency and normalized use

When first using ongoing assessment, an instructor may only be able to initiate routine assessment (number 1). As the instructor's assessment skills increase, the other methods of assessment may be tried to provide the opportunity for more refined instructional decisions (numbers 3 and 4 are discussed later in this chapter). Figure 1 provides an example of the types of measurement used by an instructor with advanced skill in ongoing assessment. (In studying this instructor's data collection schedule, it may be helpful for the reader to read through the figure once, read the remainder of this chapter, and then review the figure to see applications of the methods of assessment described.)

Constructing Task Analytic Assessment

Research on Task Analyses   Task analytic assessment and instruction have often been a component of successful instructional packages to teach life skills (Browder, Hines, McCarthy, & Fees, 1984; Cuvo et al., 1978; Spears, Rusch, York, & Lilly, 1981; Tucker & Berry, 1980). However, there has been little research on the construction of task analyses. Several authors have suggested guidelines for their construction based on extensive experience in their use (e.g., Bellamy, Horner, & Inman, 1979; Sailor & Guess, 1983; Snell, 1983). The sparse research that exists also offers some tenuous principles regarding their use. First, it may be important to use specific responses as steps of the analysis and to define stimulus control within the chain of behavior (Crist, Walls, & Haught, 1984; Thvedt, Zane, & Walls, 1984). Defining stimulus con-

Time	Schedule	Instructional priorities	Method of assessment
8:00–9:00	Arrival/free play/ restroom	Arrival routine (all)	Routine TA
		Grasp and carry (Sam)	Repeated opportunity
		Coat off (Peg & Terry)	Coat off TA
		Use communica- tion wallet (Bob & Alicia)	Repeated opportunity
		Restroom routine (all)	Routine TA
		Wash hands (Peg & Terry)	Handwashing TA
9:00	Homeroom integration	Regular class routine (all)	Routine TA
		Calendar skills— peer tutor (Sam)	Repeated opportunity
9:30	Passive leisure	Specific leisure skills (all)	Leisure skill TAs
		Choice (Bob, Alicia, Peg, Terry)	Repeated opportunity
		Integrated music class—Sam with OT	(No data)
10:00	Snack/restroom	Snacktime routine (all)	Routine TA
		Wash table (Peg & Terry)	Table washing TAs
		Snack preparation (Bob)	Cooking TA
		Restroom routine (all)	Catch-up data not done at 8:30
10:30	Active leisure or gym	Social interaction	Repeated opportunity
		General fitness	(No data)
		Integrated gym Tuesday, Thurs- day (PT works in class Monday)	Generalization data on social in- teractions
11:15	Lunch/restroom/ recess	Cafeteria routine for integrated lunch (all)	Routine TA
		Restroom	Catch-up data

(continued)

Time	Schedule	Instructional priorities	Method of assessment
12:00	Domestic routine simulation/rest (teacher break)	Toothbrushing (all)	Toothbrushing TAs
		Shoes off (Peg) Listen to story with lunch aide	Shoes off TA (No data)
1:00	Afternoon special		
	Vocational theme (Monday, Wednesday)	Work on task alone Cleaning (Peg, Terry)	Duration recording Custodial TAs
	Community-based instruction (Tuesday, Thursday) (PT accompanies Sam)	Store routine (all) (Ratio in store is 2:1; do leisure skills in van with aide while waiting turn)	Routine TA (Record data after return to van)
	School-wide clubs	Regular class routine	(No data)
2:00	Departure routine	Departure routine (all)	Routine TA

Figure 1. Sample schedule for ongoing assessment. The teacher has selected the type of assessment that best supports instructional priorities for each student in this elementary class. The teacher's ideal is to collect data daily on all priorities. However, if she collects data three times a week on a priority, an instructional decision can be made in 1–2 weeks. (PT = physical therapist, TA = task analysis, OT = occupational therapist.)

trol within the chain of behavior helps the instructor identify the natural cues to move from one step of a task analysis to the next. Second, instructors may include steps that are nonessential to the task for teaching purposes (e.g., saying the price aloud in using a vending machine), but these should be excluded from data summaries used to determine progress (Williams & Cuvo, 1986). Third, instructors may want to consider evaluating individual steps of a task analysis, as well as summarizing all steps together (T.G. Haring & Kennedy, 1988). Finally, when speed of performance is important, instructors may want to apply engineering principles in defining the task analysis (Lin & Browder, 1990). These research principles, as well as practical experience, are the bases for the guidelines offered to construct task analyses.

Routine Task Analytic Assessment As mentioned previously, the most important task analyses for ongoing assessment are those for daily routines. In a life skills approach, increased participation in routines of daily living are the instructional priority. Assessment needs to reflect this priority. Ongoing

Assessment using a task analysis of a specific skill like stuffing envelopes can be useful for evaluating progress.

assessment of routines helps the instructor evaluate both whether a person knows *how* to perform a skill and whether he or she knows *when* to perform it. Although extremely important, little research exists on the development of routines. However, Neel and Billingsley (1989) described the development of routines for assessment and instruction. (The guidelines discussed in this section are adapted from their IMPACT curriculum, to which the reader is referred for more information.) An important distinction should be noted between routine assessment as used here versus the work of Neel and Billingsley (1989).

Neel and Billingsley (1989) used the term routine to refer to any chain of responses that begins with a natural cue and ends with a critical effect (i.e., the naturally occurring outcome for performing the routine). Here, the term routine also applies to a chain of responses that begins with a natural cue and ends with a critical effect—but the chain represents an activity. If instructors use activity-based instruction, this is an important distinction. A lesson may have many task analyses, but usually only one activity. Routine task analytic assessment measures the person's active performance from the beginning to the end of the activity. To qualify as a routine, the activity must be planned to begin with a distinct natural cue and end with a critical effect. Sometimes there will be several subroutines with critical effects within the activity, especially if it is a long activity. While these subroutines may be considered for instruction, for routine task analytic assessment the focus will be on the entire activity.

Most individuals' days have natural breaks or transitions between routines. By identifying these transitions, the instructor can identify the routines in a person's day. For example, the elementary school students for whom assessment is shown in Figure 1 have the routines of arrival, restroom use, regular class routines, passive leisure, snack, active leisure, lunch, a domestic or vocational simulated routine, community-based instruction, and departure. To define the responses in the routine, a three-step planning process is required:

Step 1: Identify the natural cue for performing the routine
Step 2: Identify the critical effect
Step 3: Identify the responses to be assessed in the routine by selecting priority
IEP/IHP skills that enhance participation

The potential natural cue and critical effect for routines can be difficult to identify. It may be helpful to watch how children or adults without disabilities know when to begin a routine and what outcome seems to serve as their critical effect. Table 2 illustrates examples of these beginning and ending points for routines.

Once the beginning and ending of a routine have been defined, the intermediate responses can be selected. These responses will be IEP/IHP objectives that enhance participation in the routine. To keep the routine manageable for assessment and instruction, Neel and Billingsley (1989) recommended that about 15 responses be selected. The specific responses selected should be based on the priorities discussed in Chapter 2. For example, the instructor should consider which responses will increase the person's choice and control of the events in the routine, thus enabling him or her to become a more active participant.

Table 2. Examples of beginning and ending points for routines

Examples of routines	Natural cue to begin	Critical effect at end
	Recess routines (elementary)	
Preparation	Teacher announces	Being outside
Playtime	Peer swings	Stimulation of swinging
Return to class	Bell rings	Get water inside
	Community job routines (adult)	
Departure	Clock time	Relax on bus
Arrival	Bus stop	Get coffee
Photocopy	Papers in bin	Peer praise
Departure	Clock time	Relax on bus
	Family-style mealtime routines (any age)	
Preparation	Clock time	Food served
Eating	All seated	Consume dessert
Clean up	All finished	Watch the news

An example of a routine developed by Neel and Billingsley (1989) is shown in Figure 2. This figure shows how the routine is used for assessment once it is constructed. First, baseline assessment is conducted to determine the level of assistance the person requires to perform each response in the routine. Once identified, these levels of assistance are specified on the data sheet for instructor reference during instruction. For example, in Figure 2, Gary needs only the verbal cue "go to class" to walk down the aisle of the school bus.

The second step in developing the routine for ongoing assessment is to identify the speed of performance targeted for each response. Neel and Billingsley (1989) advocated that in order for individuals to experience the natural reinforcers for skills, performance must be fluent. If too slow, others may lose patience and perform the response for the person. Or, the person may resort to a faster, maladaptive response to achieve the same critical effect. Thus, the duration for each response is specified as shown in the second column in Figure 2.

Once the baseline assessment has been completed and instructional levels and durations have been identified for each response, the instructor is ready to use the form for ongoing data collection while teaching the routine. (It should be noted that Neel and Billingsley [1989] provided a second form for ongoing assessment that has more columns for additional days.) During instruction, the educator records the highest level of assistance needed for the person to perform each response. Duration is recorded on a less frequent schedule—about twice per month. The method used to summarize these data for instructional decisions is discussed in Chapter 4.

Task Analytic Assessment of Specific Skills As mentioned earlier, assessment of routines is most important to functional instruction. However, instructors will often also want to assess a specific skill within a routine that is targeted for increased independence (e.g., vocational assembly, putting on a shirt). An outline for the steps to develop a task analysis and use it for assessment are shown in Table 3.

In constructing the task analysis, the instructor should consider the following:

1. How effectively and efficiently does the learner currently perform the skill?
2. What is the "best" way to perform the skill (e.g., safest, most nutritious, hygienic, socially normative, fastest)?
3. What are the simplest and most efficient motoric responses that can be used to perform the skill effectively?
4. Can these motoric responses be further simplified by the use of adaptations (e.g., jigs, caregivers' arrangement of materials)?
5. How can responses be arranged or modified so that the discriminative stimuli for each response in the chain are clear?
6. Is the end analysis effective? By following the steps, is the activity achieved?

Assessment Data Sheet

Manager: _____ Helen _____

Name: _____ Gary _____

Date: _____ Bus to Classroom _____

Routine: _____ Bus to Classroom _____

Beginning natural cue: _____ Teacher approaches Gary _____

Critical effect: _____ Participation in classroom activities _____

Latency: _____ 3 seconds _____   Duration of routine: _____ 3 min., 10 sec. _____

Types of assistance:
FP = Full physical assistance
PA = Partial physical assistance
G = Gestural cue
V = Directive verbal cue
I = Natural cue or independent
Ⓒ = Communication target

[Note: Includes 3 seconds latency for each step.]

Steps	Duration	Date	Date	Date	Date	Type of assistance for instruction (describe)
1. Ⓒ Requests help with seatbelt	2 sec	FP	FP	FP	V/FP	V/FP Say "Show me 'help.'" Mold sign for "help."
2. Walks down aisle	15 sec	V	V	V	V	V "Go to class."
3. Picks up lunch box or other materials	10 sec	I	V(ED)	I	I	I [Note: No duration errors occurred with type of assistance selected for instruction.]
4. Exits bus	5 sec	PA	PA	I	I	I
5. Walks to building entry	35 sec	PA	PA	PA	PA	PA Hold his hand while walking
6. Ⓒ Requests help with door	2 sec	FP	PA	FP	V/FP	V/FP Say "Show me 'help.'" Mold sign for "help."
7. Enters building	2 sec	PA	PA	PA	PA	PA Hold his hand while entering building
8. Walks to classroom	60 sec	PA	FP	PA	PA	PA Hold his hand while walking
9. Puts away lunch box and other materials	10 sec	PA	G	PA	FP	FP Take his hands and guide to shelf
10. Takes off coat	7 sec	I(ED)	I	I(ED)	FP	I [Note: Record duration errors during instruction.]
11. Ⓒ Requests help finding hook	2 sec	FP	FP	FP	FP	V/FP Say "Show me 'help.'" Mold sign for "help."
12. Hangs up coat	4 sec	G	PA	G	V	4th trial, G | G — Point at hook

Figure 2. Example of routine task analytic assessment. (From Neel, R.S., & Billingsley, F.F. [1989]. *IMPACT: A functional curriculum handbook for students with moderate to severe disabilities* [p. 76]. Baltimore: Paul H. Brookes Publishing Co.; reprinted by permission.)

Table 3.   Steps to task analytic assessment

Step 1.   Plan the task analysis.
—Consider the student's current performance.
—Consult resources on the best way to perform the task.
—Identify simple motoric responses.
—Simplify the task further with adaptations.
—Enhance stimulus control.

Step 2.   Write the task analysis.
—Write the sequence of steps using action verbs.
—Clarify steps as necessary.
—Try the task following the written steps.
—Write the steps on a data collection sheet.

Step 3.   Plan the assessment.
To plan probes:
—Decide how to secure attention, enhance motivation.
—Identify the discriminative stimulus to begin the task.
—Decide the latency for responding.
—Plan how to handle errors.
—Plan how to end the assessment.
—Write these plans and scoring key on data sheet or the instructional plan.
To plan instructional data collection:
—Decide what will be scored.
—Plan when to record data during instruction.
—Write these plans on the data sheet or plan.

Step 4.   Conduct the assessment.
—Follow the assessment plan.
—Schedule reliability observations when possible.

Observing Current Performance   Before writing the task analysis, the instructor may first want to observe the person attempting to perform the task. If the person is told to brush his or her teeth, what happens? This open-ended, initial observation can help the instructor define and build on existing responses. Once the instructor has defined the analysis, it may be difficult to step back and observe the person's way of performing the skills since the analysis supposedly represents the "correct" way. This few minutes of time to observe current performance may provide a beginning list of responses or an indication that the person has no skill in this area when given the materials and instructions to perform the skill.

Identifying "Best" Practices   Instructors of people with severe disabilities often find themselves planning instruction for skills for which their own training has been minimal. Life skills instruction requires knowledge of home economics, industrial trades, nursing, and so on. Relying on one's own practices may not lead to identifying the safest, most hygienic, or nutritious practice. For example, in food preparation, instructors may choose recipes based on their own preferences and teach them according to their own cooking styles. When these plans are reviewed, it may become evident that: 1) foods selected are not the best for the person's dietary needs, 2) the person does not like the menu, 3) the preparation style may be inefficient or unsafe, and 4) the instructor may omit critical hygienic steps (e.g., washing hands before handling food). The work of Cuvo and his colleagues has well illustrated methods instructors may use in developing task analyses for skills for which their own training is minimal. For example, Cronin and Cuvo (1979), Cuvo et al. (1981) and B.F. Johnson and Cuvo (1981) consulted with a professor of home economics to develop task analyses for cooking, laundry, and mending. To develop an emergency telephone use analysis, Risley and Cuvo (1980) consulted with the telephone company and emergency stations. These authors also observed people without disabilities performing these skills, to validate their task analyses. While the instructor may not have the time for such extensive validation of each task analysis, other sources of information that are readily available might be consulted. For example, the instructor might check a public library for a book on the subject, call a high school teacher with expertise on this subject (e.g., a home economics teacher), or keep a file of popular magazine articles and government booklets on various life skills that can be consulted quickly when writing task analyses. The person's caregivers may also have expertise in specific areas, and ideas and preferences for how certain skills should be performed.

Defining Simple Motoric Responses   The design of a task and the type of motor movements taught can affect how efficiently and fluently the task is peformed. Bellamy et al. (1979) described methods to minimize the response difficulties of vocational tasks, and Browder, Shapiro, and Ambrogio (1986) demonstrated how more efficient responses can be taught. One way to achieve identification of the most efficient motoric responses and task design is to use an industrial engineering principle known as *motion study*. In motion study, extraneous movements are eliminated, necessary motions are simplified, and the most efficient movement sequence is selected (Niebel, 1982).

In the 1920s, two engineers named Frank and Lillian Gilbreth classified all human movement into 17 categories that they called "therbligs"—which is their last name spelled backward, with the last two letters reversed (Gilbreth & Gilbreth, 1917). These movements were further classified as efficient and inefficient. These therbligs have been used by engineers for over 65 years to construct what special educators call task analyses. Table 4 provides the definitions of the 17 therbligs and Table 5 states which are most efficient. Figure 3 provides a checklist for further sequencing the therbligs for overall efficient task performance. Interestingly, if two engineers analyze a task, their steps will be nearly identical because of the application of therbligs. Recently, Lin and Browder (1990) demonstrated the benefits of applying therbligs in teaching vocational tasks. Instructors may want to refer to Tables 4 and 5 and Figure 3 when writing the steps of a task analysis for vocational skills, or any task, to try to select the most efficient responses for fluent performance. Figure 4 shows an example of a therblig-written task analysis compared to a traditional, nontherblig analysis.

Table 4. Definitions of 17 fundamental motion therbligs

1. *Search:* The basic operation element employed to locate an object.
2. *Select:* The therblig that takes place when the operator chooses one part over two or more analogous parts.
3. *Grasp:* The elemental hand motion of closing the fingers around a part in an operation.
4. *Reach:* Represents the motion of an empty hand, without resistance, toward or away from an object.
5. *Move:* The basic division to signify a hand movement with a load.
6. *Hold:* The basic division of accomplishment that occurs when either hand is supporting or maintaining control of an object while the other hand does useful work.
7. *Release:* The basic division that occurs when the aim of the operator is to relinquish control of the object.
8. *Position:* An element of work that consists of locating an object so that it will be properly oriented in a specific place.
9. *Preposition:* An element of work that consists of positioning an object in a predetermined place so that it may be grasped in the position in which it is to be held when needed.
10. *Inspect:* An element included in an operation to assure acceptable quality through a regular check by the employee.
11. *Assemble:* The basic division that occurs when two mating parts are brought together.
12. *Disassemble:* The reverse of assemble. It occurs when two mating parts are disunited.
13. *Use:* A completely objective therblig that occurs when either or both hands have control of an object during that part of the cycle when productive work is being performed.
14. *Unavoidable delay:* An interruption beyond the control of an operator in the continuity of an operation.
15. *Avoidable delay:* Any idle time that occurs during the cycle for which the operator is solely responsible, either intentionally or unintentionally.
16. *Plan:* The mental process that occurs when the operator pauses to determine the next action.
17. *Rest to overcome fatigue:* The duration of rest that does not appear in every cycle but is evidenced periodically in order to overcome fatigue.

From Lin, C., & Browder, D. M. (1990). An application of the engineering principles of motion study for the development of task analyses. *Education and Training in Mental Retardation, 25,* p. 371; reprinted with permission.

A second consideration in defining the motoric movements that will be the steps of the task analysis is the degree of specificity for each step. For example, in the task of watering houseplants, the first step might be "Fill watering can." This "big" step actually includes many motoric responses. By contrast, the first steps could be "Grasp watering can. Walk to sink. Grasp cold water knob. Turn knob on. Move can under faucet. Turn knob off." The specificity of each response defined will obviously influence the number of steps in a task analysis.

Table 5. Summary of therbligs

Efficient therbligs
1. Physical basic divisions
   a. Reach
   b. Move
   c. Grasp
   d. Release
   e. Preposition
2. Objective basic divisions
   a. Use
   b. Assemble
   c. Disassemble

Inefficient therbligs
1. Mental or semimental basic divisions
   a. Search
   b. Select
   c. Position
   d. Inspect
   e. Plan
2. Delay
   a. Unavoidable delay
   b. Avoidable delay
   c. Rest to overcome fatigue
   d. Hold

Adapted from Niebel (1982).

While Crist et al. (1984) found some support for using longer task analyses with learners with more severe retardation, it would be an overgeneralization to assume that people with severe disabilities need long task analyses for every task. Rather, the instructor will want to match the specificity of the analysis to the learner's current ability to perform the task. The instructor will not want to make steps so specific that they create responses "frozen" in mid-air while teaching (note that to "hold" or to "rest" are classified as inefficient therbligs). For example, in putting on a sweater, a step may be "Move arm through sleeve." The instructor would not want to define an analysis with "one inch into sleeve, second inch into sleeve," and so on, because this step is typically one fluid motion.

Simplifying Responses with Adaptations Some persons will have difficulty with the task because certain motoric responses are not in their repertoire due to physical disabilities or delay in motor development. The instructor may be able to overcome these barriers to independent performance of the task analysis by building in the use of adaptations. For example, an occupational therapist may be able to provide a dressing hook for a learner who cannot reach down to put on his or her pants. Toothpaste pumps can eliminate the need to screw on and off caps. Velcro tennis shoes eliminate difficult shoe tying. Some individuals' physical impairments are so extensive, however, that the instructor

	Yes	No
Elimination		
1. Eliminate all possible jobs, steps, or motions.	___	___
2. Eliminate irregularities in a job so as to facilitate automaticity. Provide fixed places for things.	___	___
3. Eliminate the use of the hand as a holding device.	___	___
4. Eliminate awkward or abnormal motions.	___	___
5. Eliminate danger.	___	___
Rearrangement		
1. Distribute the work evenly between the two hands.	___	___
2. Arrange for a straightforward order of work.	___	___
Simplification		
1. Use the smallest muscle group capable of doing the work.	___	___
2. Reduce eye travel and the number of fixations.	___	___
3. Keep work in the normal work area.	___	___
4. Shorten motions.	___	___
5. Adapt handles, levers, pedals, buttons, and so on to human dimensions and musculatures.	___	___
6. Use the simplest possible combination of therbligs.	___	___
7. Reduce the complexity of each therblig.	___	___

Figure 3. Checklist of general suggestions for improving jobs based on the principles of motion economy. (Adapted from Niebel, 1982.)

cannot identify or design the technology to overcome the barriers to independent performance of the skill. L. Brown, Branston-McLean, et al. (1979) advocated that when such disabilities exist, the instructor target partial participation as a goal for the activity. When the goal is partial participation, the instructor can define the task analysis to enable the person to perform as many of the responses in the chain as are feasible and practical in daily living. An example of a task analysis based on partial participation is shown in Figure 5.

Enhancing Stimulus Control In performing a chain of responses, some stimuli set the occasion for the chain to be performed. Each response in the chain then sets the occasion for the next response to be performed. It is unclear whether the response itself becomes the discriminative stimulus to perform the next response, or whether changes in the environment created by a response set the occasion for the next response (Sulzer-Azaroff & Mayer, 1977; Thvedt et al., 1984). Giving consideration to how each response can be defined to cue the next response may minimize the instructor-delivered prompts during teaching. To do this, the instructor needs to define what the discriminative stimulus is for each response in the chain. This was illustrated and described well by Bellamy et al. (1979). An example of a task analysis with defined stimuli for each step is shown in Figure 6.

THERBLIG TA		PRIOR TA

Left Hand	Right Hand	PRIOR TA
*1. Reach for insert A	Reach for insert B	1–3. Did not use both hands together, to pick inserts. Rather picked up A with right hand, then picked up B with right.
*Grasp insert A	Grasp insert B	
Move insert A to workplace	Move insert B to workplace	
2. Release insert A	3. Grasp insert A while holding insert B	
*4. Reach for envelope		4. Step was "Pick up envelope"-not typically grasped at opening.
Grasp envelope at opening		
Move envelope to workplace		5. Step not specified in prior TA.
5. Hold envelope		
	6. Move inserts into envelope	6–10. Steps were "Put inserts in" and "Drop in bin." Did not teach to use fluid left to right motion to release insert into envelope and keep moving to bin.
	7. Release inserts	
	8. Reach for right side of envelope	
9. Release hold	**10. Grasp envelope	
	Move envelope to finished bin	
	Release envelope	

Figure 4. Example of therblig-written task analysis compared to a nontherblig task analysis for the envelope insertion task. (From Lin, C., & Browder, D. M. [1990]. An application of the engineering principles of motion study for the development of task analyses. *Education and Training in Mental Retardation, 25*, p. 373; reprinted by permission.) (* = steps were combined into a "get insert/envelope" step during training, ** = steps were combined into a "put envelope away" step during training.)

Defining responses to enhance stimulus control can be a challenging procedure. Instructors may consider the following in trying to enhance stimulus control:

1. Can a response be introduced early in the chain that sets up materials to serve as cues for what comes next (e.g., when clearing the table, lining up the dishes by glasses, silverware, plates, and pots to cue the order for washing or loading the dishwasher)?

2. Can the responses be sequenced so that a distinctive visual or auditory effect is created that cues the next response (e.g., loading glasses in the dishwasher from back to front by rows so that one glass is a cue for where the next glass belongs)?

3. Can the movement of the chain of responses be defined so that the learner moves toward the next response (e.g., bathing by soaping a sponge or washcloth well, scrubbing from face to toes, rinsing the cloth, and rinsing from face to toes, as opposed to soaping the cloth, washing the face, rins-

Task:	Tape recorder use with flipper switch and Yes/No tape choice				Week of:	4/8–4/12		
Teacher	S^D	Response	4/8	4/9	4/10	4/11	4/12
Asks choice	"Want tape?"	Yes or no signal	+	+	+	+	+
	"Want Grandma's tape?"	Yes or no signal	+	+	+	+	+
	"Want Uncle's tape?"	Yes or no signal	NA	+	+	NA	+
	"Want the music tape?"	Yes or no signal	NA	NA	+	NA	+
Opens tape player	—	—					
Gives student tape	Tape in hand	Insert tape.	–	–	–	–	–
Snaps tape in	—	—					
Shuts cover	Cover clicks.	Push switch on.	+	+	+	+	+
	Tape plays to end.	Push switch off.	–	–	–	–	–
Rewinds tape (repeat sequence)	—	—					

Figure 5. Example of task analytic assessment designed for partial participation. (S^D = discriminative stimulus; + = correct response; – = incorrect response; NA = not applicable, makes prior choice.) (Adapted from a task analysis designed by Doris Martin for use in her classroom in the Bucks County Intermediate Unit, Pennsylvania, with a student who is blind and has severe spastic quadriplegia.)

ing the face, soaping the cloth, and needing to remember to move to the neck after soaping again)?

Writing Task Analysis Based on this Planning The ideas given for planning task analyses are a resource to improve, as well as develop, task analyses. The instructor need not try to develop the perfect task analysis, but rather should keep in mind the guidelines suggested to make each task analysis the best possible, given time and logistical constraints. When this planning has been done, the instructor is ready to define the responses in the chain that will be the task analysis. To do this, the instructor will:

1. State each response as an observable behavior (see therbligs in Table 4 as a guide)

S^D	Response
13 Parts in bin	Pick up bearing and place on table
12 Bearing on table	Place hex nut in one bearing corner
11 Nut in one corner	Place hex nut in second corner
10 Nuts in two corners	Place hex nut in third corner
9 Nuts in three corners	Place cam base in bearing
8 Cam in bearing	Place roller in bearing
7 Roller in bearing	Place red spring in bearing
6 Red spring placed	Rotate bearing and cam 180°
5 Bearing rotated	Place roller in bearing
4 Roller in bearing	Place green spring in bearing
3 Green spring placed	Wipe bearing with cloth
2 Bearing cleaned	Place camed bearing in bag
1 Cam in bag	Place bag in box

Figure 6. A task analysis data sheet indicating task acquisitions across 20 training probes. Slashes indicate correct responses on a step. Circles show total number correct. (S^D = discriminative stimulus.) (From Bellamy, G.T., Horner, R.H., & Inman, D.P. [1979]. *Vocational habilitation of severely retarded adults* [p. 75]. Baltimore: University Park Press; reprinted by permission.)

2. Write the stated behavior beginning with an action verb stated in the second person (e.g., "Grasp the waistband," "Move the knob to turn on water")

3. Write the responses in the order they are to be performed

4. Review the list of responses to clarify any that are ambiguous or that have special criteria for performance (e.g., "Grasp waistband—both hands")

5. Watch someone perform the task following the steps written, to see if doing so results in performance of the activity

6. Record the steps on a data sheet

Example of Development of a Task Analysis The planning and writing of a task analysis can be illustrated with an example from John's case study. The instructor developed a task analysis for John to pour his drink from a thermos during lunch. If not assisted, John would open and pour the drink on the table and himself. When Ms. M. observed John before writing a task analysis, she noted that he could open the thermos alone but then poured the entire contents downward without aiming toward the cup or judging when the cup was full. She decided to include the response he had mastered of opening the thermos to help define what correct response should follow. Since John's pouring skills were complicated by his lack of vision and hearing (i.e., he could not see or hear the spill), Ms. M. asked a vision specialist for ideas about the best way to teach John to pour. The vision specialist showed Ms. M. how to insert a finger on the inside of the rim of the cup to feel when the liquid filled the cup. Ms. M. next considered how to define the specific motor responses to make them as efficient as possible by reviewing the list of therbligs (see Table 4). By practicing with her eyes closed, she came up with these responses:

1. Search for thermos.
2. Hold thermos with left hand.
(Next steps are for right hand.)
3. Grasp cup.
4. Move (unscrew) cup.
5. Preposition cup on table.
6. Search for lid.
7. Grasp lid.
8. Move (unscrew) lid.
9. Preposition lid on table by cup to avoid search for cup.
10. Reach finger into cup.
11. Move thermos to pour (left hand).
12. Release thermos to table (left hand) when finger reached.
13. Reach (remove) finger from cup.

Ms. M. considered adaptations to simplify the above responses. She considered a thermos with a spout, which would minimize spilling. However, she decided to try to teach the skill without this adaptation for two reasons: 1) John's current coffee thermos looked more typical of the type of thermos used by adult men, and 2) John showed a strong preference for his thermos and became concerned on occasions when he did not find it in his lunchbox.

When Ms. M. reviewed the task analysis to consider stimulus control, she noted these natural cues to perform each response:

The open lunch box already cued the pouring activity for John. No verbal direction to pour would be needed.
John typically unscrewed the cup and lid once he got his thermos out of the box.
Putting the lid down would need to serve as a cue to put his finger in the cup. This seemed like a weak cue.
The finger on the rim also could be used for tactile feedback for when the thermos was on the edge of the cup so he could pour into the cup (i.e., tilt thermos to touch finger).
The feel of the liquid on his finger would be a distinct cue. It could be more distinct if the liquid was very cold or hot (not scalding).

Ms. M. was generally pleased that all of the responses had clear stimuli, except for John's putting his finger in the cup. She decided to have him move his hand immediately from holding the thermos while unscrewing the lid to the cup, without placing his hand on the table or his lap. Now, she was satisfied that she had planned a good task analysis with which to begin instruction. Ms. M. tried pouring a drink with her eyes closed while a friend read the steps and was satisfied that the defined chain of behavior worked well for pouring.

Conducting Task Analytic Assessment

Once a well-defined task analysis has been constructed, the instructor can develop the task analytic assessment procedure. In planning this procedure, the instructor should consider several questions:

1. How will attention to the task be secured and maintained? How will the person be motivated to do his or her best?
2. What stimulus should set the occasion to begin the chain of responses?
3. How much time should the person have to begin the task and how much time should be allowed between steps?
4. What will be done if the person does not perform a step correctly?
5. How will the assessment end?

Attention and Motivation   One of the challenges of assessment is motivating persons to perform to the best of their ability. Ideally, assessment approximates naturally occurring environmental events. A person who performs a routine such as cleaning the house can do so with few to no prompts to attend to the task, or perform the task for praise for performing well. Sometimes an instructor may be able to conduct task analytic assessment simply by watching the person perform the task, without interacting with the person. This would be ideal for tasks typically performed without social interaction. However, if the person does not perform the task, the instructor may not know whether the person cannot do the task or will not do the task. Additional motivation may be necessary to try to assess performance of the skill. For example, the instructor might praise the person for "working hard." Or, some preferred activity might be scheduled to follow performance of the skill to be tested. In rare instances, every response in the chain might receive reinforcement (e.g., praise) if the instructor wants to determine exactly what the person can do if highly motivated. In research on motivation during testing with people with severe behavior disorders, Handleman, Powers, and Harris (1981) found that providing reinforcement for every response on the test, regardless of whether or not the response was correct, enabled the tester to evaluate the performance of individuals who previously would not respond. Some people have serious and high rates of interfering behaviors that constitute most of their responding throughout the day. For example, an instructor may be using differential reinforcement of other behavior (DRO) to decelerate self-injurious behavior. Such reinforcement would typically also be used during testing to obtain the person's best performance. The use of these contingencies should be exceptions in ongoing assessment if the goal of instruction is for the person to respond given the naturally occurring contingencies available in the environment.

Discriminative Stimulus to Begin Responding   Similar to the goal of assessing individuals under conditions of natural contingencies, it is preferable for assessment to be conducted with natural cues to begin and continue responding. Often instructors get into the habit of giving verbal directions for all tasks because individuals respond to these directives. However, the functional use of many daily living skills requires responding to environmental cues that are not a stated direction. For example, entering the classroom is the natural cue to walk to the closet and take off a coat, not someone saying "Take off your coat." If a person is still dependent on the instructor's directions to get through daily routines, the instructor may wait for the person to respond to natural cues and then give one verbal prompt to see if the person can perform the task if told to do so, even if environmental stimulus control has not yet been achieved.

Response Latency   The instructor must decide how long to wait to see if the person will begin the task, and how long to wait between steps before providing assistance or ending the assessment. For example, Browder et al. (1984) allowed 3–5 seconds for the person to begin responding and to begin each response in the chain.

Incorrect or No Response   A special problem that arises in assessing a chain of responses is that if one response is not made, the rest of the responses in the chain cannot be assessed. The instructor may use several methods to handle the failure to respond correctly prior to the end of the chain of responding. These include the single opportunity method, the multiple opportunity method, or the *variation* method (Snell, 1983). In the single opportunity method, the instructor ends the assessment as soon as the person fails to respond or to respond correctly in the given latency period (e.g., 5 seconds). Credit is only given for steps performed up to the failure to respond correctly. The rationale for this approach is that often in the natural environment, continuation of the activity is unsafe or impossible if failure to respond correctly occurs (e.g., street crossing, cooking, telephone use). This method requires no instructor intervention, so it has the advantage of allowing the instructor to step back and observe performance under natural conditions. The disadvantage is that the instructor has no idea whether or not responses that occur later in the chain can be performed correctly. In the multiple opportunity method, the instructor intervenes to perform the step when the person fails to respond. The person is not prompted to respond, but rather the instructor gets materials to the point that the person can continue the chain of responding. This intervention is repeated as necessary until the entire chain has been performed. In the variation method, certain steps may be omitted if a critical response is not performed, but then the instructor skips to a later point in the chain to continue assessment.

Figure 7 illustrates each method of handling the failure to respond correctly during task analytic assessment. In the chart within Figure 7, a plus (+) shows the person responding correctly; a minus (−) indicates that the person

This example shows hypothetical performance of the same student when tested with the three methods for handling errors. In the single opportunity method, the test is stopped after the first error. In the multiple opportunity method, the teacher correctly performs erroneous responses for the student. In the variation method, the teacher does not test steps 4 and 5 if 3 is wrong because these steps are interdependent, but continues testing on step 6.

	Single opportunity		Multiple opportunity		Variation	
Response	S	T	S	T	S	T
1. Approach machine.	+		+		+	
2. Take out wallet.	+		+		+	
3. Select coins.	−	End test	−	Puts coins in S's hand	−	Goes to step 6
4. Insert coins.	−	Not tested	−	Inserts coins	−	Not tested
5. Collect change.	−	Not tested	−	Takes change	−	Not tested
6. Push choice.	−	Not tested	−	Pushes choice	−	Pushes choice
7. Reach to bin.	−	Not tested	+		+	
8. Take out soda.	−	Not tested	+		+	
Total correct	2		4		4	

Figure 7. Examples of methods to handle errors during task analytic assessment. (S = student's responses; T = teacher's responses; + = correct response; − = response not correct)

did not make the correct response. The data show how results may differ depending on the instructor's reaction to errors. In the single opportunity method shown in Figure 7, the assessment is ended when the person does not select the correct coins. Obviously, in daily living, failure to select the correct coins precludes using a vending machine. In the multiple opportunity method, the instructor selects the coins and waits for the next response. The person inserts the coins in the wrong place on the machine, so the instructor inserts them. The person does not take the change, so the instructor collects it. Then the person does not push a selection, so the instructor pushes a selection. The person can reach to the bin and pick up the soda. This multiple opportunity gives the instructor useful information about the person's ability to perform the end of the chain. If one step at a time will be trained, the instructor might instruct this person first on step 6, since he or she can then finish the chain alone. The variation method is shown in the last column of Figure 7. In this example, a single opportunity is given to perform the money-related steps 3–5, and then the instructor begins assessment again for selecting a choice and getting the soda.

Ending the Assessment The termination of assessment depends on the instructor's plan for the person's failure to respond. That is, the instructor may end the assessment at the first failure or at the end of an opportunity to perform each and every step. An alternative that has been used by Cuvo et al. (1981) is to end the assessment after a defined duration for performing the entire task or after the person communicates that he or she has finished. Some instructors like to acknowledge performance (e.g., by saying "Thank you for trying that alone"), since the person is often aware that he or she has been observed.

Example of Task Analytic Assessment The example of the pouring task can be reviewed to illustrate how task analytic assessment is planned. Figure 8 shows the data sheet with the task analysis and the assessment instructions. No special provisions are needed for motivation. The cue to begin is initiated by John whenever he opens his lunchbox. The instructor allows John only 3 seconds to begin each correct response because John typically will pour the liquid quickly and erroneously. During baseline, Ms. M. used a single opportunity method for failure to respond correctly because the natural consequence for an error creates unpleasant lunch conditions (i.e., spilled liquid) for both the instructor and John. During instruction, Ms. M. recorded data immediately after teaching John the pouring steps. She did not try to teach a step and then score a step because John would lose the opportunity to respond to the natural cues to perform the next step.

Variations of Task Analytic Assessment

Testing versus Teaching Instructors typically follow one of three patterns of data collection for teaching versus testing: 1) collecting data only during noninstructional "probes" or tests, 2) collecting data only while teaching, or 3) using some combination of probes and instructional data. The teaching example shown in Figure 8 has probes during baseline and then instructional data only are collected.

When data are collected on performance during instruction, the instructor may wish to note the level of assistance the person required to make the response. For example, in Figure 8, scoring during instruction utilizes a prompt hierarchy. This type of data can help an instructor note if the person is using less assistance across time to perform the task.

There are advantages to collecting instructional data just as there are advantages to collecting probe data. Probes obviously provide an opportunity to observe the person performing the task with natural cues and consequences and minimal instructor interaction. Collecting data during instruction has several advantages. First, this data collection may help the instructor self-monitor the accuracy of his or her own performance (e.g., Was a prompt given when not required?). A second advantage is that instructional data can help instructors make decisions about prompt fading. Such data are especially important in a procedure such as time delay, when specific fading criteria are used (Snell & Gast, 1981). For example, if the level of delay will be increased with three prompted correct responses, data are needed as a record of when these re-

Behavior: <u>Pour a thermos</u>   Name: <u>John</u>   Mastery: <u>100%/2 days</u>

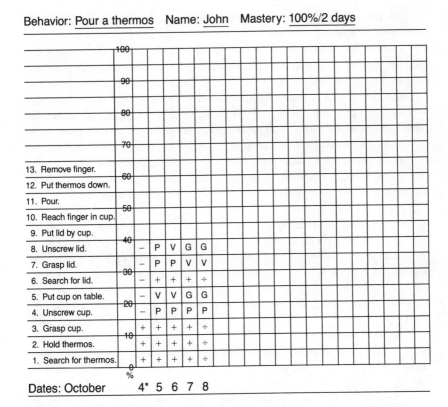

Dates: October   4* 5 6 7 8

Baseline data

Schedule: First attempt to pour at lunch on Monday
Attention/motivation: No special procedures
Discriminative stimulus to begin task: John picks up thermos
Response latency: 3 seconds to begin each step
Error treatment: Single opportunity method
Ending the test: Stop at first error and begin task again with instruction
Scoring: + = correct, − = incorrect

Instructional data

Schedule: First instructional trial each day
Coordination with instruction: Score entire TA after last step
Scoring: + = correct without help, G = correct after gesture (touch or tap),
            V = correct after verbal prompt, P = correct with physical guidance

Figure 8.   Example of task analytic assessment. (* = probes.)

sponses have occurred. Third, instructional data provide documentation of the investment of teaching that has been made for a given skill.

Despite these advantages, some instructors find data collection during teaching to have several disadvantages. A major disadvantage is that data collection can disrupt instruction by requiring the instructor to have his or her hands in two places at once. To minimize this problem, the instructor could wait until the end of the task analysis to record data. However, the instructor then may have difficulty remembering performance of early responses in the chain. A second disadvantage of this method is that instructors may record too much instructional data. Only data that are going to be used to make instructional decisions should be collected. Rarely does an instructor need to collect data on every trial of instruction for every person to make instructional decisions.

Given these advantages and disadvantages, the instructor must decide how much "teach" versus "test" data are needed. The guidelines for evaluation of data given in Chapter 4 may aid in this decision. The general model presented in this book is to use baseline probes and then, to collect data during instruction. Probes are only scheduled when a specific instructional decision hinges on this information (e.g., Has the person generalized this skill to a new setting?).

Partial Participation For some persons, performance of an entire activity chain is impossible given their physical disabilities and our current limitations in technology. For such individuals, caregiver assistance is often an ongoing reality. Given this, the instructor may design the task analysis to be interactive with a caregiver. Responses are defined for the person to participate in the task to the fullest extent possible so that he or she is an active, rather than passive, participant (L. Brown, Branston, et al., 1979). An example of an interactive chain of responding is shown in Figure 5. Both the instructor's and learner's responses are defined and sequenced for the task analysis.

Inclusion of Related Skills Task analytic assessment traditionally has included the responses critical to performance of the activity. However, related skills such as communication or academics are often performed by people without disabilities in combination with other activities in daily routines. Some instructors define and include noncritical steps in the task analysis because they enrich a person's development of communication, social, motor, or academic skills. By including them in the context of a chain of behavior, the instructor may help the person discriminate the appropriate context for the use of the skill. For example, an instructor may include communication and social skills in a task analysis for playing a game with a peer. Even though the game could be played without making these noncritical responses, most people without disabilities do communicate and socialize while playing games. Figure 9 provides an example of a task analysis that has been expanded to include related

Behavior: __Play "Cross 4"__ Name: __Nat__ Mastery: __100%/2 days__

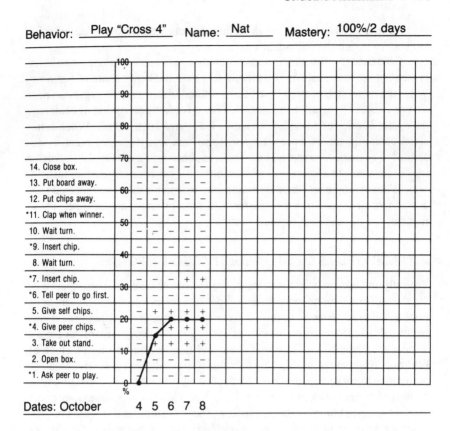

	100																								
	90																								
	80																								
	70																								
14. Close box.		−	−	−	−	−																		
13. Put board away.	60	−	−	−	−	−																		
12. Put chips away.		−	−	−	−	−																		
*11. Clap when winner.		−	−	−	−	−																		
10. Wait turn.	50	−	−	−	−	−																		
*9. Insert chip.		−	−	−	−	−																		
8. Wait turn.	40	−	−	−	−	−																		
*7. Insert chip.		−	−	−	+	+																		
*6. Tell peer to go first.	30	−	−	−	−	−																		
5. Give self chips.		−	+	+	+	+																		
*4. Give peer chips.	20	−	−	+	+	+																		
3. Take out stand.		−	+	+	+	+																		
2. Open box.	10	−	−	−	−	−																		
*1. Ask peer to play.	0 %	−	−	−	−																			

Dates: October   4   5   6   7   8

Probe data

Schedule: Wednesday with classroom peer, Friday with nonhandicapped peer
Attention/motivation: Praise for sitting
Discriminative stimulus to begin: Teacher gives game to Nat and peer
Response latency: 3 seconds to begin each step
Error treatment: Multiple opportunity method
Ending the test: After the last step, put game away
Scoring: + = correct, − = incorrect or no response

Instructional data

(will not be taken)

Figure 9. Task analytic assessment that includes related skills. (Asterisks identify the skills that are not essential to this leisure skill but help to enrich the individual's experience.) (*Note:* Data have been summarized as percent correct, not the total number. The total number of steps performed correctly on each day must first be calculated, then converted to a percentage, and then the graph line is drawn. The reader is referred to Chapter 4.)

skills. The asterisks identify the skills that are not essential to this leisure skill, but help to enrich the individual's experience.

Chaining Instructors sometimes choose to teach one step or a cluster of steps in the task analysis at a time, rather than the entire chain of behavior. When the target step or steps have been mastered, the instructor targets the next step or cluster of steps for instruction. (For a further description of chaining, the reader is referred to Sailor & Guess, 1983, and Snell, 1987). When using serial chaining, the instructor may still use task analytic assessment as described to evaluate how much of the chain has been obtained. Or, the instructor may choose only to assess the single response that has been targeted for instruction. When a single response is chosen, the instructor may use repeated trial assessment or a time-based assessment to note progress across time. These methods are described in the next sections.

REPEATED TRIALS OR OPPORTUNITIES TO RESPOND

Typically in task analytic assessment, the instructor assesses performance of the chain of behavior no more than once per session, per person. The data to be used to measure progress in this case are the number of steps performed correctly and independently on the task analysis. Sometimes, the instructor targets a specific response to be acquired alone and later introduced into a chain of behavior. Assessment of this target response is usually based on repeated opportunities to make the response. Evaluation of progress is then based on the number of correct responses per day or session. These opportunities may occur together or across time (massed or space). The opportunities to respond may be given for one specific response or for several responses that are conceptually or functionally related (distributed trials). Sometimes, the opportunities to respond will not be instructor-controlled "trials," but naturally occurring opportunities that are observed. These naturally occurring opportunities may be episodic or nearly continuous (free responding). To help the instructor develop these types of repeated opportunities to respond, each is described, with examples.

Before considering each, however, it is important to review again the necessity of assessing person performance in the naturally occurring events of daily activities. If a person is able to make a response 9 times out of 10 opportunities, but cannot make it once when required to do so in daily living, the skill has not been mastered. It is also notable that comparative research has suggested that distributed trials and task analytic instruction may be more effective ways to schedule instruction than massed trial instruction (Kayser, Billingsley, & Neel, 1986; Mulligan, Lacy, & Guess, 1982). Repeated trial assessment can be a convenient way to assess whether or not a response is emerging, but cannot substitute for assessment of the person's ability to make the response in a functional context.

Methods of Repeated Opportunity Assessment

One Discrete Response: Massed or Distributed Trials Sometimes, in initial instruction of a new and difficult response, the instructor decides to measure that response alone. For example, for a person who does not yet use symbolic communication, the instructor may target a requesting response (e.g., pointing to object desired). The instructor's initial goal is for the person to use the pointing response across materials. One method to assess this response would be to schedule repetitions of presentations of objects in a session and to ask the person, "What do you want?" This repeated trial assessment provides *massed trials* of opportunities to make the same response. A second method would be for the instructor to present opportunities across the day and ask, "What do you want?" This repeated trial assessment would use *spaced trials* (i.e., not occurring together in time) that would also be *distributed* (i.e., many other responses would be made between pointing to objects).

The instructor might wonder which is the best way to assess a single response such as pointing. Massed trials present rapid, repeated opportunities for the instructor to assess and for the person to practice the response. Trials that are presented throughout the day provide a better picture of functional use of this response and will be preferable for assessing many single responses. Massed trials are never adequate alone, since they do not provide information on functional use in other contexts. But, the instructor might note acquisition of a response such as pointing earlier in these massed opportunities and thus consider it worthwhile to use both a quick, massed trial assessment and a generalization assessment across the day. Figure 10 provides an example of a massed trial assessment and instruction that supplements the functional use of this skill.

Response Class Assessment Sometimes the goal of instruction is the acquisition of a *response class*. A response class is a set of differing responses that are made to the same discriminative stimulus. For example, for the discriminative stimulus of the instructor's asking the question "What do you want?" the person's response might be any one of a class of responses he or she has learned (e.g., "apple," "sweater," "juice," "crackers," "game," "go outside"). Similar to a single response, the instructor may give the opportunities for responding together in time or may schedule them throughout the day. In either case, the opportunities are for the person to make varied responses and thus, each response is distributed across trials (e.g., for a response class assessment, the instructor would not give repeated opportunities for the person to respond, "apple"). To evaluate progress, the instructor would note the number of correct responses. If some specific response or responses did not yet occur, these might be targeted for single response assessment and then reintroduced in the response class assessment. For example, perhaps the person responds to some opportunities to communicate for juice, crackers, sweater, and so on, but never uses the picture or sign for "game." Rather, the person indicates interest in performing the game by reaching for it and whining. The instructor may

Behavior: __Select quarter__ Name: __John__ Mastery: __90%/2 days__

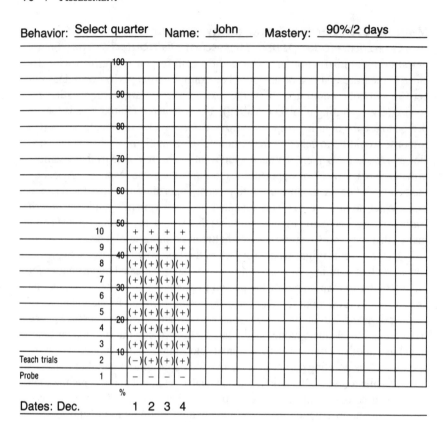

Teach trials 2
Probe 1

Dates: Dec.   1 2 3 4

Probe data

Schedule: Just prior to vending machine use; 10 trials
            Probe first trial; teach nine trials.
Attention/motivation: No special procedures on probe; praise during instruc-
                        tion.
Discriminative stimulus: Change purse plus teacher request to "find two
                           quarters."
Response latency: 10 seconds to find each quarter
Error treatment: Single opportunity method for probe
                   Present quarter as a model with time-delay fading during
                   instruction.
Ending the test: Only probe first trial, then teach.
Scoring: + = correct without help, − = incorrect without help, (+) = correct
           with model, (−) = incorrect after model

Figure 10.   Data collection for repeated opportunity (massed trial) assessment: An example of assessment of a single response. (*Note:* This assessment and instruction is a supplement to John's instruction in vending machine use that includes coin identification in context
of machine use.)

target repeated opportunities to sign "game" so the person can master this specific vocabulary item and may evaluate this separately from the person's emerging response to the question "What do you want?" Figure 11 provides an example of assessment of a response class in the use of a picture communication wallet.

Functionally Related Response Cluster: ICS Assessment The individualized curriculum sequencing (ICS) model provides a method for sequencing assessment and instruction by using skill clusters (Guess et al., 1978; Holvoet et al., 1980). Individual target responses are linked together and taught across activities. Responses from traditional skill areas such as motor, language, and self-care are selected that can be *functionally related* and taught across activities. For example, the skill cluster might be to request an item, to use the item, and to pass a material to a peer. This cluster might be taught across eating, grooming, and leisure activities. Assessment would also be conducted across these activities during the day. The instructor could describe progress in several ways: 1) number of correct responses across the day, 2) number of correct performances of the cluster across the day, and 3) number of correct performances for each response within the clusters across the day (e.g., number of correct responses for requesting and using items, and for passing materials). Figure 12 shows an example of assessment of a response cluster used across activities.

Frequency Counts of Naturally Occurring Responses One of the important, but difficult types of responses to assess is the *naturally occurring* (i.e., person-initiated) *response*. For example, the person approaches the instructor and points to a desired object. This may occur while the class is in the grocery store, walking down the sidewalk, preparing to go home, and other occasions when the instructor may not have or cannot have the person's data sheet for pointing close by. Yet, this may be an important personal accomplishment. If the initiation is very infrequent (less than daily), the instructor might note it on the graph of instructor-initiated opportunities, with an asterisk under that day's date. If the responses occur throughout the day, the instructor may want to obtain a count of the number of responses. This might be done by using a simple method to keep a tally, such as pennies to be transferred from pocket to pocket for each occurrence, masking tape to be moved from sleeve to sleeve, or use of a hand-held clicker. There is an obvious limit on how many such responses an instructor can count across the individuals in his or her classroom. Perhaps only one or two of the highest priorities in the classroom may be feasible for such counts across the day. Some opportunities such as a break or independent play might allow more counts for that one period (e.g., of social initiations). Noting that at least one initiation occurred during the day by starring a graph of instructor-initiated opportunities could be feasible for several responses and individuals. An especially difficult type of response to record is a high-rate problem behavior that occurs throughout the day.

Behavior: <u>Use picture wallet to request</u>   Name: <u>Nat</u>   Mastery: <u>81%/2 days</u>

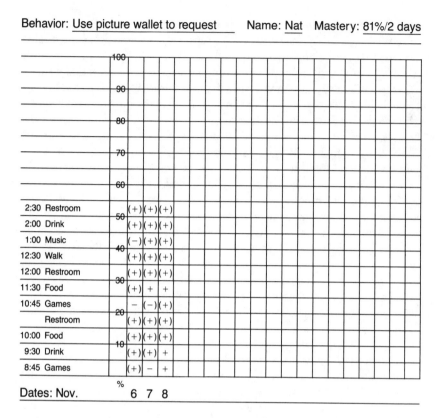

		Nov. 6	7	8
2:30	Restroom	(+)	(+)	(+)
2:00	Drink	(+)	(+)	(+)
1:00	Music	(−)	(+)	(+)
12:30	Walk	(+)	(+)	(+)
12:00	Restroom	(+)	(+)	(+)
11:30	Food	(+)	+	+
10:45	Games	−	(−)	(+)
	Restroom	(+)	(+)	(+)
10:00	Food	(+)	(+)	(+)
9:30	Drink	(+)	(+)	+
8:45	Games	(+)	−	+

Dates: Nov.   %   6 7 8

Instructional data

Schedule: During each break that follows lesson (10 per day)
            Assess one break per day—different break each day.
Attention/motivation: Natural consequence—give item requested.
Discriminative stimulus: Display objects and ask, "What do you want?"
Response latency: 5 seconds.
Error treatment: If no selection indicated, say, "I'm sorry. I'm not sure what you want." Delay presentation of item. In instruction, model use of wallet with time-delay fading and give item if Nat imitates model.
Scoring: + = correct without help, − = incorrect without help, (+) = correct after model, (−) = incorrect after model.

Figure 11.   Data collection for repeated opportunity assessment: An example of a response class assessment.

An all-day frequency count is sometimes feasible by using one of the portable methods of tallying mentioned above. An alternative is to count the frequency within one or more sample time periods during the day. Or, the instructor might use a less precise but practical assessment, known as a scat-

Behavior: <u>Store/carry belongings</u>   Name: <u>Ann</u>   Mastery: <u>100%/2 days</u>

	%				
DEPARTURE	100				
3. Walk to van.	90	−	P	−	M
2. Carry bag.		−	P	−	P
1. Grasp bag.	80	−	M	−	V
CLEAN-UP					
4. Release bag.	70	−	V	−	M
3. Walk to trash can.		−	P	−	V
2. Carry bag.	60	+	P	−	P
1. Grasp trashbag.	50	+	M	−	M
WORK PREP.					
4. Release box.	40	−	M	−	M
3. Walk to table.		−	P	−	M
2. Carry box.	30	−	P	−	P
1. Grasp box.		−	V	+	+
ARRIVAL	20				
4. Release bag.		−	M	−	P
3. Walk to shelf.	10	−	P	−	P
2. Carry bag.		−	P	−	P
1. Grasp bag.		−	P	−	P

Dates: October   4* 5* 6* 7

Conditions
Baseline data

Schedule: Four times per day
Attention/motivation: No special procedures
Discriminative stimulus: Allow 2 minutes for Ann to follow others. Then say, "Ann, get (or put away) your things for lunch (or from home)."
Response latency: 30 seconds to begin, 5 minutes to finish
Error treatment: Single opportunity method
Ending the test: End the test when Ann does not begin in 30 seconds, stops responding for 1 full minute, or after 5 minutes. Then, begin instruction.
Scoring: + = correct, − = incorrect

Instructional data

Schedule: Each instructional trial
Coordination with instruction: Score after teaching each response.
Scoring: + = correct without help, G = gesture, V = verbal prompt, M = model, P = physical guidance.

Figure 12.   Data collection for repeated opportunity assessment: An example of assessment of functionally related skills. (* = probes.)

terplot, of occurrence or nonoccurrence in each 15- or 30-minute period (Touchette, MacDonald, & Langer, 1985). These periods might correspond to instructional sessions and the tally might be kept on the data sheet for instructed skills. The data to be summarized might be, for example, the percentage of lessons in which self-abuse occurred. This approach not only has the advantage of being simple to utilize, but it also provides information on the occurrence of problem behavior by specific lesson, which can help the instructor evaluate the interaction of skill acquisition and deceleration of behavior by lesson. (Problem behaviors are also amenable to time-based assessment, which is discussed later in this chapter.) Figure 13 provides an example of a frequency-count assessment of a person-initiated response.

Developing and Implementing Repeated Opportunity Assessment

The following are guidelines to assist the instructor in developing repeated opportunity assessment:

1. The instructor should select either a single response, response class, stimulus class, or skill cluster to assess.
2. The instructor should define the response(s) in observable, measurable terms. The criteria for correct responding must be explicit (e.g., Does the person have to point with the index finger or just extend the hand toward the desired object?).
3. The instructor should define the stimuli that set the occasion for the response—preferably cues that occur in the natural environment. (This step may not be possible for problem behaviors.)
4. The instructor should decide how opportunities to respond will be scheduled (e.g., massed or spaced trials, instructor- or person-initiated responses).
5. The instructor should design a method to record each response.
6. The instructor should follow the schedule to assess the response(s).

Skill: <u>Initiate conversation by touching arm</u>   Student: <u>Nat</u>

   Schedule: <u>Student-initiated</u>

   Attention/motivation: <u>Natural consequence–social exchange</u>

   Discriminative stimulus: <u>Others greet Nat</u>

   Response latency: <u>5 seconds</u>

   Error treatment: <u>If whines or grabs, prompt touching</u>

   Scoring: <u>Tally number of touches to initiate by transferring penny from right to left pocket</u>

Figure 13. Data collection for repeated opportunity assessment: An example of assessment of person-initiated responding.

TIME-BASED ASSESSMENT

When a person is first learning to perform a skill, the instructor will typically use the task analytic or repeated opportunity assessments previously described. This initial phase of learning is called *acquisition*. After a person acquires the skill, the instructor will write objectives for *extended performance* of the skill to meet normalized criteria for performance (e.g., improved fluency). For example, when a person is learning to prepare a lunch for school or work, the instructor will probably use task analytic assessment of the person's acquisition of this skill. Once the person can perform all the steps of the task analysis, his or her performance may still be too slow—in the time constraints of the family's routine—to prepare lunch daily. Thus, the instructor would set an objective for extended performance of this skill to meet a normalized time criteria to make it usable in the family setting. Assessment of this extended performance often requires time-based assessment.

This time-based assessment might include measurement of *rate, duration,* or *latency* of responding. In the above example for lunch preparation, the family's concern is for the duration of the task. To measure duration, which is the length of time required to complete the task, the instructor can note the time when the person starts and the time when the person stops the task. A stopwatch is a useful tool for time-based assessment. The instructor can simply start the watch when the person begins the task and stop it when the person completes the task. Rate, which is the number of responses per some unit of time (e.g., number per minute), is often the concern in vocational assembly work in which placement and pay may be based on rate. To calculate rate, the instructor can set a predetermined time period for the time-based assessment (e.g., 30 minutes) and provide the person with adequate materials to work throughout the time period. At the end of the time period, the total number of pieces completed are counted. To calculate rate, the number of responses are divided by the number of minutes (i.e., responses per minute). Latency, or time to initiate a response, may also be a concern when the instructor assesses extended performance of an acquired skill. For example, the instructor might provide a picture schedule for the person to perform custodial tasks. The instructor may then measure the number of minutes or seconds from the time the schedule is assigned until the person begins the first task. Figures 14, 15, and 16 show examples of data collected for each of these time-based assessments.

In conducting time-based assessments of extended performance, the instructor is usually observing performance only. To assist the person in meeting the criteria set for the rate, duration, or latency of performance, the instructor might be using procedures such as teaching the person to self-monitor the response or providing consequences based on meeting the time criteria. However, the instructor typically will not interact with the person during the time-based assessment itself.

Extended performance objectives may also target criteria other than im-

| Student: | John | | Behavior: | Stuff envelopes | |

Student: John   Behavior: Stuff envelopes
Assessment: Record the time that session begins and ends, and count the
number of envelopes stuffed (letter and inserts collated and
inserted into envelope).

Date	Session	Time started	Time ended	Number	Rate
2–7	1	9:00	9:30	60	2/min.
	2	9:35	10:00	45	1.8/min.
	3	10:15	10:43	52	1.9/min.
	4	10:45	11:30	67	1.5/min.
	5	12:15	1:05	37	1.4/min.
	6	1:10	1:45	42	1.2/min.

Daily summary:
  Sessions worked: all 6
  Average rate: 1.6
  Average session length: 35 minutes
Comment: Teacher graphs average rate for the day.

Figure 14.   Example of data collection for time-based assessment—rate.

proved fluency. The instructor may set objectives for generalization across materials or settings, or for maintenance of performance as artificial reinforcement and instructor presence is faded. Such objectives can be measured using the time-based, task analytic, or repeated opportunity methods described. (Further discussion of evaluation of these extended performance objectives is provided in Chapter 4.)

In some cases, the instructor may want to work on acquisition and fluency of performance simultaneously. As described earlier in this chapter, routine task analytic assessment can include a measure of duration of responding. The advantage of this time-based measurement is that even while a person still requires some prompting, increased fluency may be noted in the activity. For example, a person who requires physical guidance for a restroom routine may learn to interact better with the caregiver, responding more quickly to physical guidance. Because the entire activity now takes less time, although still guided, this is important progress.

The time-based assessment suggested here relies on the simple use of a clock, watch, or stopwatch, and can be conducted while teaching or assessing other persons in the group. The time-based assessment that is frequently used in applied behavior analysis research is interval recording, using intervals of a few seconds (Sulzer-Azaroff & Mayer, 1977). In interval recording, a cue tape or other device is used to signal observers to record occurrence or nonoccurrence of defined target behaviors within given intervals. These intervals may be as short as 10 seconds, but are rarely longer than 1 minute. Two advantages can be derived from using interval recording. First, agreement between two ob-

Behavior: <u>Raise hand for "hello"</u>   Name: <u>Nat</u>   Mastery: <u>2 sec./2 days</u>

Number of seconds latency to raise hand after "Hello"

```
20 20 20 20 20 20 20 20 20 20 20 20 20 20 20 20 20 20 20 20 20
19 19 19 19 19 19 19 19 19 19 19 19 19 19 19 19 19 19 19 19 19
18 18 18 18 18 18 18 18 18 18 18 18 18 18 18 18 18 18 18 18 18
17 17 17 17 17 17 17 17 17 17 17 17 17 17 17 17 17 17 17 17 17
16 16 16 16 16 16 16 16 16 16 16 16 16 16 16 16 16 16 16 16 16
15 15 15 15 15 15 15 15 15 15 15 15 15 15 15 15 15 15 15 15 15
14 14 14 14 14 14 14 14 14 14 14 14 14 14 14 14 14 14 14 14 14
13 13 13 13 13 13 13 13 13 13 13 13 13 13 13 13 13 13 13 13 13
12 12 12 12 12 12 12 12 12 12 12 12 12 12 12 12 12 12 12 12 12
11 11 11 11 11 11 11 11 11 11 11 11 11 11 11 11 11 11 11 11 11
10 10 10 10 10 10 10 10 10 10 10 10 10 10 10 10 10 10 10 10 10
 9  9  9  9  9  9  9  9  9  9  9  9  9  9  9  9  9  9  9  9  9
 8  8  8  8  8  8  8  8  8  8  8  8  8  8  8  8  8  8  8  8  8
 7  7  7  7  7  7  7  7  7  7  7  7  7  7  7  7  7  7  7  7  7
 6  6  6  6  6  6  6  6  6  6  6  6  6  6  6  6  6  6  6  6  6
 5  5  5  5  5  5  5  5  5  5  5  5  5  5  5  5  5  5  5  5  5
 4  4  4  4  4  4  4  4  4  4  4  4  4  4  4  4  4  4  4  4  4
 3  3  3  3  3  3  3  3  3  3  3  3  3  3  3  3  3  3  3  3  3
 2  2  2  2  2  2  2  2  2  2  2  2  2  2  2  2  2  2  2  2  2
 1  1  1  1  1  1  1  1  1  1  1  1  1  1  1  1  1  1  1  1  1
 0  0  0  0  0  0  0  0  0  0  0  0  0  0  0  0  0  0  0  0  0
```

Dates: Nov.   12 13 14 15 16 19 20 21 22 23 26 27 28 29

Assessment: Time latency with stopwatch; round to nearest second; begin timing from moment someone says "Hi, Nat."

Figure 15.   Example of data collection for time-based assessment—latency.

servers to check the reliability of assessment can be more easily and accurately determined by comparing intervals. Second, the interval recording lends itself to time sampling (i.e., recording some estimation of the occurrence of the behavior). For example, the observer may only record if the behavior occurs during the time interval (partial interval), throughout the time interval (whole interval), or at a certain moment in time (momentary time sampling).

Unfortunately, interval recording is difficult to implement during instruction and rarely portable for instruction in community settings. While momentary time sampling is the interval recording procedure that does not require constant observation, it also may not be adaptable to teaching situations because of the short intervals required to get a representative sample of the behavior. In research to compare interval lengths, Lentz (1982) found that 30-second intervals were required to get a momentary time sample comparable to

Behavior: __Walk to seat__ Student: __Ann__ Mastery: __1'/3 days__

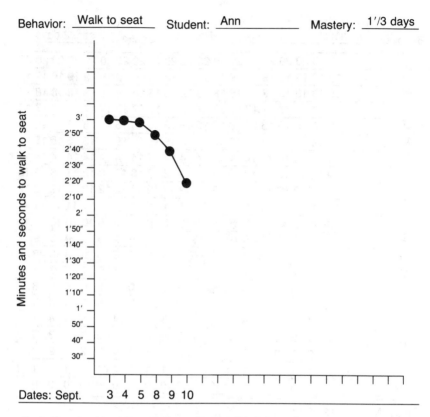

Dates: Sept.   3 4 5 8 9 10

Assessment: Use stopwatch to time walking from first step in the door to moment pupil touches chair; round to nearest minute and seconds; end assessment after 3 minutes if not at chair. Mastery is 1 minute for 3 consecutive days.

Figure 16. Example of data collection for time-based assessment—duration.

the actual rate or duration of the response. Obviously, an instructor cannot teach a group of persons and conduct 30-second-interval momentary time sampling. Because of these logistics, this book does not cover interval recording except for the use of scatterplots by instructors or the use of brief intervals by supervisors who typically observe without interaction with learners (see Chapter 9).

QUALITATIVE ASSESSMENT AND RELIABILITY

The traditional approach to measurement in applied behavior analysis is to count observable responses. This approach will be the foundation for most ongoing assessment of objectives. However, the instructor may sometimes wish to evaluate the quality of responding to judge criteria for normalized use of a skill. Often this judgment will be recruited from experts or significant others in the person's life. This qualitative assessment comprises both *social validation* and *reliability*. Social validation was described in detail in Chapter 2 as it relates to skill selection. The same procedures (e.g., peer comparison, expert judgments) are also applicable to the validation of treatment outcomes. For example, the instructor may send the parents a questionnaire to determine if the person's emerging skills are usable in the home environment. Or, an employer may be asked to rate an employee's performance. These qualitative assessments alone are rarely adequate to evaluate progress. However, they can help the instructor determine if the criteria of performance achieved will be encouraged and/or tolerated by the significant people in the person's environments.

While the social validity of performance is important in evaluating progress, the reliability of the direct assessment of target objectives is also important in qualitative assessment. That is, when an instructor hopes to see improvement, data may be biased toward change rather than accurately reflecting responses made. Such fluctuations in measurement have been demonstrated in research (Fixsen, Phillips, & Wolf, 1972; Romanczyk, Kent, Diament, & O'Leary, 1973). Reliability checks by a second observer can influence observers to be more consistent in recording (Craighead, Mercatoris, & Bellack, 1974). Unfortunately, scheduling a second observer for assessment in teaching settings can be extremely difficult. The instructor is faced with the dilemma of needing reliable data to make instructional decisions, but not having the means to obtain data on reliability. The compromise in teaching settings is that reliability data will be taken much less frequently than is typical of research situations. However, even if infrequent, demonstrations of reliability can help instructors make instructional decisions with more confidence that the data evaluated are reliable. In this book, reliability observations are suggested as a role for the supervisor and are described in further detail in Chapter 9. Methods to schedule reliability observations and to calculate coefficients of agreement have been described in detail in other resources (e.g., Kazdin, 1980; Sulzer-Azaroff & Mayer, 1977).

SUMMARY

Ongoing assessment enables the instructor to engage in formative evaluation of progress and to make changes in instruction, if necessary, to improve the person's success. The most important type of ongoing assessment is routine task analytic assessment. Only in assessing routines can an instructor determine if a person knows both when and how to perform a skill. Besides assessing routines, acquisition of specific tasks will typically be assessed as either task analytic or repeated opportunity assessments.

Task analytic assessment requires planning and writing steps in the chain of responses to perform a task in the most effective and efficient way. Once a well-developed task analysis has been planned, the instructor can follow the steps to assess the person's performance of this chain of responses. During non-instructional probes, the instructor might give the person one opportunity to perform this chain and then end assessment, or several opportunities to begin the chain again after errors. The instructor might also assess performance during instruction by noting the level of assistance needed to perform each step.

Repeated opportunity assessments may include the instructor's initiation of these opportunities or trials in close succession or distributed across the day. For other behaviors, the instructor may note the frequency of person-initiated responding (e.g., for problem behaviors).

When skills have been acquired, time-based assessment of rate, duration, or latency can help the instructor assess extended performance of skills to meet normalized criteria. While interval recording may be used by supervisors, it rarely will be feasible for implementation by teachers. Reliability checks also are difficult to schedule in teaching settings, but may be provided occasionally by supervisors to evaluate the consistency of measurement.

Sometimes, the educator may solicit evaluation of the person's quality of performance by asking significant others in the person's environments to rate this performance. Once these ongoing procedures have been developed and implemented, the instructor is ready for the next step of assessment—evaluation to make instructional decisions.

STUDY QUESTIONS

1. What are the four steps to follow in planning ongoing assessment to *keep instruction functional?*
2. Why does the author recommend using routine task analytic assessment as the foundation for ongoing assessment? When are specific skill task analyses or repeated opportunity assessments used?
3. What are the steps in defining a routine for ongoing routine task analytic assessment?
4. What are some considerations in developing specific skill task analytic assessment? What are therbligs and how might they be applied to this process?
5. What are the types of repeated opportunity assessment? What are some examples of skills for which this assessment is applicable?
6. What are some examples of skills for which qualitative or time-based assessment would be applicable?

FOR FURTHER THOUGHT

1. Review the schedule of your day and consider the extent to which you are teaching activities versus isolated, specific skills. For the ac-

tivities you are teaching, how might routine task analytic assessment as described in this chapter be applied?

2. How could the schedule be further developed into instruction of routines?
3. Consider developing a chart like Table 1. Note the types of assessment you currently use. Consider new options that could be developed.
4. What are your priorities for specific skill task analyses or repeated opportunity assessment?
5. Would it be helpful to follow the therblig definitions in writing specific skill TAs?

chapter 4

EVALUATION OF ONGOING ASSESSMENT

INSTRUCTIONAL ASSESSMENT HAS three phases. First, as described in Chapter 2, assessment is conducted to identify skills for instruction (initial assessment, which includes comprehensive and annual assessment). Second, as described in Chapter 3, assessment is developed to track progress on these priority skills (ongoing assessment). The third phase, the focus of this chapter, is the evaluation of the data collected through ongoing assessment. Evaluation makes ongoing assessment *purposeful* by using data to make instructional decisions. For example, if a person's objective is to learn snack preparation, the instructor may conduct task analytic assessment of the steps in the selected snack preparation. However, what if the learner does not progress? Will task analytic assessment and instruction be continued indefinitely? Will the instructor conclude that the person cannot learn snack making and discontinue instruction? What if the data are highly variable? How can a determination of progress be made? These questions exemplify the need to make instructional decisions, given certain data patterns.

To make instructional decisions, the instructor needs to: 1) collect data on a regular schedule, 2) summarize the data, and 3) consider the instructional decision implied by the data pattern. While the need for instructional changes may be obvious when no learning occurs, mastery also implies the need to change instruction. For example, when mastery occurs it may be important to extend performance by helping the person to become more fluent in skill performance or to generalize the skill to new situations.

The use of systematic data evaluation to make these instructional decisions can enhance both the accuracy of instructor judgments (Holvoet, O'Neil, Chazdon, Carr, & Warner, 1983; Utley, Zigmond, & Strain, 1987) and the amount of person progress (Browder, Liberty, Heller, & D'Huyvetters, 1986; Fuchs & Fuchs, 1986; N. Haring et al., 1980). However, educators often need a practical system for this data review. Research with instructors who record data has revealed inconsistency across instructors in how data are reviewed (Farlow & Snell, 1989), and a reliance on clinical judgment, rather than data patterns, in making decisions (Grigg, Snell, & Lloyd, 1989). This research suggests that it is not enough for instructors to acquire skills in data collection and summary (e.g., graphing, trend lines): Instructors also need explicit guidelines for data-based instructional decisions, and evidence that the individuals whom they teach benefit from the use of these rules. This chapter provides an overview of options for data evaluation and explicit guidelines for data-based instructional decisions.

TYPES OF DATA-BASED DECISIONS

In Chapter 2, descriptions were given for ongoing assessment of routines (e.g., routine task analytic assessment) and of specific skills (e.g., task analytic assessment, repeated opportunity assessment). In Chapter 8, options are described for ongoing assessment of problem behavior. Assessment of routines, specific skills, and problem behavior generates different types of data that require different types of decisions. Routines may involve a complex array of skills that are targeted for increased independence and fluency across time (e.g., more than 1 year). Also, the specific responses assessed within routines are highly diverse. Within the same routine (e.g., morning arrival), an instructor may assess duration of walking, latency of a greeting, and physical assistance required to release the handle of a gym bag. Summarizing the assessment of these responses into one "total" may not make sense for ongoing decision making about progress, but may help longitudinal evaluation of increased participation in a routine.

By contrast, mastery of specific skills is typically targeted within one IEP/IHP year. The same type of measurement is applied to all the responses to perform the skill (e.g., level of assistance to make the response on a task analytic assessment). Summary of the "total" correct is logical (e.g., percentage of steps performed correct independently). With this summary, data-based decisions can be a highly precise means of fine tuning instruction to achieve the objective of mastery within the year.

Ongoing assessment of problem behavior focuses on deceleration of undesirable behavior and the concurrent increase of a functionally equivalent response. Criteria for progress may require qualitative judgment (e.g., Is the topography of the undesirable behavior getting less serious?) as well as evaluation of two concurrent data trends. This chapter focuses on evaluation of a skill that is not a specific alternative to problem behavior, and includes discussion of both routine and specific skill data. Chapter 8 provides guidelines for the evaluation of problem behavior data.

Since the research on data collection has focused on specific skill data, this method is described first. Some of this research has been conducted by the author in the model programs at Lehigh University. As an example of a data evaluation system, the Lehigh model is described in detail. Later in the chapter, data evaluation for routines is described.

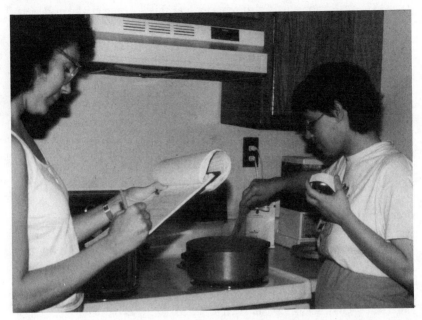

Instructors should collect only as much data as needed to make decisions. This teacher is assessing an adult's skills in a meal preparation routine to evaluate her progress.

DATA-BASED DECISIONS: SPECIFIC SKILL DATA

Preparation for Data Evaluation

How Often to Collect Data The first requirement for making instructional decisions is to collect data on a regular and frequent schedule. While little research exists to guide instructors in knowing how much data is enough, a study by Munger, Snell, and Lloyd (1989) suggested that instructors may need to collect data more frequently than once a week to make consistent judgments about a person's progress based on data trends. However, instructors probably do not need to, and often cannot, record every response every person makes during instruction. Thus, the parameters for data collection for specific skills seems to be more often than once a week, but less than every response made during instruction every day. In Chapter 3, consideration was also given to "probe" (noninstructional) data versus data collected during instruction.

Thus, while no firm answers exist for how much data should be collected, the rule-of-thumb is to *Collect no more data than needed to make an instructional decision.* Rather than asking, "How often should I collect data?" an instructor should ask, "How much data do I need to make a decision by this given date?" The instructor should also consider how this decision can be made relative to several types of skills and evaluation schedules.

If an educator wants to make every effort for a high-priority skill (e.g., expression of choice, handwashing for a hepatitis carrier) to reach mastery within a year, frequent data evaluation is warranted. The instructor may then decide to take data daily on this priority skill and make an instructional decision as soon as there are enough data points to determine a trend (i.e., about 6). However, it must be noted that for skills on which instruction is repeated (e.g., handwashing), data may only need to be taken during one instructional session (e.g., first trip to restroom). The rest of instruction for the day can be "data free." Thus, daily data collection is the answer to how much data is needed to make decisions as soon as possible on high-priority skills. By contrast, the instructor may teach other skills that are lower priorities (e.g., using a microwave oven), or those that can only be taught on a weekly schedule (e.g., making a purchase). The schedule for evaluation may then be some regularly occurring progress review (e.g., 6-week report cards, quarterly reviews). Weekly data collection may thus be sufficient, since it permits summaries for these less frequent reviews.

Finally, not all evaluation need be data based. Farlow and Snell (1989) found that the instructors they surveyed collected daily data on about 75% of their objectives, with an average of about 10 objectives per learner. Some instructors specify an order of priority for objectives at IEP/IHP time. High-priority objectives are targeted for daily data and frequent review. Medium-priority objectives receive weekly assessment and less frequent (e.g., quarterly) review. For lower priority objectives, or those that require more qualitative appraisal, informal notes are kept and anecdotal summaries are utilized.

Whether or not to use noninstructional probes also depends on how the data will be evaluated. Many educators review instructional data to make decisions, and find noninstructional probes to be unnecessary. Noninstructional probes help others, at the beginning of instruction—as a "baseline" against which to contrast progress. For some, noninstructional probes answer questions about how well a person performs a skill under generalization conditions. Further, noninstructional probes can be an alternative to instructional data if an instructor simply cannot teach and take data at the same time. Figures 1, 2, and 3 illustrate these options. In Figure 1, the instructor took daily data in the school 4 days per week and used noninstructional probes once a week on a press-bar door in a community setting to assess generalization. In Figure 2, the instructor made all decisions based on instructional data and no probes were utilized. In Figure 3, the instructor found it too difficult to take data while guiding Ann out the door and to the van. As an alternative, she taught Ann 3 days per week and took probe data (instead of teaching the skill) 2 days per week.

In the Lehigh University model for data evaluation (Browder, 1987; Browder, Demchak, Heller, & King, 1989), data are collected daily on high-

Behavior: <u>Open bar-press door</u> Name: <u>Ann</u> Mastery: <u>100% / 2/3 days</u>

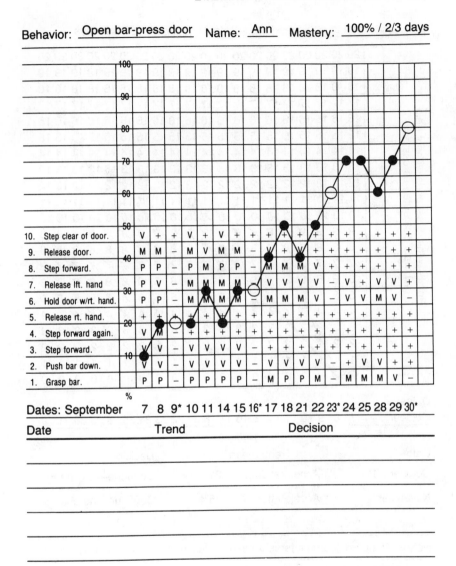

Figure 1. An example of instructional and probe data on a combination data collection and graph form. Probes, indicated by asterisks, are shown as open circles.

priority, specific skills, and the instructors make biweekly data-based instructional decisions. A minimum of 6 data points is needed to analyze the data trend. By setting the goal of daily data collection, at least 6 data points are usually achieved despite learner or instructor absence, assemblies, problem behavior, illness, and so on. If all is going well, instructors can take a day off from data collection (e.g., Fridays) and still obtain 6 data points in the 2 weeks.

Behavior: <u>Point to choice.</u> Name: <u>Nat</u> Mastery: <u>80%/2 days</u>

Points within 5 seconds without help (10 trials distributed across day)

100	20	20	20	20	20	20	20	20	20	20	20	20	20	20	20	20	20	20	20	20
90	19	19	19	19	19	19	19	19	19	19	19	19	19	19	19	19	19	19	19	19
	18	18	18	18	18	18	18	18	18	18	18	18	18	18	18	18	18	18	18	18
80	17	17	17	17	17	17	17	17	17	17	17	17	17	17	17	17	17	17	17	17
	16	16	16	16	16	16	16	16	16	16	16	16	16	16	16	16	16	16	16	16
70	15	15	15	15	15	15	15	15	15	15	15	15	15	15	15	15	15	15	15	15
	14	14	14	14	14	14	14	14	14	14	14	14	14	14	14	14	14	14	14	14
60	13	13	13	13	13	13	13	13	13	13	13	13	13	13	13	13	13	13	13	13
	12	12	12	12	12	12	12	12	12	12	12	12	12	12	12	12	12	12	12	12
50	11	11	11	11	11	11	11	11	11	11	11	11	11	11	11	11	11	11	11	11
	10	10	10	10	10	10	10	10	10	10	10	10	10	10	10	10	10	10	10	10
40	9	9	9	9	9	9	9	9	9	9	9	9	9	9	9	9	9	9	9	9
	8	8	8	8	8	8	8	8	8	8	8	8	8	8	8	8	8	8	8	8
30	7	7	7	7	7	7	7	7	7	7	7	7	7	7	7	7	7	7	7	7
	6	6	6	6	6	6	6	6	6	6	6	6	6	6	6	6	6	6	6	6
20	5	5	5	5	5	5	5	5	5	5	5	5	5	5	5	5	5	5	5	5
	4	4	4	4	4	4	4	4	4	4	4	4	4	4	4	4	4	4	4	4
10	3	3	3	3	3	3	3	3	3	3	3	3	3	3	3	3	3	3	3	3
	2	2	2	2	2	2	2	2	2	2	2	2	2	2	2	2	2	2	2	2
	1	1	1	1	1	1	1	1	1	1	1	1	1	1	1	1	1	1	1	1
0	0	0	0	0	0	0	0	0	0	0	0	0	0	0	0	0	0	0	0	0

****

Dates:
October   7   8   9 10 11 14 15 16 17 18 21 22 23 24 25 28 29 30 31   *

Reviews

Date	Trend/mean	Decision
October 18	Acceleration, $\bar{x}$ = 21%	Continue—no change
November 1	Acceleration, $\bar{x}$ = 56%	Continue—no change

Note: Standard quarter intersect line has been drawn to show trend for each period of review.

Figure 2. Example of self-graphing data collection sheet for instructional data. (Asterisk indicates that Nat was absent from school on November 1.)

How to Summarize Data   Before data can be evaluated, they must be summarized. In applied behavior analysis, this summary is typically an equal interval linear graph (see Figure 3). Most instructors find this type of graph easy to construct and review. Numerous resources on applied behavior

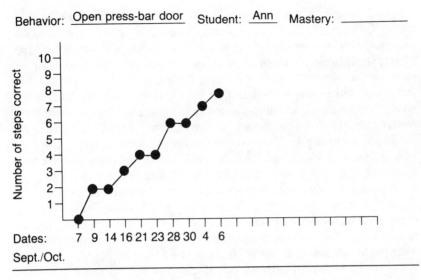

Behavior: Open press-bar door   Student: Ann   Mastery: _____

Figure 3.   An example of an equal interval graph used to summarize data that are collected on a separate form. This graph summarizes probe data only, not instructional data.

analysis have provided descriptions for the construction of equal interval graphs (e.g., Sanders, 1978; Sulzer-Azaroff & Mayer, 1977). These graphs can be constructed by using plain paper, and drawing the ordinate and abscissa (i.e., vertical and horizontal axes) with a pen and ruler, or by using graph paper.

Figure 3 illustrates the use of the equal interval graph to summarize task analytic assessment. In all graphs, the vertical axis (ordinate) reflects the unit of measurement of the target skill. In Figure 3, the unit of measurement is the number of steps correct on the task analysis. The horizontal axis (abscissa) reflects the frequency of measurement. In Figure 3, the frequency is semi-weekly probes. It also is important to give the dates on the horizontal axis for graphs used in making instructional decisions, since the data pattern may be influenced by interruptions in the program (e.g., due to school vacations).

A variation of the equal interval graph that can simplify graphing is the "self-graphing" data collection sheet. That is, the graph is made directly on the data collection sheet. This self-graphing approach is shown in Figures 1 and 2. In Figure 1, independent correct responses during instruction are summarized with closed circles on the graph. Probes of performance without assistance are shown with open circles. In Figure 2, the numbers listed are used for both data collection and graphing. The instructor slashes each trial on which the person responded correctly without help. The slashes are counted, and this number is indicated with a closed circle. The closed circles are then connected to form a graph.

Equal interval graphs are not the only types of graphs that can be used to summarize progress. The 6-cycle semilogarithmic graph (see Figure 4) and the columnar numerical semilog paper (see Figure 5) have also been used. The 6-cycle semilogarithmic graph has been a trademark of the precision teaching model that began with the work of Lindsley (1964), and has been applied to data for learners with severe disabilities by N. Haring et al. (1980). Typically in the precision teaching model, time-based data are collected (e.g., rate data) for correct and error responses, and are summarized on a standard precision teaching graph (see Figure 4). The advantage of the precision teaching graph is its standardization, which simplifies data review across objectives and learners. N. Haring et al. (1980) also developed a set of decision rules based on pupil performance summarized on semilog graphs. One of the advantages of the logarithmic vertical axis is that it "straightens" the typical S-shaped learning curve. Most human behavior changes slowly at first and then accelerates rapidly to acquisition. This slow initial progress looks like the bottom curve of the "S" when plotted on equal interval graph paper (see Figure 6).

Another method of graphing that also adjusts to the learning curve was recommended by Sailor and Guess (1983). In this method, a 2½-cycle semilog columnar numerical paper is used. Figure 5 provides an example of task analytic assessment graphed on columnar numerical paper. In this example, the instructor is also using serial chaining (i.e., instruction on one step at a time). By constrasting the summary of serial chaining in Figure 5 to the equal interval graph of whole chain instruction shown in Figures 1 and 3, the reader will note that the data evaluation requires differing judgments. In Figure 5, the instructor determines whether 2 or more data points are above the criterion line. In Figures 1 and 3, the instructor evaluates instead the trend of the data.

In this chapter, and throughout this book, equal interval graphs are recommended because of two distinct advantages. First, most figures in research articles are presented as equal interval graphs. Therefore, the model that instructors have to guide their ongoing professional development in data management is the equal interval graph. Second, equal interval graphs can be constructed easily and adapted to the same form as that used for data collection.

Further, if graphs are drawn by hand in a nonstandard manner, it is easy for data to be distorted because of different proportions used for the horizontal and vertical axes across graphs. Instructors are thus encouraged to make one graph that will be standard across data evaluation, to avoid misjudgments created by differing forms. For example, the forms shown in Figures 1 and 2 lend themselves to a wide range of data collection and could be easily adopted as a standard form.

Throughout this book, three standard forms of graphs are used (these forms are shown in Appendix D at the end of the book). These graphs have been set up for a scale of 20 on both the vertical and horizontal axes. Data are converted to percentages to conform to the 20-interval scale on the vertical axis.

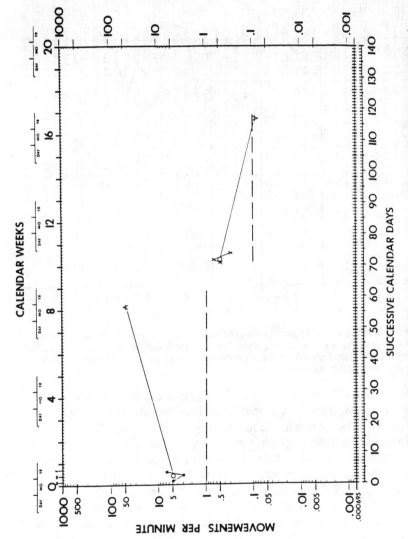

Figure 4.   Example of the 6-cycle semilogarithmic graph used in precision teaching. Data summarized are time-based data (e.g., rate). (From White, O. R., & Haring, N. G. [1980]. *Exceptional teaching.* Columbus, OH: Charles E. Merrill; used with permission of author.)

119

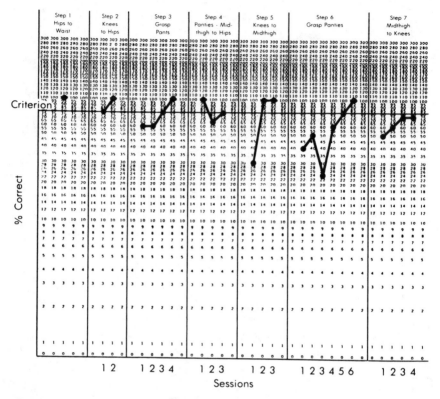

Figure 5. Clothing removal progress data plotted on columnar numerical paper. Instructor's use of chaining is evident in the steps listed. (From Sailor, W., & Guess, D. [1983]. *Severely handicapped students: An instructional design* [p. 168]. Boston: Houghton Mifflin; reprinted by permission.)

The horizontal axis represents days. These graphs can hold 20 school days (4 weeks) of data. Again, the advantage of this standardization is that it may facilitate data review and improve its accuracy.

Even when a standard graph is used, however, the scale of measurement must represent enough of a range of response opportunities to show change over time. For example, if the scale is from 0 to 2, the person's progress may be masked by this limited range for the data display. By contrast, if the range is too large (e.g., a 40-step task analysis), it may also be difficult to pinpoint instructional problems. Ideally, the instructor should use a scale of measurement with about 10 responses. Throughout this text, the scale of measurement that will be used will be at least 8, but no more than 20 responses. This scale is typically converted to percentages for uniform intervals across graphs.

Obviously, the horizontal axis (i.e., frequency of data collection) also requires standardization to prevent data distortions. Once the instructor selects this pattern, it should be shown on the horizontal axis. If days are missed, these

Student: __John__   Behavior: __Stuff envelopes__

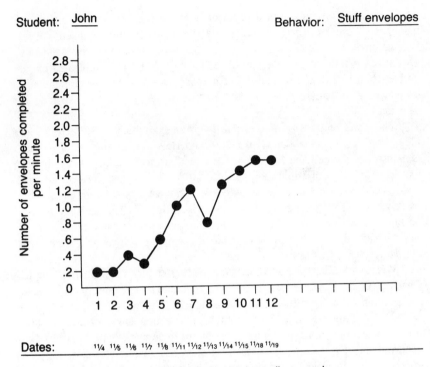

Dates: ¹¹/₄ ¹¹/₅ ¹¹/₆ ¹¹/₇ ¹¹/₈ ¹¹/₁₁ ¹¹/₁₂ ¹¹/₁₃ ¹¹/₁₄ ¹¹/₁₅ ¹¹/₁₈ ¹¹/₁₉

Figure 6. An example of rate data summarized on a linear gaph.

omissions can be shown as missing data points. The standard graphs used throughout this book are based on daily data collection, with data omissions (e.g., absences) left as blank columns.

In addition to these data summary considerations that can influence evaluation of ongoing assessment, the educator also must consider whether instruction has been implemented as planned. That is, it would be unfair to judge a person's progress as poor if he or she had not had the opportunity to learn. Opportunities may have been limited by the person's illnesses or by disruptions in the program (e.g., instructor absence, snow days). Thus, one of the first considerations that the instructor should make in reviewing the graphs is whether there are sufficient data in the period of evaluation to make a decision about progress.

Biweekly Data Evaluation

Once the data have been collected on a regular schedule (e.g., daily), and the graphs for each data set have been prepared, the educator is ready to begin evaluation of the data to make instructional decisions. As discussed in conjunction with how often to collect data, an instructor's schedule for data review will depend on the priority of the objective and the time frame for mastery. In this book, a biweekly schedule of data review is presented because this allows no more than 2 weeks to pass before ineffective instruction is changed. (*Note:* Evaluation of skill acquisition for specific skills is reviewed next, and evaluation of routines is presented at the end of the chapter. In Chapter 8, evaluation of problem behavior data is reviewed; in Chapter 9, evaluation of generalization is presented. All of these types of data are equally important for instructional decision making.)

The *Lehigh model for data evaluation* is an example of a biweekly schedule of data review. Browder et al. (1989) and Browder, Liberty, et al. (1986) demonstrated the benefit of adherence to a standard method for data evaluation that included a set of empirically derived guidelines for making instructional decisions. The entire data review, which is conducted for each graph on a biweekly basis, is summarized as a task analysis in Table 1. The decision rules to be followed are shown in Table 2. The following paragraphs describe these steps in more detail, giving references to alternative practices instructors may consider.

When to Change Instruction Using a Standard Method to Evaluate the Data Pattern The prerequisite to data pattern review is to determine if there are sufficient data to conduct evaluation (i.e., at least 6 data points). If not, the educator should continue instruction and reschedule evaluation. The second consideration for data pattern review is whether mastery has occurred during the period of review. If mastery has occurred (as defined by the criteria in the objective for the lesson), the instructor will plan extended performance instruction as described next in *what* to change. A third consideration is whether any change has occurred. If all data points are at the same level as when instruction began (e.g., at 0), an instructional change is clearly needed. If enough data are present, and some learning has occurred, but mastery has not occurred, then the instructor must determine whether the data pattern shows adequate acceleration, inadequate acceleration, a plateau, or deceleration. This discrimination may require using some standard method for data inspection, as described next.

In single-subject research, visual analysis of graphed data has been considered an appropriate alternative to statistical analysis (Hersen & Barlow, 1976; Kazdin, 1982). Unfortunately, visual analysis alone can lead to inaccurate conclusions about the data pattern. For example, research has shown inaccuracy in visual analyses conducted by instructors (Liberty, 1972), graduate students (Wampold & Furlong, 1981), and experts (DeProspero & Cohen, 1979). By contrast, using a standard method of data inspection has been shown to improve this accuracy (Bailey, 1984; White, 1972).

One method to evaluate the trend of the data is called the standard quarter intersect method (White, 1972). This method is used to draw a "learning picture" or line of progress. To draw this line of progress, the instructor follows these steps:

Table 1. Lehigh model for data-based decisions

1. Prerequisite review
    1.1 Were data collected six times in 2 weeks?
    1.2 Is the scale of measurement no less than 8 and no more than 20 responses (e.g., steps of the task analysis)?
    1.3 Is the period of review continuous, without program breaks due to illness or vacation of 4 or more consecutive school days?
    1.4 Are the data summarized on the standard data collection graph sheet (e.g., Figure 1) with the vertical axis representing percentage correct and the horizontal axis representing week days?
    1.5 If the answer to 1.1–1.4 is "yes," proceed with review of this graph. If not, the guidelines may not be applicable.

2. Simple data patterns (visual analysis adequate)
    2.1 Has the person met the criteria for mastery at any time in this review period (cross to last period of review to note mastery)? If so, note "Mastery" as the data pattern and proceed to section 4 to make the instructional decision.
    2.2 Has the person failed to progress at all on this skill? If so, note "No progress" as the data pattern and proceed to section 4 to make a decision.

3. Data patterns that require standard estimation of trend
    3.1 Draw the line of progress using the first 3 data points and the last 3 data points. Note intersections with a plus sign (+). Decide if this line is going up (accelerating), going down (decelerating), or flat. (See Figure 7 for help in intersections.)
    3.2 Calculate the mean for *all* data points in the period of review. If you have not already done so, calculate the mean for the last period of review. Decide if the mean is higher by at least 5%, higher but not by 5%, lower, or the same as the last period of review.
    3.3 On the graph, under "Data Pattern" note the trend (accelerating, decelerating, flat) and mean.

4. Making the instructional decision to match the trend
    4.1 Refer to the "Decision Rules" shown in Table 2 and select the decision that matches the trend. Write this on the graph under "Decision."
    4.2 If you decide not to follow the decision rule suggested by the guidelines, write out the rationale.
    4.3 If the decision requires an instructional change, mark a phase change line on the graph and label the specific change you make (e.g., "Use time delay to fade verbal prompt").
    4.4 If the decision requires new measurement and graphing, note this on the graph (e.g., "Graph discontinued—new task analysis").
    4.5 If changes are required, be sure to write these into the systematic instruction plan for this skill.

Note: Developed and evaluated by Browder, Demchak, Heller, and King (1989).

Table 2. Rules for data-based decision making

Category	Data pattern	Decision rule
PART I. Biweekly reviews		
1. Mastery	Criteria achieved during decision phase.	Extend performance (e.g., fluency, generalization).
2. No progress	Same mean as baseline. *or* No independent responses.	a. First period of review, wait 2 more weeks—change. b. After 4 weeks, simplify skill.
3. Adequate progress	Trend is accelerating or flat, and mean is higher by 5% or more.	Make no changes.
4. Inadequate progress	Trend is accelerating or flat, and mean is higher by less than 5%. *or* Trend is flat, same mean.	Improve antecedents (e.g., prompting strategies).
5. Motivation problem	Trend is decelerating regardless of mean change. *or* Trend is accelerating or flat, and mean is lower.	Improve motivation.
Part II. Quarterly reviews[a]		
1. Adequate progress	Net gain across months and magnitude of gain satisfactory to parents/instructor/learner. Most biweekly decisions were Rule 3—adequate progress.	No change.
2. Inadequate progress	No net gain or gain is unsatisfactory. Most biweekly decisions were Rule 4—inadequate progress.	Plan new instructional strategies for faster acquisition.
3. Motivation problem	No net gain or regression (negative number). Most biweekly decisions were Rule 5—motivation problem.	Reevaluate importance of objective or plan new motivational strategies.

Note: Categories are ranked according to complexity of decision based on amount of data summary required.

[a]To compute net gain, subtract first biweekly phase mean from most recent biweekly phase mean.

1. Identify the first 3 data points of the series. Find the second highest data point. Find the second day's data point. Mark a + at the intersection of the second highest point and the second day's point.
2. Identify the last 3 data points of the series (e.g., the last 3 days). Repeat the procedure in #1 to find the intersection. That is, find the second highest data point and the midday of these 3 points and mark a + at the intersection.
3. Connect the two +s with a straight line. The slope of the line will be shown by this straight line and will be either accelerating (going up), decelerating (going down), or flat. (See Figure 7.)

This method for evaluating the data trend is recommended for application of the instructional decision rules in Table 2. However, two other methods of data review merit consideration. The first is to compare the learner's rate of progress to an expected rate of progress. N. Haring et al. (1981) described how to draw the "minimum 'celeration (acceleration) line" on the graph. To draw this line, the instructor marks and "A" or aimstar on the intersection of the date and level of performance to show when mastery should be achieved. A line is then drawn from the midpoint of the learner's current performance to this aimstar. This is the minimum 'celeration line. Progress is compared to this minimum acceptable rate of progress (see Figure 8). One advantage of the minimum 'celeration line is that the instructor need not wait to collect 6 data points to see when progress is not adequate. This may be especially useful for programs that are implemented infrequently (e.g., weekly community instruction). The difficulty in applying the minimum 'celeration line is that instructors may not be able to set a date for mastery unless there is some naturally occurring deadline, such as the end of the individual's last year of school.

A third method for evaluating the data, described by Sailor and Guess (1983), is a variation of both the standard quarter intersect and minimum 'celeration line approach. In this evaluation, the instructor first draws a line of progress as shown in Figure 7 (standard quarter intersect). Then the instructor extends this line to predict when mastery will be achieved at the current rate of progress. This method can be helpful in making the decision of whether current acceleration is too slow (e.g., mastery will take several years). This prediction line is shown in Figure 9.

Again, the method of data inspection that is used throughout this book is the standard quarter intersect method shown in Figure 7. This method helps the instructor determine the *slope* of the data pattern by observing whether the line is going up (accelerating), going down (decelerating), or remaining flat. In addition to the slope of the data, instructors should also compare the *magnitude* of change. To compare the magnitude of change, the instructor must calculate the *mean* performance for the previous data period (e.g., the previous 2 weeks) and the current period of review. In comparing these means, the instructor can note

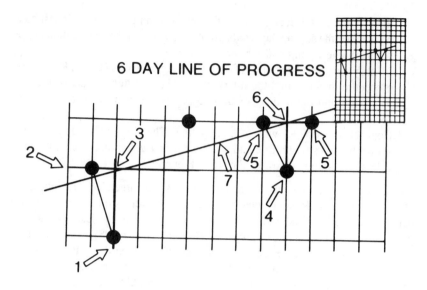

1 mid-day of first 3 days

2 mid-level of first 3 days

3 intersection

4 mid-day of last 3 days

5 mid-level of last 3 days when 2 are the same, that will be the middle

6 intersection

7 connect intersections

Figure 7. The standard quarter intersect method of trend estimation. (From Haring, N., Liberty, K., & White, O. [1980]. Rules for data-based strategy decisions in instructional programs: Current research and instructional implications. In W. Sailor, B. Wilcox, & L. Brown [Eds.], *Methods of instruction for severely handicapped students* [p. 170]. Baltimore: Paul H. Brookes Publishing Co.; reprinted by permission.)

whether the average performance is better and adequate (mean higher by 5%), better but inadequate (mean higher by less than 5%), worse (lower mean), or the same (same mean). Thus, the instructor makes two discriminations in reviewing the data pattern: 1) the slope of the data trend (accelerating, decelerating, or flat) and, 2) the mean of the current period versus the previous period of review (higher, lower, or same).

What to Change When Pattern Suggests Need for Change—Applying "Rules" to Improve Success of Instructional Decisions Unless the data pattern shows an acceptable rate of acceleration, an instructional change is necessary. The choice of change need not be made randomly or from "hunches," but can be based on the data pattern itself. Research by N. Haring et al. (1981) produced a set of rules that can help educators match instructional decisions to data patterns, and improve the success of their decisions. N. Haring et al. (1981) found that when educators' instructional deci-

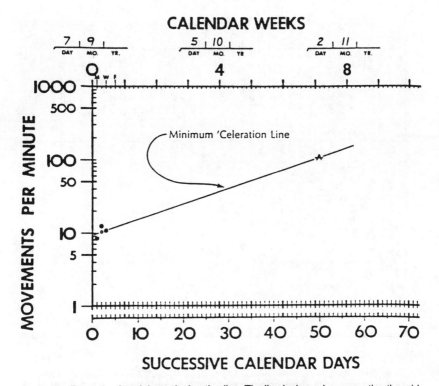

Figure 8.   Example of a minimum 'celeration line. The line is drawn by connecting the mid-point of current performance to the "A" aimstar. The aimstar is estimated by selecting the criterion and date for mastery (e.g., 100 movements per minute in 50 days is the aimstar selected above). (From White, O., & Haring, N. [1980]. *Exceptional teaching*. Columbus, OH: Charles E. Merrill; used with permission of author.)

sions adhered to the suggested rules, substantially more instances of learner improvement resulted than when they chose not to follow the rules. While the N. Haring et al. (1981) research utilized semilog graphing, subsequent studies by Browder et al. (1989) and Browder, Liberty, et al. (1986) applied an adaptation of the rules to nonstandard equal interval graphs. It was found that instructors' self-monitoring improved their accuracy in evaluating the data pattern and rule-based decisions, and that rule-based decisions resulted in substantially more cases of learner improvement than non–rule-based decisions.

   Browder, Liberty, et al.'s (1986) research on standard data review focused primarily on the slope of the data pattern. Subsequent research by Browder et al. (1989) focused also on the increment of change, by comparing the current and previous phase changes. From their research, Browder et al. (1989) generated a revised list of decision rules, shown in Table 2. One of the changes in these rules since the first edition of this book (Browder, 1987) is the requirement of a 5% mean increase. Progress at less than 5% per 2 weeks will not

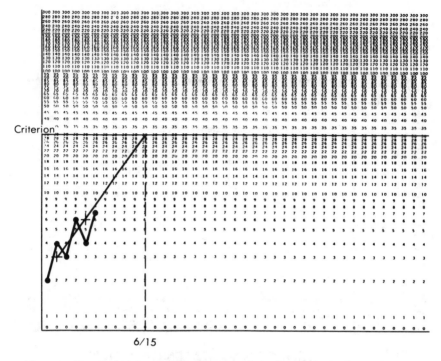

Criterion

6/15

Figure 9. Hypothetical data set illustrating a prediction line, a criterion line, and resultant intersect with ordinate to show projected date of criterial performance. (From Sailor, W., & Guess, D. [1983]. *Severely handicapped students: An instructional design* [p. 178]. Boston: Houghton Mifflin; reprinted by permission.)

result in mastery within a program year. By contrast, progress at 1% per 2 weeks sets the aim of about 5 years for mastery to occur! Interestingly, Browder et al. (1989) found that, in most cases, when progress occurred it was more than 5%.

A second change from the guidelines in the first edition of this book is in the definition of an acquisition problem. If a 5% gain is the definition of adequate progress, a gain of less than 5% is inadequate progress and reflects an acquisition problem. Since the data system is based on increasing the number of independent responses, a low mean increase reflects poor transfer of stimulus control from prompts to the natural cues of the task. Improving antecedents, especially methods to transfer stimulus control, can enhance progress. In the Browder (1987) guidelines, acceleration of slope with the same or lower mean was considered an acquisition problem. Further field testing has revealed this to be a motivation problem. If the trend is acceleration, but the mean is not also increasing, there must be variability in the data since the previous review (usually regression occurred at the beginning of the 2 weeks of review). Instructional changes that improve motivation can enhance progress in this case.

Finally, in a third departure from Browder (1987), further field testing has revealed that attention to the variability of the data pattern is not necessary. In every case, variability was redundant with either a lower mean or deceleration in the slope. Since variability can be difficult to judge, eliminating this discrimination simplifies the decision-making process.

Quarterly and Annual Data Evaluation

The disadvantage of biweekly reviews without a minimum acceleration line is that longitudinal progress is not evaluated. To be sure longitudinal progress is adequate, it is important to supplement biweekly reviews with periodic reviews of the data. These periodic reviews can correspond to person summaries such as report cards or quarterly reviews. As described in Chapter 2, an annual data summary can also enhance the development of the next year's IEP/IHP. However, few resources have described how to link data-based evaluation to reports of personal progress.

In the Lehigh model, the data summary required for progress summaries is simple to calculate. The summary is based on the *increment* of progress, expressed as percentage points that the person has gained during the quarter or year. Since many caregivers understand percentage and the goal of achieving 100% (or some other percentage), this system may be more useful than graphic displays for communicating gains. To summarize progress for a quarter, the steps are:

1. Write down the most recent biweekly mean for the quarter.
2. Write down the first biweekly mean for the quarter.
3. Subtract the first biweekly mean from the most recent mean.
4. Note if progress has occurred. The answer will be a positive number (gain), a negative number (regression), or zero (no gain).
5. Decide what instructional changes should be made to redesign programs that have had overall regression or lack of gain for the quarter. (These decisions are shown in Table 2.)

The following paragraphs illustrate the calculation of progress summaries for three objectives for Nat, for an April 10 summary:

In *handwashing*, Nat's mean for the period of March 27–April 10 was 58%. His mean for the first 2 weeks of this quarter, January 16–30, was 34%. His increment of progress was calculated as: 58% − 34% = 24%. This was a positive gain. The instructor wrote on the progress summary: "Handwashing. Progress of +24% (range 34% to 58%). No change in instruction."

In *using a communication wallet*, Nat's mean for March 27–April 10 was 65%. His mean for January 15–30 was 75%. The increment of progress was calculated as 65% − 75% = − 10%. This negative number indicated a regression of 10% across the quarter. The instructor wrote on the progress summary: "Communication wallet. Regression of − 10% (range 75% to 65%). Change wallet to include new leisure items Nat prefers."

In *wiping the table*, Nat's mean for the beginning of April was 35% and his mean for the last 2 weeks of January, when the quarter started, was 35%. In looking at Nat's biweekly data, he had made minimal progress all quarter, with biweekly means and decisions as follows:

January 30: 35% (no change)
February 13: 32% (inadequate progress; use time delay)
February 27: 27% (motivation problem; schedule before recess)
March 13: 35% (no change)
March 27: 42% (no change)
April 10: 35% (Quarterly decision)

In looking at these biweekly decisions and the lack of progress for the quarter, the instructor realized Nat's tablewashing program needed to be revamped. She decided that she had not identified a critical effect for Nat to clean the table. Although the instructor scheduled recess after the table was finished, Nat had learned that it did not matter how well he cleaned the table to get recess. The instructor would guide him to wipe it. Thus, the instructor decided to help Nat realize that the table needed to be clean before moving on to a new activity. She would make sure it had noticeable crumbs and spills, delay prompting by longer intervals (15 seconds), and have the aide begin helping other children line up for recess as she helped Nat wipe the table. She hoped to teach him that by doing more steps for himself, he could get outside faster. She wrote on the report: "Wiping tables. No progress, 0%, due to progress followed by regression (range 35% to 35%). Enhance natural cues and critical effect."

As the above example illustrates, it is during longitudinal reviews of progress that major program changes are made. The biweekly reviews usually result only in the "fine tuning" of programs—not in redeveloping them. Figure 10 provides an example of a longitudinal progress summary for Eva Ortiz.

A similar method can be used for the annual summary of progress. To compute an annual increment of progress, the instructor should:

1. Identify the mean of the most recent 2 weeks (Annual summaries often have to be done before the end of the program year and may even be done in the third quarter. The instructor should use the most recent 2 weeks and report the date used.)
2. Identify the mean of the first 2 weeks for this objective, *or*, if a baseline probe was used before instruction, use this baseline mean.
3. Subtract the first 2-week mean (or baseline) from the most recent mean.
4. Determine if the number reflects progress, regression, or no progress.
5. Record the increment of progress.

(A discussion of annual assessment for IEP/IHP development was provided at the end of Chapter 2, along with an example of reporting these annual progress summaries in Figure 13 of that chapter.)

EASTERN LEHIGH SCHOOL DISTRICT
SPECIAL EDUCATION QUARTERLY REPORT

NAME: Eva Ortiz   QUARTER: 3rd

TEACHER: Mr. N.   PLACEMENT: Integrated Sp.Ed./8th Grade
                                              at Eastern Middle

Skill Area	Evaluation	Teacher comments
Routines		
Arrival	76 pt = 95% mastery 5'2" (2' faster)	Excellent progress (No change)
Cafeteria	34 pt = 29% mastery 28'15" (5'32" slower)	Regression—assign peer partner.
Regular class	47 pt = 38% mastery 24'10" (1'5" faster)	Good progress (No change)
Specific Skills		
Follow schedule	+28% (31% to 59%)	Good progress
Social conversation	+48% (6% to 54%)	Excellent progress
Group games	+37% mastery	Extend to new games
Menstrual care	−14% (64% to 50%)	Regression—incentive needed
Play basketball	0% (12% to 12%)	Simplify task analysis.
Others		
Purchase item	+20% (weekly data)	Good progress
Clothing selection	Clothing has been clean, age appropriate	
Assertiveness *vs.* Screaming behavior	Assertiveness used five times Screaming used five times	Good progress

Comments: Eva has had an excellent quarter especially in interpersonal skills. I'll be offering more support for the cafeteria routine and menstrual care.

Figure 10. Example of a quarterly summary of student progress.

DATA-BASED DECISIONS FOR ROUTINE DATA

The concept of defining a routine for assessment and instruction is a recent development for programs for individuals with severe disabilities. Neel and Billingsley (1989) described this methodology in detail, and their guidelines for developing a routine for assessment were described in Chapter 3. The research on data-based decisions to date has focused on specific skill data, not routines. As described in Chapter 3, routines often comprise a greater diversity of skills. The "steps" of a routine may even require different scales of measurement for each step (e.g., duration recording for one, latency for another). Thus, systems that compress data into one unit (e.g., trends, means), may have limited applicability for routine data. Rather, a system is needed that allows for each response in the routine to be analyzed separately.

T.G. Haring and Kennedy (1988) described the problem of adding up responses into one unit (e.g., percent) with respect to task analyses. That is, relevant information on individual response progress are masked by these summaries. Thus, the within-response summary to be described next has applicability to task analytic assessment of specific skills. Within-response summaries are especially critical, however, to routine task analytic assessment, where responses are more divergent in topography.

IMPACT Model for Evaluation of Progress on Routines

The Neel and Billingsley (1989) method for data-based evaluation provided a model that instructors can use or adapt for routines. In Chapter 3, a description was given for developing the routine and using it for a baseline assessment to determine the level of assistance for each response. Figure 2 in Chapter 3 provided a reproduction of an IMPACT assessment data sheet. The reader is referred to that figure to follow the description in the next paragraph. (For another example of a routine data summary with decisions, see Chapter 9, Figure 1.)

The data summary for routines is not an equal interval graph. Rather, the raw data are reviewed for each response in the routine. The schedule for review is every 3 data points. However, these data points may be collected less than daily (e.g., weekly). Since no data summary is needed (i.e., the raw data are reviewed), the instructor can proceed to make a decision once three trials have been assessed. The flowchart for these decisions is shown in Figure 11. As the chart indicates, a change in instruction is only made if less than two "correct" responses are obtained. However, a correct response is not necessarily independence, but rather the level of prompt that is targeted for instruction. If three corrects are obtained, independence is increased by using a less intrusive prompt, fading any training reinforcers, or increasing the fluency of the response (e.g., decreasing the time to make the response).

For example, as shown in Figure 2 in Chapter 3, Gary has three "corrects" for requesting help with his seatbelt. Corrects were defined as cooperating with Gary's hand being molded for "help" when told, "show me 'help.' " Since he has done this, the instructor will now only slightly lift his hand so that he must gain independence in forming the sign for "help." As the next three dates show (the last three columns), Gary had two corrects. The decision for this first response (decision not shown in figure) would then be to continue instruction without change, as indicated in the flowchart in Figure 11. The reader is encouraged to review the rest of the responses in Figure 2 in Chapter 3 to see how each decision was made for each response. (Also see Neel & Billingsley, 1989, for more information on routines.)

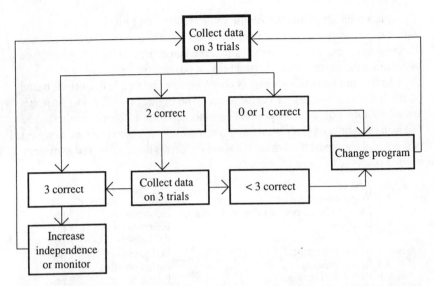

Figure 11. Decision rules flowchart for application of instructional change in individual steps of routines. (From Neel, R.S., & Billingsley, F.F. [1989]. *IMPACT: A functional curriculum handbook for students with moderate to severe disabilities* [p. 89]. Baltimore: Paul H. Brookes Publishing Co.; reprinted by permission.)

Quarterly and Annual Evaluations of Routines

Personal progress summaries are also needed for routine assessments. For these quarterly and annual evaluations of progress, a summary of all responses in the routine may be logical. Two ways the routine can be summarized are: 1) by the duration the entire routine requires, which indicates how fluent the person's performance is; and 2) by the level of independence the person has acquired. The following paragraphs describe the Lehigh model, an adaptation of routine assessment for quarterly and annual evaluations that is being field tested at Lehigh University.

To summarize the routine, first the person's performance of the entire routine with necessary instructor assistance is timed using a stopwatch. Time is the first component of progress reported by noting whether the person is faster or slower than the previous quarter in performing the routine.

Next, the entire routine is summarized by the level of assistance required by using the following scoring:

Independent . . . . 7 points
Nonspecific verbal prompt . . . . 6 points
Gesture . . . . 5 points
Specific verbal prompt . . . . 4 points
Model . . . . 3 points
Partial physical guidance . . . . 2 points
Full physical guidance . . . . 1 point
Resists guidance . . . . 0 points

Adding up all points across the entire routine will yield a "score." This score can'be a source of comparison across quarters and years. For convenience of communication with caregivers, the score can be converted to a percentage by dividing the current score by the highest possible score.

An illustration of this scoring is now given for Figure 2 in Chapter 3, based on the last three columns of performance. The highest possible score for this arrival routine would be 84 points (7 points each for a 12-step routine). The following is a tally of Gary's current score on each step (scoring based on best two out of three trials; if all three trials are different, highest level of assistance needed is scored):

1.	Requests help with seatbelt	Full physical	1 pt.
2.	Walks down aisle	Specific verbal	4 pts.
3.	Picks up lunch box or other materials	Independent	7 pts.
4.	Exits bus	Independent	7 pts.
5.	Walks to building entry	Partial physical	2 pts.
6.	Requests help with door	Full physical	1 pt.
7.	Enters building	Partial physical	2 pts.
8.	Walks to classroom	Partial physical	2 pts.
9.	Puts away lunch box or other materials	Full physical	1 pt.
10.	Takes off coat	Independent	7 pts.
11.	Requests help finding hook	Full physical	1 pt.
12.	Hangs up coat	Partial physical	2 pts.
	TOTAL SCORE =		37 pts.

The instructor would then record on the quarterly report of progress, "Arrival routine: 37 pts. = 44% of score needed for independence, which is 84. Duration of routine is 3'10" (new routine, so comparison of fluency is not yet possible)." (The quarterly summary in Figure 10 includes reports of routines as well as specific skills.)

The limitation of the Lehigh model method of summarizing data for routines is that it assumes prompt fading is accomplished by moving through a hierarchy of routines (a *multimodal* prompt approach). Neel and Billingsley (1989) advocated the use of a *unimodal* approach to prompting; that is, selecting one type of prompt and fading it (e.g., by decreasing physical assistance). If a unimodal approach is employed, a similar scoring approach can be used, if each level of fading can be defined. For example:

No assistance .... 5 points
Touch elbow .... 4 points
Guide wrist... 3 points
Guide hand, minimal pressure........................... 2 points
Full hand guidance..................................... 1 point
Resists guidance .... 0 points

However, fading a one-prompt system is sometimes highly subjective, and such an appraisal would not be applicable because the level of fading could not be defined. In this case, for ongoing evaluation, the instructor would simply calculate the total percentage independent correct and the duration of the routine.

SUMMARY

This chapter provides guidelines for utilizing performance data to make instructional decisions. These data-based decisions help the instructor to reap the investment of the time and effort required to conduct ongoing assessment. The instructor who does not use data, but simply collects and graphs them, will probably soon tire of this exercise. By contrast, the instructor who uses data to make instructional decisions may be rewarded with increased personal progress and the documentation to show this progress.

Data-based decisions for routine assessment are the simplest to master because minimal data summary is required and the guidelines for instructional decisions are simple. Since routines are also the most important unit of measurement in a life skills program, an instructor may want to master this method of data review first. However, routines are a new methodology and no research exists on the benefits of this method of data analysis.

While the benefits of data-based decisions for specific skills assessment have been well validated by research, instructors sometimes fail to use "best practices" for this precise method of evaluation. This chapter has provided a step-by-step guide for data-based decisions for evaluation of specific skills that may help the instructor learn this complex methodology.

This chapter focused only on evaluation of ongoing assessment of skill acquisition data. Ongoing assessment and evaluation of problem behavior data and generalization data (including extended school year) are described in Chapters 8 and 9.

STUDY QUESTIONS

1. How much data should be collected?
2. What important points should be followed in summarizing data?
3. What support can be found in research for following a standard procedure for data summary and review?
4. Using real or simulated graphs, try to apply the Lehigh model for data evaluation following the decision rules given in Table 2.
5. How can data-based summaries be used for quarterly reviews or report cards?

FOR FURTHER THOUGHT

1. Consider developing data-based evaluation as described in this chapter. If you made a chart at the end of Chapter 3, review it now

and ask yourself the question, "How much data do I need to make sound instructional decisions?"

2. If you find you are collecting more data than you use for decisions, consider whether you need to schedule time for decision making or eliminate some data collection. If you collect less data than you need, plan how to enhance this assessment. Try following the Lehigh model for data evaluation for several programs across students for three months. Then evaluate whether this process has enhanced your instructional decisions.

chapter 5

ASSESSMENT IN AND FOR THE HOME

Linda M. Bambara and Diane M. Browder

TRADITIONALLY, ASSESSMENT IN the home domain has focused on the identification of basic self-help and housekeeping skills. However, with the increasing emphasis on facilitating full community integration and enhancing the quality of life for people with severe disabilities, assessment in and for the home has become a much more complex and challenging undertaking. The goal of assessment for the home is to identify skills needed to function independently within domestic environments and to participate as a contributing member of the family, the household, and the immediate community (Eshilian, Haney, & Falvey, 1989).

Participation in the home as a valued member of the family and community will thus require that assessment go beyond the simple identification of task-related daily living skills. First, assessment must address questions about *long-range plans* for community living options. For example, will the individual live with his or her family or in his or her own apartment with support staff? Second, assessment must reflect the *culture* and *values* of the family and the community. Skills needed for domestic functioning must fit within the social milieu of the family and the surrounding community. Third, to ensure that selected skills are indeed meaningful to the functioning of the individual and to his or her family, assessment must reflect individual *preferences* of the learner and other family members. Fourth, assessment must address skills in *personal autonomy* such as choice making, household management, and self-scheduling, for without these skills individuals will be relegated to assume a passive role, rather than an active, contributory role. Finally, assessment in the home needs to reflect the *interpersonal skills* required to be a good neighbor, to maintain friendships, and to negotiate and share responsibilities with other family members or housemates.

This chapter provides strategies for planning and implementing assessments for the home across four domains: 1) personal maintenance, 2) recreation and socialization, 3) housekeeping and food preparation, and 4) preparation for community outings. Following the sequence of the three assessment phases discussed in Chapters 2 and 3, specific illustrations for conducting a comprehensive assessment, an annual assessment, and an ongoing assessment for the home are presented. In addition, two preliminary assessment steps are introduced: getting to know families and conducting personal futures planning. Combined, they set the contextual backdrop for conducting meaningful assessments for the home and set a longitudinal plan for personal integration in the home and community.

PRELIMINARY ASSESSMENT FOR THE HOME

Getting to Know Families

Active family involvement in the identifiction and prioritization of long- and short-term goals is central to the assessment process, especially within the home domain. (The term *family* is used in this chapter to refer to people who live together and care for each other. They may be a biological family, foster parents and children, or unrelated adults such as residents in a group home. The term *caregivers* is used for the people who provide care to the person with severe disabilities, and may refer to the biological parents, foster or adoptive parents, a guardian, a sibling, or paid support staff.) Parents, family members, and support staff are most familiar with the demands of their home settings and the goals and dreams that they have for individual family members. Family members and caregivers can provide thorough information on the daily routines of their household; the customs, beliefs, and traditions of their family; and their plans for future living alternatives. They can also provide an accurate appraisal of the learner's preferences, abilities, and needs, and may have, prior to professional involvement, already identified priority goals that will enhance greater household/family participation. Without some family involvement, it would be difficult, if not impossible, to identify ecologically valid skills for the home. Beyond information sharing, collaboration between professionals and family members is desirable because it respectfully recognizes that the family has a pivotal role "in the nurturance, socialization, education, and career development of its individual members" (Turnbull, Barber, Behr, & Kerns, 1988, p. 82).

This chapter provides a number of strategies for working with families to prioritize skills for assessment and instruction in the home domain. However, before active collaboration is pursued, it is critical that professionals obtain some basic information about the families with whom they are endeavoring to work. The *family systems theory* as described by Turnbull and her colleagues (Benson & Turnbull, 1986; Turnbull et al., 1988) provides practitioners with a useful framework for understanding the dynamic nature of families, gathering preliminary assessment information, and structuring initial and ongoing assessments.

Family Systems Theory   The family systems perspective views individual families as social systems comprising individual family members with unique characteristics and needs. The basic tenet of the family systems perspective is that all components of a family are interrelated. Events affecting one component or one individual family member are likely to affect other components and other family members.

Benson and Turnbull (1986) and Turnbull et al. (1988) described the family system as comprising four interrelated major components:

1. *Family resources* (inputs): Refers to the structure of the family that includes individual membership characteristics (e.g., parents, siblings, extended family members, unrelated housemates, friendships, paid support staff), and cultural (e.g., ethnicity, religion) and ideological (e.g., family beliefs, personal coping process) mechanisms of the family. These resources define the family's style, and its ability to meet the individual and collective needs of the family.

2. *Family interaction* (process): Refers to the constant interaction among the family subsystems, which, in a traditional nuclear family, may include the relationships among the family and the outside community, relationships between the husband and wife, the relationship between parents and children, and relationships among siblings. Since family members often share membership with more than one subsystem, participation in one will often compete with the others in terms of time and resources (e.g., spending time as a mother versus as a wife).

3. *Family functions* (outputs): Refers to the numerous tasks, functions, or outputs a family produces in order to meet its individual and collective needs. Families are called upon to provide economic security, educational and vocational guidance, nurturance, affective support, health care, recreation, socialization, and respite.

4. *Family life cycle* (change): Refers to the sequence of changes that a family experiences across time. These changes, or stress factors, whether developmental (e.g., birth, early childhood, school age, adulthood, death) or episodic (e.g., divorce, natural catastrophes), will have a substantial impact on the interplay of each of the other three components.

Implications for Collaboration   From the family systems approach we can derive four main implications for working with families to assess the needs of an individual family member. First, teachers and other professionals should develop a shared working relationship with families rather than a directive one. As one of its primary functions, education and nurturance is the business of the family. This needs to be respected in both philosophy and practice.

Second, teachers and other professionals need to be sensitive to the values and strengths of a family before planning assessment. Individual families are diverse and unique in respect to the composition of their members and their values, cultures, and beliefs. It cannot be overemphasized that an appropriate assessment for the home will require professionals to become familiar with the structure and culture of individual families, and accept individual family differences—without evaluative judgment.

Family compositions come in all shapes and forms. The traditional nuclear family of mother-father-siblings is one of many constructions. Many families may have a single parent as head of the household, or in the case of group living arrangements, family members may be completely unrelated. Similarly, primary caregivers may vary tremendously across families, moving well beyond the stereotyped notion that mothers assume the primary role. Knowledge of family membership characteristics has important implications for who is involved in making educational decisions on behalf of the learner (Benson & Turnbull, 1986). For example, in many Puerto Rican families, it is customary for the maternal grandmother to assume primary responsibility for child care while the mother is out working. In addition to her central role in child rearing, the maternal grandmother is frequently consulted with regard to family problems and health-related issues (Comas-Diaz & Griffith, 1988). Thus, in families in which the maternal grandmother provides the most care, it may be as important or more important to involve this person than parents in assessing daily routines and identifying potential personal care goals.

Knowledge of family culture and beliefs also has strong implications for identifying priority assessment areas that are ultimately functional for the individual *within the context of the family*. Functionality cannot be viewed in isolation. What is functional for the individual must also fit within the cultural context of the family. For example, professionals might view domestic skills such as housekeeping and cooking to be critical to the achievement of domestic independence for all individuals with severe disabilities. Yet, families of various ethnic cultures and religious beliefs may place a different emphasis on independence—especially across gender. Families that uphold a clear role differentiation between males and females may view housekeeping and cooking to be stigmatizing for a teen-age boy. Other families with certain religious beliefs may see their primary role as lifelong care providers for their children with severe disabilities, and thus may find little value in facilitating domestic independence or preparing their family member for independent living in the community. Professionals need not agree with family beliefs, but should recognize that skills will be far more meaningful if they are supported by the culture of the family.

The third implication for collaboration is that instructors need to be sensitive to the demands of everyday family life. Families are very busy just fulfilling their basic daily needs. Professionals need to remember that the caregivers' primary responsibility is to maintain a nurturing, normalized environment for *all* members of the family, including themselves—not just the individual with severe disabilities. Moreover, nurturance is just one of several major functions that families need to fulfill on a daily basis. When an equilibrium is established, families balance multiple responsibilities through the establishment of routines, scheduling, and role delineation among family members. However, stress can easily upset the balance, forcing families to reorganize their schedules, resources, and even priorities. For example, while most families would agree that education is a chief concern, it should not be assumed that it is a priority for all families. Faced with financial, medical, or emotional crises, a family may have no option but to place education as a lower priority, until the impending stressors are relieved.

Given that caregivers' collaboration in both initial and ongoing assessment is highly desirable, but complicated by the many demands and stresses in a family, the professional needs to communicate carefully with the family to set priorities for participation. Conducting an assessment within a family can strain, as well as support, a burdened family. Professionals need to be sensitive to how their relationship will fit in the web of family interactions (e.g., the father is the spokesperson at IEP/IHP meetings, but the mother is the primary contact person for daily care issues).

Families will vary with the extent to which they can collaborate in the assessment process. When the caregivers are group home staff who are paid to teach and assess, as well as provide care, a larger role may be played in conducting the assessment of home skills. In the more typical family where caregivers are parents or guardians, the instructor will probably assume the primary responsibility for assessment and instruction. Family collaboration may then include participation in skill selection, anecdotal reports of progress, and, depending on family resources to participate, assessment and instruction of some priority skills. Collaboration in ongoing assessment can be suggested, but needs to be realistic based on the family's values, its daily schedule, and the interaction pattern among its members. Professionals must be willing to develop assessment procedures that are minimally intrusive, and adaptable to family style.

The fourth implication for collaboration concerns the need for professionals to be flexible and adaptable to family change. Families are dynamic systems. As discussed, developmental lifestyle change, as well as unanticipated or episodic change, can greatly affect the structure and interplay of family resources, family interaction among subsystems, and family functions. This strongly suggests that instructors must adapt their assessment approach when working with interfamily differences and intrafamily change. For example, parent preference may be given considerable weight when planning assessment for a young child. By contrast, when conducting assessment for an adult, parent preference will need to be balanced across input from friends, advocates, and employers, and especially from the individual with special needs.

The dynamic nature of families also underscores the necessity of involving family members in at least yearly prioritization of objectives. Goals or objectives previously identified for instruction may no longer be critical to the overall day-to-day functioning of the family. Or perhaps as families move through natural life cycles, family plans for the individual with disabilities may change substantially. Thus, although assessment should be based on a longitudinal plan, both long-range goals and short-term objectives are subject to change.

Preliminary Assessment of Family System   Like most relationships, "getting to know families" is an ongoing process that evolves with time. However, as a first step to the initial assessment, professionals should obtain basic information regarding individual family structure, interactions among family members, family functions, and the life cycle of the family. Table 1 provides examples of the types of questions that instructors might find useful. This information may help educators to become sensitized to demands and stresses of families, as well as to acquire a basic understanding of home routines and family culture. In addition, self-assessment questions are included in the table to assist instructors in translating the information generated by the questions into direct implications for facilitating instructor-family collaboration. To facilitate maximum effectiveness, educators are urged to adapt these questions to suit individual family needs and program interests. In fact, many of the questions may be answered through casual interactions with the family. Additionally, considerable adaptation may be required when these questions are applied to group home or supportive living arrangements.

Methods for gathering basic information about a family include direct observations, interviews, and self-report instruments such as questionnaires and surveys. Spending time with families in their home, perhaps through an afternoon visit, will provide the richest source of information. Observing families can provide tremendous insight into how families meet the demands and routines of daily life. If a home visit is not feasible, open-ended interviews—whether conducted in the home, over the telephone, or in the school setting—have the advantage of providing specific information about family structure and function through the perspectives of individual family members. Written questionnaires or surveys also provide specific information, but only to a finite set of questions: they do not offer an opportunity for the give-and-take of a personal interaction. Interviews allow spontaneous elaborations, while self-report instruments do not.

Selecting the most appropriate method to become acquainted with a family will largely depend upon the interests and resources of both the instructor and the family. A home visit plus an interview may be the most desirable combination for a new learner or for a comprehensive assessment. However, given the busy schedules of most instructors and families, a written survey followed up by a brief telephone call may be the most feasible for an annual update.

Before ending this discussion about families, a word of caution is in order: Regardless of the method selected, professionals must guard against intrusive questioning. That is, families should never feel pressured into providing more information than they want to give.

Table 1. Assessment guide for obtaining basic information about families

Family structure
Membership
1. Who are the members of the family?
2. What are the ages and genders of the members?
3. What are the occupations of family members?
4. Are there friends, extended family members, or support staff who play a significant role in the functioning of the family?
5. Is there a chief spokesperson for the family?

Self-assessment: Am I familiar with all the key players in the individual's life? Have I been careful to respect the primary contact person?

Culture and values
6. What is the ethnic background of the family?
7. What is the family's/individual member's religious preference?
8. What traditions does the family uphold?
9. What impact do the family's religious beliefs or ethnic background have on the individual's functioning within the home?
10. What does the family value?

Self-assessment: What have I done to understand this family's values, especially if they are different from my own? What else do I need to do (e.g., talk with a professional who shares these values, read resources on this culture)?

Family interactions
11. How are daily responsibilities negotiated among family members?
12. Do all family members have the opportunity to speak for themselves, including the individual with severe disabilities?
13. What activities do family members share together?
14. Do all members of the family understand the nature of the individual's disabilities?
15. How have the individual's disabilities affected family interactions?

Self-assessment: Am I aware of how family members perceive the family member with disabilities? Do I carefully avoid contests for my loyalty or taking sides with family members in conflict (e.g., separated parents)?

Family functions
16. What is the established routine of the family on weekdays and weekends?
17. What are each member's roles and responsibilities in maintaining daily routines?
18. What impact have the individual's disabilities had on the family's ability to recreate, socialize, and fulfill basic duties inside and outside the home?
19. How does the family member with disabilities contribute to overall family functioning?
20. What is the family's current priorities?

Self-assessment: How will I schedule my assessment to be compatible with this family's schedule? Have I determined how involved this family will be in the assessment, based on preferences, past involvement, and current stress? Do I

(continued)

Table 1. (*continued*)

remain respectful of family members even if they choose to be minimally involved in assessment?

Life cycle

21. What general life-cycle stage is the family currently experiencing (e.g., early childhood years, school-age years, preparation for retirement?)
22. What are the primary stressors that are affecting the family now?
23. What plans and/or visions for the future does the family have for the member with disabilities?

Self-assessment: Have I reassessed the family's views and future plans for the family member with disabilities in this current developmental life cycle?

Adapted from Benson and Turnbull (1986).

Conducting Personal Futures Planning

Personal futures (Mount & Zwernik, 1988) or lifestyle planning (O'Brien, 1987) is a process that brings together concerned family members, friends, advocates, and professionals to describe a desirable future for an individual with severe disabilities. It is a process that evaluates an individual's quality of life in integrated community settings and results in an action plan that organizes and mobilizes resources toward that future. It requires that each participant on the planning "team" make a commitment to seeing that the plan is implemented, including dealing with obstacles such as the lack of needed supports or resources.

As a preliminary step to the initial assessment phase, a personal futures plan can provide the organizing framework for keeping subsequent assessments and instructional activities focused toward a unified long-range goal—one that emphasizes quality living in integrated settings. Because developing a personal futures plan is a time-intensive process, it is not recommended as a preliminary assessment step for all individuals. However, it is recommended when there is an expressed concern or dissatisfaction with the individual's current or projected lifestyle. Personal futures planning is also useful to reevaluate and to set new directions during transitional periods (e.g., moving from adolescence to young adulthood, moving from one area of the country to another) and during crisis situations (e.g., behavioral problems, social/emotional difficulties).

Borrowing heavily from the work of Mount and Zwernik (1989) and O'Brien (1987), the basic procedure for conducting a personal futures plan is outlined below. For more specific information, the reader is encouraged to consult these sources directly.

Reviewing the Individual's Current Lifestyle Lifestyle planning typically takes place across two sessions, with each session lasting 3–4 hours. In the first session, key participants, those who play a significant role in the focus person's life and who are willing to invest time and energy in the planning process, review the focus person's current lifestyle across five quality-of-life indicators: community presence, choice, competence, respect, and community participation. The aim is to describe the individual's accomplishments or experiences within each of the five areas rather than to identify specific skill deficits. Sample questions that can be used to guide the review process are presented in Table 2. The following is a summary description of each of the five quality-of-life areas:

1. *Community presence:* Refers to the extent to which the individual with severe disabilities is present in the community, frequenting everyday ordinary places and activities that make up community life. Frequent participation across a variety of community settings reflects high levels of physical integration.

2. *Choice:* Refers to the extent to which opportunities for choice making and decision making are present in the individual's daily life. This includes participating in decisions that occur during routine activities, such as what to eat and what to wear, as well as major life decisions regarding where to live and work. Choice making and decision making are fundamental to the establishment of personal autonomy, for without them individuals with severe disabilities will be forever relegated to a passive role.

3. *Competence:* Refers to the skills and abilities that an individual has to care for him- or herself and to participate in meaningful, valued community activities.

4. *Respect:* Refers to having a valued place or role in the community, a role that others hold in esteem. Opportunities for respect are increased when persons with severe disabilities do what other respected people do in the company of other respected individuals. Conversely, segregated activities are associated with low-status positions (e.g., mindless table work at sheltered workshops) and stereotyped notions (e.g., persons with developmental disabilities must be supervised for the welfare of themselves and others).

5. *Community participation:* Addresses the individual's social relationships, particularly friendships and family involvement. Typically, persons with severe disabilities have limited relationships outside of the people within their immediate household. However, increased community involvement is in part dependent upon the establishment of a social network of close friends and community acquaintances.

In addition to the five quality-of-life areas, the key participants discuss and list the individual's preferences, dislikes, and when possible, the individual's own image for the future. To facilitate creativity and lively discussion, the futures planning process makes use of symbols, colored markers, drawings, and maps to record information and illustrate a person's life. Figures 1 and 2 illustrate the recorded review process for a 32-year-old woman named Cathy (Mount & Zwernik, 1988).

Table 2. Questions to describe lifestyle outcomes

Community presence

What community settings does the person use regularly (daily, weekly, occasionally)?

To which of these places does the person go alone? as part of a group of two or three? as part of a larger group?

Does the person have any significant problem using any of these places?

What other community settings would it be in the person's interest to use, or to use more independently?

What would it take to increase the number of community settings the person uses completely? (Consider changes in the person's skills, changes in available assistance, negotiating changes in the setting, or changes in service patterns.)

Choice

What decisions are regularly made by the person?

What decisions are made for the person by others? For which of these could decision making be transferred to the person himself or herself?

What are the person's strongest interests and preferences that make him or her unique?

What would it take to increase the number, variety, and importance of the decisions the person makes?

What would it take to increase others' knowledge of the person's interests and preferences?

Competence

What skills could the person develop that would offer the most opportunity for increased presence, choice, respect, and participation?

What strategies for instruction and assistance have been most effective for the person?

Are there more efficient strategies than instruction, such as environmental modification or provision of additional personal assistance?

Are there any health-related threats to the person's continuing development? How can these be managed effectively with minimal disruption of good quality life experiences?

What would it take to increase the person's competence in more valued activities?

Respect

What are the valued community roles the person occupies and what percentage of time is spent in each?

Which community roles offer the person the best opportunity to express individual gifts and talents?

What would it take to increase the amount of time the person spends in a valued community role? in roles that express the person best?

What images and ideas about a desirable future are available to the person?

Does the person display any characteristics that reinforce stereotyped perceptions of people with severe handicaps?

Are there any characteristics of the person's environment that reinforce stereotyped perceptions of people with severe handicaps? (Consider the images

(continued)

Table 2. *(continued)*

projected by activities, schedules, expectations, and the way the person is spoken to or about.)

What would it take to decrease the stigma the person experiences?

Community participation

With whom does the person spend the most time on a daily and weekly basis? How many of these people are other clients/students in the same program? How many are program staff? How many are people without apparent handicaps?

Are there other important people in the person's social network with whom the person spends time occasionally?

Who are the person's friends and allies? Who knows the person intimately? Who will act as an advocate for his or her interests?

What would it take to provide better support for the person's present network of relationships?

What would it take to develop more friends or allies?

What would it take to increase the number of nonhandicapped people, including age-peers, who know and spend time with the person as an individual?

From O'Brien, J. (1987). A guide to life-style planning. In B. Wilcox & G.T. Bellamy, A comprehensive guide to *The activities catalog: An alternative curriculum for youth and adults with severe disabilities* (p. 182). Baltimore: Paul H. Brookes Publishing Co.; used with permission.

Describing a Personal Future   In the second session, the participants reconvene to plan a desirable future for the focus individual. After reviewing the individual's personal profile, and discussing any major trend or event likely to have an impact on the individual in the near future (e.g., graduating from high school, moving to another residence, changes in family structure), members of the planning team share their ideas about what images they have for an ideal future for the individual who cannot express his or her own ideas. The group is encouraged to think creatively in terms of the individual's preferences and interests, and in terms of what nondisabled similar-age peers would envision for themselves. Where would they live, work, go to school, recreate? Who are their friends? Ideas about the future can also be clustered around the five quality-of-life areas, asking a series of "what will it take" questions (O'Brien, 1987). For example:

What will it take to increase the individual's participation in valued community activities?

What will it take to increase competence in these activities?

What will it take to facilitate increased friendships?

Ideas about the future are then discussed until a vision is shared among all members of the group. Next, the members work on translating the vision into a workable action plan. This process begins breaking down the future into long-range goals, and into goals that can and should be worked on immediately. The

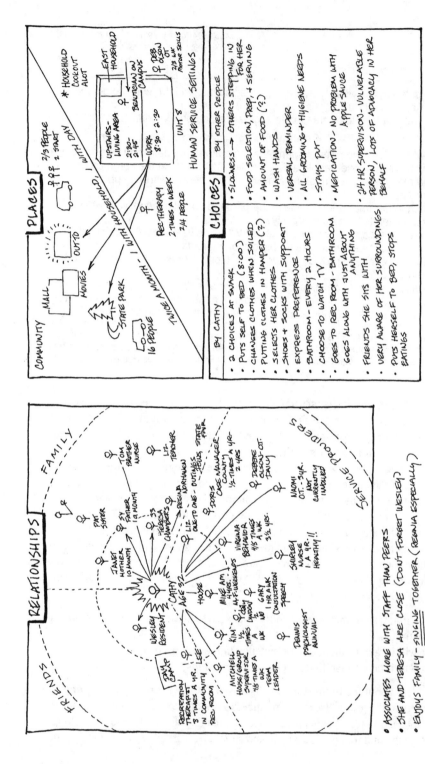

Figure 1. Cathy's personal profile: relationships, community presence (places), and choices. (From Mount, B., & Zwernik, K. [1988]. *It's never too early, it's never too late: A booklet about personal futures planning* [p. 11]. St. Paul: Minnesota Governor's Planning Council on Developmental Disabilities; reprinted by permission.)

THINGS THAT "WORK" CREATE INTEREST, ENGAGEMENT	PREFERENCES	THINGS THAT "DON'T WORK" CREATE UPSET, FRUSTRATION, BOREDOM

THINGS THAT "WORK" CREATE INTEREST, ENGAGEMENT	THINGS THAT "DON'T WORK" CREATE UPSET, FRUSTRATION, BOREDOM
• REACHES FOR HAND RAILS	• STEPPING FROM SIDEWALK TO GRASS - UNEVEN GROUND (STAIRS) (GO FOR SINGLE FLOOR)
• SUNDAY NIGHT DANCE, COUNTRY MUSIC/DANCES	• MEDICAL EXAMS - MUST HAVE RAPPORT WITH PHYSICIAN - NEED TO PREPARE DOCTOR
• STAIRS WITH RAILS	
• FAMILY INVOLVEMENT	
• IS HELPFUL	• HAVE TO GO TO BATHROOM BEFORE TALKING ABOUT IT
• FOOD RELATED - SHOWS CHOICE	
• SINGING - KNOWS SONGS, HAPPY BIRTHDAY	• ATTENTION SPAN IS SHORT
• ARTICULATES MORE CLEARLY WHEN SINGING	• PUSHES AWAY THINGS SHE DOESN'T LIKE
• LIKES TO LISTEN	• BEING IN A HURRY - NEEDS LOTS OF TIME
• SMILES FOR CERTAIN PEOPLE	
• OUTINGS, MOVIES, OUT TO EAT	• WEARING GLASSES
• OUTSIDE FRENCH FRIES	• SLOW IN DRESSING - NEEDS TIME - YOU GET TIRED OF WAITING
• BASKETBALL	
• NEED TO HAVE GLASSES	• THINGS THAT TWIRL
• DOESN'T CRAWL - GOOD PROTECTIVE MECHANISMS - DOESN'T FALL	• GROUPS AND CROWDS
• PRETTY AGILE	• NOT EATING = NOT FEELING WELL
• STACKING, FOLDING, SORTING	• DOESN'T LIKE WATER, CARBO DRINKS
• HAND MOVEMENT - PATTYCAKE - TACTILE STIMULATION	• PRONE TO COLDS
• LOVES TO CLAP • FOR EXCITEMENT	• DIDN'T NOTICE CHILDREN MAY NOT SEE THINGS
• LIKES LIQUIDS - NOT ICE/CARBON	
• SIT BY WESLEY	
• NEAT EATER, PRECISE	
• LOVES PRAISE!!	
• LIKES TIME TO HERSELF - STAYS IN BATHROOM	
• STAYS WITH A GROUP WELL	
• SLEEPS VERY WELL	
• WATER - BATHS - ENJOYS WATER SPLASHING	
• OBSERVANT ON OUTINGS - SMILING, AWARE	
• LIKES TO WATCH PEOPLE	
• CAR RIDE	
• ROCKING (CHAIR)	
• LIKES COOKOUTS - HELPS WITH PREPARATION, STIRS	
• LIKES TO VACUUM	

Figure 2.   Cathy's personal profile: preferences. (From Mount, B., & Zwernik, K. [1988]. *It's never too early, it's never too late: A booklet about personal futures planning* [p. 12]. St. Paul: Minnesota Governor's Planning Council on Developmental Disabilities; reprinted by permission.)

Since this man obtained a community home and has begun enjoying events like vacations to Florida, his quality of life has improved.

members then identify obstacles and opportunities that may hinder or facilitate these goals, brainstorm methods for eliminating barriers, and revise the vision if necessary. By the end of the session, the group identifies five action steps that will be implemented immediately by individual members. The meeting is adjourned with plans for follow-up meetings to review progress, develop new action plans, and address obstacles that interfere with the plan to move forward. Figure 3 illustrates a vision of the future for Cathy (based on information in Figures 1 and 2), with identified long- and short-term goals.

Summary   As a preliminary step to the initial assessment, the futures plan can keep all subsequent assessment and instructional activities, including those in the home, community, and related area domains, focused toward one desirable goal. Without a clear sense of direction for the future, assessment may become disjointed, resulting in fragmented skills that do not advance the individual toward greater integration. Additionally, the futures plan may serve as the foundation for the development of an individualized comprehensive curriculum that will guide the selection of skills to be assessed, and facilitate cross-planning among the assessment domains. Using the futures plan to develop an individualized curriculum is discussed in more detail in the next section of this chapter.

INITIAL ASSESSMENT TO DEVELOP THE CURRICULUM PLAN

In Chapter 2, a plan was outlined for the initial comprehensive assessment that focused on skills for the home, skills for the community, and related skills.

Cathy's Future Plan

Cathy, 32, lives in a group home with four housemates and attends a day program for adults with developmental disabilities. Her vision for the future includes:

- Housing in an apartment (first floor), with a paid roommate to support her daily living needs
- A part-time job involving food preparation in a restaurant or collating/sorting in an office
- Increased involvement in community life: singing in the church choir, swimming at the "Y," attending sports events
- Good friends, good neighbors

Long-term goals

1. Locate suitable housing
2. Find appropriate roommate
3. Identify suitable employment and training support
4. Establish friendships and neighborhood acquaintances through increased community involvement

Short-term goals

1. Participate in swimming program at the "Y," attend church choir rehearsals, take long walks in neighborhood (*community presence*)
2. Improve grooming skills (*competence, respect*)
3. Develop food preparation skills (*competence, respect*):
   a. in the home
   b. at day program, to make work more enjoyable and meaningful
4. Develop home leisure skills that reflect preferences and that can be shared with a friend (*competence, respect*):
   a. listen to music, operate tape player
   b. garden, share vegetables
5. Increase choice opportunities within daily routines (*choice*)
6. Increase opportunities for social relationships (*relationships*):
   a. increase community presence
   b. teach greetings and how to make invitations

Figure 3. A vision of Cathy's future, based on information provided in personal profiles (see Figures 1 and 2).

Skills for the home can be broadly classified as: 1) personal maintenance, 2) recreation/socialization, 3) housekeeping and food preparation, and 4) preparation for community outings. The first step in developing this curriculum plan is to identify specific environments for assessment and tentative priorities to guide the assessment plan. Two preliminary assessment activities were already discussed in this chapter: gathering information on family structure, culture, and values; and personal futures planning. Each of these activities can identify potential priorities, and environments and subenvironments that are relevant to the home domain. In addition, a general survey, such as the one illustrated in Figure 4, Chapter 2, may be used to gather preliminary information.

Selection of Skills for Assessment

The next step in conducting an initial assessment is to select skills for direct assessment. Three methods for selecting skills are: review of records, ecological inventories, and curriculum-based assessment.

Review of Records   Records will often reveal objectives not yet mastered that still have relevance for the individual. This information may be obtained from previously conducted assessments, such as adaptive behavior scales, and records of IEPs/IHPs. Not all unmastered objectives present skills deficits. Some may indicate the individual's lack of interest in the activity (e.g., the individual hates to mop the floor), or a prevailing medical problem (e.g., a spastic bladder may contribute to toileting problems). Potential causes such as these should be considered before assuming a skill deficit or learning problem with unmastered objectives. Therapeutic and medical evaluations may also provide relevant details needed for assessment for the home. For example, diet restrictions will need to be considered in planning food preparation instruction. Severe neurological damage may preclude independence in toileting, and may require alternative management strategies. Allergies may require care in selection of cleaning products and detergents. Additionally, the individual's chronic health problems may suggest areas of health care, personal hygiene, and wellness in need of assessment, such as self-medication and self-catheterization.

Ecological Inventories   Ecological inventories are useful in that they identify specific skills that are needed to function in current and future settings. Many different examples of ecological inventories may be found throughout this book. To the extent that the assessment guide for getting to know parents and the futures planning process yield specific skills needed for functioning in home environments, these assessment strategies may also be classified as examples of home inventories. Three additional home inventory approaches are illustrated here: open-ended surveys, assessment of daily routines, and discrepancy analyses. Instructors may elect to use one or all three approaches when conducting an inventory of the home.

Open-Ended Survey   In this approach, the instructor generates specific questions that will identify potential target skills in the areas of personal maintenance, housekeeping and food preparation, recreation/socialization, and preparation for community outings. Information may be obtained through written questionnaires, informal interviews, and home observations. The home inventory in the IMPACT curriculum (Neel & Billingsley, 1989) provides an excellent example of this approach. Figure 4 illustrates a section of the home inventory that asks parents to assess their child's leisure/recreational abilities.

Assessment of Daily Living Routines   As discussed by Dever (1988) in his curriculum, *Community Living Skills: A Taxonomy,* routines may be categorized into weekday routines, weekend routines, nondaily weekly routines (e.g., Monday: food shopping, clean cupboards; Tuesday: swim class at the "Y"; Wednesday: banking, arts-and-crafts club), holidays, and even seasonal

What Does Your Child Do Most of the Time?

This section is designed to give us an idea about the number and types of activities your child participates in during the week. We are interested in where, when, and with whom your child interacts. We especially want to know the problems you and your child face on a day-to-day basis. Be sure to add any additional comments you feel will help us understand what goes on during a typical week. This information will be used to aid us in designing a functional program for your child.

What does your child usually do between school and dinner?

_____

_____

_____

Which of these activities does your child do:

Independently _____

With members of the family _____

_____

With friends and/or neighbors _____

_____

What special problems, if any, occur during those times?

_____

_____

_____

What does your child usually do between dinner and bedtime?

_____

_____

_____

Which of those activities does your child do:

Independently _____

With members of the family _____

_____

With friends and/or neighbors _____

_____

(continued)

Figure 4.   Example of home inventory illustrating an open-ended approach to an ecological inventory. (From Neel, R.S., & Billingsley, F.F. [1989]. *IMPACT: A functional curriculum handbook for students with moderate to severe disabilities* [pp. 146–148]. Baltimore: Paul H. Brookes Publishing Co.; reprinted by permission.)

Figure 4. (*continued*)

What special problems, if any, occur during those times?

_____

_____

_____

What does your child usually do on weekends?

_____

_____

_____

Which of those activities does your child do:

Independently _____

With members of the family _____

_____

With friends and/or neighbors _____

_____

What special problems, if any, occur during those times?

_____

_____

_____

Does your child play with other children? ____ Yes ____ No

If yes, with whom?

_____

_____

_____

What activities does your family do for entertainment *at home*?

_____

_____

_____

_____

Which activities does your family do for entertainment *away from home*?

_____

_____

_____

_____

Figure 4. *(continued)*

Which, if any, of these activities does your child enjoy?

_____

_____

_____

_____

When your child does participate in one of the activities that the family uses for recreation, does he or she participate in a special way, or with special rules, that are only understood by the members of the family? ____ yes ____ no
    If yes, please describe the special adaptations that you have made.

_____

_____

_____

What, if any, are some of the problems you have with your child during vacation (when there is no school)?

_____

_____

_____

What are some of the ideas you have that might make these times easier for your child and you?

_____

_____

_____

routines (e.g., Fall: store lawn furniture, put on storm windows). An individual's routine may be identified by asking caregivers, either through an interview or questionnaire, to list the family's or individual's daily routines. Next, in order to identify possible targets for instruction, the instructor may ask the caregiver to identify specific activities within the routine that the individual does independently or for which assistance is required. Figure 5 provides an example of this approach.

Like other ecological inventory strategies that assess the individual's functioning in current environments, assessment of routines may be limiting in that it identifies skills that are needed to function within the "status quo"—not what may be needed in future settings. Additionally, if the individual's "quality of life" is poor, then the identification of skills through routines may do little to enhance the individual's overall lifestyle. Thus, when identifying potential assessment targets through this process, it may be wise to compare the individual's routine against a typical routine of a similar-age peer without disabilities

Learner: <u>Ann</u>   Date: <u>September 10</u>
Instructor: <u>Ms. P.</u>   Environment: <u>Ann's home</u>
Source of information: <u>Telephone interview with caregiver (group home staff person)</u>

Weekday routine

A.M.

7:00 Caregiver wakes up Ann and takes her to toilet.*
7:30 Caregiver dresses Ann.*
8:00 Caregiver helps Ann eat breakfast.*
8:30 Caregiver brushes Ann's teeth and gets her belongings ready.*
9:00 Car picks up Ann; driver escorts Ann to car (9:00 A.M.–3:00 P.M. at center).

P.M.

3:00 Car delivers Ann; caregiver escorts Ann to house, stores her belongings.
3:30 Caregiver takes Ann to toilet.
4:00 Ann watches television.*
5:00 Caregiver helps Ann eat dinner.*
5:30 Caregiver helps Ann carry her dishes to the sink.
6:00 Ann watches television; caregiver washes dishes and clothes.
7:30 Caregiver gives Ann a bath and dresses her for bed.
8:30 Ann watches television; caregiver helps roommates.
10:00 Ann is escorted to bed.

Weekend routine

A.M.

7:30 Caregiver takes Ann to toilet.*
8:00 Caregiver dresses Ann.
8:30 Caregiver helps Ann eat breakfast and brush teeth.*
9:00 Ann watches television; caregiver cleans house.*

P.M.

12:00 Caregiver helps Ann eat lunch.*
12:30 Caregiver takes Ann to toilet.*
1.00 Weekend special—caregiver takes Ann and roommates somewhere such as grocery store, movies, or for a walk. On Sundays, friends and family sometimes come for a visit at this time.
3:30 Ann watches television; caregiver cleans or cooks.
5:00 Caregiver helps Ann eat dinner.*
5:30 Caregiver helps Ann take dishes to sink.
6:00
to
10:00 Same as weeknights

Figure 5. Example of an ecological inventory for the home that identifies skills needed by outlining the family's weekday and weekend routines. (* = activities that the instructor and caregivers identified as possible targets for Ann's instruction.)

(e.g., What routine would a typical 4-year-old follow? A 15-year-old?), and against routines that might be required in the future (e.g., What might the individual's day be like at 25 years of age, living semi-independently in an apartment complex?). To assist in this process, Dever (1988) provided several daily and weekly routines that generically represent the typical sequence of events followed by independent adults. These preidentified routines may help caregivers and educators to think more broadly about important skill areas beyond the individual's current environmental demands. A weekday routine is shown in Figure 6.

Discrepancy Analysis This approach involves comparing the individual's performance against the performance of peers without disabilities within a given activity. For example, the activity "phoning a friend" would be task analyzed by observing the steps performed by a peer without disabilities. Then the learner would be observed to determine whether or not he or she is able to perform the same skill steps that make up the activity (e.g., dials the telephone, uses social politeness, responds appropriately to telephone signals). Discrepant skills would be targeted for instruction.

Traditionally, discrepancy analyses have been used to assess individuals' abilities to perform specific activities. However, as suggested previously, entire chains of activities or daily routines can also be assessed using a discrepancy approach. For example, Dever's (1988) routine as shown in Figure 6 could serve as the comparative basis for determining the extent to which an adult with severe disabilities is able to perform independently similar routine activities.

In addition to assessing specific activities and daily routines, discrepancy analyses may also be used to evaluate skills that are distributed across activities and routines, such as communication and choice-making skills. For example, Table 3 lists some fundamental choices of daily living (e.g., what to wear, what to eat, where to work) that are generally made available to adults without disabilities, but are frequently unavailable to adults with developmental disabilities (Kishi, Teelucksingh, Zollers, Park-Lee, & Meyer, 1988). Using these choices as a base, a nondisabled person inventory can be conducted. As shown in Table 3, a nondisabled person inventory was conducted with a 4-year-old and with an adult to determine the extent to which these options are made available to them. A discrepancy analysis may then be implemented by comparing the choice-making opportunities made available to similar-age individuals with severe disabilities. Discrepancies would suggest that opportunities need to be significantly broadened or that choice-making skills need to be taught directly.

Curriculum-Based Assessment As indicated in Chapter 2, published curricula are becoming an increasingly popular method for identifying potential instructional targets. *The Syracuse Community-Referenced Curriculum Guide* (Ford et al. 1989b), *Community Living Skills: A Taxonomy* (Dever, 1988), and *The Activities Catalog: An Alternative Curriculum for Youth and Adults with Severe Disabilities* (Wilcox & Bellamy, 1987a) are excellent resources for home assessment. Although individual curricula vary in scope, sequence (*The Activities Catalog* and *Community Living Skills: A Taxonomy* are not sequenced curricula), and in categories of subdomains, many of the skills identified for independent living are essentially the same. Table 4 presents some of the major skill areas found in written curricula. For continuity pur-

Routines

a. Weekday Routine (Monday-Friday, Except Holidays)

1. Rise
2. Toilet
3. Groom self
4. Check weather conditions and select workday clothing
5. Dress
6. Make bed
7. Prepare breakfast
8. Eat breakfast
9. Prepare sack lunch
10. Clear table and wash dishes
11. Tidy kitchen
12. Brush teeth
13. Select outerwear for weather conditions
14. Check lights and appliances
15. Leave and secure house
16. Travel to work
    •
    •
    •
    (Perform work routine)
    •
    •
    •
17. Travel home (see also payday routine)
18. Collect mail
19. Store outerwear
20. Exercise
21. Select evening clothing (for chore/leisure routine)
22. Bathe
23. Groom and dress
24. Store dirty clothing (and linen, if applicable)
25. Tidy bathroom
26. Set table
27. Prepare supper
28. Eat
29. Clear table and wash dishes
30. Tidy kitchen
31. Tidy living room
32. Perform chore/leisure routine
33. Toilet and dress for bed
34. Set alarm
35. Sleep

c. Saturday Routine

    •
    •
    •
    (#1-12 same as daily routine, except select Saturday chore clothing)
    •
    •
    •

(continued)

Figure 6.   Example of a weekday routine (Monday–Friday, except holidays) that characterizes adult life. (From Dever, R.B. [1988]. *Community living skills: A taxonomy* [p. 29]. Washington, DC: American Association on Mental Retardation; reprinted by permission.)

Figure 6. (continued)

13. Select morning chores (see chore/leisure routine)
14. Check weather conditions and select outerwear according to chore
    (if outdoor chores required)
15. Do morning chores
16. Prepare lunch
17. Eat
18. Clear table and wash dishes
19. Tidy kitchen
20. Select Saturday leisure activity (see chore/leisure routine)
21. Select Saturday leisure clothing
22. Bathe and dress
23. Select outerwear according to weather conditions and activity
24. Perform leisure activity (see daily activities #14-16 if travel is involved)
25. Return home (if "away")
    •
    •
    •
    (same as #26-30 on daily routine, unless going to restaurant)
    •
    •
    •

26. Select Saturday evening leisure clothing (change if necessary)
27. Select leisure activity
28. Check outerwear according to weather conditions (if "away")
29. Leave and secure house
30. Travel to leisure activity
31. Perform leisure activity
32. Return home
    •
    •
    •
    (same as #33-35 on daily routine)
    •
    •
    •

poses, these skills areas are categorized according to the four home subdomains used in this book.

Using the curriculum for initial assessment, the individual's abilities are considered for each skill in the curriculum. Several approaches may be used. In one approach, the instructor may list the skills from the curriculum that seem appropriate to the individual's home setting and chronological age (preliminary ecological inventories are most useful for defining the skills presented to the caregiver). Next, using a checklist approach, the caregiver can check whether the individual possesses or lacks skills, and rate the importance of each skill for the home environment. Figure 7 provides an example of this approach.

In another strategy, the goals developed from an individual's futures plan may be used to generate an individualized curriculum plan. In this approach, the instructor and caregiver would consider each long- and short-term goal generated from the futures plan and ask, "What skills or competencies must the

Table 3. Discrepancy analysis of choice-making opportunities available to a preschooler and an adult

Does the individual choose . . .	Nondisabled person inventory: 4-year-old	Learner inventory	Nondisabled person inventory: Adult	Learner inventory
What to eat for a meal or snack?	Given limited options to choose (e.g., Jello or apple)		No restrictions, except diet and negotiations with other family members	
What to wear?	Given limited options to choose		No restrictions, except social	
Leisure activities to do on days off and evenings?	Free play generally unrestricted, options limited to family activities		No restrictions	
What TV show to watch?	Given limited options, restricted times to watch TV		No restrictions	
How to spend money not committed for expenses?	Negotiated		No restrictions	
Whether to participate in a group activity?	If non–school-related, has free choice		No restrictions	
Where to live and with whom?	No choice		No restrictions	
To make a phone call to a friend?	Needs to ask permission?		No restrictions, except finances	
Whether to stay up late at night?	Weekends and holidays, 1 hour past regular bedtime		No restrictions	
To sleep in on days off?	Saturday, free choice		No restrictions	
Where to work?	Not applicable		No restrictions	

Table 4.　Sample curriculum domains for home assessment

Personal maintenance

Dressing
　Basic mechanics
　Dresses appropriately for the weather/season/event
　Coordinates color/style
Eating
　Basic skills
　Table manners
Maintains personal cleanliness/hygiene
　Bathes/showers
　Routine handwashing
　Tidies self throughout the day
　Toileting
　Menstrual care
　Brushes/flosses teeth
　Uses deodorant
　Grooming
　Hair care and styling
　Trims nails
　Shaves
　Applies make-up
　Maintains neatness
Wellness
　Exercises
　Eats balanced diet
　Regulates food quantities
　Maintains appropriate sleep cycle
　Self-medicates
　Controls use of caffeine, tobacco
Safety
　Aware of danger
　Proper care of dangerous/hazardous materials
　Follows accident/emergency procedures (e.g., fire, blackouts, flooding)
Care of illness
　Recognizes/communicates illness or injury
　Applies first-aid
　Follows routine procedures for treatment

Housekeeping and food preparation

Housecleaning
　Basic skills (e.g., dusting, vacuuming, washing)
　Identifies when to clean
　Schedules/follows routine
Yard care
　Basic skills (e.g., raking, mowing, gardening)
　Identifies when to care for yard
　Schedules/follows routine
　Trash removal

(continued)

Table 4. (*continued*)

Housekeeping and food preparation (*continued*)

Food preparation
  Prepares meals
  Purchases food
  Operates appliances
  Cleans up
  Recognizes spoiled foods
Clothing care
  Washes clothes
  Irons
  Sorts
  Repairs
  Uses dry cleaners
Household maintenance
  Maintains/repairs interior (e.g., paints, replaces light bulbs)
  Maintains linens
  Responds to seasonal changes (e.g., changes storm windows)
  Maintains exterior
  Decorates
Household management
  Schedules chores
  Follows home safety procedures
  Maintains food stock

Recreation/socialization

In-house leisure
  Crafts/hobbies (e.g., paints, knits)
  Plays games (e.g., cards, puzzles)
  Uses media (e.g., TV, videos, radio, magazines)
Events
  Attends outside activities (e.g., movies, fairs)
  Prepares for holidays
  Prepares for celebrations
Friendships
  Invites friends to visit
  Dates
  Maintains contact (e.g., telephones, writes)
  Does something nice (e.g., bakes, offers help)
Neighbors
  Appropriate greetings
  Offers assistance
  Borrowing and lending skills
Family/housemate relations
  Respects privacy of others
  Respects others' belongings
  Shares household responsibilities
  Communicates

(*continued*)

Table 4. (*continued*)

Preparation for community outings

Scheduling
  Schedules community events
  Makes medical appointments
Money/finances
  Associates money with specific purchases
  Budgets
  Banks/maintains account
  Allocates funds appropriately
Time
  Associates time with specific activities
  Tells time
  Uses calendar
Prepares for departure
  Takes necessary materials
  Secures house
  Knows personal information and carries ID
  Uses telephone

---

individual demonstrate in order for this goal to be achieved?" Using a published curriculum as a reference guide, a number of skills may be identified. For example, in looking at Cathy's short-term goal for increasing community presence (Figure 3), several personal maintenance and preparation for community outing skills may be considered; including: dressing appropriately for the community event and season, maintaining neatness, scheduling community events, and preparing for departure.

Prioritizing Skills Selected for Assessment From the skills identified by records, ecological inventories, and curriculum assessments, a long list of potentially appropriate targets may be generated. The instructor needs to set priorities for the skills that will be further assessed. At this point, it may help to list potential targets identified by the categories suggested: 1) personal maintenance, 2) recreation/socialization, 3) housekeeping and food preparation, and 4) preparation for community outings. Skills that have been identified by caregivers as priorities and those that reflect the individual's preferences or interests should be starred. Additionally, if a futures plan has been developed, then those skills that reflect specific competencies needed to reach long- or short-term goals should also be starred. Then, the instructor should note which of these priority skill areas require further assessment to identify the individual's specific skill needs. Also, if one or more categories reveal inadequate information (e.g., no information on recreational skills because the individual has not had the opportunity to use many materials), more assessment may be planned. The instructor may also wish to use the priority ranking form presented in Figure 13 in Chapter 2.

Student's name: Nat	Date: September 21
Teacher: Ms. S.	Environment: Home
Source of information: Survey mailed to caregivers	

Please identify whether Nat currently performs the skills below. For each skill, please also rank how important you think this is for Nat at this time.

Skills	Performs the skill	Importance of skill
Personal maintenance		
1. Undresses.	yes	2
2. Dresses.	no	1
3. Eats finger food.	yes	3
4. Eats with spoon.	somewhat	2
5. Eats with fork.	no	3–4
6. Drinks (no spilling).	somewhat	2
7. Eats a varied diet.	no	3–4
8. Uses toilet.	yes	1
9. Has no toilet accidents.	somewhat	1
10. Selects clothes.	no	3
11. Selects food.	yes	3
Recreation/socialization		
1. Plays alone.	yes, too much	4
2. Plays with siblings.	no	1
3. Plays with toys.	somewhat	2
4. Has hobbies.	no	3
Housekeeping/food preparation		
1. Performs some chores.	no	3
2. Pours own drink.	no	2
3. Makes simple snacks.	no	2
4. Picks up belongings.	no	2–3
5. Sets table.	somewhat	2
6. Puts laundry in hamper.	no	2
Preparing for the community		
1. Obtains belongings.	no	2
2. Puts on coat.	no	1

Figure 7. Example of a curriculum-based assessment for a home environment that uses a skill checklist. This approach identifies both skill deficiencies and caregivers' priorities in one survey. (1 = top priority, 2 = important, 3 = somewhat important, 4 = not important.)

Assessment of the Individual

When more information is needed because of inadequate information, assessment may be conducted in several ways. The instructor may use task analytic assessment (e.g., routines, specific leisure skills), observations of the individual that are guided by checklists or anecdotal notes (e.g., of independent eating), repeated trial assessments (e.g., using pictures to follow a housekeeping schedule), or frequency counts (e.g., toileting accidents). Resources on instruction for people with severe disabilities provide many examples of the assessment and instruction of domestic skills (e.g., Falvey, 1986; Gaylord-Ross

& Holvoet, 1985; Sailor & Guess, 1983; Snell, 1987; Wehman et al., 1985; Wuerch & Voeltz, 1982). The reader is encouraged to consult these resources for illustrations of task analyses for each area of home assessment that is discussed. In the following sections, examples of this initial assessment are illustrated by considering how each home category was addressed in the case studies.

Personal Maintenance Personal maintenance is an area that is often included in adaptive behavior checklists. Sometimes, this information, combined with the home inventory to note priorities, is enough to plan personal maintenance goals for the 3- to 5-year curriculum. In other cases, the instructor may not have sufficient information in this area. Such was the case for Ann's skill deficiency in toileting. Ms. P. knew from the adaptive behavior survey completed by the group home staff, and from her own work with Ann, that Ann had toileting accidents. However, she did not have a clear impression of whether or not Ann had an elimination pattern that would make schedule training a realistic goal. Therefore, Ms. P. recorded both the frequency and schedule of Ann's elimination for 2 weeks. She recruited the assistance of the group home staff to fill in the schedule of elimination each day in the evening hours. To make sure that the staff conducted this assessment daily, Ms. P. asked them to send the copy of this schedule to her each morning. Each afternoon, she wrote a brief note to thank them for the previous day's schedule and included the current day's data form. Through this cooperative assessment, Ann's schedule of elimination could be evaluated. This is shown in Figure 8. From this information, Ms. P. concluded that schedule training should be attainable. Because this was a top priority for Ann, she made this a first-year objective. The group home staff agreed to continue recording Ann's schedule of elimination to provide ongoing assessment of Ann's progress in toilet training in her home environment.

In Dennis's case, Ms. K. noted that his parents had difficulty suggesting goals for Dennis because they were discouraged by his lack of progress to date. The adaptive behavior scale had revealed that Dennis had virtually no skills in personal maintenance. Ms. K. felt that she needed to observe Dennis and his mother engaged in a care routine to identify potential responses that Dennis could make to participate to some extent in this routine. Ms. K. wrote a routine for dressing, bathing, and eating to use as a guide in observing the responses that Dennis's mother currently performed, but that might be targeted for Dennis. She used a schedule to make notes of the order of activities so that she could plan for his participation in the transition, as well as the activities. A summary of her notes is shown in Figure 9. Dennis's mother was pleased with this assessment and felt that it acknowledged the many activities that she performed with Dennis that could be developed further for instruction and assessment. She offered to keep a calendar with notes on new responses that she observed Dennis attempt during the care routine. Ms. K. welcomed this anecdotal method to report generalization and to identify new responses as they emerged.

Student's name: Ann   Date: October 1–7
Teacher: Ms. P.

	Sun.	Mon.	Tues.	Wed.	Thurs.	Fri.	Sat.
7:00							
7:30	U+		U−			U+	
8:00		U−		U−	U−		U+
8:30							
9:00							
9:30							
10:00	U−	U+				U+	
10:30			U+	U−	U+		U−
11:00							
11:30							
12:00						U−	
12:30	U+	U+	U+				U+
1:00				U−	U+		
1:30							
2:00							
2:30							
3:00	U+	U+				U−	
3:30			U−	U+			U−
4:00							
4:30							
5:00							
5:30							
6:00	B+	B+		B+			B+
6:30							
7:00							
7:30	U−		U+	U+	U−	U+	
8:00							U−
8:30							
9:00							
9:30							
10:00							

Figure 8.   Example of schedule of elimination used in assessment for toilet training. (U+ = urination in toilet, U− = urination in pants, B+ = bowel movement in toilet, B− = bowel movement in pants.)

Nat's parents asked Ms. S. to pay particular attention to Nat's dressing skills. Getting Nat dressed in the morning often created havoc in the family's routine because he neither dressed himself nor cooperated with family members' efforts to dress him. Ms. S. evaluated Nat's dressing skills using task analyses for pants, shirt, shoes, and socks (on and off). She also used a discrep-

Student's name: Dennis		Date: October 3
Teacher: Ms. K.		

Schedule	Activity	Ideas for Dennis
7:00	Changes diaper	Greeting, indicate wet
7:30	Dresses Dennis	Head up to signal ready; indicate clothing choice
8:00	Prepares Dennis's food	Operate blender
8:30	Feeds Dennis	Indicate food choice
9:00	Cleans Dennis and wheelchair	Grasp cloth; wipe tray

Figure 9. Assessment of a caregiver's routine to identify responses for partial participation.

ancy analysis to identify other skills that Nat needed to cope with this activity (e.g., communication of choice). This discrepancy analysis is shown in Chapter 8, Figure 6. Nat's father was especially interested in Ms. S.'s efforts to find new ideas for Nat. He wanted to observe these assessments and brainstorm with Ms. S. She negotiated times for Nat's father to observe and contribute (e.g., during a home visit, in a visit to the classroom) and also scheduled times to observe Nat during the daily school routine. (This schedule was shown in Chapter 2, Figure 12.) Ms. S. considered Nat's father's interest to be an asset to Nat, and planned to discuss with the father possibilities for ongoing home instruction and assessment.

Recreation/Socialization Adaptive behavior scales often do not provide adequate coverage of home leisure skills. Since Ann typically used few leisure materials besides television and magazines, Ms. P. considered it important to evaluate both her interests and skills. She developed a checklist of home leisure skills, shown in Figure 10, by asking Ann's caregivers to suggest materials that Ann had tried or might learn to use. Ms. P. then gave Ann these materials and assessed her interest and skills in using them. Her results are shown in Figure 10.

Ms. K. noted that Dennis's home leisure materials were primarily toys designed for young infants (e.g., mobile toy animals, rattles). She wanted to help his parents find age-appropriate materials that required simple responses. Ms. K. assessed Dennis's use of a flipper switch to activate a toy bus by using task analytic assessment. Dennis moved his hand slightly against the switch after being shown that it would activate the bus. Ms. K. decided that this, or another switch, could be developed so that with training, Dennis would be able to operate battery-operated toys or a tape player. Dennis's grandparents were especially pleased with this new idea for Dennis and offered to buy new toys to be adapted with switches. Again, this seemed to be an area that Dennis's mother might report anecdotally to the instructor on an ongoing basis.

Ms. M. discovered from John's records that he once enjoyed geographic

Student's name: Ann   Date: October 7

Teacher: Ms. P.

Code for interest:
    Yes—Shows definite interest in material by, for example, smiling, laughing, holding material, using material
    Some—Shows some interest in material (e.g., looks at it; picks it up; touches it)
    No—Shows no interest in material or pushes it away

Code for skill:
    Yes—Uses material in its intended manner
    Some—Makes some of the responses to use the material
    No—Does not use the material

Materials	Interest	Skill
Radio		
—Upbeat music	Yes	Some
—Easy listening	Some	Some
Cassette player		
—Upbeat music	Yes	No
—Comedian/laughter	Yes	No
Simon game	No	No
Electronic self-playing piano	Yes	Yes
Photo album	Some	No
Camera	No	No
Stamp collection	No	No
Cards	No	No
Magazines	Yes	Some

Figure 10. Example of an assessment of leisure skills and preferences for an adult.

magazines and writing simple leters. Since his loss of sight, his caregivers had obtained a radio that broadcast talk shows, the weather, news, and so forth. Because of his hearing loss, John listened to the radio with earphones. However, his attention span for these shows was short. Ms. M. wanted to assess John's listening comprehension to determine if such shows were meaningful to him. She read him passages from magazines and asked him questions about the passages. She discovered that John could only comprehend passages that were simple and contained familiar information (e.g., passages about hits and runs in baseball, names of food, lists of familiar names). However, he enjoyed these simple, familiar passages. Ms. M. noted that John's independent leisure time could be enhanced if he learned to operate a tape player without help, and to use a selection of tapes that he understood and enjoyed.

    Housekeeping and Food Preparation   When Ms. K. assessed Dennis's use of an adaptive switch, she got an idea for teaching him to participate in his food preparation. Dennis's food was blended because of his eating difficulties. Ms. K. talked with Dennis's parents about having a blender adapted to be used with a flipper switch so that Dennis could blend the food after a

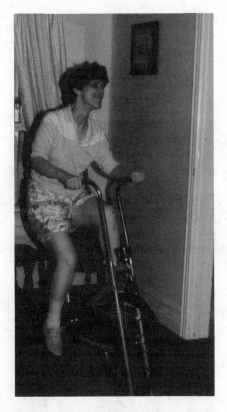

Assessment of home leisure skills should respect the learner's choices. For example, this woman prefers an exercise bike to other forms of aerobics.

family member placed it in the blender (see Figure 9). Dennis's mother thought this would be an exciting way to get him to participate more in his daily routine, so this was included in Dennis's curriculum plan.

In John's case, Ms. M. was surprised to learn that John's caregivers reported that John performed no housekeeping or food preparation activities. His caregivers were concerned about John's safety and did not allow him in the kitchen or laundry room nor allowed him to operate a vacuum cleaner. At work, John had learned quickly to clean the lunch table by moving from chair to chair and counting each chair until he reached the sixth one. Ms. M. decided that she needed to consult with a person who was independent in daily living, but was also blind, to help the caregivers understand what precautions were or were not appropriate for John. From this ecological inventory, Ms. M. concluded that John could be expected to learn to perform most of his housekeeping and food preparation routine. Safety could be taught concurrently with the activities introduced. Since Ms. M.'s curriculum plan was for an adult continuing education program that was primarily work oriented, she included housekeeping

Good communication with caregivers can help instructors know what to assess and teach. In this photo, the instructor has selected operating a mixer to make a family recipe for bread pudding.

goals that were appropriate to the work setting but would also be useful to his home setting (e.g., sweeping, cleaning windows, making coffee). She recommended that the caregivers give John more opportunities to participate in his home routine, and noted that the skills he would be using at work would be good activities to expect John to perform at home. Since John's caregivers were paid staff who were responsible for teaching John home skills, Ms. M. gave the staff task analyses for several domestic activities that John might learn to perform, and shared her system of data collection.

Preparation for Community Outings A fourth category of home skills is preparation for community outings. This includes such skills as using the telephone to make an appointment, getting ready for work, consulting a bus schedule, or keeping an appointment calendar. Ms. P. noted that Ann needed skills in preparing to leave to go to her educational program on weekdays. Her caregivers reported that she sat passively until dressed in her coat and escorted to the van. Through her ecological inventory of the home, Ms. P. had identified the steps that Ann needed to perform to prepare to leave. These steps were identical to those needed to prepare to go home in the afternoon. Therefore, Ms. P. wrote a routine task analysis for preparing to leave and used it to assess Ann. The task analysis is shown below.

1. Go to coat room.
2. Put on coat.*
3. Put on hat.*
4. Put on gloves.*
5. Walk to refrigerator.*
6. Get lunchbox.*
7. Walk to bathroom.
8. Get gym bag with spare clothes.*
9. Carry lunchbox and gym bag to car.

Ms. P. found that some steps of the routine required a specific skill task analysis for ongoing assessment. These are marked by an asterisk. For example, step 6 (task analysis for getting lunchbox) is broken down into the following smaller steps:

1. Grasp refrigerator door handle.
2. Pull door open.
3. Reach and grasp lunchbox by handle.
4. Pull lunchbox from shelf.
5. Push refrigerator door closed.

These examples of the initial assessment conducted in each case study help to illustrate how this information is obtained. The specific skills selected for each individual are shown in Appendix A at the end of this book. One of the most difficult steps in assessment is selecting the skills that will be the most important for the next 3–5 years, and those that should be taught the first year. While Chapter 2 provided guidelines for setting priorities, some examples of prioritization from the case studies may also help to illustrate this point.

In John's case, Ms. M. was concerned about John's lack of participation in his home routine. But Ms. M. had an overall priority for John of increasing his vocational skills and productivity. Therefore, she only selected from his home routine those skills that were common to his work routine, and referred his home needs to his caregivers (who were paid to teach him, as well as care for him).

In Dennis's case, Ms. K.'s criteria for skill selection were to increase Dennis's active participation in his home routine, and to teach him to make choices about his personal care. Since Dennis's progress to date had been minimal,

Ms. K. also wanted to build a repertoire of activities on a few responses to be trained (i.e., a "yes" response, movement of one hand, holding his head erect). Therefore, she wrote a home environment curriculum based on using these few motoric responses to perform some part of each category of home skills.

For Nat, his preferences and his family's preferences gave Ms. S. some clear priorities for instruction. Nat's parents' expectations were for him to learn to "pull his weight" in the family's busy early morning routine by learning to dress himself. Nat's entire family wanted him to participate in their enjoyment of family leisure activities and conversations. Therefore, Ms. S. selected skills that would make Nat more independent in his routine sooner (e.g., teaching him to dress in elastic-waist pants rather than ones with snaps), and based Nat's leisure instruction on some of the family's favorite pastimes (e.g., taking walks together, playing board games).

ONGOING ASSESSMENT AND EVALUATION OF PROGRESS

The ideas for ongoing assessment and evaluation of progress described in Chapters 3 and 4 can be applied to skills needed for the home environment. A specific challenge for applying this methodology to home assessment is the potential imposition of data collection in a home environment. If the assessment of home skills is implemented by an educator during instruction (e.g., community-based instruction in a home setting during the school day or in a home economics suite), then both routine and specific skill assessments can be utilized. The instructor can use these highly precise data to make instructional decisions to enhance progress, as described in Chapter 4. Paid staff in community living arrangements may also collect daily data and make data-based instructional decisions. By contrast, few professionals would find it acceptable to be responsible for collecting daily data when "off duty," in the contexts of their homes. Nor should they impose this expectation on families of individuals with severe disabilities. However, some caregivers might welcome the opportunity to participate in the assessment of progress if unintrusive strategies can be identified. These unintrusive strategies might include anecdotal notes (e.g., a daily log) or evaluation of routines on a lean schedule (e.g., weekly, monthly). The application of routine task analytic assessment to home settings is now described.

In Figures 11 and 12, the same daily chores routine is provided. However, the applications of the routines vary based on the individual's entry skills. Lester is a 60-year-old man who resides in a community living arrangement. For most of his life, the bulk of his daily routine has been performed for him by caregivers. Lester is beginning to learn to participate more actively in self-care and the care of his home. In the routine task analytic assessment for daily chores shown in Figure 11, Lester is expected to carry his own dishes to the sink, carry out the garbage, feed the cat, carry out the newspaper, and put away

Assessment Data Sheet

Manager: ___Ms. K.___

Name: ___Lester (age 60)___
Date: ___9-15-90___
Routine: ___DAILY CHORES – Housekeeping___
Beginning natural cue: ___Dinner is over___
Critical effect: ___Listen to music after chores or take a walk.___
Latency: ___5 seconds___ Duration of routine: ___30 minutes___

Types of assistance:
- FP = Full physical assistance
- PA = Partial physical assistance
- G = Gestural cue
- V = Directive verbal cue
- I = Natural cue or independent
- © = Communication target
- ED = Duration error;

Steps	Duration	Date	Date	Date	Date	Type of assistance for instruction (describe)
1. Clean up after dinner	5'	FP	PA	PA		PA to carry dishes to sink.
2. Take out the garbage	3'	6	PA	PA		PA to carry tied bag to can outside.
3. Feed pets	5'	FP	FP	FP		FP to pour cat food in bowl.
4. Straighten living room	5'	G	V	V		V to carry newspaper to recycle box
5. Do one weekly chore	12'	PA	PA	PA		PA to put away "materials (e.g. "vacuum cleaner)

Figure 11.   Example of routine task analytic assessment for a man with few current skills to participate in home routines. (Blank form courtesy of Neel, R.S., & Billingsley, F.F. [1989]. *IMPACT: A functional curriculum handbook for students with moderate to severe disabilities* [p. 136]. Baltimore: Paul H. Brookes Publishing Co.; reprinted by permission.)

173

Manager: _Ms. S. / Nat's Father_

Assessment Data Sheet

Name: _Nat (age 6)_
Date: _9-5-90_
Routine: _DAILY CHORES — Housekeeping_
Beginning natural cue: _Dinner is over_
Critical effect: _Play with toys_
Latency: _5 seconds_   Duration of routine: _15 minutes_

Types of assistance: FP = Full physical assistance
PA = Partial physical assistance
G = Gestural cue
V = Directive verbal cue
I = Natural cue or independent
ED = Duration error; Ⓒ = Communication target

Steps	Duration	Date	Date	Date	Date	Type of assistance for instruction (describe)
1. Clean up after dinner	3'	PA	V	V		V to take his plate to kitchen.
2. Take out the garbage	5'	PA	PA	PA		PA to tie bag and put in outside can.
3. Feed pets	2'	G	I	G		G to feed the fish.
4. Straighten living room	2'	V	G	V		V to pick up one toy and put away.
5. Do one weekly chore	3'	PA	PA	PA		PA to do what picture schedule shows
						(e.g., take garbage to curb, dust one table, put dirty clothes in washer)

Figure 12. Example of routine task analytic assessment for a child whose parents want him to learn to do chores independently. (Blank form courtesy of Neel, R.S., & Billingsley, F.F. [1989]. *IMPACT: A functional curriculum handbook for students with moderate to severe disabilities* [p. 136]. Baltimore: Paul H. Brookes Publishing Co.; reprinted by permission.)

cleaning equipment to help out a housemate. Lester will be accompanied by a staff person who does part of the skill and then teaches Lester to do his part. For example, the staff person puts water in the cat's bowl and gets the cat food. Lester is then taught to pour the food in the bowl. The ongoing assessment for Lester is conducted by this staff person (a paraprofessional) on a weekly basis, using the routine task analytic assessment shown in Figure 11. Decisions about changing the level of assistance to increase Lester's participation are made in monthly staff meetings with the house supervisor (a professional trained in special education) based on the data obtained.

The application of this routine to 6-year-old Nat, as shown in Figure 12, illustrates two points about routines. First, the degree of participation within a routine can range from discrete responses for partial participation, as shown for Lester, to independent performance of the entire chain of responding, as targeted for Nat. Second, routine assessment may be feasible for parents who wish to participate in evaluating their child's progress. The instructor spent time with Nat's family to become familiar with their family system. Nat's parents believe it is important for children to take responsibility and maintain a neat and orderly home. Nat's father is in business administration and wants to "give Nat some manners." Having Nat's father teach him to do chores can set up opportunities for him to praise Nat. By evaluating progress with data, his father can also learn to appreciate the subtle achievements Nat will make. Nat's father teaches Nat to do his chores daily and "tests" him on Saturday evening. After 3 weeks, the data are sent to the instructor, who reviews it and sends a note home suggesting how to decrease assistance or get Nat to work faster. Ms. S. also teaches a variation of this chores routine after lunch at school so that progress can be compared (e.g., Nat cleans his place, takes out the garbage, picks up a toy, and follows a picture schedule).

Besides this routine assessment, Nat's instructor would be likely to have some specific skill assessments for his skills for home living. These might include task analyses for handwashing, playing a board game, and pouring a drink. A frequency count might be used to assess how often Nat communicates his need for help during dressing, rather than screaming or hitting. Duration recording might be used to assess how fluent Nat has become in putting on his shoes to see if these skills are adequate for use within the busy routines of his family. If the instructor notes progress at school, but the parents do not observe these skills at home, a generalization evaluation might be conducted (see Chapter 9). While the instructor might not use all of these assessments, these illustrate the variation of ongoing assessments available for use in or for the home.

SUMMARY

Assessment in and for the home requires consideration of caregivers' interests and resources for collaboration in this assessment. This collaboration can be facilitated through instructor and caregiver communication to set expectations for the caregivers' participation and instructor's progress reports. Even if the caregivers cannot assess the individual due to family stresses, the instructor will still want to invite their opinions about environments and priorities for the curriculum plan. The ecological inventory will be an important step in identifying the specific skills for the home environment. This inventory might be conducted through an interview, survey, or observation. However the information is obtained, it is important for instructors to respect the many differences in family lifestyles in planning life skills instruction for this domain.

STUDY QUESTIONS

1. What are the implications of family systems for planning assessment? What are the types of basic information about a family that are needed before conducting assessment?
2. What is a personal futures plan and how is it developed?
3. How are the steps to developing a comprehensive assessment applied to assessment in and for the home?

FOR FURTHER THOUGHT

1. For the individuals with whom you work, review Table 1 to determine how well you know their families. What do you need to do to become better informed about some individuals' families and/or to become more sensitive to their cultural or other differences?
2. What is the quality of life of the individuals you instruct?
3. Consider how you might initiate a personal futures plan for someone whose current options are limited.
4. If you planned to conduct comprehensive assessments after reading Chapter 2, consider how what you learned in this chapter can be used in this process.

chapter 6

ASSESSMENT
IN AND FOR
THE COMMUNITY

Diane M. Browder
and Phillip J. Belfiore

IN THE PAST, people with severe disabilities were often excluded from community settings because of their disabilities. Through litigation (e.g., *Halderman v. Pennhurst State School and Hospital*, 1977; *Lloyd v. Regional Transportation Authority*, 1977; *Pennsylvania Association for Retarded Citizens* [PARC] *v. Commonwealth of Pennsylvania*, 1972) and legislation (e.g., PL 94-142), such community discrimination has been discouraged. Full service integration has become, and remains, the priority for the education and habilitation of people with severe disabilities.

Instructors who endorse the principle of community integration face challenges in planning, implementing, and adapting instruction to achieve this goal. Traditionally, behavior analysts worked in analogue settings where clipboards, interval recording, and stopwatches were the standards for accepted analysis. When these same instruments and procedures are used in the community, the goal of integration may be undermined by the intrusiveness of measurement. Thus, instructors must develop discreet methods of assessment that also include the rigors of behavior analysis. Another problem is that individuals with severe disabilities, due to a history of discrimination, may lack the basic skills required to blend into the community. Providing intensive support to the individual in a nonintrusive manner and collecting data may seem an impossible challenge. For example, an instructor who helped an individual make the transition from a 45-year-long institutionalization at Pennhurst commented, "How can I measure his skills as I escort him to stores and restaurants? He is overwhelmed by the many new sites and experiences of life outside the one building where he spent most of his life." Still another challenge to community-based assessment is time constraints. An instructor who has implemented frequent community-based instruction may realize the logistics of taking a small group of people with severe disabilities into a community setting (e.g., transportation costs, time, safety precautions) and may question devoting precious teaching time to assessment. Yet, without evidence of learner progress, administrative support for long "trips" away from school may be discontinued.

Community-based assessment presents challenges to the extent that it *competes* with integration. However, if planned well, this assessment can *support* integration by documenting its benefits for individuals who participate by guiding instructors in knowing how and what to teach. This chapter provides guidelines for community-based assessment based on: the guidelines that have been developed as the current "best practices" emerging from the community instruction research, and applications by instructors in developing assessment procedures in the community when no formal guidelines exist. By carefully planning assessment in the community, the investment of time and energy required by community instruction may be appreciated.

CONSIDERATIONS FOR PLANNING COMMUNITY ASSESSMENTS

Community assessment may be divided into two broad areas of daily life: 1) vocational/work, and 2) other community-based skills that may include recreation, travel, and use of community facilities. Different issues may arise in planning assessment for each of these areas. For example, in planning a vocational skills assessment with the ultimate goal of a long-term, quality "job match," it will be important for the instructor to know the community vocational needs and job availability, the required and accepted behavior of employees in a potential job site (social and vocational), and the interests and skill level of the person being assessed. By contrast, in recreation or leisure assessment, the individual's own interests are of primary importance. A preference assessment may be designed to target leisure activities to enhance enjoyment and relieve stress.

As mentioned earlier, the community's acceptance of social validation of assessment procedures is another consideration in planning assessment *in* community settings. Two procedures that can be used for social validation are *subjective evaluation* and *social comparison* (Kazdin, 1982). Subjective evaluation solicits the opinions of others most familiar with the environment selected for assessment. For example, the manager of a fast-food restaurant or store, the custodial staff, the bus driver, and the aquatics instructor are all staff who may be able to predict which assessment methods will draw unwanted attention to instructors and to learners with severe disabilities.

A second way to validate the assessment procedure is by social comparison: identifying and collecting data on a peer group in a specific setting. By collecting normative data, instructors might make lists of the various ways that people in the setting record information. Examples of some of the normalized (i.e., unobtrusive) data collection procedures may include a hand-held stroke counter (frequency counts), a page attached to a newspaper (multiple skills), and a Walkman cassette player. All of these systems might be adaptive for specific data collection during assessment. Table 1 lists data collection systems that are designed to: provide adequate collection of data and appear normal in the specific community setting. Some instructors may wish to wait to record data after they return to their vehicle or classroom. If data are to be recorded some time after skill performance is observed, a simple (e.g., number of independent responses) rather than complicated (e.g., level of prompt) method of recording is needed.

Table 1. Materials for unobtrusive data collection in community settings

Task analytic or multiple skill data collection
1. *Checkbook:* Responses are written like check entries.
2. *Stenographer spiral notebook:* Skills are written on the left and data marked on the right.
3. *Ledger analysis pad:* Task steps are written in left column and data checked in adjoining column.
4. *Magazines, books:* Task analysis is attached to one page. When not collecting data, instructor appears to be carrying reading materials.
5. *Newspapers:* Task analysis is attached to one page.

Frequency counts
1. *Small spiral notebook* (pocket size)
2. *Hand-held stroke counter/clicker:* Many golf shops and grocery stores sell hand-size golf stroke counters or adding machines. With an adding machine, the instructor can count two behaviors under 100 occurrences if the instructor uses the dollar for one and the cents for the other.
3. *Calculator*
4. *Masking tape:* Occurrences are marked with tallies on a piece of tape attached to the cuff of the instructor's sleeve.
5. *Coins in pockets:* A coin is transferred to a different pocket for each occurrence of a response.
6. *Wrist counters:* These look like wrist watches, and can be ordered through PRO-ED Enterprises (5341 Industrial Oak Blvd., Austin, TX 78735).
7. *Old watches:* The minute hand can be manually moved one number for each occurrence of a response.

Time-based data
1. *Walkman cassette player:* This can be used to give prerecorded time cues for interval recording (e.g., every 15 seconds) by an observer who is not teaching.
2. *Microcassette player:* With an earphone, this can give time cues for interval recording.
3. *Stopwatch with neckstrap:* Time duration or latency can be recorded. With casual clothing and a jacket, the watch may be concealed.
4. *Runner's wrist watch:* Time duration or latency can be recorded with any runner's watch that has a stopwatch mode.
5. *Hand-held computer:* Small computers can be programmed to record events and responses while an internal clock monitors time.

The suggestions in Table 1 can help the instructor plan data collection procedures to minimize the potential reactive effect of data collection and instructor presence on the person's normalized inclusion in the community. The instructor may also need strategies to minimize the effects of his or her presence. For example, an instructor who accompanied her class to a fast-food restaurant was pleased that one person who was nonverbal approached the cashier on his own initiative and showed the cashier a card that said "Would you show me where the bathroom is located, please?" Unfortunately, the cashier yelled across the restaurant to the instructor, "Do you want to watch him do this too?" Many instructors who have escorted individuals in community settings for instruction have experienced similar situations in which either people in the community altered their behavior to try to accommodate the instructor and the person with special needs, or individuals have waited for the instructor to be observing before performing the skill. Two strategies for minimizing the influence of instructor reactivity to assess person performance in the community environment are: 1) to allow people in the community setting to become acclimated to the presence of the instructor and the individual with severe disabilities, and 2) to observe the individual from as natural a position as possible by "blending" into the community setting.

For example, in research, experimenters will at times introduce a prebaseline assessment phase to allow the subjects to become familiar with the data collection system. After this period, it may be assumed that the behavior of the subject returns to a pattern similar to before the system was in place. If the behavior is observed to be similar to previous levels, it may be hypothesized that the behavior of the subject is no longer reactive to the presence of the data collection system. When the behavior does not return to preobservation levels, the observer may be made more unobtrusive by blending into the setting (e.g., by recording information in the same manner used by others in that environment). Repeated exposure to a recording system and unobtrusive observations are just two ways to decrease the reactivity of observations, staff presence, and the general public to assessment of the target behavior. If the instructor will be making repeated observations or assessments in the same setting, it may be helpful to talk with employees about the importance of their treating individuals with severe disabilities the same as they would other customers or employees.

ASSESSMENT IN AND FOR VOCATIONAL SETTINGS

A quality job placement with potential for advancement is one of the highest priorities for adults and adolescents. Most adults work outside their residences for wages. Others work in the home with another means of financial support (e.g., wage-earning family member) or in the community without wages (e.g., volunteers). However, this pattern differs across age groups. Many young adults continue to attend school. Most adults who are older retire from their primary wage-earning jobs, and spend more time engaged in recreation and leisure activities, volunteer work, and/or new wage-earning pursuits. Vocational placement for adults with severe disabilities should follow the same wage-earning employment patterns.

By definition, *vocation* is a strong inclination to follow a particular activity or career. The goal of educators is to assist individuals to pursue a vocation. What this entails is both an understanding of the person's abilities and interests, and a knowledge of the potential job market in a given community.

Vocational assessment has a differing focus depending on the age of the person with severe disabilities. For young learners, the most important factor for instructors to consider is their employability after schooling has been completed. Vocational training, including community-based experiences, should be made available throughout the learner's public school years. A foundation of work experience is one component that assists in the development of job placement for quality employment. Assessment will focus on skills that may generalize across jobs (e.g., communicating one's name) as well as specific job skills that are matched to the community-based experiences (e.g., rolling silverware in napkins for a restaurant, cleaning restrooms in businesses). As learners enter the transition years (age 14 and above), assessment becomes more focused on these specific job skills and less on general work behavior. In the last years of public school, the assessment is the same as for an adult. Situational assessment is utilized before job placement in specific job tryouts; assessment of the specific work requirements is conducted once a job is obtained (Moon, Inge, Wehman, Brooke, & Barcus, 1990).

Instructors may face a difficult challenge in considering vocational options for some adults or adolescents with profound skill deficits. Such individuals may not only have severe physical impairments, but may lack basic communication systems, toileting skills, or self-help skills. Thus, it may be difficult to attain the goal of job placement, let alone *quality* employment.

Currently, several alternate routes have been suggested for people who have been classified as having profound disabilities. The most beneficial route would be to develop creative adaptations to make the person employable at minimum wage or above. This option should not be eliminated from the futures plan for an individual who is of employment age. Further, it is important not to set up invalid criteria for vocational training and experience. Hanley-Maxwell, Rusch, Chadsey-Rusch, and Renzaglia (1986) sited the most frequent cause for job termination was related to production, not to specific social characteristics. Current research does not support "readiness" criteria for employment, but rather a focus on the support services made available that will enable people to contribute vocationally. Thus, exposure to stimuli in community-based job experiences may be more important to the success of employment than many characteristics previously used to exclude people with severe disabilities from employment opportunities.

A second route would be to place people with severe disabilities in an integrated work setting at a reduced wage (e.g., through application for the Handicapped Worker's Certificate). In this approach, people with complicated needs (e.g., medical or physical disabilities that preclude working at the expected pace or performing without continued support) that make meeting employer expectations difficult may still earn more than a sheltered workshop placement would allow, and would have increased opportunities for normalized employment relations with co-workers and customers/clients. Although some advocates have suggested that meaningful work without any type of wages may be preferable to segregated placements with less meaningful activities (L. Brown et al., 1984), others have argued that work without wages sets up a dangerous precedent for discrimination (Bellamy et. al., 1984). Since working for minimum wage or above is strongly valued in American society, vocational alternatives at reduced wage or on a volunteer basis may be a compromise that is pursued for the gain of integration, but neither as a first choice nor as a permanent placement for individuals of employment age. However, as Bates (1989) noted, unless people with profound disabilities receive exposure to an array of community vocational environments (i.e., wage earning, volunteer), they will have very little self-control over their vocational participation.

Vocational assessment can be a step toward achieving the goal of quality employment and long-term job security. The following six components make up vocational assessment:

1. Conducting a job market analysis to know what types of jobs are most prevalent in the community.
2. Planning priorities for job placements by assessing the priorities of the person with severe disabilities and his or her caregivers.
3. Conducting ecological inventories of community jobs to be used for community experiences for school-age students, or job tryouts or placement for adults. For younger students, curricula may also be developed for initial assessments that are based on inventories of employers' expectations.
4. Conducting assessment of the skills that have been identified in these community settings, for employability and job matching.
5. Conducting assessment of the skills needed in the job that has been identified for job tryout or placement. For school-age students, some simulated setting assessment may also be used.
6. Developing the curriculum chart and individualized plan (i.e., IEP for younger learner, individualized transition plan [ITP] for learner in transition years, job placement plan or IHP for adult).

How these components of vocational assessment are applied differ for school-age individuals who are increasing their employment options through skill building versus adults who are seeking a job regardless of their skill level.

Job Market Analysis

Prior to any specific person assessment of vocational skills, an analysis of the potential job market from the community in which the person lives should be completed. Such an analysis leads to improved job retention and job match. If a person leaving school or moving into a new community can anticipate and "scout" the job potential in that community, he or she can plan vocational experiences, prioritize vocational selections, and identify possible resources (e.g., transportation).

The first step in becoming familiar with the current community job market in which the person lives is to monitor the classified ads in local newspapers and trade journals to identify positions that are frequently advertised and new businesses opening in the area. A second way to analyze the community job market is to obtain employment listings from large companies and services (e.g., hospitals). Through analysis of the local job market, the instructor and the person seeking employment can get a general idea about job availability. Some professionals (e.g., Bates, 1989) have suggested that the job analysis should also in-

In ongoing assessment of job skills, the instructor might observe a specific task, such as photocopying.

clude a comprehensive assessment of nonpaid (e.g., volunteer) vocational options in the work community for individuals with more profound disabilities.

If the person being assessed is an adult, this market analysis is followed by job development. The best job matches for some individuals with severe disabilities are jobs that have been created for them. By isolating one aspect of a job that provides steady, repetitive work, an employer may create an opportunity for a person with disabilities to make a unique contribution to a business. Some examples of jobs that have been created for people with severe disabilities include: folding towels in a hospital laundry, rolling silverware in napkins for a restaurant, distributing advertising fliers for a business, photocopying for an office, vacuuming carpet in a store, and cleaning restrooms for a shopping mall.

Prioritization Planning

Once the instructor has some idea of the current job market from the community in which the person anticipates living, the second step should be an assessment of learner priorities. Any type of vocational assessment, either targeting wage earning or volunteer work, must include some indication of the person's preferences. Job satisfaction, job maintenance, and long-term employment all hinge on the acceptance of the vocation by the person performing the job. No job match can be considered complete or accurate if the preference of the person is omitted. Prioritization planning may require scheduling person interviews and visits to types of work in a given geographic area, asking the individual about different types of work presented to him or her in the past, interviewing caregivers to determine their aspirations for the learner, and interviewing instructors about their observations of the learner's preferences. Figure 1 gives some general questions an instructor may ask a caregiver for prioritization planning.

The process of prioritization planning is longitudinal, and the instructor should be aware of the potential for long-term employment, wage adequacy, and promotion. An IEP objective for the elementary years might be for the learner to communicate preference regarding different types of work. As the time for vocational assessment becomes shorter (e.g., in programs for adults who do not yet have specific vocational skills), a more pragmatic approach may be needed in which the instructor presents the jobs currently available, and helps the person select from a limited list. Figure 2 presents a broad list of jobs an instructor might consider in designing a prioritization/preference assessment.

When a person's disabilities create a significant challenge to employment, it can be helpful to utilize personal futures planning to envision job options. (Chapter 5 described the steps for personal futures planning.) To apply this strategy to job development, a support group would be identified that would meet with the person to develop a dream for the individual's employment. This group would identify the person's strengths rather than focusing on the challenges of his or her disabilities. Together, members of the group would set goals for pursuing

Client name _____   Date _____

Instructor _____

Caregiver interview

1. What progress has this individual made that you hope will be maintained for future employment?

_____

_____

2. What skills do you think are especially important for this person's continuing education and employment?

_____

_____

3. Should paid work be a priority for this person at this time? Why or why not?

_____

_____

4. What type of work (paid or volunteer) has this person enjoyed in the past?

_____

_____

5. What type of work (paid or volunteer) do you think this person would enjoy in the future?

_____

_____

6. Are there other concerns you have in general regarding the current services provided to this person?

_____

_____

7. Please list what you consider to be the top five priorities for this person's future vocation?

_____   _____   _____

_____   _____

Figure 1.   Caregiver questions for prioritization planning.

employment options, and, individually, each would commit to strategies for creating these lifestyle changes. Such a support group may be a key component of an ITP for adolescents or an adult services plan (e.g., part of a strategy to transition someone from an adult day program to work).

Ecological Inventory of Job Setting

Job market analysis and prioritization planning are important prerequisites for the instructor in designing a vocational assessment. Once current job availability and the person's preference are monitored, the instructor can initiate the third step of the assessment: conducting ecological inventories of potential employers to determine what social, vocational, and/or academic skills will be needed to secure and maintain this type of employment. This step of the assess-

Check which of the following apply for each job type

Job type	Community availability	Learner familiarity	Learner preference	Caregiver preference	Wage adequacy	Integration	Longitudinal expectancy	Promotion potential
1. Factory								
Benchwork								
Assembly								
Bagging								
Machining								
Construction								
Stockperson								
Other:								
2. Business (e.g., banks, offices)								
Clerical								
Delivery								
Mailroom								
Custodial								
Stockperson								
Other:								
3. Service (e.g., schools, grocery store)								
Foodline server								
Caregiver								
Custodial								
Clerical								
Dishwasher/ busperson								
Stockperson								
Bagger/handler								
Other:								
4. Transportation (e.g., public transportation, gas station)								
Car wash attendant								
Custodial								
Clerical								
Stockperson								
Maintenance								
Other:								

Figure 2. Vocational priority planning chart.

(continued)

Figure 2. (continued)

Check which of the following apply for each job type

Job type	Community availability	Learner familiarity	Learner preference	Caregiver preference	Wage adequacy	Integration	Longitudinal expectancy	Promotion potential
5. Arts/leisure (e.g., sports arena, museum)								
Foodline server								
Ticketer								
Custodial								
Clerical								
Other:								

ment process differs substantially depending on the age of the individual and whether or not a specific job has been obtained. For younger students, inventories are used to develop curricula to enhance employability. (This is discussed in the next section.) For adults to be placed on the job, the inventory is conducted prior to job placement, to prepare for on-the-job training, and is highly specific to the particular job.

The job inventory process that is conducted prior to a specific job placement has been defined and discussed in detail by Moon and colleagues (Moon, Goodall, Barcus, & Brooke, 1985; Moon et al., 1990) in their guides for job trainers. The inventory process should include two general analyses: an *environmental analysis* and a *job analysis*. In the environmental analysis, the job trainer observes an employee performing the targeted job in its various phases. As the employee is observed, the job trainer notes the physical areas in which the job is performed, the major subjobs performed in each area, and the specific skills required for each of these subjobs. The duration of each job is also noted by the job trainer. Once the job trainer has observed the job being performed, he or she then conducts a job analysis that consists of interviews with the employer and co-workers, and of further observations. This analysis is conducted to identify specific skills needed in such areas as time management, mobility, communication, work initiation and maintenance, and social behavior. The analysis also includes questions concerning job logistics such as the work schedule and transportation needed. The information obtained through this inventory clarifies what task analytic, work productivity, and vocationally related skills will need to be assessed for the person. Figure 3 provides an example of a job analysis interview.

The Moon et al. (1985) method to conduct an ecological inventory with potential employers has been defined for adolescents and adults who will be

VIRGINIA COMMONWEALTH UNIVERSITY
REHABILITATION RESEARCH AND TRAINING CENTER
EMPLOYER INTERVIEW FORM

Company: *Mall*   Date: *3-29*

Address: Telephone:

Person interviewed: *Mr. (   )*
Title: *Food Court Maintenance Supervisor*

Job title: *Restroom attendant*   Rate of pay: *4.15/hour*

Work schedule: *Tuesday–Saturday 8:00–4:00*

Company benefits: *2 weeks of annual leave after 1 year of employment; 6 paid holidays including New Year's Day, Memorial Day, Independence Day, Labor Day, Thanksgiving Day, and Christmas Day; 1 paid day of funeral leave for immediate family member; 3 days of sick leave per year; annual bonus at Christmas, which may equal 1 week's pay.*

Size of company (or number of employees): *18 in food court maintenance*

Volume and/or pace of work: *Overall the pace is steady to slow. There may be some periods of time when the pace is fast . . . mostly during holidays and Saturdays.*

Number of employees in this position: *One for maintaining both restrooms*

Written job description available? *no*

Description of job duties: *(Record on Sequence of Job Duties Form)*

Availability of supervisor: *The supervisor is in immediate area but is not interested in providing more than 10% of his time to supervision of the cluster placement employees.*

Availability of coworkers: *There are approximately 10 coworkers in the food court area.*

Orientation skills needed (size and layout of work area): *The food court is 5,700 square feet. The restroom attendant position requires minimal orientation skills, since the individual will be in one small area, except during break times.*

What are important aspects of the position:
Speed _____ vs. Thoroughness __X__ Judgment _____ vs. Routine __X__
Teamwork _____ vs. Independence __X__ Repetition _____ vs. Variability _____

Other: *Neat appearance is a must . . . uniform is required and provided by the mall management. The uniforms will be cleaned weekly by mall.*

What are the absolute don'ts for employee in this position: *Stealing, drinking, excessive absences*

Describe any reading or number work that is required: *None*

What machinery or equipment will the employee need to operate: *Minimal . . . use of a mop and broom*

Atmosphere: __X__ Friendly, cheerful   _____ Aloof, indifferent
              __X__ Busy, relaxed (sometimes)   _____ Busy, tense
              __X__ Slow, relaxed (mostly)   _____ Slow, tense
              _____ Structured, orderly   _____ Unstructured

Comments: *Excellent benefits; management is very positive; coworkers are friendly; regular merit raise after 90 days; good opportunity for social integration during breaks; opportunity for skill development in other areas of the mall.*

Figure 3.   Example of employer interview form. (From Moon, M.S., Inge, K.J., Wehman, P., Brooke, V., & Barcus, J.M. [1990]. *Helping persons with severe mental retardation get and keep employment: Supported employment strategies and outcomes* [p. 41]. Baltimore: Paul H. Brookes Publishing Co.; reprinted by permission.)

placed in identified jobs for future employment. Instructors of younger individuals also need to identify skills for future placement—the more distant future. Since the instructor probably will not know which specific job the young student will secure in the future, a broader array of skills may be targeted. To identify these target skills, the instructor of young learners can replicate the job analysis approach across several potential jobs. While initially this may be time consuming, the information can be used for planning across several years. Another approach to identifying employer expectations is to review published surveys (Hanley-Maxwell et al., 1986; Rusch, 1983; Shafer, Rice, Metzler, & Haring, 1989). The potential weakness of this latter approach is that some of the skills may be specific to the types of jobs and geographic areas surveyed. The obvious advantage is that the published surveys provide far more extensive information than can be feasibly obtained by a single instructor.

Assessment for Employability and Job Matching

A market analysis yields information on work typically available in a community. The ecological inventory or job analysis defines the skills and support (e.g., transportation) needed for a job. For younger persons, assessment focuses on identifying a repertoire of skills to increase the employability in the transition years. This assessment may take three forms: 1) assessment of skills identified in research that increase competitive employment, 2) assessment of work behavior that is age appropriate and builds job skills, and 3) assessment of job tryouts on a wide variety of jobs. These three formats are shown in Figure 4.

When job placement is the priority (i.e., for an adult or youth in transition), assessment has a different focus. Rather than a focus on how to make the person more employable, assessment is used to find a job that *matches* the individual's current strengths and weaknesses. Figure 5 shows a job-match assessment for Al. While this example is an individual assessment, Moon et al. (1990) described how it can be applied to job tryouts as a situational assessment. This direct, situational assessment will be the best means to consider a job match when resources permit its implementation.

Assessment of Skills for a Specific Job

In the job-matching process, the instructor has developed a list of skills the person already has in his or her repertoire, and skills he or she will need for the future job environment. This list of assets and needs has been determined from an array of assessment procedures, including a job market analysis, a prioritization planning outline, an ecological inventory of specific job environments, and an assessment for job matching. The next step is to assess directly the performance of the person on these skills. This may be done as an individual is placed in a community job, during a job tryout, or during simulated work or chores. Assessment formats to consider are checklist observations; task analytic assessment; and time-based assessments for latency, rate, and duration of

---

Name: <u>Nat</u>   Date: <u>May 1, 1990</u>

I. Vocational skills checklist to increase employability (condensed and adapted from Rusch, 1983)

Skill	Person's current skills	Possible target for instruction
Provide personal identification	Carries I.D. card	Show I.D. card
Communicate illness/fatigue/pain	Cries when ill	Gesture "rest"
Follow work instructions	Requires physical guidance	"Sit," "put," "stop"
Add/subtract	No skill	Counting jig
Respond to change without disruptive behavior	Hits self when confused	Use picture wallet to indicate "help"
Move safely about workplace—avoid obstructions	Minimal orientation	Walk to restroom unassisted
Ask for help/supplies	Sits and waits	Tap shoulder for attention/indicate "help"
Maintain personal grooming/self-care	Partial participation in self-care	Eliminate drooling/increase participation in self-care
Work alone 30–60 minutes	Works 2 minutes alone	Unsupervised responding
Follow time schedule	Relies on teacher	Follow picture schedule
Work for money	Unaware of money's value	Use money daily
Read work-related words	No skill	"Read" pictures
Learn new task in 6–12 hours	Learned to wash table in 8 months—about 160 hours	Teach wide repertoire of job skills

II. Age-Appropriate Job Skills

Age	Skills	Possible target for instruction
Kindergarten	Classroom chores	
Elementary school	More complex classroom chores/school "jobs"	Nat can clean lunch table and sweep floor; help clean restroom; empty trash; photocopy; help with school mailings

(continued)

Figure 4. Formats for assessing vocational skills of a younger individual to enhance employability.

Figure 4. *(continued)*

II. Age-Appropriate Job Skills *(continued)*

Middle school	Varied community- and school-based job training
High school/transition	Increase community job training/specific job placement

III. Job tryouts

Market analysis of major employers	Potential jobs	Job tryout ideas*
Lehigh University	Custodial; photocopying; food service	Nat can do photocopying/custodial work at school; tour Lehigh
AT&T Communications	Sorting wire by color; custodial	Teach Nat benchwork, sorting wires; tour AT&T
Over 25 motels	Custodial	Nat can make beds in community home
Area hospitals	Laundry; food service; custodial; mail service	Community instruction; tour hospital

*Ideas are for elementary-age child.

learned skills. At the skills assessment phase, the instructor does not try to make the assessment specific enough for ongoing evaluation, but rather to make it useful for skill selection. Some examples of skills for selection may be communicating when assistance is needed, remaining on one part of a job until completion, and selecting work materials needed for a job. Over a period of days, the instructor would present each task and note whether or not the person could perform the task. The instructor would then note if the person had mastery of the skill, partial mastery of the skill, or no mastery of the skill.

One type of checklist observation that might be performed is a vocational routine assessment. The idea of assessing skills in the routine incorporates the stimuli that make up a natural workday. By assessing skills around natural routines, the instructor can also assess what natural stimuli on the job site initiate, maintain, and terminate the target skills. Without assessing in natural routines, the instructor may only observe if the individual knows *how* to perform a skill, but not *when* to perform it. Another concern of not assessing around natural routines is that instruction may also take place out of the natural work environment, limiting job performance when on the job site. The instructor should structure the assessment to follow the employer's typical routine, noting whether or not the person can perform job skills, manage time, and follow a

Skill	Rating	Comment
1. Physical strength	+	Can lift 50-lb. weights
2. Endurance	+	Good physical stamina
3. Orientation skills	+	Locates areas of school alone
4. Physical mobility	+	No physical problems
5. Independent work rate	−	Only works when observed
6. Appearance	+	Well groomed
7. Communication	+	Converses
8. Social interactions	−	Inappropriate and bizarre comments
9. Perseverance on task	−	Easily distracted by people, objects
10. Sequence job duties	+	Can follow picture/word list
11. Initiative/motivation	+	Wants to work; begins work eagerly
12. Adapts to change	−	Cries, runs when upset
13. Reinforcement needs	−	Needs daily "pay" or privilege
14. Caregiver support	+	Parents value securing a job
15. Discriminate work supplies	+	Reads common product names
16. Time management	+	Follows digital watch/picture schedule
17. Functional academics	+	Uses calculator, some sight words
18. Street crossing	−	Not reliable in looking both ways
19. Handle criticism/stress	−	Aggressive when criticized
20. Problem behavior	−	Grabs females to get their attention
21. Bus riding	−	Not reliable in identifying destination
22. Community work experience	+	5 hours/week in food co-op
23. Use of money	+	Has bank account; needs support
24. Home/school experience (chore)	+	Housekeeping chores

Key: + potential strength; − potential weakness

Individual preferences: Enjoys public settings; likes custodial work; does not like to sit for long periods of time.

Job match: Al is well suited for a job where he can be active and use his physical strength. He can probably learn to read simple schedules and product labels, and compute simple arithmetic. Although he likes being in public, he has severe social problems and is easily distracted. Al may work best in a job where he works away from the public and then socializes with co-worker support (e.g., motel cleaning, cleaning restrooms, back-room stock work).

Figure 5. Example of assessment to enhance job match for adults or youths in transition. (Adapted from Moon, Inge, Wehman, Brooke, & Barcus, 1990.)

schedule. Figure 6 presents an example of a daily routine assessment. (The procedures to conduct a routine assessment were described in Chapter 3 and evaluation of routine data was provided in Chapter 4.)

The instructor probably will also conduct some task analytic assessments of the job skills identified on the job site (e.g., dishwashing, collating, floor waxing). For skills that are already mastered, the instructor should also assess: 1) the rate of productivity, 2) the latency to begin a new task or move to a second component of one task, and 3) the duration of job completion (e.g., floor waxing). Information on rate, latency, and duration are important variables to assess to increase longevity for the person on the job. This information can be used when writing the individualized plan.

For older persons or adults who will be trained for specific jobs, it will be especially important to conduct the assessment in the job setting, and around the natural work routines. Even for the younger learner who is receiving training for future vocational placement, the instructor needs to remember that assessments of skills in simulated settings (e.g., the classroom) may not be indicative of performance in the actual community work setting (see Snell & Browder, 1986, for review).

Curriculum Chart and Individualized Plan

Once the initial assessment has been completed, the instructor is ready to prioritize the specific skills to be trained. For an adult who will be placed on a job, a curriculum chart may be developed with the priority of the skills needed immediately to meet employer expectations (e.g., locating supplies, beginning the job on time, using dishwasher or other equipment) and longer range goals that will enhance the person's satisfaction with the job (e.g., social skills for breaks, use of vending machines). For an adolescent who is in transition, a curriculum chart may be developed that identifies skills to be addressed each year until graduation and ideally, job placement. This chart can be translated into an individualized transition plan (see Figure 7 for a component of an ITP). For the younger student, the priority skills will be written in the community-vocational section of the curriculum chart. Priorities for the first year are then written as goals and objectives in the vocational section of the IEP.

Ongoing Evaluation

For each objective on the individualized plan, ongoing evaluation is necessary. This assessment needs to be sensitive to subtle changes across days. For example, if the job is industrial dishwashing, the ongoing evaluation might be a breakdown of a "big-chunk" task analysis into "small-chunk" task analyses for dishes, pots, garbage, and material storage. The vocational routine, as illustrated in Figure 6, may also be used for ongoing assessment and evaluation. Ongoing evaluation should also include a component of quality control. Maintenance of a job depends not only on the routine of the job being done accu-

Instructional Data Sheet

Manager: _____

Name: _____
Routine: _Work arrival_
Date: _10/5/90_

Beginning natural cue: _Exits bus_
Critical effect: _Social greeting by co-workers_
Latency: _____   Duration of routine: _____

Dura-tion	Step	Job Coach Assistance	Date	Date	Date	Assistance	Date	Date	Date
	1. Walk to company.	Verbal cue re: streat							
	2. Enter employee door.	Point to entrance.							
	3. Store belongings.	Model							
	4. Punch timecard.	Model							
	5. Greet supervisor.	Model							
	6. Start work.	Model							

Total duration: _____

EL = Latency error
E = Response form error
ED = Duration error
C = Correct

© = Communication target

Program changes:
/ = Change in assistance
// = Change in consequence

Figure 6. Example of daily vocational routine assessment. (Blank form courtesy of Neel, R.S., & Billingsley, F.F. [1989]. *IMPACT: A functional curriculum handbook for students with moderate to severe disabilities* [p. 137]. Baltimore: Paul H. Brookes Publishing Co.; reprinted by permission.)

194

SEQUENCE OF STEPS TO ACCOMPLISH GOALS

Student: Ed Jones   Date: 1–12–87

Liaison: School	Comp. Date	Liaison: Rehabilitation	Comp. Date	Liaison: MR/DD	Comp. Date
1. Monitor students full time at community-based training site.	9–87	1. Attend regularly scheduled ITP meetings beginning on 1/12/87.	1–87 1–88 1–89	1. Introduce the range of available MR Adult Services in this community.	1–88
2. Provide an opportunity for the student to experience at least three different types of employment opportunities	12–88	2. Assist schools with selecting/identifying competitive employment placements.	1–89	2. Assist family with adjustments needed with SSI benefits, notification of employment, etc.	3–89
3. Look for a full-time employment opportunity 6 months prior to graduation.	1–89	3. Begin paying for transportation training.		3. Assign individual responsible for employment management.	5–89
4. Meet with student and family prior to accepting job position.	3–89				
5. Begin full-time job-site training 2 months prior to graduation. *Transportation training would also begin at this time.	3–89				
6. Phase out assistance and provide follow-along support.	5–89				
7. Transfer employment management to MR adult vocational services.	6–89				

EMPLOYMENT

Figure 7. Example of a component of an individualized transition plan (ITP) for adolescent in transition. (From Wehman, P., Moon, M.S., Everson, J.M., Wood, W., & Barcus, J.M. [1988]. *Transition from school to work: New challenges for youth with severe disabilities* [p. 84]. Baltimore: Paul H. Brookes Publishing Co., reprinted by permission.)

195

rately, but also on customer satisfaction. The person may be completing all the dishes and pots, but if some are not thoroughly cleaned, job termination may be imminent. Assessment of social and communication skills might also be included in these task analyses or scored on separate checklists.

For assessments in vocational settings to be effective, instructors should plan for moving from the individualized transition plan constructed at the school to a transition plan designed to meet the needs of the community employment setting. Initially, individualized plans implemented from the school provide a means of assessment and training of skills necessary for maintenance of a vocation on the job site. The transition plan is designed specifically to meet the needs of the person for long-term employment (e.g., transportation, ongoing and long-term follow-up, wage analysis).

Case Study Examples

The following case studies provide examples of how the vocational assessment procedure can be applied to various persons. For each example, a brief description details how skills were selected, which procedures were used for initial assessment, and how ongoing assessment was developed for evaluation of progress.

Assessment of a Young Elementary Student: Nat   Nat's case provides an example of planning for a young child who may be an excellent candidate for transitional planning and supported employment by the time he reaches high school, if he is provided with longitudinal planning and instruction. Ms. S. began this longitudinal planning by focusing on Nat's job exposure, current work repertoire, and cooperation with teaching. To select skills for assessment, Ms. S. conducted a market analysis by reviewing newspaper help wanted ads. She also interviewed a supported employment job coach about the current community job market and skills needed for these jobs. Ms. S. then interviewed Nat's parents to determine their priorities for him. Nat's parents agreed that he needed to develop independent work skills and were interested in his acquisition of skills to do as chores. Ms. S. spoke with the high school teacher and discovered that the most prevalent jobs in the area involved custodial skills, benchwork sorting, photocopying, laundry services, or food services. She then assessed Nat's skills, as shown in Figure 4. From this information, she developed initial assessments of specific skills that included: 1) a routine assessment for an active job—cleaning tables and making beds, and 2) a sitdown job—sorting wires by color. She also assessed the skill of showing a personal identification card (name, address, age) and communication skills. Her ongoing assessment included task analyses for active work routines, such as tablewashing and benchwork sorting. She timed his in-seat behavior with a stopwatch when he was assigned to work alone. For personal information and job-related communication, a repeated trial assessment with generalization probes was used for social interactions with other personnel and students in the school. Also targeted for Nat during his elementary years are field trips to major employers in his community.

Obviously, Ms. S. has targeted skills that will require later generalization to community job sites. For example, Nat will be taught to sort items along several dimensions (e.g., color, size) and will be taught a wide range of cleaning skills. Once he acquires benchwork assembly and custodial skills, these tasks will be used to shape productivity and working for extended periods of time without instructor interaction. Once Nat enters high school, these skills will be trained and probed on the job sites. The extent of Nat's generalization will depend on how well the instructor has matched his longitudinal instruction in generalization to the actual stimulus and response generalization required in these settings. Thus, even though Nat is still young, the instructor needs to be familiar with the skills required in community employment settings in order to plan longitudinal instructions.

Planning for an Individual Who Will Enter Transitional Instruction for Supported Employment: Al Al was an excellent candidate for supported employment training. To select skills for Al, Mr. A. first noted job availability by scanning the local help wanted ads and by calling several area companies for job listings. He summarized Al's strengths and weaknesses to enhance job matching, as shown in Figure 5. He then conducted an ecological inventory (environmental and job analyses) of two locations for which Al communicated a preference and in which jobs were available. Mr. A. spoke to the bowling alley manager about an advertised custodial job, and decided to pursue this specific placement for Al. Until a job was obtained, Mr. A. would conduct situational assessment of Al in the school and in an area business where job tryout could be arranged. Mr. A. also arranged for Al to begin job training with a job coach once the job was procured. For initial, specific skill assessment, Mr. A. used task analyses of cleaning the restrooms and cleaning the snack bar. He also used a checklist of social behaviors for interactions with customers, and another for time management. For ongoing assessment and evaluation, Mr. A. developed task analyses for mopping, restroom sink cleaning, and toilet cleaning, and a vocational routine assessment. He was able to use his time management and social interaction checklists for ongoing evaluation without adaptation. For time management, he counted the number of work sessions correct (e.g., if Al moved correctly to his next job or break). For social behavior, he counted the number of staff and customer interactions that met all the criteria on the checklist.

Planning for an Adult with Few Independent Adaptive Responses: Ann As Ann was an adult with very limited adaptive responses in her repertoire, job success would depend on careful job development and ongoing, intensive support. Ms. P. began planning for Ann by recruiting a support group for her. This group, which comprised Ann's primary caregiver in her supported living situation, her aunt, an advocate (a previous instructor), and Ann's current continuing education instructor, met with Ann to brainstorm options for her. They identified that Ann had several important strengths. She smiled when spoken to and many people enjoyed her companionship. Ann also could use one arm and had learned some discrete responses such as pushing a door and lifting her lunchbox. Ann's caregiver said Ann could use extra money to do more in the community and urged consideration of wage-earning, as well as volunteer, jobs.

Ms. P., Ann's instructor, committed to try to develop a job for Ann and to conduct an initial assessment. From a job market analysis of potential employers in the community, Ms. P. identified a mail service enclave as a good match for Ann because of the ongoing support offered. (An enclave may be described as a program for employment that is centered in an integrated worksite such as a factory or office that includes ongoing training and support.) Ms. P. then conducted a job analysis of the mailroom jobs to develop a job for Ann and to conduct specific assessment. From this analysis, Ms. P. made a checklist of skills needed in the office setting (e.g., eliminate toileting accidents, social skills with potential co-workers). From this direct job skills assessment, she selected photocopying and delivery as jobs available in the office enclave in which Ann could engage in a meaningful and necessary part of the job with some independence (e.g., activate the copy machine, carry completed copies to management). Other related skills targeted were communicating basic needs, increasing independence of job set-up and delivery routines, increasing toileting independence, and initiating and responding to co-worker social salutations.

The support group met with the manager of the enclave prior to Ann's beginning work in this setting to identify who would provide Ann with training and ongoing support. Ms. P. negotiated to provide the initial training and to write the plans and assessment for ongoing evaluation, which would be taken over by the staff in that setting. Ongoing evaluations would include task analytic assessments of job tasks, duration of wage-earning time, frequency of toileting accidents per day, frequency of salutations per day, levels of assistance for daily work routines, and related social interactions with co-workers.

USE OF COMMUNITY FACILITIES

Initial Assessment

Living in the community requires frequent use of public facilities to shop, receive health care, participate in recreation, and so forth. Some of the skills required for any one of these settings are applicable to most of the other settings. Others (e.g., bowling, swimming) are setting specific. Prior to the initial assessment, the instructor may want to conduct a community analysis, similar to the job market analysis, to identify community activities that are specific for that area or that time of year. The community analysis or "activities catalog" will yield information on times and dates of specific community events and/or classes (e.g., YMCA/YWCA, community college). The community analysis will also assist the instructor in identifying ongoing community activities. In developing the individual's community plan, the instructor may want to assess skills for recreation, shopping, health care, and general public behavior. Similar to the job assessment, the community assessment should also incorporate an ecological inventory of identified community sites, preference/prioritization planning from the individual and his or her caregivers, community assessment, and ongoing evaluation.

Recreation Skills As technological advances in home care and employment have created more time for leisure pursuits, recreation and leisure activities have become increasingly important in American society. Even when an individual has long job hours, the scheduling of recreation or leisure time becomes important to maintain mental and physical well being. For people with severe and profound disabilities, leisure time is even more important. Often, vocational opportunities are limited and/or provide limited stimulus for enjoyment. For individuals who do not work outside the home, community recreation provides opportunities for social interactions. For those working in the community, recreation provides increased opportunities for interactions with co-workers outside of a job setting. For any individual, community recreation provides avenues for continued integration.

Community recreation skills selection will vary greatly across geographical areas. The instructor may begin the ecological inventory process by noting the types of recreation available in the current community, and by asking caregivers and friends about outings. Sometimes, outings will be limited by the person's current skills deficits. In other instances, facility accessibility will be the barrier to active participation. While the latter problem is one that requires political and legal action, skill deficits can be addressed in assessment to improve both the person's and the family's access to community recreation. Figures 8 and 9 provide two examples of community ecological inventories for potential recreation and leisure activities. Figure 9 provides an ecological inventory most applicable to small- and medium-size cities, such as those in the Lehigh Valley area of Pennsylvania where this inventory was developed. In more rural areas, community recreation often is centered around friends, neighbors, and prominent human services organizations such as a church or civic group. Public schools and colleges also provide the setting and impetus for special cultural and sports events.

Under ideal circumstances, the assessment of community recreation skills would be conducted by taking the person to the various settings and events and observing his or her current skills in each of the settings and events. However, sometimes such assessments are not feasible for instructor and person. Community recreation events are available usually after school hours, and some events may take place some distance from the school. To make the assessment more feasible, the instructor may conduct an interview based on the ecological inventories presented in Figures 8 and 9. Although not as precise as actual com-

Site _____ Interviewee _____

Date _____ Instructor _____

1. Travel/location (answer by traveling to site): What method of transportation will be needed for this site (e.g., pedestrian skills, van, public transportation)?
   a. Is the site accessible to wheelchairs?
   b. Is parking available for easy access?

2. What are the primary activities of the site (e.g., services, if public facility; activities, if leisure facility; curriculum, if public classroom; jobs, if vocational facility)?

3. What is the schedule of the site (e.g., class times, hours open)? What are the best times for integrated instruction (e.g., less busy times in public facility, instructor's preferred time for regular class)?

4. To what extent are orientation/mobility skills required (e.g., seated in one place for the duration, multiple rooms, stairs)?

5. How important is a neatly groomed appearance? Any other considerations regarding public appearance?

6. What type of communication, if any, is required (e.g., placing orders, asking for help, buying tickets, asking for a locker)?

7. What type of social interaction skills is required (e.g., working with a group)?

8. What type of help/assistance is available to individuals (e.g., peer instruction, information booths, attendants, waiters)?

9. How often does the site change routines or physical layout?

10. To what extent are other people in the site expected to be quiet, versus tolerance for a range of behaviors (e.g., museum or theater versus football game or night club)?

11. What natural cues (i.e., reminders) and contingencies (i.e., rewards) are available?

12. What is the interviewee's attitude toward people with disabilities participating in the site?

13. Will escorted assistance in restrooms and for eating or dressing be acceptable?

14. Are there any other special considerations for instruction for and in the site?

Figure 8. Community ecological inventory for integration planning.

Phase I.   Place and event selection

Type	List available places	Check if family participates	Check if learner prefers
Spectator:			
1. Sports	_____		
2. Theater	_____		
3. Movies	_____		
4. Art gallery	_____		
5. Other	_____		
Games and Hobbies:			
1. Dancing	_____		
2. Camping	_____		
3. Arts and crafts	_____		
4. Photography/video camera	_____		
5. Video gameroom	_____		
6. Fishing	_____		
7. Horseback riding	_____		
Fitness Activities:			
1. Swimming	_____		
2. Aerobics	_____		
3. Walking/hiking	_____		
4. Cycling	_____		
5. Bowling	_____		
6. Golfing	_____		
Civic/social:			
1. Church	_____		
2. Scouts, clubs	_____		
3. Volunteer groups	_____		
4. Library	_____		
5. Educational class	_____		

Figure 9.   Ecological inventory for community recreation.

(continued)

Figure 9.   (*continued*)

Phase I.   (*continued*)

Type	List available places	Check if family participates	Check if learner prefers
Friends' homes: 1. Visits 2. Parties	_____ _____ _____ _____		

Phase II.   Identification of activities and skills needed

List places identified with potential events for learner's recreation. Check skills needed in each. Circle skills the learner has not yet mastered (i.e., needs to acquire).

	Places			
	1. _____	2. _____	3. _____	4. _____
1. Sits quietly				
2. Purchases tickets				
3. Shows identifi- cation				
4. Purchases food				
5. Consumes food				
6. Uses rest- room				
7. Communi- cates with people be- sides family				
8. Communi- cates with family				
9. Learns special skills (e.g., dancing, exercise)				
10. Keeps up with special equipment (e.g., camera)				
11. Other				

munity assessments, an interview of the caregivers may reveal which skills the person has. Sometimes, the instructor may find through the interview that the person has had few community experiences because of behaviors not tolerated in public (e.g., taking others' food, grabbing people, toileting accidents). If the interview is the primary source to obtain information, the instructor should attempt to plan at least one community outing to assess related skill deficits as a supplement to the interview. With the interview information and at least one community observation, the instructor may then begin direct observation of community-based recreation skills for the identification and selection of objectives to be taught. Because community recreation skills cannot always be either assessed or taught in the setting in which they were designed, instructors may simulate some community activities. For example, a checklist of skills may be used during a school assembly to assess participation in a community spectator event (e.g., college wrestling match). The school gymnasium might also be used as a simulated setting for assessment of skills used in aerobic classes such as those available at the YMCA, YWCA, or fitness center. An example of an initial assessment task analysis for an aerobics class follows:

1. Dress in appropriate clothing.
2. Join group before class begins.
3. Stand in appropriate area, facing instructor.
4. Imitate instructor for warm up.
5. Imitate instructor for aerobics.
6. Imitate instructor for cool down.
7. Return to locker room with others.
8. Dress in street clothes.

If the person cannot perform any of the exercises or dance steps used in the aerobics classes, task analyses of the exercises or steps most frequently used should be developed.

From this information, the instructor is ready to select recreational objectives for instruction. As the ultimate goal is for the person to participate in recreational events in the environment for which the events were designed, any ongoing assessment should take place in the actual community setting in which the events occur.

Shopping Skills A frequent and useful community activity is shopping, which may include small purchases at a neighborhood store, drugstore purchases, or larger purchases of groceries or clothes. These various shopping activities share common responses that may be assessed and taught for generalized shopping skills to be acquired. In the ecological inventory to identify skills to be assessed, the instructor will identify skills specific to those observed in the shopping setting. The instructor should observe various shopping sites in the community and the people present in those sites.

Following the ecological inventory, initial assessment may be designed. Figure 10 provides an example of a checklist of some common shopping skills

Assessment of community skills requires in vivo observations. In this photo, the instructor (not shown) assesses the man's grocery shopping skills.

that may be used during an interview with caregivers, or during observations of the individual in a shopping environment. Again, similar to the initial assessment of recreation skills, every effort should be made by the instructor to obtain information from a number of direct observations of the person in the shopping settings in the community.

Initial task analytic assessment can also be conducted for purchasing, walking to the corner store, giving a prescription to the pharmacist, choosing a sandwich at the deli, and so forth. Below is a task analysis that is designed for direct assessment of purchasing an item in a store with aisles and a front check-out counter (e.g., grocery store).

1. Walk to entrance of store.
2. Open door and enter store.
3. Walk across front of store to locate aisle.
4. Walk down aisle to correct item display area.

Skill	Never	Sometimes	Most of the time
1. Walks in correct door			
2. Manipulates shopping cart			
3. Identifies money; selects item within budget			
4. Determines items			
5. Reads aisle signs			
6. Reads shopping list			
7. Gives correct money			
8. Carries bags			
9. Takes items out of cart, puts on counter			
10. Asks for information			
11. Opens refrigerator doors			
12. Takes clothes off hangers			
13. Uses elevators or escalators			
14. Reads numbers for floors			
15. Reads tags/labels			
16. Uses coupons			
17. Returns shopping cart			
18. Tries on clothes			
19. Puts clothes back on hangers			
20. Reads dates on items			
21. Grasps item			
22. Releases items into cart			
23. Walks and carries object			
24. Takes number for waiting			
25. Climbs stairs			
26. Takes free samples			
27. Finds appropriate places to sit (rest areas)			
28. Uses restroom			
29. Uses pay phone			
30. Uses drinking fountain			
31. Uses tongs (means of selecting food)			
32. Knows not to sample merchandise			
33. Is aware of other people (traffic)			

Figure 10. Checklist of common shopping skills.

5. Pick up item.
6. Walk up aisle to front of store, carrying the item.
7. Locate an open checkout counter.
8. Wait in line holding item.
9. Place item on the counter.
10. Take out and open wallet.
11. Give cashier money.
12. Collect and pocket change.
13. Return wallet to pocket.
14. Carry bag to exit.
15. Open door and exit store.

From this task analysis, the instructor can select objectives, design assessments of the specific skills, and implement instruction.

Health Care People with severe and multiple disabilities often have health problems that require frequent visits to health care professionals. Sometimes, unpleasant experiences may cause the person to respond to health care professionals with fear, resistance, and even aggression. Assessment of the skills needed to participate actively in health care, and to improve communication about procedures, may assist the person in tolerating these frequent visits. Instructors may gain information needed for the initial assessment, instruction, and ongoing assessment through: 1) interviews with caregivers concerning the type and frequency of appointments, 2) interviews with health care professionals concerning routines and any participation needed during examinations and treatments, and 3) direct observations of the person in the health care facility. From the information obtained, the instructor may then design a checklist of skills needed, task analytic assessments, and instructional programs.

General Public Behavior, Travel, and Mobility Depending on the person's skills, different expectations may exist for the ways in which the person will use community resources. For some individuals, further instruction may provide the skills to use resources alone or with companions who do not instruct or supervise. For others, brief opportunities may be made available for independent participation in community activities while an escort waits nearby. Some individuals will always be with an escort while in the community. To determine the feasibility of independent use of community facilities, the instructor might use a checklist of skills required to be safe alone in public (Figure 11). A community match of person preference, public availability, and level of assistance may increase both the quantity and quality of community involvement.

Another important set of skills is needed for travel and mobility within the community. Checklists and inventories should be designed to assess skills such as congested street crossing, locating a destination, and using public transportation. For the person who will always be escorted in the community, the instructor may observe the person's cooperation when being escorted across the street, speed in exiting a bus, or head control when being pushed in a wheel-

Skill	Never	Sometimes	Most of the time
1. Verbally recites full name			
2. Verbally recites home address, on request			
3. Verbally recites phone number, on request			
4. Produces I.D. card when asked address, phone			
5. Uses telephone			
6. Uses restroom			
7. Enters and exits building			
8. Communicates basic need, sickness, and asks for restroom			
9. Maintains proper grooming			
10. Communicates need for help			
11. Reaches destination			
12. Has independent pedestrian skills			
13. Waits in line			
14. Responds appropriately to danger alarms (e.g., fire)			
15. Uses money correctly			
16. Acknowledges people known, but ignores strangers			
17. Uses social pleasantries (e.g., "Excuse me")			

Figure 11. Checklist of skills needed to be safe alone in the community.

chair on sidewalks. An example of a checklist for community travel and mobility is shown in Figure 12.

Case Study Example:
Lester and his Integrated Retirement Services

Lester's case study provides a good example of how initial assessment can be conducted for someone who is gaining entry to new community opportunities. Lester received his first educational services as a senior citizen. He spent most of his life in an institution and did not have the benefit of a public education because he was of school age prior to PL 94-142. Lester was referred to Lehigh University's adult services program to receive support for his life as a senior citizen who had recently obtained a community living placement. Even though Lester had never worked, employment was not a priority because of his age (68) and health. Lester was viewed as "in retirement." Although his retirement was

I. Pedestrian skills

   A. Walking (escorted)
1. Walks with head erect   ____
2. Stays with escort   ____
3. Hands at side or carrying objects   ____
4. Quiet or communicates appropriately   ____
5. Crosses streets when prompted by escort   ____
6. Has stamina to walk to destination   ____

   B. Wheelchair (escorted)
1. Rides with head erect   ____
2. Quiet or communicates appropriately   ____
3. Has stamina to ride to destination   ____

   C. Orientation to destination
1. Walks or wheels self in correct direction   ____
2. Makes appropriate turns   ____
3. Arrives at destination   ____
4. 1–3 for simple, familiar destinations   ____
5. 1–3 for complex (several turns) familiar destinations   ____
6. 1–3 for new destinations with directions   ____

   D. Street crossing
1. Waits if traffic approaches   ____
2. Crosses with light   ____
3. Crosses by observing traffic   ____
4. Stops if car pulls out or turns   ____
5. Crosses at appropriate speed   ____

   E. Street types mastered (crossing stimuli)
1. "Walk" signs   ____
2. Traffic light (red, green, yellow)   ____
3. Stop sign for traffic   ____
4. Uncontrolled intersection   ____

   F. Street types mastered (traffic conditions)
1. One-way traffic   ____
2. Two-way traffic, two lanes   ____
3. Two-way traffic, four lanes   ____
4. Slow traffic   ____
5. Fast traffic   ____
6. Numerous vehicles   ____
7. Infrequent vehicles   ____

II. Car/van transportation
1. Enters/exits vehicle alone   ____
2. Fastens seat belt   ____
3. Does not touch door handle en route   ____
4. Operates window   ____
5. Has stamina to ride to community locations   ____
6. Sits quietly or communicates appropriately   ____

(continued)

Figure 12. Checklist of skills needed for travel and mobility.

Figure 12. (continued)

       7. Communicates needs during travel (e.g., restroom, eating, too hot) ——
       8. (Wheelchair) Participates in transfer from chair ——

III. City bus transportation
  A. Bus alone
     1. Identifies correct bus ——
     2. Pays fare ——
     3. Quiet or appropriate communication on bus ——
     4. Locates destination and departs ——

  B. Bus with escort
     1. Waits at bus stop with escort ——
     2. Gets on/off bus at appropriate speed ——
     3. Inserts fare in slot ——
     4. Sits quietly or communicates appropriately with escort ——
     5. Sits with head erect ——
     6. Departs with escort ——

actually from an institution rather than from a job, Lester had needs similar to other older adults who must make the transition from a highly structured day (i.e., a job for other adults, an institution's routines for Lester) to having substantial leisure time in the community. Lehigh would provide Lester with support for an integrated retirement experience.

The retirement specialist, Ms. C., began Lester's initial assessment by interviewing other senior citizens about how they spent their days and the settings to which they went. She discovered that certain fast-food restaurants at certain hours of the morning were popular hangouts for older adults. She also identified a club, a craft center, and the YMCA as popular community spots. Ms. C. then conducted ecological inventories of the YMCA, craft center, and senior citizen club to identify skills for Lester. (In Lester's case, his records were of little use for this initial assessment.) She then developed a draft of a curriculum chart that included activities such as playing music, dancing, swimming, gardening, painting, doing crafts that require cutting and gluing, running errands, doing volunteer work (i.e., Red Cross mailings), and playing golf. In conducting the assessment, Ms. C. was determining both Lester's entry skills and his preferences. Since Lester had never experienced some of these activities, exposure was a key component of this assessment.

From these tryouts, Ms. C. was able to develop a curriculum chart for Lester's community recreation that was based on his preferences. This community assessment also revealed the need for enhancing some of Lester's communication and motor skills. Lester also had some interfering behavior that reflected social deficits that created some dilemmas during the community tryouts. For example, when he tired of swimming during a YMCA water walking class, Lester hit the retirement specialist. He had not learned to terminate an activity by asking to stop. Interestingly, the other class participants, who were not disabled, said, "He doesn't feel well. Let him rest." (Lester's chart is shown in Appendix A at the end of the book.)

Ongoing Assessment

After the instructor analyzes the current community environment, conducts ecological inventories, and conducts community-based assessments to plan for a curriculum of community skills, the individualized plan is written, and ongoing assessment is developed. Objectives should be developed and implemented for each area of community involvement.

For instance, for recreational skills, specific ongoing assessment might include a task analysis of bowling, photography, or vending machine use. Task analyses might be more specific for those who learn slowly or have few entry-level skills (e.g., a task analysis for grasping a soda can, opening a wallet, or making a selection on a vending machine). Figure 13 provides an example of ongoing assessment.

Frequency counts might be used for behaviors targeted for deceleration, such as grabbing objects and shouting. The instructor might use time-based data for assessment of fluency, such as latency of taking selected items to the counter, or duration of time watching a movie without disruptions.

SUMMARY

People learn to *enjoy* their communities by experiencing and becoming acquainted with an array of social activities, developing and communicating preferences, and developing and maintaining friendships. People *enhance* their communities by developing and maintaining a vocation that is integral and purposeful for their community. As people become more independent financially and in terms of their lifestyles, their ability to integrate themselves increases.

The purpose of assessment in community settings is to help the community as a whole and people with severe disabilities create and develop a "match." Job and recreation matches take the best from both person and community in the development and maintenance of personal futures. Further, the application of behavioral assessment helps the instructor identify specific objectives for the appropriate level of community independence, and to evaluate the effectiveness of instruction to achieve it. For while some individuals will learn to maneuver successfully without an escort, others will rely on lifetime companionship to open doors to community resources.

STUDY QUESTIONS

1. What are the components of a vocational-based assessment? How can this assessment enhance employment options or job matching?

Behavior: __Grasp soda can.__ Name: __Ann__ Mastery: __100%/2 days__

Figure 13. Example of ongoing assessment for grasping a soda can. The figure shows the combination data collection/graph and data review described in Chapter 4. A slash (/) indicates the number of independent correct responses.

Date	Reviews Trend/mean	Decision
10/16/85 (not shown)	Acceleration; $\bar{x} = 10\%$	No change
11/12/85	Acceleration; $\bar{x} = 10\%$	Inadequate progress—improve prompts; delay verbal
11/14/85	Acceleration; $\bar{x} = 34\%$	No change

2. What must be considered in assessment in community settings?
3. What are some examples of assessments of use of community facilities?

FOR FURTHER THOUGHT

1. Consider your assessment of community-based instruction. Do you fit into either of these profiles: the instructor who conducts no assessment of community instruction or the one whose assessment is noticable to everyone in public (e.g., clipboards)? If so, what ideas have you gleaned from this chapter to improve community assessment?
2. What is the difference between a "readiness" orientation to vocational assessment and an employability/job match orientation?
3. How might you use assessment to focus on employability and job match without falling into the trap of vocational readiness?

chapter 7

ASSESSMENT
OF RELATED SKILLS
COMMUNICATION,
MOTOR SKILLS, ACADEMICS

TRADITIONAL SPECIAL EDUCATION curricula have often focused on skills that are common to daily activities, including communication, gross motor skills, fine motor skills, and functional academics. However, when these skills are addressed out of the context of their daily living use, the activities chosen for instruction become nonfunctional; or, that is, of limited utility in daily activities. Communication, motor, and academic skills have more use for the individual in his or her daily life if they are related directly to daily activities. For example, instead of teaching a learner to identify coins in a tabletop activity, the instructor can present coin identification activities during vending machine, laundry, and shopping instruction. Instead of teaching a learner to point to objects and sign his or her name in an isolated communication lesson, the instructor can have the learner sign to request objects needed for lunch, self-care, work, leisure, and so on. Instead of having a learner improve fine motor skills with pegboards and bead stringing, the instructor can have the learner practice fine motor skills while playing board games or preparing snacks. Thus, this chapter refers to the skill areas of communication, motor, and academic skills as *related skills,* to emphasize the fact that these skills should be directly related to specific daily activities to enhance their generalized use in these activities.

Sometimes, to avoid identifying nonfunctional communication, motor, or academic skills, educators have focused assessment only on daily activities. When assessment focuses only on the domains of daily living, related skills may be underdeveloped. For example, an individual can be taught cooking skills with no consideration given to communication, motor, or academic skills. By contrast, if motor and academic skills are taught in the context of cooking instruction, generalization may be enhanced. For example, the person may improve his or her grasp across a variety of materials while cooking—if attention is given to setting up opportunities to use this skill during this activity. Or, a learner may be able to generalize cooking skills to untrained recipes if taught to read recipe words. Similarly, cooking provides an activity that can stimulate communication and socialization.

This chapter provides guidelines for the instructor to assess related skills with the priority of selecting those that enhance home and community activities that are considered most important for the particular learner. In the areas of communication and motor skills, this assessment will require a multidisciplinary effort if the individual receives speech, occupational, or physical therapy. Liz's case study, presented in the next section, illustrates how a comprehensive assessment can be conducted as a multidisciplinary effort.

MULTIDISCIPLINARY COMPREHENSIVE ASSESSMENT

The comprehensive assessment that would be provided from the perspective of the speech-language pathologist, occupational therapist (OT), or physical therapist (PT) are beyond the scope of this book. Rather, the focus here is on how the contribution of these specialists can help the instructor develop a comprehensive educational assessment.

Campbell (1987) described how educators and therapists can work together as an integrated programming team, and recommended that a team coordinator synthesize assessment results to guide the team by: selecting functional skills within each content domain and determining integrated methods to teach desired skills. To make the comprehensive assessment a multidisciplinary effort to support integrated therapy, the instructor can serve as the coordinator of this effort.

In Liz's case, however, an educator other than the classroom teacher served as the coordinator, since the comprehensive assessment was new to the team (the author served as the coordinator). The team included a physical therapist, occupational therapist, speech-language pathologist, Liz's teacher, and the special education supervisor. Liz's mother also became a team member during the skill prioritization phases. The team first met to review the steps of a comprehensive assessment (described in Chapter 2, and shown in Table 2 in Chapter 1). Next, the team members clarified their roles in how skills would be identified for assessment. The team decided to gather information from Liz's records by having each professional bring recent results from testing (a state requirement) to the next meeting. The teacher would also bring Liz's final report card summary of her progress for the year and the most recent IEP. The coordinator was identified as the person to conduct the home ecological inventory, to obtain a list of parent priority skills from which the team could focus its efforts.

At the next meeting, the parent-generated list of skills was used like a curriculum to summarize all of the information known about Liz's skills and to identify areas needing further assessment. Liz's teacher and therapists also added skill priorities to this list based on their work with Liz. Through reviewing this list, the team became aware of areas requiring further assessment. First, Liz had not yet received community-based instruction. Although Liz's parents took her many places in the community, her mother mentioned that she preferred not to shop with Liz because of her difficult behavior in stores. The teacher wanted more information on how Liz would respond to instruction in a store setting and an ecological inventory was planned. The entire team was interested in the extent to which Liz generalized her skills. Also, while Liz attended a regular school, her integration into regular classes was sparse. Since Liz was attending an integrated summer camp, this seemed to be an excellent opportunity to conduct an assessment of her generalization and response to peers without disabilities. One of Liz's greatest areas of skill need was communication. The speech-language pathologist and team coordinator decided to work together trying different types of picture symbols with Liz in various school and playground environments. Also, the teacher was asked to contribute to the communication assessment by trying these symbols in the context of the community-based store assessment. The occupational therapist wanted more information about Liz's fine motor skills and tactile defensiveness. Since the mother had expressed strong concern about Liz's lack of independent play skills, the coordinator suggested that the OT assess Liz with a variety of play materials and consider sensory and motor development in the context of Liz's skills and preferences for play materials. The physical therapist felt Liz was often unmotivated to complete her therapy exercises. The team selected a playground assessment, in a playground near her home and with other children present, to be conducted by the team coordinator, OT, and PT, to see Liz use her skills in a motivating and functional context. The PT would also be able to assess Liz's skills in entering and exiting a car.

For the third meeting of the team, each participant brought informal notes on his or her assessment results and Liz's mother was invited. Prior to the meeting, the team coordinator discussed with Liz's mother the type of assessments that were being conducted. The coordinator also discussed Liz's mother's role in prioritizing Liz's 3-year curriculum chart. At the meeting, each professional gave a brief presentation on his or her findings, and Liz's mother had the opportunity to ask questions and express further concerns. The coordinator then led the group through generating the 3-year curriculum chart. For each item, Liz's preferences were considered by noting how she responded to the activity (e.g., laughed with other children, resisted having her hair brushed). If anyone on the team disagreed with a priority suggested for the chart (including Liz's preferences), the group paused to discuss it and to reach a consensus. Liz's preferences and her mother's preferences were given considerable weight in reaching this consensus.

Subsequent to the meeting, each professional provided a formal, written report of his or her assessment, including results from the published assessments used prior to the team meetings (to meet state requirements) and the recent informal assessment. The team coordinator wrote the comprehensive educational assessment report based on the work of the team (this report is provided in Appendix B at the end of the book). At the end of this assessment, the team members were ready to prioritize skills from the chart for the IEP and to discuss role clarification for their integrated therapy approach with Liz in the coming year. For example, each professional would give Liz opportunities to use her skill to nod "yes" (e.g., while choosing toys during OT). The teacher and therapist would work together to develop Liz's picture communication system. The teacher would implement and assess the system daily. Then, the speech-language pathologist would update the system and provide weekly therapy in the context of the classroom. Similarly, role clarification was obtained for encouraging motor skill development in the context of Liz's daily routines.

As this example has illustrated, the instructor's contribution to the multidisciplinary assessment of language and/or motor skills can be the identification of responses that will most likely be used and maintained in daily activities. Thus, the instructor may lead the planning of the language and motor *functions* to be targeted. Functions are the purposes for the language or motor responses to be acquired (e.g., to ambulate to the cafeteria, to cross a street, to open a drink can, to request items, to make choices). The advanced training of the therapist often enables him or her to better identify the language and motor *forms* for these functions. Forms are the topography of the responses used for the functions (e.g., self-ambulation in an electric wheelchair with a chin control, use of a picture communication book, manual signing).

Obviously, both instructor and therapist will have ideas for form and function, but the instructor's identification of skills needed in the home and community makes him or her especially aware of specific functions needed for language and motor skills. This chapter is a guide for the instructor to assess functions for the related skills of communication and motor skills, with some discussion given to the forms for these functions. At the end of the chapter, assessment of another set of related skills, functional academics, is presented. Specific guidelines for assessing communication and motor skills are now provided.

COMMUNICATION ASSESSMENT

Warren and Rogers-Warren (1985) noted that functional language affects the listener in specific intended ways. The function of a communicative response is established when a person experiences the consequences for the response and when these consequences are reinforcing. New forms are established when consequences are made contingent on their expression to achieve a function. McLean, Snyder-McLean, Sack, and Decker (1982) described early nonlinguistic forms that have clear communicative functions. Sometimes, one form (e.g., crying) can serve several functions (e.g., to get help, to get attention).

Assessment of related skills can be conducted in the context of a daily routine. Using the telephone provides an opportunity to assess reading names and numbers and communicating information.

The individual learns language as new forms are tried that achieve these and other functions that are reinforced by others in the environment. Thus, if the instructor assesses the functions of communication currently used by the individual in either linguistic or nonlinguistic forms and considers the functions and forms needed by current and future environments, communication objectives can be identified that will be related to daily use and will improve the person's repertoire of forms and functions.

Several language experts have developed approaches to language that have either defined or implied procedures to assess functional use of language. For example, MacDonald (1985) developed a language curriculum that uses a conversational model. The conversation skills targeted include social recognition events; purposive social contacts; joint activities; turn taking; chains; initiations; responses; topic initiations, shifts, and closes; and off-topic behavior. All behaviors can be verbal or nonverbal. MacDonald, Gillette, Bickley, and Rodriguez (1984) have begun to field test assessment and training of these conversational behaviors. Another approach to functional language is described in the Vermont Early Communication Curriculum (Keogh & Reichle, 1985). This approach concentrates on the language functions of requesting, rejecting, and describing. McLean et al. (1982) used the term *transactional* to describe their language approach, which focuses on language function, content, and form.

A comprehensive assessment of communication should reflect this priority of focusing on communicative *function* and can follow the same procedure described in Chapter 2: 1) select skills for assessment, 2) conduct assessment, and 3) prioritize skills for a longitudinal curriculum chart. In selecting skills for assessment, the instructor can begin by reviewing the learner's records and noting which skills have been the most recent focus of instruction and therapy and what progress the individual has made. Next, an ecological inventory with the primary caregiver is needed to determine how the individual currently communicates needs, desires, information, and feelings. This inventory helps the instructor determine what forms the learner currently uses for various communicative functions. These forms may represent idiosyncratic (e.g., clapping to express wants) or aberrant (e.g., screaming to express refusal) behavior or may be symbolic (e.g., manual sign, picture system, speech).

Identification of Current Functions and Forms

To conduct this inventory with the caregivers, the instructor needs to be familiar with communicative functions and the various ways these functions may be achieved with adaptive and maladaptive behavior. Donnellan (1984) provided a format to consider how problem behavior may be communicative. Neel and Billingsley (1989) offered a detailed ecological inventory on communication skills that is administered as a parent interview. Table 1 provides a synthesis of several resources on communicative function that can serve as a guideline for assessing how a learner currently communicates. Figure 1 provides a sample format for this assessment. (In Chapter 8, more information is given on understanding the communicative function of problem behavior.)

Through the interview with the caregiver and through the instructor's own knowledge of the learner, using a format such as that shown in Figure 1, the instructor begins to identify communicative strengths and weaknesses. This information can then be summarized, to begin planning communication goals. As shown in Figure 2, Liz had only limited vocalizations and had not made much progress in learning either speech or augmentative systems of communication in her 5 years of speech therapy, with the exception of learning an adapted manual sign for "eat" and to nod "yes." However, Liz came from a highly social family and had learned her own style of communicating with them. She called out to them with an "eh," and expressed affection with hugs. She expressed her wants by calling "eh," then waiting for family members to guess what she wanted, and confirming their guess by waving both hands. When distressed, she cried loudly, similar to the manner in which a toddler would respond. As Liz gets older, and develops new friendships outside the family, she will need to develop more sophisticated communication. As shown in Figure 2, Ms. G., the evaluator, has developed some tentative ideas for what

Table 1. Language functions: definitions and examples

I. *Instrumental functions:* Language that is used to obtain more than socialization. The person's intent is to get the listener to perform some action or to stop the listener from performing a proposed action.

    1. *Request object.* Examples: saying "Please pass the salt" or "More juice"; signing to ask for food; pointing to a ball to get it.

    2. *Request help.* Examples: crying to signal discomfort; pointing to untied shoes; saying "Help."

    3. *Request permission.* Examples: saying "May I go now?"; pointing to a peer's toy to ask to play.

    4. *Request action.* Examples: pulling at instructor's arm to get him or her to push the swing; pointing to picture to ask to dance.

    5. *Get attention.* Examples: vocalizing loudly to get instructor or caregiver to look; saying instructor's name to get him or her to look; tapping caregiver's arm.

    6. *Get information.* Examples: asking "What is this?"; pointing to question mark on communication board in context of introduction of new item or activity; signing "What?"

    7. *State a preference or choice.* Examples: signing "no" when asked if wants water; consenting by pointing to "yes" when asked if peer can sit beside person; saying "I want the cherry juice" when given a selection of drinks; saying "Leave me alone."

II. *Social functions:* Language that is used for socialization. The speaker's primary intent is to engage the listener in an exchange that may be as brief as a polite greeting while passing, or an extended conversation.

  A. *Initiations.* Language that is the first response in an exchange.

    1. *Greeting.* Examples: saying "Hi"; raising a hand in greeting; pressing a symbol on an electric board that activates a voice to say "Hi, my name is John."

    2. *Questions.* Examples: asking "How do you like this weather?"; signing "What is your name?"; pointing to a symbol for "Would you like to talk awhile?"

    3. *Declarations:* Examples: repeating jokes, compliments, or well-known social expressions that serve as conversation starters (e.g., saying "It sure is hot," signing "Pretty dress").

  B. *Responses.* Language in response to another person's initiations.

    1. *Answer.* Examples: saying "My name is Sally"; signing that one would like to talk for a while.

    2. *Replies.* Examples: returning a greeting; saying "Yes, it is hot"; signing "thank you" after a compliment.

    3. *Social links.* Examples: asking "What else would you like to talk about?"; touching the speaker's arm to ask him or her to keep talking.

    4. *Closings.* Examples: signing "Goodbye"; saying "I'll see you later"; waving goodbye.

III. *Personal functions:* Language that is used for self-expression. It is intended neither to initiate a social exchange nor to get some desired object or action. However, this type of communication often occurs in the context of a social exchange.

(continued)

Table 1. *(continued)*

1. *Express emotions.* Examples: pointing to symbol for "happy"; signing "I'm sad"; saying "I'm angry."
2. *Label.* Examples: saying "This is a car"; pointing to shoes when someone says the word "shoes."
3. *Rehearse.* Examples: repeating the instructor's directions while performing an action; stating a sequence of steps aloud.
4. *Entertainment.* Examples: repeating a word while playing; saying a rhyme to oneself.

Adapted from Lucas (1981); MacDonald (1981); and McLean, Snyder-McLean, Sack, and Decker (1982).

Liz needs to learn. From this information, Ms. G. can decide what further assessment is needed. Often, further ecological inventories will be helpful. For example, Ms. G. may list all the environments and activities in which Liz is involved (e.g., playing at school, attending class at church, participating in dressing at home) and specific communication that can enhance each of these activities. The chart provided in Figure 1 in Chapter 2 can be useful for this cross-planning. (An example of cross-planning is shown later in this chapter, in Figure 6.)

With this information regarding the learner's communicative strengths and weaknesses, the instructor is ready to determine what further assessment is needed. If the speech-language therapist has not been involved up to this point, the instructor and therapist will probably want to review the information obtained to date to determine what further information is needed. In Liz's case, further assessment was needed regarding how she used her communication in the context of the community and how she would respond to various types of pictures (e.g., photographs, line drawings).

Neel and Billingsley (1989) noted that communication problems typically fall into one of several patterns. While individuals without communication problems have adequate forms to express a wide variety of functions, individuals with problems may have: 1) adequate forms but limited functions (e.g., an individual with emotional disturbance who can talk, but does not know how to influence others with language), 2) limited forms but multiple functions (e.g., the example of Liz in Figure 2), and 3) limited or unidentifiable forms and functions (e.g., an individual without a communication system and who passively accepts caregiving).

Obviously, the function of communication is most important. If an individual achieves a critical effect for a communicative behavior, it is likely to be used again and maintained. However, refining communicative form may also be important to help increase the ability of the individual to be understood by unfamiliar people (e.g., people in the community) and to have more age-appropriate communication if less mature forms are being used.

Individual's name _____ Evaluator _____

Source of information _____ Date _____

Directions: Any observable behavior that achieves the critical effects listed below may be considered communication. The form of this communication may be speech or augmentative systems such as manual signing picture systems or gestures. It may also be idiosyncratic (unique to the individual), such as tapping the table to request food. Communication can also be in the form of aberrant behavior such as aggression, self-injury, stereotypy, running, tantrums, screaming, crying, and echolalia. For each communicative function, list the behavior the individual currently uses to achieve these critical effects.

Communicative Function. I. Instrumental function to request

Communication/Critical effect	Current communicative behavior and example
1. "I want to eat."/Gets food	_____
2. "I want this."/Gets object	_____
3. "I want to do this."/Gets activity	_____
4. "I want to go."/Leaves building	_____
5. "I need you."/Gets attention	_____
6. "I'm bored."/Gets stimulation	_____
7. "I choose this."/Gets choice from options	_____
8. "What's this?"/Gets information	_____
9. "I'm tense."/Gets tension released	_____
10. (Other)	_____

Communicative Function. II. Instrumental function to refuse or end distress

Communication/Critical effect	Current communicative behavior and examples
1. "Help me."/Problem resolved	_____
2. "Stop this."/Activity ends	_____
3. "I need a break."/Interaction ends	_____
4. "Not this one."/Object withdrawn	_____
5. "Not here."/Move to new location	_____
6. (Other)	_____

Communicative Function. III. Social functions and feelings

Communication/Critical effect	Current communicative behavior and examples
1. "Hello."/Starts interaction	_____
2. "Let's interact."/Keeps others talking	_____

(continued)

Figure 1. Example of form used to assess communicative function.

Figure 1. *(continued)*

3. "Let's play."/Gets others to play	_____
4. "I need a hug."/Gets affection	_____
5. "I care about you."/Expresses affection	_____
6. "I'm excited/happy."/Pleasurable event occurs	_____
7. "I'm afraid."/Gets reassurance	_____
8. "I'm angry/frustrated."/Gets attention/ ends activity	_____
9. "I'm hurt/annoyed."/Interaction ended	_____
10. "Share information."/Maintaining attention	_____

Assessment to Refine Communicative Form

The forms of communication for speech are *Phonology, morphology, syntax,* and *semantics*. Phonology is the study of the production and comprehension of speech sounds (e.g., the initial consonant *b* in the word *butter*) and of prosodic features of speech (e.g., loudness, duration, pitch). Morphology is the study of the smallest unit of meaning in speech. For example, the letter *b* obviously has no meaning of its own. However, root words, suffixes, and prefixes do have meanings (e.g., *-ing* is used to mean a continuing process, as in *swimming*). Syntax is the study of the production and comprehension of recognized sentence structures. Semantics is the study of the content of communication (e.g., vocabulary). While phonology, morphology, syntax, and semantics all are relevant to the specific form of communication, their importance is determined by the extent to which they enable a person to convey his or her purpose for communicating. Being able to convey one's purpose for communicating and to obtain the desired response from others are the focus of the study of *pragmatics*.

If an individual uses a nonspeech form of communication, some of the speech forms of communication may not be applicable. For example, in picture communication, the study of phonology, morphology, and syntax do not apply unless pictures are sequenced into sentences (which probably is not necessary to convey meaning). Syntax in American Sign Language differs from spoken syntax, and individual speech sounds or letters are not signed for most words. Thus, considerations of form for nonspeech communication focus on the mode and symbols for communication. Sometimes, syntax may be assessed and developed in the nonspeech form. In speech, consideration is also given to whether or not the individual's production and comprehension of speech sounds and sentence structures are adequate for communication.

Selection of Communication Mode and Symbol System In Figure 3, a screening checklist is given to help the instructor make a referral to a speech-language pathologist or a speech-and-hearing clinic for further eval-

Individual's name Liz   Evaluator Ms. G.

Source of information Mother   Date 6/1/90

I. Summary of current adaptive communication

Communication	Plan to improve form
1. Signs "eat" for eating or drinking	1. Sign to begin meal, then point to food choice during meal; also introduce pictures for eating versus drinking
2. Nods "yes" if asked "Do you want _____?"	2. Teach nodding "no" to refuse
3. Hugs to express affection	3. Handshake or "slap 5" for less familiar people
4. Waves "hello"	4. —No change needed—
5. Gets bathing suit to request pool	5. Picture communication

II. Summary of aberrant forms of communication

Behavior observed	Alternative communication form
1. Pulls away/falls down to stop activity	1. Nod "no"
2. Screams/cries to get help or to protest	2. Reach out for "help" or nod "no"/vocalize "uh-uh"
3. Screams/cries if denied an inappropriate choice	3. Teach to comprehend "later," "wait"

III. Summary of idiosyncratic forms of communication

Behavior observed	Symbolic form to be targeted
1. Vocalizes "eh" to get attention	1. Tap shoulder also
2. Waves both hands for "I want"	2. Tap table and point to object; also introduce picture wallet
3. Turns head away to refuse	3. Teach nodding "no"

IV. Summary of functions not observed

Function	How will be taught
1. Get information	1. Hold object up or point
2. "I need a break"	2. Put head down to indicate "tired"

Figure 2. Example of communication assessment summary and instructional planning form.

uation of the selection and development of a response mode and a symbol system for communication. As the figure suggests, this evaluation may be conducted to identify more than one form for instruction. It may be difficult to identify one form for an individual with limited communication that will be applicable across functions. For example, signing may not be functional for

I. Response mode selection

Check all responses that the individual makes voluntarily. Circle any responses that the individual makes frequently and consistently as well as voluntarily.

_____ 1. Speaks words
_____ 2. Speaks phonemes (e.g., "baba")
_____ 3. Vocalizes sounds that are not recognizable phonemes
_____ 4. Nods "yes" or "no" (does not have to be used correctly yet)
_____ 5. Moves head other than nodding
_____ 6. Focuses eyes on objects
_____ 7. Focuses eyes on one picture or symbol in an array
_____ 8. Uses fingers independently (e.g., "OK" sign, shows age)
_____ 9. Points to objects
_____ 10. Uses hands to manipulate objects (e.g., pulls up pants, feeds self)
_____ 11. Moves arm and hand together across body and overhead
_____ 12. Slightly moves arm and hand together a few inches
_____ 13. Does not move hands, but can move other body parts independently (e.g., shoulder, foot, knee) (State part that can be moved.)
_____ 14. Other observable, voluntary responses (e.g., tongue clicking, eye blinking) (State response.)

II. Symbol selection

For each of the following symbol systems, note if the individual: 1) responds to the symbol system (e.g., makes differential responses to spoken words), 2) uses the symbol system (if so, note the approximate number of symbols in the individual's vocabulary), and 3) if the symbol system can be adapted to the individual's response modes (if not used currently).

Symbol system	Responds to (yes/no)	Uses (no. of symbols)	May use adaptations (yes/no)
1. Speech			
2. Printed word			
3. Bliss or other symbols			
4. Pictures			
5. Photographs			
6. Objects (e.g., points to)			
7. Manual signs			

(continued)

Figure 3. Communication forms to be targeted for instruction. The instructor may complete this screening checklist and then share the information with therapists to aid selection of communication forms.

Figure 3. (*continued*)

III. Other

_____ 1. Does the individual come from a bilingual or non–English speaking home?

_____ 2. Should an electronic board be considered?

ordering in a restaurant. A communication board will not be available to communicate the need for help during bathing, and may be too awkward for use during strenuous activities such as exercising. Some combination of pictures or gestures would be applicable across these differing functions. A clinical evaluation can help the instructor and school-based therapist know whether or not speech is physiologically possible, if structural difficulties are influencing articulation, and if hearing is normal. If this clinical evaluation includes multidisciplinary assessment, the PT and OT may advise the instructor regarding augmentative forms for communication (e.g., feasibility of turning pages in a communication wallet given impaired gross and fine motor ability) and how to position a learner with physical disabilities for best expression of communication.

Assessment of Syntax Sometimes, individuals with severe disabilities have developed a sizable vocabulary and may have some phrases and sentences in their expressive repertoire. The instructor may then be interested in expanding the syntactic repertoire of the learner. Waryas and Stremel-Campbell (1978) described how syntax can be assessed and trained along with semantics and pragmatics to improve an individual's overall communicative ability. Using their language assessment, language objectives are targeted for functions, grammar, semantics, and nonlanguage behavior (e.g., tantrums). Grammatical training is an area in which it is easy to lose sight of the functional use for these improved forms. For example, a learner who masters plurals in daily sessions of 20 trials of stating the plural may make little use of this skill in other activities. Thus, grammatical training needs to be linked with language functions (e.g., stating requests for one cookie or two cookies). To help the instructor consider how to improve syntactical form, a skill sequence is given in Figure 4 to shape a learner's form from nouns to sentences. This grammatical assessment could be applied to speech or to augmentative forms of expression that allow for expansion of syntax (e.g., Signing Exact English, Blissymbols, typing, other printed word communication systems.)

Assessment of Semantics and Vocabulary Consideration of semantics, and, specifically, of vocabulary to be taught, should be linked to the activities in which communication will be required. This vocabulary can be identified by reviewing the ecological inventories that are used to identify skills needed in home, community, and work environments. Instructors often select vocabulary for nonvocal communication systems that is based on the functions

Information for this checklist may be obtained by observing the student's communication and recording each word, or by testing the student's use of a vocabulary list that the teacher develops from the student's daily activities. For each category, note the number of words observed in spontaneous use, the number of words tested, and the percentage of words correct on the test.

	Number observed	Number tested	Percent correct on test
1. Noun imitation			
2. Nouns			
3. Verbs			
4. Noun–Verb			
5. Verb–Noun			
6. N–V–N			
7. "Wh" questions			
8. Prepositions			
9. Adverbs			
10. Negation			
11. Articles			

Figure 4. Skill sequence checklist for assessment of development of grammar. (Adapted from Waryas & Stremel-Campbell, 1978.)

of getting help or objects from caregivers (e.g., pictures or signs for "toilet," "eat," "drink"). However, due to the many functions for communication and the numerous settings used to plan the individual's curriculum, such content, while important for self-care, is insufficient for the learner's participation in daily activities. For example, social communication requires that the person possess the vocabulary to talk about activities and to ask and answer questions.

Methods to Assess Communicative Form   One of the best methods to assess an individual's current communication forms is to observe him or her during periods when the motivation to communicate is high. For example, the instructor might introduce a recreational activity followed by a snack. During the activity, opportunities could be given to request new materials, to engage in conversation with the instructor and peers, to express feelings and preferences, and to describe the activity or give instructions. During this activity, the instructor might use one of two methods to record communication observed, depending on the frequency and content of communication.

If communication is brief and infrequent, the instructor could use *language logs*. These involve a verbatim recording of all communication over several days, noting the circumstances and what the person did. Later, the instructor can analyze not only the form and content of each communication, but also the function observed. MacDonald (1985) also recommended noting the communication provided by significant others. If feasible, the instructor might spend part of the activity watching an aide, parent, or peer without disabilities initiate communication with the learner to note the types of communication typically received. If the individual's own communication is limited, the communication of others to the individual may be limited in frequency, form, and functions. This sets up a self-perpetuating cycle for limited communication. Thus, it may be helpful to note the opportunities to communicate, as well as the actual communication observed.

When an individual has more frequent or lengthy communication, the instructor may wish to record a *language sample*. A language sample is a verbatim recording of an exchange of spontaneous utterances between two people (Carrow-Woolfolk & Lynch, 1982). The use of language samples has had broad variation, from collecting a sample from 3 minutes to collecting samples of over 30 minutes and from 50 to 1,500 utterances (Bloom, 1970; R. Brown, Fraser, & Bellugi, 1964; Lee, 1974; Muma, 1978). While Carrow-Woolfolk and Lynch recommended collecting a sample of about 100 utterances, this may be too ambitious for assessment of individuals with severe disabilities. However, to improve the chances of obtaining a representative sample, the instructor may collect samples across three or more 30-minute sessions and combine these for analysis. Obviously, these sessions should provide motivation to communicate, such as the recreational activity described earlier. The best way to collect the sample is by audiotape, later transposing what was said. However, if the communication is nonverbal, the instructor may make a written record or videotape during the observation. The analysis of the sample will depend on the level of expression.

As Figure 5 illustrates, several analyses can be performed for the language sample: 1) listing the language functions observed, 2) counting the vocabulary variety (the first use of each word), 3) noting correct and erroneous grammatical forms observed, and 4) calculating mean length of utterance (MLU). Calculation of mean length of utterance can be based on words or morphemes, and can show progress in language development across years that is more meaningful than age norms. One utterance is defined as a verbal string that is marked by inflection—either rising or falling. This verbal string may or may not be a grammatical sentence. The simplest method to calculate MLU is to count words (McLean & Snyder-McLean, 1978). The only components not counted as words in the language sample would be "fillers" (e.g., "um," "uh"). Commonly connected words also count as one word (e.g., "Burger King"). To calculate MLU, the total number of words is divided by the total number of utterances. This calculation is illustrated in Figure 5. (For further discussion of the uses of language samples, the reader is referred to Miller, 1980).

Student's name: Al   Date: 1/11

Context of sample: Al was shown photographs of his daily activities and asked to describe them to his gym teacher while the classroom teacher made this observation. Al then played basketball with the gym teacher.

		Grammar	Function
1.	Al: "Mr. Sear!" Mr. S.: "Hey, Al."	N	S: Greet
2.	Al: "Look my pictures." Mr. S.: "Nice. What are you doing in these pictures?"	V-PN-N	I: Get attention
3.	Al: (as shows each picture) "cooking, cleaning, ride the bus, pay at K-Mart, count my money" Mr. S.: "That's nice. You stay busy."	N, N, V-A-N, V-P-N,* V-PN-N	S: Reply
4.	Al: "It's a two. Pay three dollars." Mr. S.: "What? I don't understand."	PN-A-N V-Adj-N	P: Rehearse
5.	Al: "You got any gum?" Mr. S.: "No, I don't."	PN-V-Adj-N	I: Get object
6.	Al: (stares at Mr. S. and moves face close to his) Mr. S.: "Do you want to play ball?"	Nonverbal	S: Link*
7.	Al: "Yeah!" Mr. S.: "Here, we'll play catch."	Affirmative	I: Choice
8.	Al: "No. Basketball."	Negative-N	I: Choice

Vocabulary variety: 23 different words

Mean length of utterance: 3.5 (28 words in 8 utterances)

Comments: Al shows a variety of vocabulary and sufficient overall grammatical development to be able to communicate with an acquaintance.

Figure 5.   Example of the analysis of a language sample. (Grammar column: N = noun; V = verb; PN = pronoun; A = article; P = preposition; Adj = adjective. Function column: S = social; I = instrumental; P = personal; asterisks indicate potential needs for instruction including: omission of personal pronoun "I," failure to respond to listener's need for clarification, or need for an appropriate social link.)

While the language observation will be sufficient for some learners, for others, the use of one or two tests may provide additional information. Many tests have been developed for language assessment that provide either norm- or criterion-referenced scores. However, the utilization of these tests has several limitations. The first is that many of the available language tests do not analyze language skills to the extent that they can be utilized with individuals who have limited language ability. Second, language tests are typically only oriented toward speech communication. Third, language tests may not provide information that is specific enough to plan intervention. The observations of communication described earlier often provide far more information than can be obtained on a test. For example, in research conducted with children with language impairments, Blau, Lahey, and Oleksiuk-Velez (1984) found that more goals for intervention could be generated with a language sample than with a language test. Finally, a language test might not provide an adequate assessment of an individual's language skills because the test format does not provide adequate motivation to communicate (e.g., many language tests use repeated trials of pointing to pictures).

Given these limitations, the instructor may want to focus primarily on observations of language use. However, tests may be used to try to identify language forms that the individual can use, but infrequently uses. When this testing approach is taken, the instructor needs to keep in mind the limitations described. Table 2 provides a list of some of the language tests available that may be useful for some individuals with severe disabilities (e.g., individuals like Al, in the case studies). The instructor may find it more beneficial to use self-constructed tests that will focus on the specific assessment question he or she wishes to address. For example, if the instructor wants to test grammar, a repeated trials assessment may be appropriate. Vocabulary also can be tested in a repeated trial format using pictures, objects, or activities, and asking "What is this?"

Case Study Example: Nat

In Nat's assessment, the instructor was concerned with expanding his communication functions, with developing forms to supplement signing, and with developing his comprehension of spoken language. Through the caregiver interview and her own knowledge (using the formats shown in Figures 1 and 2), Ms. S. noted that Nat needed to expand his adaptive skills for communicative functions. His current adaptive forms only included requesting objects with signing. His current form was signing one-sign initiations or replies. His vocabulary was limited to a few common objects and needs (e.g., "go," "eat," "shoe," "brush teeth"). In reviewing the settings and activities that had been selected as priorities for Nat's home and community-related instruction, Ms. S. noted the specific need for the social function of communication to be developed, and that Nat needed vocabulary to request or refuse help and to describe his daily schedule in conversation.

In planning for 5 years, Ms. S. targeted greetings (initiating by asking "What is it?"), expressing likes and dislikes, and short conversations based on questions about his daily activities. These priorities were endorsed by Nat's parents, who were eager to see him communicate more in family conversations.

Table 2. Examples of published tests to aid in the assessment of related skills

Language Tests

Peabody Picture Vocabulary Test
  American Guidance Service
  Publishers Building
  Circle Pines, MN 55014

Environmental Language Inventory
  Charles E. Merrill
  1300 Alum Creek
  Box 508
  Columbus, OH 43216

Receptive-Expressive Emergent Language Scale
  PRO-ED
  5341 Industrial Oaks Boulevard
  Austin, TX 78735-8898

Motor Tests

Milani-Comparetti Motor Development Test
  Meyer Children's Rehabilitation Institute
  University of Nebraska Medical Center
  444 South 44th Street
  Omaha, NE 68131

Peabody Developmental Motor Scales
  Teaching Resources
  50 Pond Park Road
  Hingham, MA 02043

Bruininks-Oseretsky Test
  American Guidance Service
  Publishers Building
  Circle Pines, MN 55014

Erhardt Developmental Prehension Assessment
  RAMSCO
  P.O. Box N
  Laurel, MD 20707

Pre-Feeding Skills: A Comprehensive Resource for Feeding Development
  Therapy Skill Builders
  3830 E. Bellevue
  P.O. Box 42050-P
  Tucson, AZ 85733

Nat's instructor also targeted the use of pointing and the use of pictures as forms to supplement his signing. Since spoken language would be used in his conversation training and throughout his daily instruction, no additional receptive language goals were targeted.

These goals reflect the use of several priority guidelines. The language goals have utility both across activities and across Nat's lifespan. The responses targeted can enhance development of social interaction with his nondisabled peers and his family. The goals also take an efficient approach by emphasizing functions while using simple forms such as pointing and pictures to supplement signing. By contrast, the instructor did not plan to delay Nat's communication development by focusing on articulation of phonemes. Speech development would be a long and possibly unsuccessful procedure, given Nat's age and clinical evaluation.

Generalization

Another important step in developing a 5-year curriculum is to plan for generalization, rather than simply hope it will occur (Stokes & Baer, 1977). Generalization can be planned in two ways. First, communication skills, as well as the other related skills, are targeted for use across daily living activities. Second, criteria for mastery are defined as generalized use of a response. For example, for Nat's greeting response, the instructor might use the sufficient exemplar approach (see Chapter 9). In such a case, the criteria for generalization might be to greet two adults and two peers without disabilities whom Nat has not been directly trained to greet. Settings might also be targeted. The criteria for settings might be to greet in two natural settings not used in training (e.g., playground, home, neighborhood).

Another type of generalization that Warren (1985) targeted focuses on linguistic structures for response generalization. These linguistic structures are selected from specific pragmatic categories (i.e., functions). For example, Nat has the goal of responding to social questions about his daily activities. One linguistic structure that might be targeted for this is the first-person pronoun and a verb. For example, Nat would sign "I play(ed)," when asked "What did you do in school?" The pragmatic function that this form addresses is a social answer. Response generalization will have occurred when Nat uses some of the signs he now uses as labels as social replies. Thus, the criteria for generalization might be for Nat to make three untrained social answers using signs in his repertoire. This response generalization might be supplemented with some stimulus generalization goals. For example, the instructor might also target for Nat to give social answers to his parents, sister, and two peers without disabilities in a variety of settings. In the first criterion of generalization, the instructor might assess response generalization by using repeated, massed trial assessment. For example, Ms. S. might have a conversation period at the end of the day in which she probes the learners' communication about their day. The second generalization criterion might be evaluated by keeping a tally of Nat's social replies throughout the day and/or by setting up situations in the natural environment in which someone asks Nat a question and the instructor observes his reply.

Ongoing Assessment of Communication

The curriculum charts and individualized plans in Appendices A and B at the end of this book illustrate how the assessment information is developed into instructional plans. Ongoing evaluation of communication warrants further discussion because of the complexity created by the cross-planning approach. In the domain areas of curriculum planning, ongoing assessment is straightforward. For example, a task analysis is developed for eating with a spoon. Or, productivity rate is used for a vocational task such as packaging. Related skills are more complex because they are part of these other routines. The instructor may use several approaches for ongoing assessment of communication. *Whichever approach is used for assessment, it is assumed that instruction is scheduled during the activity in which the communication typically occurs.*

One approach to ongoing assessment is to use massed, repeated trials for assessment of the acquisition of the target function and form and to supplement these with checklist observations for generalization use. For example, for Nat's use of "what?" Ms. S. might spend 10 minutes presenting Nat with novel objects and pictures to give him 10 opportunities to ask "what?" in a highly structured situation. She would also have a checklist of times when the use of "what?" could be appropriate (e.g., with a peer at lunch who often brings toys and pictures from home, when a new vocational task is introduced, when a new material is introduced in the classroom). The instructor might then graph both the number of responses in the structured probe and the percentage use of "what?" out of opportunities presented across settings. The first might be a graph of daily data to use the decision rules on rate of progress (see Chapter 4). The second might be a weekly graph of the percentage use of "what?" out of opportunities targeted for use across a school week, and could be used to determine when mastery based on generalization is achieved (e.g., used two out of four opportunities for 2 weeks). A second approach to ongoing assessment is to rely solely on assessment of use in context. Rather than using a probe approach, the instructor might assess the skill in the context of routines throughout the day when the use of "what?" would be appropriate. That is, for each routine, Ms. S. would record whether Nat used "what?" alone or with prompts. This latter approach is simpler in that it requires only one graph. Whichever approach is used, similar planning for ongoing assessment will also be needed in the other related skills—motor and academics.

ASSESSMENT OF MOTOR SKILLS

Motor skills, like communication, require careful interdisciplinary planning. The assessment described here is intended to assist the special education teacher in working with occupational and physical therapists to plan instruction to improve motor skills.

Components of Motor Ability

Prior to discussing this assessment plan, it may be useful to examine the components of motor ability. While sensation and perception are related to motor ability, this chapter focuses on observable, voluntary motor responses that can be targeted for instruction. The therapist will often be concerned with sensation, perception, and involuntary responses (e.g., reflexes) as well as voluntary responses. The instructor will want to work closely with the therapist to understand and implement recommendations related to discouraging abnormal reflexes and improving tolerance for sensory input. For more information, the reader is referred to resources that describe therapeutic approaches in further detail (Ayres, 1981; Bigge, 1982; Campbell, 1983; Fraser & Hensinger, 1983).

Observable responses that relate to motor ability can be classified by traditional terminology. Fine motor skills are movements that require small muscle groups, such as the fingers, eyes, and those muscles used for speaking. Gross motor skills are movements involving large muscle groups, such as those used in walking, dressing, or climbing a flight of stairs. Physical fitness, while often associated with cardiovascular fitness, also includes strength, coordination, flexibility, and posture.

Motor Assessment Plan

Approaches to motor assessment often use tasks not encountered in daily living, but tasks selected to evaluate specific motor responses. For example, stringing beads might be used to assess fine motor skills such as finger dexterity and eye-hand coordination. Unfortunately, such assessment also often leads to instruction using nonfunctional "fine and gross motor materials" such as balance beams, pegboards, obstacle courses, and so on. By contrast, if the instructor avoids the use of such traditional motor development materials, it can be difficult to distinguish motor instruction from all other instruction since all responses are in fact "motoric." But this lack of distinction between motor instruction and other instruction may be ideal since it focuses on motoric responses needed in daily living. However, defining specific motor skills to be developed in other instruction may help to ensure that these are not underdeveloped.

The approach recommended here is somewhat similar to that suggested for language. The therapist's evaluation and recommendations often provide the motor forms that need development (e.g., static balance). The instructor then provides the functions for their use. The steps to developing a motor assessment plan are:

1. Review medical and therapeutic evaluations and treatment recommendations.
2. Observe motor skills.
3. Test motor skills.
4. Evaluate motor needs for daily living skills.
5. Conduct further testing as needed to assess performance of motor skills for daily living routines.
6. Set priorities and plan for generalization.
7. Develop the 3- to 5-year curriculum plan.

8. Write the first year's annual plan and develop ongoing assessment for each objective.
9. Conduct ongoing evaluation of data for each objective.

Many of the above steps involve procedures that are discussed in detail in other chapters. The following paragraphs concern only those that are specific to motor assessment.

Review of Medical Evaluations and Therapy Plans The first step in the assessment of motor skills is to review medical and therapy evaluations to obtain information related to planning motor development. Bleck and Nagel's (1975) medical atlas can be a valuable resource to help educators understand this information. Discussion with the parents and with the individual's current physician and therapists may also be necessary to understand recommendations, as well as any specific limitations the individual may have.

Motor difficulties often are associated with central nervous system damage and may be manifested as a general delay in motor development or movement difficulties. Campbell (1983) described an evaluation of movement difficulties that is based on neurodevelopmental therapy. In her approach, the therapist assesses the basic processes underlying movement competence, including tonicity, patterns of movement (e.g., postural fixations), and quantity of movement. From this information, the therapist develops an individualized education planning sheet. Such planning can then be shared with the instructor. Treatment strategies may include, for example, proper positioning of the individual, proper use of adaptive equipment, the use of fast or slow movement when working with the individual, and strengthening weak muscles.

The instructor may need to work closely with the therapist to master the recommended procedures required to implement his or her suggestions. In research on inservice training, Inge and Snell (1985) demonstrated two instructors' mastery of therapeutic interventions (e.g., transferring, positioning prone over a wedge, two-person lift) when the therapist used applied behavioral techniques to instruct them. That is, the therapist used a task analysis, demonstrations, verbal and model prompts, corrective feedback, and praise to teach specific techniques with learners in the instructors' classrooms.

Motor Skills for Daily Living: Observation and Testing Through interdisciplinary planning, the individual's optimal motor forms can be identified and targeted for use across daily living skills. Similar to communication, the instructor conducts general assessments of the learner's motor forms and functions. Then the instructor notes the motor forms and functions needed in the settings and activities that have been selected for the curriculum plan (e.g., see Figure 6). Finally, the instructor selects priorities for instruction and plans for generalization of motor responses across several activities.

To assist the instructor in working with the therapist in assessing and planning for motor development, fine motor skills are listed by traditional categories, with examples of functional activities, in Table 3. Figure 7 provides

Student's name: John   Date: 10-4

Instructor: Ms. M.

Setting	Activity	Related skills needed	Student has skill (yes, no)
Snack bar	Purchasing snack	1. Coin identification 2. Conversation with peers 3. Orientation and mobility to locate cashier and seat	1. No 2. No 3. No
Home	Planning social events	1. Reading a schedule 2. Reading/following calendar 3. Using a talking clock 4. Dialing phone	1. No 2. No 3. No 4. No
Work (mailroom)	Working on task	1. Asking for supplies 2. Counting inserts 3. Signing checks	1. No 2. Yes, inaccurate 3. Somewhat, writes off of check
Restaurant	Eating with friends	1. Stating order 2. Greeting friends 3. Waiting for friends to eat 4. Conversing 5. Walking to restaurant	1. Yes 2. No, hugs and kisses excessively 3. No, wanders and screams 4. No, inconsistent 5. No, shortwinded

Generalization planning—What related skills are needed across activities?

Communication: 1) Conversing with other adults, 2) stating need for supplies

Motor: Orientation and mobility, 2) stamina to walk 3–4 blocks

Academics: 1) Identifing coins, 2) following schedule calendar, 3) using talk-ing clock, 4) signing checks, 4) counting work pieces

Figure 6. Example of cross-planning to identify related skills needed in daily living.

illustrations of the grasps that are listed for fine motor skills. These may be reviewed in collaboration with therapists to select forms to teach to the learner that would enhance absent or inefficient motor functions. For example, the individual may be unable to open bar-press doors because he or she lacks a firm grasp. The individual's poor grasp also may be apparent in other daily activi-

Table 3. Fine motor skills and functional activities

Skill	Activity
1. Movement of fingers in any direction and with control	Turning book pages
2. Individual finger use	Dialing telephone
3. Individual thumb use	Clothes snaps
4. Coordinated finger use	Typing, playing musical instruments, shoetying
5. Arm placement	Placing arm on small table or in water basin
6. Placing objects in/on other objects	Jar lids, box tops, records/tapes
7. Using both arms for holding and carrying	Carrying cafeteria tray
8. One hand holding, one hand manipulating	Painting, stirring, gardening
9. Hook or shovel grasp	Toothbrushing, racquet sports
10. Pincer grasp	Buttoning, zipping, sewing
11. Lateral pincer grasp	Using scissors
12. Spherical grasp	Throwing and catching, eating/drinking

From Moon, M. S., & Bunker. L. (1987). Recreational programming. In M. E. Snell (Ed.), *Systematic instruction of persons with severe handicaps* (3rd ed). Columbus, OH: Charles E. Merrill; reprinted with permission of Merrill, an imprint of Macmillan Publishing Company. Copyright © 1987, 1983, 1978 by Merrill Publishing.

ties (e.g., grasping bar in restroom to sit on toilet alone). From this review, a tentative list of forms may be generated to compare with functions that the learner lacks.

The skills in Table 3 can be used by the instructor as a checklist to identify deficits in specific motor forms. Some commercially available motor assessments are also useful in this regard (see Table 2). However, these instruments do not provide the most efficient approach to identifying motor functions needed by older learners (e.g., jumping and hopping would typically not be assessed for older learners unless identified as components of a leisure skill such as dancing).

Motor functions have not been defined in the literature to the extent that language functions have. However, by reviewing the gross and fine motor demands of daily living, some common functions can be suggested. These motor functions are:

1. *Ambulation:* This motor function is accomplished when an individual moves him- or herself across the floor or ground. Some examples are: walking, using a wheelchair, crawling, walking with a walker.
2. *Sitting/standing:* Many daily living skills require the function of moving from sitting to standing, and vice versa. (Wheelchair use may bypass this

ILLUSTRATION OF THE TYPICAL GRASPS

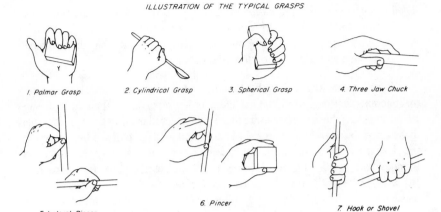

Figure 7. Illustrations of typical grasps for fine motor skills. (From Snell, M. E. [Ed.]. [1987]. *Systematic instruction of persons with severe handicaps* [3rd ed.]. Columbus, OH: Charles E. Merrill; reprinted with permission of Merrill, an imprint of Macmillan Publishing Company. Copyright © 1987, 1983, 1978 by Merrill Publishing.)

function.) Some examples are: sitting on a bus seat, standing at a fast-food restaurant counter, standing with the assistance of braces and crutches.

3. *Negotiating changes in levels of landings* (e.g., stairs): This motor function has been accomplished if the individual safely reaches a different level of landing within buildings and walkways. Some examples are: walking up and down stairs, ramps, street curbs; using an elevator.

4. *Goal-directed ambulation (orientation):* When an individual can reach a near or far destination, he or she has achieved goal-directed ambulation. Some examples are: walking to the restroom in a workshop or to one's assigned seat in the classroom, using a cane or sighted guide to find the cafeteria, holding the instructor's arm to cross the street.

5. *Opening doors:* Most homes and community facilities require entering passageways by opening doors. Some examples are: turning a doorknob and pulling a door open, pushing a crossbar, walking on an automatic door opener.

6. *Entering/exiting vehicles:* Community travel often requires movement into and out of vehicles. Some examples are: moving onto the seat of a car, stepping onto a van, walking up bus steps.

7. *Opening/closing containers and fasteners:* This function is achieved when the container needed is opened or closed, or when a fastener is used in dressing. Some examples are: opening a latch-type lunch box, or a zippered gym bag, closing a thermos.

8. *Object manipulation:* Many daily living skills require manipulation of objects. Some examples are: grasping a cereal box and releasing it into a cart, carrying a gym bag, grasping socks from a drawer.

9. *Locomotion and gross motor skills for recreation:* Recreational activities require skills that are unique to specific sports and games. Some examples are: swimming strokes; hopping and jumping in aerobic dancing; ball skills such as rolling, throwing, and catching.

Figure 8 provides a checklist that the instructor can use to review the motor functions that the individual has in his or her repertoire. The materials suggested to assess these functions are those encountered in adult living rather than those often found only in motor skills instruction (e.g., balance beams, stacking rings). By checking inefficient or inadequate functions with deficits noted in motor forms, the educator develops a list of potential skills for instruction. However, these skills should then be checked against the settings and activities chosen for the curriculum plan (see Figure 6) to make sure that they are needed in, or can be used to enhance, these priority activities. The instructor may also wish to review the task analytic assessment conducted for recreational planning to note the specific activities that can be used for motor instruction (see examples of these task analyses in Chapters 5 and 6).

Setting Priorities and Assessing Generalization A review of one of the case studies can illustrate how consideration of priorities applies to the motor component of the assessment. As mentioned previously, Ann had limited independent responses. From her therapy and medical evaluations, Ms. P. learned that Ann had reduced strength and coordination in one arm due to an accident. Ann's motor development was generally delayed. She walked with an unsteady gait. Ann's range of arm motion was about half that typical of adults her age. Pronation of the pelvis contributed to her unsteady gait and limitations in range of motion. The physical therapist's treatment plan included exercises for Ann's arm strength and pelvis (which she would implement) and a seat insert to encourage correct pelvic alignment. The OT was concerned that Ann learn to use her thumb and forefinger in opposition to learn tasks such as snapping and zipping. After using the checklist in Figure 8, Ms. P. noted that Ann needed to improve the speed of her ambulation so that she could keep pace with a group of adults without disabilities during outings. Her goal-oriented ambulation was very poor, to the extent that Ann could not find the restroom in the adjoining room of her educational center. She also could not open doors. Ann used a spherical grasp on a spoon to feed herself, and a palmar grasp on a glass to drink. Neither grasp was efficient, and Ann had considerable spilling while eating.

In reviewing Ann's life domains, Ms. P. noted Ann's goals in the area of eating, simple housekeeping, dressing, vocational assembly, leisure skills, and community travel, which seemed especially relevant for concurrent development of motor skills. For the 5-year curriculum plan, Ms. P. recommended that Ann acquire a spherical grasp that would generalize across pulling up her pants, drinking from a glass or soda can, and opening doors. She also targeted Ann's development of strength, and use of a hook grasp to carry her gym bag, push a

Individual's name: _____   Date: _____

Instructor's name: _____

For each of the following motor skills, note the level of assistance that the individual needs to perform the skill. If necessary, provide an opportunity to perform the skill and observe performance. Scoring code:

    5—No deficiency
    4—Performs alone, but inefficient or slow
    3—Performs alone most of the time
    2—Needs partial physical assistance most of the time
    1—Needs full physical assistance

1. **Ambulation**
   _____Walks
   _____Walks with adaptive equipment (e.g., crutches, walker)
   _____Ambulates in a wheelchair
   _____Walks or wheels self length of average room*
   _____Walks or wheels self 1–2 city blocks*
   _____Walks or wheels self 3–5 city blocks*
   _____Walks, wheels, or jogs for 15 minutes*

2. **Sitting/standing**
   _____Sits and stands from armless chair
   _____Sits and stands from chair with arms
   _____Sits and stands from toilet
   _____Stands for 5–15 minutes (e.g., to wait for bus)

3. **Negotiating changes in levels of landing**
   _____Ascends stairs alternating feet
   _____Ascends stairs without alternating feet
   _____Descends stairs alternating feet
   _____Descends stairs without alternating feet
   _____Walks up/down ramp
   _____Ambulates wheelchair up/down ramp
   _____Uses elevator alone
   _____Steps up/down from street curb

4. **Goal directed ambulation**
   _____Locates restroom in work setting or school
   _____Locates assigned seat
   _____Ambulates to van or bus
   _____Ambulates to community destination 2–3 blocks away

5. **Opening doors**
   _____Opens door by using key to unlock it
   _____Opens door with door knobs
   _____Enters/exits door with crossbar by pushing
   _____Enters/exits door by pulling handle
   _____Enters/exits door that is opened by escort
   _____Enters/exits automatic door

6. **Entering/exiting vehicles**
   _____Gets in/out of car
   _____Transfers from wheelchair to car

(continued)

Figure 8.   Checklist to assess motor skills for daily living. (* = cardiovascular fitness.)

Figure 8. *(continued)*

6. **Entering/exiting vehicles**
   _____Gets in/out of van
   _____Gets on/off bus

7. **Opening/closing containers and fasteners**
   _____Opens/closes plastic lids on food lunch containers
   _____Uses can opener to open cans when cooking
   _____Opens/closes plastic lunch bags
   _____Opens/closes latch-type lunchbox
   _____Opens/closes zippers on gym bag or pants
   _____Opens/closes Velcro on lunch bag or shoes
   _____Screws jar lids on and off

8. **Object manipulation**
   _____Grasps and releases objects with both hands (e.g., grocery bag, basketball)
   _____Grasps and releases hand-size objects such as socks, fruit
   _____Pours from a small jar or pitcher
   _____Grasps and releases finger-size objects such as coins, comb
   _____Carries lightweight item such as bag with small purchase
   _____Carries medium-weight item such as nylon suitcase
   _____Carries heavy item such as vacuum cleaner
   _____Carries backpack or purse
   _____Grasps and pulls clothing on and off
   _____Grasps and pushes mop or vacuum

9. **Locomotion and gross motor skills for recreation**
   (Individual only neds enough of these skills to participate in targeted leisure and fitness activities)
   _____Runs or jogs
   _____Jumps in aerobic exercises or dancing
   _____Hops in games or exercises
   _____Rolls a ball
   _____Catches a ball that is rolled
   _____Throws a ball
   _____Catches a ball that is thrown or hit
   _____Strikes a ball with a bat or racquet
   _____Kicks while swimming with assistance
   _____Kicks and strokes to swim without assistance
   _____Pedals a stationary bicycle
   _____Rids a regular bicycle

vacuum cleaner, and carry her laundry basket independently. The plan also targeted use of a pincer grasp (modified if necessary) to pick up coins to use a vending machine, perform collating tasks, and zip her pants and gym bag. Ms. P. also selected the specific fine motor skill of opening plastic lunch containers. Increased distance, speed, and direction were chosen to improve Ann's fitness and independence in ambulation with generalization targeted across: 1) walking to the restroom alone, 2) walking to the van alone, 3) keeping pace with the group to walk from the van to a store (about two blocks), and 4) taking a leisure-time walk for three to four blocks with a companion.

Ongoing Assessment and Evaluation of the IEP Similar to the ongoing assessment utilized for language, motor objectives might be assessed in the context of other activities (e.g., as one or more steps of a task analysis) or summarized across activities for evaluation of a specific motor skill. Figure 9 shows a self-graphing data sheet on which Ann's generalized use of a spherical grasp has been summarized. The vertical axis shows the activities in which the grasp was assessed. The instructor would also have task analytic assessment graphs for each of these activities. As mentioned in the section on communication, such cross-evaluation is a time-consuming task. Further, this method of evaluation is not feasible for all related skills targeted. For some, evaluation of their use in the context of activities will suffice. For one or two high-priority related skills, this cross-evaluation might also be utilized. Figure 9 also shows the decisions Ms. P. made in evaluation of Ann's progress on the acquisition of this motoric response. While the first evaluation showed minimal progress, revision of prompting enhanced performance across the time period used for the second evaluation. An alternative method for ongoing assessment would be to embed Ann's motor skills in routine task analytic assessment. Each skill would be evaluated based on the level of assistance Ann required to perform the response (see Chapter 4).

FUNCTIONAL ACADEMICS

Many daily living skills can be performed without mastery of academic skills such as math or reading. Browder and Snell (1987) described three approaches to academic instruction for people with severe disabilities. The first is to teach generalized academic skills (e.g., functional literacy). The second is to teach specific limited academic skills as they arise in planning daily living instruction (e.g., the prices on a drink machine). The third is to teach the use of academic prostheses that minimize the skill complexity (e.g., a money matching card). In addition to these instructional approaches, Browder and Snell (1987) noted that many individuals with severe disabilities have other skill needs of higher priority; academic tasks might be performed for these individuals by the instructor and caregivers (e.g., handing an individual the correct coins needed to purchase a soda).

The assessment of the math and reading skills needed for literacy are beyond the scope of this book. However, the instructor might consider some specific academic skills that are often encountered across daily living tasks. These include the use of money, use of a calculator, telling time, sight reading words, and writing a signature. A skill checklist for these specific functional academic skills is shown in Figure 10. As the figure illustrates, academic skills are also considered in cross-planning to enrich the instruction of life skills.

Behavior: Spherical grasp   Name: Ann   Mastery: 90%/2 days

New Prompt Fading

	100	20 20 20 20 20 20 20 20 20 20	20 20 20 20 20 20 20 20 20 20
		19 19 19 19 19 19 19 19 19 19	19 19 19 19 19 19 19 19 19 19
	90	18 18 18 18 18 18 18 18 18 18	18 18 18 18 18 18 18 18 18 18
		17 17 17 17 17 17 17 17 17 17	17 17 17 17 17 17 17 17 17 17
	80	16 16 16 16 16 16 16 16 16 16	16 16 16 16 16 16 16 16 16 16
		15 15 15 15 15 15 15 15 15 15	15 15 15 15 15 15 15 15 15 15 15
	70	14 14 14 14 14 14 14 14 14 14	14 14 14 14 14 14 14 14 14 14 14
		13 13 13 13 13 13 13 13 13 13	13 13 13 13 13 13 13 13 13 13 3
	60	12 12 12 12 12 12 12 12 12 12	12 12 12 12 12 12 12 12 12 12
		11 11 11 11 11 11 11 11 11 11	11 11 11 11 11 11 11 11 11 11
E = Grasp door.	50	10 10 10 10 10 10 10 10 10 10	10 10 10 10 10 10 10 10 10 10
L = Grasp glass.		9 9 9 9 9 9 9 9 9 9	9 9 9 9 9 9 9 9 9 9
R = Grasp pants.	40	8 8 8 8 8 8 8 8 8 8	8 8 8 8 8 8 8 8 8 8
R = Grasp door.		7 7 7 7 7 7 7 7 7 7	7 7 7 7 7 7 7 7 7 7
R = Grasp pants.	30	6 6 6 6 6 6 6 6 6 6	6 6 6 6 6 6 6 6 6 6
R = Grasp door.		5 5 5 5 5 5 5 5 5 5	5 5 5 5 5 5 5 5 5 5
L = Grasp glass.	20	4 4 4 4 4 4 4 4 4 4	4 4 4 4 4 4 4 4 4 4
R = Grasp door.		3 3 3 3 3 3 3 3 3 3	3 3 3 3 3 3 3 3 3 3
R = Grasp pants.	10	2 2 2 2 2 2 2 2 2 2	2 2 2 2 2 2 2 2 2 2
V = Grasp soda.		1 1 1 1 1 1 1 1 1 1	1 1 1 1 1 1 1 1 1 1
************	%	0 0 0 0 0 0 0 0 0 0	0 0 0 0 0 0 0 0 0 0

Dates: January 4 5 6 7 8 11 12 13 14 15 18 19 20 21 22 25 26 28 29 30
(Absent)

Reviews

Date	Trend/mean	Decision
1/17/86	Flat/x̄ = 14%	Inadequate progress—
	(same x̄ as 1/3/86)	improve prompt fading
1/30/86	Acceleration/x̄ = 50%	No change

Figure 9. Self-graphing sheet. Example of cross-evaluation for the specific motor skill—a spherical grasp. The instructor evaluated the use of this grasp in the context of the activities listed on the vertical axis, but summarized this specific response to assess generalized use. The instructor's evaluation of progress and decisions are also shown. (V = vending, R = restroom, L = lunch/snack, E = exit building.)

Student's name: ——————————————   Date: —————

Teacher's name: ——————————————

Check the academic skills that the student currently demonstrates in at least one activity of daily living. Circle any items that the student needs to acquire, improve, or generalize across activities that have been identified in recreational, vocational, domestic, or community skill planning.

1. **Sight reading**
   - ____ 1. Performs action shown in one picture
   - ____ 2. Follows series of picture instructions
   - ____ 3. Follows instructions with pictures and words
   - ____ 4. Discriminates between edible/nonedible groceries when shown packages
   - ____ 5. Selects given product from grocery shelf
   - ____ 6. Selects food from picture menu or cafeteria food line
   - ____ 7. Selects food from printed word menu
   - ____ 8. Selects soda choice by pushing correct button
   - ____ 9. Identifies numbers to use phone, bank machine
   - ____10. Selects purchases from picture store fliers
   - ____11. Uses grocery store aisle names or numbers
   - ____12. Locates bus or street by sign
   - ____13. Locates correct restroom
   - ____14. Discriminates cleaning products by label

2. **Signature**
   - ____1. Writes name
   - ____2. Makes distinctive mark with pen or pencil
   - ____3. Uses rubber name stamp

3. **Money use**
   - ____1. Uses a 1-dollar bill for small purchase
   - ____2. Uses quarters for vending machines
   - ____3. Discriminates need for dollar versus quarters
   - ____4. Uses 10-dollar bill for larger purchase
   - ____5. Discriminates need for 1- versus 10-dollar bill
   - ____6. Counts 1-dollar bills to pay close to price under $10
   - ____7. Counts 10-dollar bills to make large purchase
   - ____8. Reads prices to select purchase within budget

4. **Time management**
   - ____1. Follows others' activities to stay on schedule
   - ____2. Matches printed schedule and digital clock or watch to follow schedule.
   - ____3. Uses digital watch to follow unwritten, familiar schedule
   - ____4. Uses digital watch to make unfamiliar appointment time
   - ____5. Punches in at a time clock before time to begin work

5. **Computation/math**
   - ____1. Adds prices with a calculator
   - ____2. Subtracts prices with a calculator
   - ____3. Uses calculator to follow budget while shopping
   - ____4. Uses calculator to plan purchase within budget
   - ____5. Identifies numbers to dial phone, use bank machine
   - ____6. Counts items for vocational assembly

Figure 10. Checklist for functional academics. (Adapted from Browder & Snell, 1987.)

SUMMARY

Communication, motor skills, and functional academics may be underdeveloped if an instructor focuses only on life domains in assessing a learner to design an individualized curriculum. However, when these skills have been taught, instruction has too often been isolated from their functional use. That is, people do not communicate in isolation (e.g., in repeated trials about "What is this?"), but rather they communicate about their daily lives in the context of other activities. Similarly, motor and academic skills are typically embedded in the routines of daily living. To meet the dual goals of developing these related skills and planning functional use of these skills, cross-planning is needed. The instructor first plans the individual's life domain skill needs, then plans related skill needs, and finally compares these assessments to see how communication, motor skills, and academics can be taught in the context of other instruction. Sometimes, to make sure these related skills are not lost in other instruction, the instructor will keep separate graphs of skills such as signing, but will not necessarily teach these in isolation from other activities. The individualized curriculum charts at the end of this book (see Appendix A) illustrate the results of this cross-planning.

STUDY QUESTIONS

1. Describe how a comprehensive assessment might be conducted by a multidisciplinary team.
2. What are the types of assessment for communication form? For communication function?
3. What are some examples of assessing motor skills for daily living?
4. What skills might be assessed in the area of functional academics?

FOR FURTHER THOUGHT

1. Read Liz's assessment report in Appendix A. To what extent do professionals in your setting coordinate their assessment efforts?
2. What are some ways this multidisciplinary effort might be improved?
3. Share the ideas you learn from this chapter with therapists, teachers, or other professionals in your setting to begin clarifying how each will address assessment of communication and motor skills.
4. Compare the ideas for communication and motor assessment to procedures you currently use. What new ideas might you try that will help you identify functional skills for individuals with whom you work?

chapter 8

ASSESSMENT OF SOCIAL SKILLS AND INTERFERING BEHAVIOR

Diane M. Browder and Barbara J. West

INTERPERSONAL SKILLS GREATLY influence a person's friendships and job success. Examples of these skills include responding to social invitations, greeting acquaintances, and handling conflicts. When people with severe disabilities live and learn in segregated settings, they may not learn the social interactions typical of their age and cultural group. In fact, follow-up research on people with mental retardation who have left institutions has revealed that social skills deficiencies interfere with vocational and community living success (Gaylord-Ross, 1979; Greenspan & Shoultz, 1981).

The social context must be considered when addressing interfering or problem behavior because behavior is only "maladaptive" to the extent that it is unacceptable to society. Behavior that is considered aberrant in one culture may be adaptive to another culture or time. For example, many people in the early 1900s would have labeled women who wore slacks in public as "aberrant." Besides the social context of behavior, the function of behavior must also be considered. That is, what critical effect (i.e., natural reinforcer) does the behavior achieve? Does it enable the individual to rest, get attention, or get food or other preferred items?

Historically, research and practice have focused on problem behaviors in isolation. A program to decelerate self-abuse or stereotypic behavior was implemented with no concurrent instruction in alternative adaptive behaviors. Unfortunately, for some people with severe disabilities, "maladaptive" behaviors constituted most or all of their leisure and social behavior repertoire. Further, instead of dealing with social skills deficits and opportunities to form relationships, professionals too often intensified deceleration programs or created more contingencies for new interfering behaviors.

By contrast, an educative approach to interfering behavior focuses on creating new opportunities for building relationships and teaching new social skills. In an educative approach, the initial assessment of social skills and problem behavior has four objectives: 1) to determine the individual's opportunities for social relationships and quality of life; 2) to identify social skills for training that will enrich relationships and opportunities; 3) to determine if annoying behavior warrants intervention; and 4) to identify the function of the problem behavior, and to identify an alternative or "equivalent" response that can achieve the same function in a more socially acceptable manner. After the educator has completed the initial assessment and selected skills for instruction, the next step is to plan ongoing assessment and evaluation of progress. Table 1 provides an overview of the steps to educative assessment for interfering behavior.

INITIAL ASSESSMENT

Environmental Assessment

Sometimes the solution to interfering behavior is a lifestyle change, rather than an intervention related to the behavior per se. If someone cannot get to work reliably because of car trouble, one solution is to get the car repaired. If the car has multiple and severe problems, getting to work may still be a problem because the car is frequently under repair. Also, the cost of repairs may add up as high as the original cost of the car. At some point, the person may decide that

Table 1. Sequence of educative assessment for interfering behavior

I. Conduct an environmental assessment
Ask questions about the quality of the person's life.
Conduct personal futures planning if quality enhancement is needed.
Begin lifestyle changes. (End assessment if lifestyle changes can resolve the problem behavior.)

II. Assess social skills
Select skills for assessment using published curricula and ecological inventories.
Conduct social skills assessment.
Begin intervention to enhance social skills. (End initial assessment if function of behavior and alternative social skill are identified. Begin ongoing assessment/evaluation of target social skills.)

III. Assess interfering behavior
Step 1. Verify the need for behavioral assessment. (End assessment if behavior does not warrant intervention.)
Step 2. Utilize anecdotal assessment: ABC/Discrepancy Analyses.[a]
Step 3. Collect data with a scatterplot.[a]
Step 4. Conduct a descriptive and functional analysis.[a]

[a]When function of behavior is identified, assess communication to select alternative skills and end initial assessment. Begin ongoing assessment and evaluation of alternative skills and interfering behavior.

the solution is not ongoing repair, but rather a new car. Similarly, people with severe disabilities may have dissatisfactory lifestyles. Rather than "repairing" problem behavior, assessment and intervention may be better directed at creating new opportunities.

To conduct an environmental assessment, the instructor can ask several questions about the individual's lifestyle (O'Brien, 1987):

1. What is the extent of the person's use of community resources? What would it take for the person to have greater access to community resources (e.g., restaurants, bowling alleys, grocery stores, parks, swimming pools, shopping malls)?

2. What decisions are made regularly by this person? What would it take for others to know and respect this person's preferences?

3. What are the valued community roles this person has (e.g., paper route, hospital volunteer, paid job, church participant)? What would it take to increase this person's status in his or her community?

4. With whom does this person spend the most time? What would it take to increase this person's opportunities for relationships with people who are not paid staff (e.g., same-age peers)?

If this initial appraisal of the person's environment and opportunities reveals the need for major changes, the instructor can organize a support group for the person and begin the process of personal futures planning. (Personal futures planning was described in Chapter 5 for the home environment, and is discussed in Chapter 9 for school integration.) The group not only brainstorms new ideas to improve the person's lifestyle, but also makes an ongoing commitment to the person to support changes that are tried.

Forest and Pearpoint (1990) described the formation of a support group of classmates for students with severe problem behaviors in regular classes. The students participated in the lifestyle assessment by offering their own opinions of what was wrong with the child with interfering behavior. The students also drew pictures of their own circles of friends and compared these with circles they drew for the child's relationships. By comparing these illustrations, the children were able to see the child's lack of friends. They then made commitments to offer friendship opportunities. The children called their friendship support the S.W.A.T. (Students Who Are Together) team. This is a summary of their evaluation of the support process:

> Our S.W.A.T. team has a weekly meeting with Mrs. Gill (the resource teacher). Jane comes to every meeting. At the first meeting we told Jane we wanted to help and be her friends. We told her that no matter what she did, we'd be there for her. We apologized for not being around enough before. Sarah invited her to a party and Sue went to visit her at home. Danny, Rose, and Linda call her a lot. Jane's happy now because she's got the S.W.A.T. team and because she has new friends. We're all making friends too. Jane's whole attitude has changed and she hasn't hit or attacked anyone since we talked to her. (Forest & Pearpoint, 1990, p. 191)

Often, assessment of interfering behavior leads to the identification of the need for social skills and networks of support.

Social Skills Assessment

After, or concurrent with, the environmental assessment, the evaluator focuses on the next objective of educative assessment for interfering behavior: the identification of social skills that can enhance relationships and community opportunities. Social skills deficits are not always as apparent as behavior problems. Sometimes, social skill deficits are present as the absence of behavior. For example, a person may not have the assertive skills to request help or to avoid discrimination. Or, the person may be withdrawn and rarely interact with others.

Selecting Social Skills for Assessment Before conducting assessment of social competence, it will be necessary to identify which skills are important to a person's current and future environments. One approach to this identification would be to conduct ecological inventories. If the instructor has already conducted inventories of the home and community, these can be reviewed to generate a list of social skills to assess. To supplement this list, the instructor might consult resources on social skills instruction to generate an expanded list (e.g., Renzaglia & Bates, 1983; St. Peter, Ayres, Meyer, & Park-Lee, 1989). This list can then be validated by asking the caregivers to rate the importance of the social skills listed. If the learner is being trained for a specific job, the employer might also be asked to respond to the list of suggested social skills. An example of an ecological inventory that could be used for this purpose is shown in Figure 1.

Individual's name: _____ Date: _____
Instructor: _____

I. (to be completed by the caregiver or employer)
Directions: Please take a moment to note the importance of each of the following social skills in your home or business. Please rate each as:
   1—Very important
   2—Important
   3—Somewhat important
   4—Not important
   5—Would not be appropriate in my setting

____ 1. Greeting others with wave or brief communication
____ 2. Greeting acquaintance with hug or touch
____ 3. Shaking hands with new acquaintance
____ 4. Engaging in conversation
____ 5. Sitting or standing at appropriate social distance
____ 6. Giving compliments
____ 7. Patting back of acquaintance
____ 8. Looking at speaker when called by name
____ 9. Walking to speaker when called by name
____ 10. Smiling when praised or in pleasant social exchange
____ 11. Accompanying caregiver or employer upon request
____ 12. Staying near group during activities
____ 13. Waiting for turn or activity to begin
____ 14. Initiating leisure activities with peers
____ 15. Participating in leisure activities with peers
____ 16. Responding appropriately to criticism
____ 17. Requesting assistance
____ 18. Asking others to stop an annoying behavior
____ 19. Avoiding unwanted social attention
____ 20. Avoiding abuse or abduction
____ 21. Choosing activities
____ 22. Managing own schedule
____ 23. Staying busy
____ 24. Using social amenities (e.g., "please," "thank you")
____ 25. Dressing like others in the environment
____ 26. Sharing things
____ 27. Making complaints

II. (to be completed by instructor)
Review the above list and circle any skills identified as important by the caregiver or employer that the individual does not have. Star any skills identified as "very important." Also, list any social skills deficits identified or implied in ecological inventories conducted for skills needed for the home and community.

Figure 1. Ecological inventory to identify social skills for assessment and curriculum planning.

An instrument that provides a scale of validated social skills is the Assessment of Social Competence (ASC): A Scale of Social Competence Functions (Meyer, Reichle, et al., 1985). Table 2 provides a summary of the skills included in the ASC and examples of each. As the table illustrates, there is con-

Table 2   Social skills

Social skill	Examples
Initiating interaction	Extending greetings, tapping shoulder to get someone's attention, joining a group for lunch
Self-regulating	Selecting own chair, checking off steps completed on job list, making own choice from menu
Following rules/routines	Following instructor's directions, requesting food at lunchtime, playing game by rules
Providing positive feedback	Smiling to show appreciation, giving a compliment, communicating "thank you"
Providing negative feedback	Communicating "no" to reject activity or item, ignoring inappropriate behavior of peers, politely refusing unnecessary help
Obtaining/responding to cues	Following hostess to table, watching screen in movie, taking change when reminded by cashier
Providing information/ offering assistance	Holding door for others, communicating own name, helping clean up spills
Requesting/accepting assistance	Communicating "help me," raising hand for instructor assistance

Adapted from Meyer, Reichle, McQuarter, Cole, Vandercook, Evans, Neel, and Kishi (1985).

siderable overlap between communication and social skills. The reader may wish to review Chapter 7 to identify other communication skills that serve a social function in developing a curriculum plan.

Conducting Initial Assessment of Social Skills   The simplest procedure to assess social skills is to complete a published checklist to summarize skills that have been observed. The ASC (Meyer, Reichle, et al., 1985), from which examples are shown in Table 2, provides a comprehensive scale for an initial assessment. This scale is based on social functions that can be achieved with varying forms that may differ across situations. The functions are intended to represent a hierarchy of increasing social sophistication. For example, the simplest level of the function of providing positive feedback is: "Positive occurs, but is not consistently related to social events." An example given for this level is that the individual "smiles or laughs inconsistently in response to events involving people and activities or objects." The highest level is: "Engages in non-preferred activities and shares highly preferred, limited resources on reciprocal basis." An example of this level is that the individual, "in order to save enough money to buy a present for a family member or close friends, restricts personal spending for leisure activities, snacks, etc."

As noted for communication assessment in Chapter 7, a more complex but informative assessment of social skills may be observations of the person in his or her community and home environments. A checklist such as the one shown in Figure 1 can be adapted as an observation checklist by scoring: 1) if the person has the opportunity to make the social response, and 2) if the social response is made. This observation can be repeated across social situations that typically arise in the person's daily living to identify skills needed in each. Some of the skills listed in Figure 1 have not been well defined (e.g., "responding appropriately to criticism"), since the acceptable behavior is situation specific (e.g., offering an apology for damaging someone's property versus ignoring insults or criticisms about one's personal values or appearance). In using the checklist as an observation guide, if the instructor notes a lack of response when one is needed (e.g., failure to apologize) or a clearly socially unacceptable response (e.g., running from the room, striking the speaker), the next step can be to operationalize a correct response based on consideration of what the person's peers without disabilities would do in that situation (e.g., after damaging materials, the person communicates "sorry").

More structured observations might be used to follow a checklist to identify potential skill needs. To measure specific properties of the behavior, the response would need to be operationalized. For example, the instructor might count the number of times a person makes eye contact when spoken to or measure the latency of responding when the person is called by name. This more specific assessment will be required for ongoing assessment of instruction, but might also be used during initial assessment to note if the behavior is similar to that of the person's peers without disabilities.

Actually testing social skills is difficult to do with persons with severe disabilities. Social skills testing typically utilizes simulations of social situations through role-play, game formats, and so on. Such simulations require complex communication about the social events to be assessed. For example, the instructor might ask, "What would you do if . . . ?" Even if the person could perform well in such a simulation, it would be uncertain whether generalization to the actual situation would occur. Observations of the defined social responses in the natural environment have the advantages of measuring generalization and eliminating the need to design simulations. Thus, observations will be the most frequently used method to assess social skills. Unfortunately, some social responses cannot be assessed through observation, because the events that require their use are infrequent (e.g., a mistake that requires an apology) or private (e.g., social sexual behavior). If such responses have been selected for assessment in the ecological inventories of the person's environments, the instructor probably can identify the specific situations that would occasion their use (e.g., bumping someone in the hallway while pushing a cleaning cart, refusing a sexual advance). Such situations might be assessed with "confederates"—people unknown to the person but instructed by the evaluator to set up the events that would occasion the target response (e.g., the confederate positions himself or herself so that the learner bumps into him or her, or the confederate asks the learner personal questions about sex).

In summary, to keep social skills assessment manageable, the instructor should: use the ecological inventory to identify the specific skills that are important and design procedures to measure these specific responses.

Example of Al's Social Skills Assessment Prior to conducting the assessment, Mr. A. reviewed the questions stated earlier in this chapter for environmental assessment. Al lived with his family in the community and frequently used community resources. In general, Al's lifestyle enhancement needs were to obtain a community job and to develop friendships outside his family, as part of his transition to adult living. Because of these goals, Mr. A. considered social skills a high priority for Al. Mr. A. chose to use the ecological inventory shown in Figure 1 as an interview with Al's job-tryout employer to select social skills for Al's assessment. In the interview, the bowling alley manager noted that he did not want his employees bothering the customers with hugging or handshakes. However, the employees enjoyed socializing together in a private break room and Al's friendliness would be welcome in that setting. The employer also considered it important to use social amenities, to avoid unwanted social attention, to avoid abuse or abduction, and to stay busy.

Using these identified social skills as a guide, Mr. A. then conducted social skills assessment. Mr. A. observed Al during the school-based vocational training times and counted the number of handshakes and hugs while working (goal would be none) and social amenities. Mr. A. also watched Al with peers during free times at school and noted that Al did not have adequate skills to solicit and maintain the social attention he sought. Further, Mr. A. kept anecdotal notes on incidents of teasing and other inappropriate social advances (usually from other students in the school) and Al's reactions to them. To assess Al's assertiveness to refuse manipulation, Mr. A. got adults unfamiliar to Al in the school to ask him to leave his work to go with them. Mr. A. then intervened to tell him not to leave a job assigned by the boss and not to go anywhere with strangers.

From this assessment, Mr. A. obtained important information about Al's social skills. Mr. A. noted that Al never hugged and rarely shook hands except to greet a new acquaintance appropriately. He also said "please" and "thank you," unless he was angry. However, as he was eager for social attention, he complied with any request to leave his work. During breaktime, he relied on the same few phrases to maintain a conversation. He reacted to teasing or stares with loud swearing. From this assessment, Mr. A. selected the following skills for the curriculum chart: 1) increasing conversational topics to enhance relationships with co-workers, 2) avoiding social bids to leave a job assigned by the boss, 3) refusing to go with strangers who do not know a special code word (selected by Mr. A. and Al's parents), and 4) ignoring rudeness by walking or looking away.

Assessment of Interfering Behavior

Given that the instructor will assess lifestyle needs and social deficits, direct assessment of interfering behavior may also be crucial to planning intervention. In the initial assessment of interfering behavior that has been determined to need formal consideration, the instructor must ascertain the potential variables that influence the person's behavior and identify alternative behaviors. Specific ways to gather this information might include an ABC analysis (Sulzer-Azaroff & Mayer, 1977), a discrepancy analysis (Evans & Meyer, 1985), a structural analysis (Touchette et al., 1985) a descriptive analysis (Mace & Lalli, in press), or a functional analysis of behavior (Durand, 1982; Iwata, Dorsey, Slifer, Bauman, & Richman, 1982; Mace et al., in press). All of these procedures have the purpose of identifying the function of the interfering behavior or potential means to prevent its occurrence. However, the resources and skill required to use these various assessment procedures span a continuum from simple anecdotal records to complex time-based data requiring someone besides direct service staff to serve as an observer.

In part III of Table 1, "Assess Interfering Behavior," a hierarchy of assessment is suggested that guides the evaluator to use simpler procedures to determine the function of problem behavior before investing in more complex procedures. The following paragraphs describe each step of this hierarchy. The first step is to determine if the behavior is serious enough to warrant the investment required to conduct the assessment and to plan intervention.

Step 1. Verify the Need for Behavioral Assessment Behaviors that are different from those exhibited by most people are not necessarily problems. Many individuals have minor quirks or bad habits with which they live all their lives, with little or no cost to their friendships, jobs, and community acceptance (e.g., nail biting, jewelry twirling, smoking, messiness, odd-spoken expressions). Evans and Meyer (1985) described this "normal" deviation as follows:

> Sometimes we choose to change such behavior, but often we do not. We may not do so because the behavior is difficult to change (that is, it is a habit), and we may "depend on it" for some reason. For example, a person who gives up nail biting may experience an increase in generalized anxiety such that she or he finds it more difficult to deal with everyday situations. . . . In some cases, the behavior itself is not as difficult to tolerate as would be an intervention program to change it!" (p. 59).

Behavior is often considered problematic if it causes physical harm to the person or to others, or if it seriously disrupts the educator's overall instruction and classroom management (Gaylord-Ross, 1980; Sulzer-Azaroff & Mayer, 1977). Behavior may also be considered serious if it places the person at risk for job loss. However, not all behavior that is viewed as problematic meets the criterion of being dangerous or seriously disruptive to the learning or work environment. Sometimes, professionals and parents are concerned with behavior that interferes with the person's attainment of friendships and access to general use of public facilities because it is repulsive or frightening to others.

Evans and Meyer (1985) developed a decision model that classifies deviant behavior in three levels:

Level I: Urgent behaviors that require immediate social attention These rare, excessive behaviors are clearly evident to the person's caregivers and instructors and are likely to result in death or permanent physical damage.

Level II: Serious behaviors that require formal consideration This consideration is only made when an individualized plan of instruction has been developed. These problematic behaviors exist despite implementation of a well-designed educational program. These behaviors may interfere with the rights of others or the person's instruction, can become more serious without intervention, and may be of great concern to caregivers.

Level III: Excess behaviors that may reflect "normal deviation" Often, these behaviors will not be targeted for instruction because modifying them creates more of a disturbance in the learning environment than does tolerating them. However, these excesses may be targeted if they create negative social consequences for the person.

The questions posed for each category of interfering behavior are shown in Figure 2.

At this phase of the assessment procedure, the instructor is simply reviewing the rationale for focusing on a behavior that is of concern to him or her or to the caregivers. By reviewing the checklist in Figure 2, the instructor and caregivers may decide that the behavior is an individual difference that does not require further attention. In this case, no data would be collected on the behavior and the assessment process would return to the consideration of needed social skills. If the behavior is categorized and identified as a problem because it interferes with the person's life or with community integration, the instructor will define and measure the interfering behavior and consider alternative behaviors. If the behavior is life threatening, an immediate treatment is needed (see Evans & Meyer, 1985, for recommendations regarding life-threatening behavior). Whether or not the behavior is Level I, II, or III, environmental and social skills assessments are still appropriate.

To verify the need for behavioral assessment, the instructor also needs to rule out medical or health problems as causes for the problem behavior. People with severe disabilities often do not have adequate communication to describe illness or chronic pain. Intense crying, head banging, and screaming may all be reactions to physical discomfort. Medical treatment may eliminate both the discomfort and the behavior of concern to the professional and/or caregivers. Such occurrences also may suggest the need for instruction in communication (e.g., to sign "hurt" and point to a body part). The interfering behavior may continue after the discomfort has been alleviated, because of the social attention the individual received while ill. In some cases, chronic pain may not be completely

---

Level I. Urgent behaviors requiring immediate social attention

____1. Is the behavior life threatening or does it cause irreversible physical harm to the student?

If yes, implement instruction to train incompatible skills, prevent the occurrence of the behavior, and if necessary, decelerate behavior through DRO or negative consequences. Also, define, measure, and analyze the behavior and begin social skills assessment.

If no, consider Level II.

Level II. Serious behaviors requiring formal consideration

____1. Does the behavior interfere with learning?
____2. Is the behavior likely to become serious if not modified?
____3. Is the behavior dangerous to others?
____4. Is the behavior of concern to caregivers?

If yes, define, measure, and analyze the behavior, and begin social skills assessment.

If no, consider Level III.

Level III. Behaviors that reflect "normal deviation"

____1. Is the behavior not improving or getting worse?
____2. Has the behavior been a problem for some time?
____3. Does the behavior damage materials?
____4. Does the behavior interfere with community acceptance?
____5. Would other behavior improve if this behavior improved?

If yes, define, measure, and analyze the behavior, and begin social skills assessment. Consider the cost versus benefits of decelerating this behavior.

If no, consider this to be "normal deviation." Informally monitor its existence as other skills are developed.

Figure 2. Checklist to identify and classify problem behavior. (DRO = differential reinforcement of other behavior.) (Adapted from Evans & Meyer, 1985.)

treatable, and the instructor will need to help the person learn to cope with daily routines despite discomfort. Whatever the situation, a physician's evaluation is needed to help the educator make decisions about instruction and further assessment. A referral for a medical examination is especially appropriate if: 1) there has been a recent onset of new and intense behavior such as crying, self-abuse, or general refusal to participate in all activities; 2) the person has not had a recent check-up; 3) previous medical examination reports suggest uncertainty in whether or not the person's behavior is related to medical problems; or 4) previous medical reports note the existence of pain that cannot be fully controlled through medication, but give no guidelines on the type of activities that should be restricted or encouraged.

Investing time in assessment of the problem behavior also may not be warranted if simple environmental changes can be made that eliminate the problem. Figure 3 provides a checklist of simple environmental changes that an instructor may make to eliminate problem behaviors. This "structural analysis" may preempt the need for time-consuming assessment of the person's behavior.

Check any change that the teacher will implement to decelerate problem behavior.

_____ 1. Minimize "dead" (noninstructional) time by using group instruction and reorganizing the schedule for better teacher time management.

_____ 2. Provide a variety of materials that the student can obtain and use without teacher assistance during times when the teacher must work with other students individually (e.g., toileting).

_____ 3. Vary the materials provided during independent time.

_____ 4. Vary the activities or materials used in instruction to promote both generalization and motivation.

_____ 5. Eliminate lessons that set the occasion for problem behavior if they are not clearly required for independent living, or modify required activities to include more reinforcement (preferably increased access to naturally occurring contingencies like frequency of pay for vocational tasks).

_____ 6. Self-monitor the schedule of social reinforcement being given to the student for engaging in alternative adaptive behavior versus the schedule of negative attention for the problem behavior. Increase the schedule of reinforcement for alternative behavior and eliminate or minimize interactions during or immediately following problem behavior.

_____ 7. Improve the general comfort level of the room and the student. Check temperature, furniture, lighting, schedules for meals and snacks, and so forth.

_____ 8. Modify the schedule to reduce fatigue (e.g., shorter lessons), or improve motivation (e.g., schedule preferred activities to follow nonpreferred activities).

_____ 9. Review the student's progress across instructional programs to note overall performance. Modify curriculum plan and instructional procedures as necessary to enhance the student's correct responses in lessons.

_____10. Talk to the parents or caregivers and previous teachers to identify simple ways to decelerate the problem behavior.

_____11. Give the student instructions to engage in alternative responses to interrupt a chain of maladaptive responding (e.g., when student begins to whimper at onset of tantrum, prompt to communicate "help").

_____12. "Teach through" problem behaviors so that the student can be prompted to get access to reinforcement with alternative responses. In future lessons, "up the ante" for reinforcement so that the student must make the response without engaging in the problem behavior to get access to reinforcement.

Figure 3. Checklist for simple environmental changes that may reduce or eliminate problem behavior.

Step 2. Utilize Anecdotal Assessment: ABC and Discrepancy Analyses The simplest assessment for problem behavior is to keep daily logs of anecdotal notes that can be used for problem solving about the behavior. These include ABC and discrepancy analyses.

ABC is an acronym for "Antecedents-Behavior-Consequences." In an

ABC analysis, the instructor keeps a daily log of the interfering behavior and the events that occur before (antecedent) or after (consequence) the behavior. In Figure 4, an example of an ABC analysis is shown for John. By keeping logs of incidents of John's screaming, Ms. M. could begin to discern patterns of events that occurred before and after the behavior.

Once the patterns have been identified, the instructor should formulate a hypothesis about the function of the behavior. Iwata et al. (1982) identified four functions of behavior, based on the consequence that follows. (Similar functions have been summarized in the Motivation Assessment Scale [Durand, 1990].) These include the functions of: 1) negative reinforcement (undesired demands, people, or situations are removed when the behavior occurs), 2) so-

---

Student's name: John   Date: September 15

Teacher: Ms. M.   Environment: Snack bar

Description of activity: John's group was given the opportunity to take a coffee break in a snack bar that was a popular location for other adults. Ms. M. escorted and assisted each adult in making a purchase at the vending machines while an assistant sat and talked with the group. The group had performed this activity on numerous other occasions. John's screaming had occurred on most previous occasions. Once, when he became very loud, the group had been asked to leave. John is totally blind and partially deaf.

Antecedents	Behavior	Consequences
John had purchased and finished his coffee and cookies. Ms. M. was assisting another student to use the vending machines. The assistant was helping one of the adults to open his package of crackers.	John stood up, pushed in his chair, and began to say, "Let's go."	Ms. M. and the assistant ignored John and continued to assist others.
	John began to scream and grabbed the arm of an unfamiliar adult who was sitting nearby.	Ms. M. went to John and told him to sit and wait for the group. She escorted him to his seat.
	John stood and screamed and reached out to find someone.	Adults at surrounding tables left the snack bar. Ms. M. escorted John out of the snack bar and the group and assistant followed.

Comments: John had nothing to do once he consumed his snack. He could not see or hear the other adults in the environment. He had no way to anticipate how long the break would last. The teacher's efforts to calm him and escort him out could be reinforcers for screaming.

Figure 4. Examples of an ABC analysis completed for John's screaming.

cial reinforcement (attention is provided when the behavior occurs), 3) tangible reinforcement (the person receives objects or edibles when the behavior occurs), and 4) sensory reinforcement (no external events are observed and the sensory feedback of the behavior itself is presumed to reinforce it). Evans and Meyer (1985) described the first three functions as "social-communicative," and further divided the last function into two categories: self-regulation (the behavior seems to be a strategy to adjust arousal level, such as when bored or uncomfortable) and self-entertainment or play (the behavior is used as a social initiation or to entertain himself or herself when alone). Donnellan et al. (1984) included all of these functions as communicative and further defined what the communicative message may be (see Figure 5).

To formulate a hypothesis about the function of the behavior, the instructor can ask, "Given the pattern of events identified in ABC logs, what is the person trying to tell me with this behavior?" Reviewing the examples given in Figure 5 may help the instructor answer this question and select an alternative skill for instruction so that the person can achieve the identified function in a socially acceptable manner. If the instructor is unsure about which function the behavior serves, it may be helpful to use Durand's (1990) Motivation Assessment Scale and then review Figure 5.

Another way to identify an alternative to the problem behavior is to conduct a discrepancy analysis. Evans and Meyer (1985) described a discrepancy analysis to identify skill deficiencies that coexist with problem behaviors. An example of a discrepancy analysis for Nat's dressing program is shown in Figure 6. As shown in the figure, the instructor observes the occurrence of problem behaviors in the context of functional daily activities. The instructor notes what a peer without disabilities would do in that activity, what the person does, and the discrepancy between the two. The advantage of this approach is that it helps the instructor identify functional, age-appropriate alternatives to interfering behavior. It also provides a way to evaluate clusters of problem behaviors that coexist because of a problem situation. The discrepancy analysis avoids defining problem behavior outside of its environmental context (e.g., to label a child as self-abusive overlooks the skill deficits in specific situations that set the occasion for self-abuse).

For many assessments of interfering behavior, anecdotal assessment will be adequate to write the curriculum plan and first year's objectives. The plan will typically focus on the acceleration of the discrepant skills. An objective may also be written for the deceleration of the problem behavior(s), but these objectives should accompany acceleration objectives related to communicative or other discrepant skills identified. Resources on management of problem behaviors (Evans & Meyer, 1985; Meyer & Evans, 1989) offer further guidelines for deceleration when skill instruction is not enough. Chapter 7 also provided more information on assessing the alternative communication skills that may be selected as functional equivalents to the problem behavior.

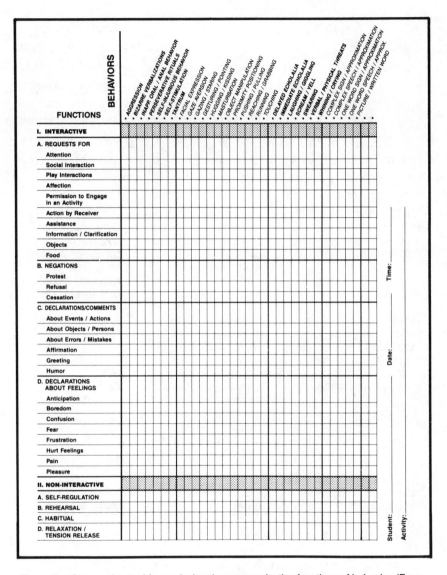

Figure 5.   Observation tool for analyzing the communicative functions of behavior. (From Donnellan, A., Mirenda, P., Mesaros, R., & Fassbender, L. [1984]. Analyzing the communicative functions of aberrant behavior. *Journal of The Association for Persons with Severe Handicaps, 9,* 210; reprinted by permission.)

Step 3. Collect Data with a Scatterplot   A daily log may not provide enough information for an instructor to formulate a hypothesis about the function of the behavior. Another method that provides a more formal "structural analysis" is the scatterplot (Touchette et al., 1985). A scatterplot can

Individual's name: Nat		Date: November 2
Instructor: Ms. S.		Environment: Dressing room

Description of activity: Ms. S. teaches Nat to undress and dress in a private area of the classroom that has been designed to simulate his bedroom at home. This activity precedes Nat's adaptive PE lesson. Nat puts on a sweat suit and sneakers for class. This lesson is taught to a group of two boys so Nat observes a classmate dress and then is instructed to dress, or vice versa.

How information on peer without disabilities obtained: Interview of a parent of a young elementary-age boy

Typical performance of peer without disabilities	Nat's responses	Discrepant skills
Puts on pants alone. Asks for help when shirt gets stuck over head.	Cannot put on shirt or pants until physically guided through a task analysis of each.	Dressing skill acquisition of one or two steps that can be learned by watching model (e.g., peer).
Refuses mother's attempt to help with shoes by pulling away and saying, "No! I'll do it by myself."	Cries loudly when guided; continues to cry for duration of lesson.	Communicating "Let me do it."
Puts on shoes alone.	Can take off shoes alone; needs physical guidance for putting shoes on; when tries to put shoes on alone and fails, crying escalates to screaming.	Communicating "Help me."
Jokes with mother when finished.	Lesson ends with Nat upset.	Initiating enjoyable social exchange.

Figure 6.   Example of discrepancy analysis conducted for Nat's dressing program.

be especially helpful when the behavior occurs too frequently to record ABCs or each occurrence, and when anecdotal records have not revealed a pattern of environmental correlates of the behavior. To make a scatterplot, the instructor uses a grid such as the one shown in Figure 7. Rates of behavior are recorded as either high, low, or zero within the time intervals. Once the grid has been completed for several days, it is compared with the class schedule, lesson plans, instructor assignment, meal schedules, and so on to determine if there is any correspondence between this information and the occurrence of interfering behavior. Once a relationship has been found, the instructor can then review Figure 5 or conduct a discrepancy analysis to select an alternative skill. Or, the

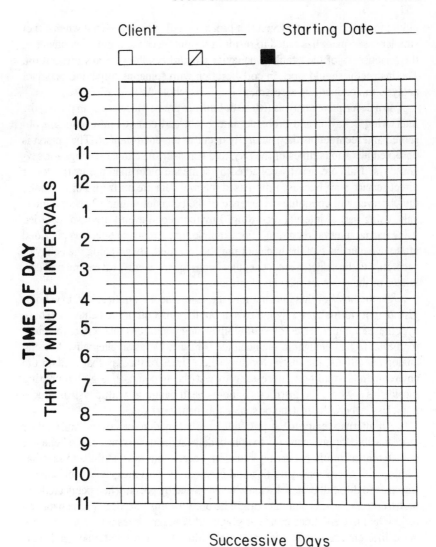

Figure 7. Scatterplot grid with a key at the top to indicate response frequencies corresponding to filled, slashed, and open boxes. Each location on the grid identifies a unique time interval on a given day. (From Touchette, P.E., MacDonald, R.F., & Langer, S.N. [1985]. A scatterplot for identifying stimulus control of problem behavior. *Journal of Applied Behavior Analysis, 18*(4), p. 344; reprinted by permission.)

instructor may review Figure 3 to note any simple environmental changes that could be made to prevent the problem behavior.

Step 4. Conduct a Descriptive and Functional Analysis
The most thorough evaluation of an interfering behavior would be to conduct a descriptive and functional analysis of behavior. Because of the resources re-

quired for this type of assessment, it probably will only be selected when either simpler assessment has failed to result in resolution of the problem behavior or the seriousness of the problem behavior jeopardizes the person's integration. The instructor should work in collaboration with someone trained in behavior analysis to conduct this assessment (e.g., psychologist).

In a descriptive analysis (Mace & Lalli, in press; Mace et al., in press), the interfering behavior and probable antecedent and consequent events are observed and recorded as they naturally occur in the environment. The person is observed at various times of the day, and across instructional settings for several days. Data are usually collected by someone other than the instructor or direct service staff because time-based interval data are utilized. For example, the observer will count the occurrence of the behavior within 10-second intervals, using partial interval recording. Environmental events are also recorded using partial interval recording. For example, occurrence of attention provided after the occurrence of the behavior may be recorded. By graphing the behavior according to the selected antecedent and consequent events, environmental correlates of the behavior may be identified.

On the basis of this information, the assessment team (teacher, psychologist, parent) formulates a hypothesis about the function of the behavior. These hypotheses are then tested by setting up analog conditions that reflect the environmental factors thought to maintain the behavior. Or, as an alternative to using analog conditions, the instructor may select times of the day that contain the environmental conditions necessary to test the hypothesis (e.g., comparing music class, where the instructor ignores head banging, with physical education class, where the instructor scolds this behavior).

An alternative approach to conducting a functional analysis that may be more feasible for instructors is to collect data on the occurrence of the behavior in different naturally occurring situations (e.g., with new adults and familiar adults, with classroom activities and community activities, with well-known lessons and difficult or new lessons, when teased by peers, when peers are loud or disruptive). Scatterplot data might be used for this purpose. These data can be graphed in trend lines or as bar graphs of cumulative responses to compare these different conditions. Figures 8 and 9 illustrate a modified functional analysis of behavior (described later in this chapter in the case studies). This type of analysis can help the instructor identify skill deficits that were not obvious in the discrepancy analysis or that apply to numerous situations (e.g., the person has no way to communicate the need for help when annoyed by others). To conduct this alternative form of functional analysis, the instructor must have some hunches about what could contribute to the problem behavior. The investment of this cross-time evaluation to find out which hunch is correct would be reserved for occasions when: 1) simple environmental evaluation has provided no clues, 2) the problem continues to exist despite skill instruction based on the discrepancy analysis, and 3) the urgency of the problem justifies the investment of time to clarify what events set the occasion for this behavior.

Definition of behavior: whining, screaming, or crying that lasts more than a few seconds

Measurement: frequency of occurrence or nonoccurrence within each defined activity across the day using a tally sheet, duration of each occurrence using a stopwatch

Conditions for analysis:

1. Physical assistance—Nat receives 10 minutes of physical guidance from the teacher to help him perform an unknown response in his life skills instruction (varied activities).
2. Short lesson, no physical assistance, variation—Nat receives instruction (gestures, modeling, verbal instruction, stimulus cues, but not physical guidance) for 10 minutes.
3. Long lesson, no physical assistance, variation—Nat receives instruction (gestures, modeling, verbal instruction, stimulus cues, but not physical guidance) for 30 minutes (measure tantrums at end of lesson to have a 10-minute sample).
4. No variation—Nat receives 10 minutes of instruction that utilizes the same materials, activity, and instructions (not physical guidance) every day.

Sample data:

Lesson	Condition	Frequency	Total duration
Shoes on	1	1	4'32"
Clean up	2	0	0
Snack preparation	3	2	4'11"
Set table	4	1	0'45"
Pants off	4	0	0
Legos (toy)	1	1	4'5"
Toy play	2	0	0
Picture recognition	3	4	3'2"

Figure 8. A modified functional analysis of Nat's tantrums.

ONGOING ASSESSMENT

Once the target behaviors have been selected for the long-term curriculum plan and the annual plan, the instructor will develop methods to measure ongoing progress. Often, the assessment of social and interfering behaviors in research utilizes complicated time-sampling procedures that are difficult or impossible to replicate while teaching. (For a discussion of the pros and cons of time-sampling procedures, see Chapter 3.) While instructors typically rely on simple frequency counts of the target responses, sometimes other characteristics of the behavior can also be evaluated. Through use of a stopwatch, an instructor can time latency (e.g., of a social response) or duration (e.g., of screaming), and continue to teach. Qualitative judgments may also be used to evaluate the intensity of an outburst or the appropriateness of a social initiation such as touching. (For more information on methods of ongoing assessment, see Chapter 3.) Whichever procedure is utilized, it is important to define the target response in clear, measurable terms.

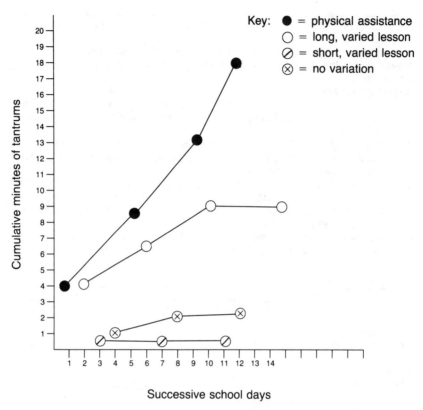

Figure 9. Graph of modified functional analysis that shows cumulative minutes of tantrums by condition.

The instructor must then decide how to get the best representative sample of the response. Some instructors record every occurrence of serious behaviors (e.g., hitting others) and their alternatives (e.g., tapping shoulder to get attention) throughout the day by using portable methods of data collection (e.g., clicker, masking tape on sleeve, pocket transfer of coins). Social responses may also occur at a rate that makes frequency counts across the day feasible. For example, an instructor can easily count occurrences of smiling when greeted by familiar people in the school and community across the day. The occasions for smiling may be as few as four or five per day. These occasions may also be embedded in a routine task analytic assessment, as described in Chapter 3. A behavior such as refusing by shaking the head "no," rather than spitting, may occur much more often, but still be easy to count. For example, early in intervention, the person may spit 10 times and communicate "no" once in a 15-minute lesson. Each occurrence of spitting and "no" could be, for example, tallied on paper or counted with two columns of a clicker. (Obviously, the instructor would arrange seating so that the person's peers were at minimal risk of being spit on until this behavior was eliminated.) Some responses, however, may not be amenable to all-day frequency counts. The instructor may then select representative times for data collection (e.g., social responses during children's recess or adults' coffee break) or use the scatterplot method (described earlier) for ongoing assessment.

As mentioned, interfering behaviors may be measured and graphed even if the treatment choice is to teach alternative skills and not to direct treatment to the interfering behavior per se. Such measurement allows the instructor to note the collateral changes in interfering behaviors as skills increase.

EVALUATION OF ONGOING ASSESSMENT

For evaluation, several data summaries may be useful: 1) lifestyle charts, 2) standard graph summaries of acceleration of communication or social skills, 3) routine summaries with embedded social or communicative skills, and 4) graphs on deceleration of problem behavior. To evaluate the summaries of communication and social skills and routines, the instructor can use the guidelines provided in Chapter 4. Chapter 10 also provides an example of a chart to evaluate lifestyle changes as part of program evaluation (see Figure 1). New guidelines are provided here for considering deceleration trends for interfering behavior.

As in collecting data on skill acquisition, a preintervention baseline is needed for problem behavior to evaluate the effectiveness of treatment. In applied settings with many serious interfering behaviors, a true no-treatment baseline may not be feasible. Rather, the "baseline" offers a picture of the pattern of behavior under preexisting intervention before a new intervention is tried. This baseline may be obtained from summaries of the number of incidents of the behavior (e.g., ABC forms), from the scatterplot data (i.e., number of intervals in which the behavior occurred), or from direct frequency counts of the behavior. The method of data collection selected for baseline should be continued during intervention to compare results.

Once the data are collected and graphed, the instructor can further summarize the data. This can be done by calculating the phase means for baseline and intervention. A second method to summarize the data is to draw a prediction line to estimate when the behavior will reach the criterion level. An example of phase means and a prediction line is shown in Figure 10.

To make a decision about continuation of intervention, the instructor can consider the typical effects of the procedure on behavior change. For example, extinction may have a delayed effect on problem behavior and may have an initial acceleration prior to deceleration (Sulzer-Azaroff & Mayer, 1977). Another consideration in extending intervention is the pattern of progress for the alternative behavior (which should also be graphed and evaluated). Figure 11 lists guidelines for instructors to make data-based decisions about intervention to decelerate unwanted behavior.

Directions: The teacher evaluates the data by comparing the mean for the baseline and intervention phases and draws a prediction line to estimate when the problem behavior would decelerate to zero.

Student: __Nat__   Behavior: __Tantrums—crying or loud screaming__

Assessment: Time each tantrum with a stopwatch. Add total minutes for the day.

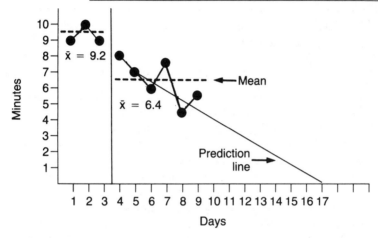

Dates: Nov.
6   7   8   11 12 13 14 15 18 19 20 21 22 25 26 27 28

Number of tantrums
3   4   2   4   3   2   4   2 3

Figure 10.   Example of data evaluation for a graph of problem behavior to be decelerated.

As part of the evaluation of treatment, the instructor may also want to review Table 1 and consider whether all steps have been followed in addressing the interfering behavior. For example, was an environmental assessment conducted? Does continuation of the problem behavior suggest that lifestyle planning is needed? Has adequate attention been given to developing an alternative response that can achieve the same function as the problem behavior? Is more extensive assessment of communication needed to select this alternative skill?

CASE STUDY EXAMPLES

A review of the case studies can illustrate how evaluators utilized these levels of assessment for individuals with interfering behaviors. In each example, the hierarchy of assessment shown in Table 1 was followed to identify an educative approach to the problem.

Trend	Other considerations	Decision
1. Clear, rapid deceleration		1. Continue intervention.
2. Evidence of deceleration ___ Intervention mean lower than baseline mean OR ___ Standard quarter intersect method shows decelerating trend	2a. Considerations to continue intervention ___ Acceleration in alternative behavior ___ First period of evaluation ___ Prediction line shows acceptable rate of deceleration 2b. Consideration to change intervention ___ None of 2a considerations present ___ Behavior presents physical danger ___ Behavior or intervention has created major disruption in instruction	2a. Continue intervention. 2b. Change intervention.
3. No evidence of deceleration (e.g., flat or accelerating or mean same as baseline)	3a. Consideration to continue intervention ___ Acceleration in alternative behavior ___ First period of evaluation ___ "Extinction burst" apparent 3b. Considerations to change intervention ___ None of 3a considerations present ___ Behavior presents a physical danger. ___ Behavior or intervention has created major disruption in overall intervention.	3a. Continue intervention. 3b. Change intervention.

Figure 11. Checklist to guide evaluation of graph for intervention to decelerate problem behavior.

Planning for Adult with Behavior
that Stigmatizes Him in Public: John

Ms. M. was concerned with John's screaming and grabbing people in public. In conducting John's environmental assessment, Ms. M. was pleased to note how much John's lifestyle had improved in recent years. He had obtained a home in the community in the last 2 years, after 40 years in an institution. In his continuing education program, John was gaining access to community facilities for the first time in his life. John typically had choices about where to go and what to purchase in the community. John's problem seemed to arise as part of his adjustment to a new lifestyle. Previously, he had not been in public settings. John's screaming was somehow related to access to the community. However, John liked to be in the community, and frequently asked to go to a restaurant or store.

Ms. M. used the Assessment of Social Competence (Meyer, Reichle, et al., 1985) as illustrated in Figure 5, to review John's social skills. Specific deficits related to the community outing were John's ability to manage his own behavior (John could not see or hear the negative reactions of others), his skill to obtain cues (John could not see when his companions were ready to leave), and cope with negatives (being asked to stay with his companions). Ms. M. began informally addressing these skill deficits as part of John's community routine. However, she also decided to give further attention to the interfering behavior itself.

When she reviewed the checklist shown in Figure 2, Ms. M. decided that while this was a Level III behavior, it warranted formal consideration because of public reaction to it (John had been asked to leave a public facility on some occasions). Since the behavior was setting specific, it seemed not to reflect a medical problem. In reviewing the environmental checklist shown in Figure 3, Ms. M. identified no ways to change the setting or John's routine to decrease the screaming and encourage his social skills. She concluded that she had verified that assessment was needed and began the ABC analyses.

Ms. M. found the results of the ABC analyses to be interesting. The function of John's screaming clearly seemed to be to leave the setting when he completed his activity (e.g., consumed his cup of coffee). In considering John's discrepant skills, Ms. M. noted that John had nothing to do in public once he had consumed his food. He could not see or hear what was going on in the environment, nor could he follow time to know how long he had to wait for his companions to be finished. Also, the functional equivalent communicative response to screaming would be for John to say "Let's go." Ms. M. selected these skills for John's curriculum: 1) state "Let's go"; 2) calm and occupy himself when asked to wait for someone, by listening to a portable radio with earphones (John could hear a radio at loud volume); and 3) interact with his companions by letting them order first, sharing food, and following their lead as sighted guides. For ongoing assessment, Ms. M. continued to use daily anecdotal records (ABCs). For each week, she summarized the number of outings with screaming and the number in which John independently used one or more of the target alternative skills. By John's quarterly review, it was clear that the days with screaming were decreasing, and John had had a few days when he used his alternative skills without prompting. Therefore, Ms. M. did not need to use the additional steps of assessment to identify the function of John's behavior problem.

Planning for Young Student's Tantrums: Nat

In Nat's case, Ms. S. and Nat's parents were concerned with his tantrums (i.e., loud, prolonged crying). Ms. S. began with an environmental assessment. Nat lived at home with his family. While other members of the family were active in community settings, Nat attended a private school and had few neighborhood friends. Ms. S. began talking with the school administrators and Nat's parents about an integrated placement for Nat. Since this lifestyle change would probably take a year of negotiation, and Nat's tantrums—which occurred in settings other than just the school—negatively affected the quality of life for Nat's family, Ms. S. decided to proceed with the assessment while advocating for a new placement for Nat.

In conducting a social skills assessment of Nat, Ms. S. noted that Nat's only means of offering negative feedback was to cry. He also could not manage his own behavior. Once upset, Nat usually cried until exhausted, which sometimes took an hour or longer. Nat also had not been observed to offer assistance. Ms. S. began teaching Nat to shake his head "no" to offer negative feedback and to help with routines at school, such as getting napkins for his classmates. Nat's tantrums, however, continued.

In reviewing Figure 2, Ms. S. concluded that while this was a Level III behavior, it required intervention because of the parents' concern and potential social reaction to Nat in an integrated setting. Ms. S. noted that Nat's medical checkups were up to date, and he indicated no cause for discomfort. Nat's tantrums also had existed for years. In a review of simple environmental changes, Ms. S. could find none to be made. Ms. S. had a schedule that involved Nat most of the day. His lessons incorporated functional skills and were designed to end in reinforcing events. Ms. S. also used a high rate of praise for Nat for responses he made during instruction and made many positive remarks to him during transitions.

Ms. S. then wrote ABC analyses for each tantrum for several weeks to look at specific activities when tantrums occurred. However, Nat's tantrums were so frequent she had trouble writing ABCs for each of them. She also could not yet identify what the function was for Nat's screaming. Ms. S. began a scatterplot assessment, using a form like the one in Figure 7. The scatterplot revealed that the tantrums were more likely to occur during certain activities of the day. One such activity was a lesson in dressing that was scheduled before physical education. When the instructor guided Nat to pull up his sweat pants, he would begin to cry. If she continued to try to help him, his cries became screams and lasted for up to an hour. The scatterplot revealed a pattern of tantrums during Nat's difficult lessons. Ms. S. decided to complete a discrepancy analysis to identify alternative skills Nat needed in activities where he was learning new and difficult skills. To identify discrepant skills, she talked to a teacher who had a young boy without disabilities about her son's dressing skills. She learned that this boy could dress without help for most items. When he could not put something on he came and asked his mother to do it. The teacher mentioned that her son also had often resisted her help when he was first learning to dress. Ms. S. noted that Nat had discrepant skills in dressing, and in signaling the need for help (he had no sign for "Help") or to be allowed to try alone (he had no sign for "I'll do it"). Since dressing was an important skill for Nat to acquire, Ms. S. decided that it was important to design instruction that motivated Nat to learn this skill with her. She selected objectives in dressing and communication. For ongoing assessment, she began to time tantrums in this and other lessons and to count the frequency of Nat's use of alternative communication for "I'll do it" (e.g., pointing to himself).

Although the dressing lesson improved, Nat continued to have tantrums throughout the day. His parents noted that their family life was seriously disrupted by Nat's continuing tantrums and once again asked the instructor to find a solution. Ms. S. decided to invest the time in a simplified functional analysis. She began to graph her data according to hunches she had about the variables maintaining Nat's tantrums.

She classified each tantrum by antecedents. For antecedents, Ms. S. noted tantrums that occurred when Nat: 1) could not perform a response and he was receiving assistance, 2) had been engaged in instruction on a skill for over 20 minutes, or 3) had received instruction on the same activity for over 2 weeks. She also measured the duration of the tantrum. Using cumulative minutes of crying, Ms. S. noted the highest number of minutes when Nat could not perform a response and she was assisting him and when the lesson was long. However, Ms. S. noted that Nat's noncumulative graph on number of minutes of crying per day had shown a sharp acceleration and now was decelerating. Ms. S. concluded that by continuing to teach Nat to sign the need for help or to try alone, selecting small amounts of behavior for Nat to learn in each lesson, and ignoring him when he cried instead of signing for help or to try alone, his tantrums would continue to decrease. These strategies were written and shared with the parents. Ms. S. also showed Nat's parents how to keep logs of Nat's behavior using the ABC format so that she and they could evaluate his generalization of alternative skills to the home environment. Ms. S.'s functional analysis data for Nat are shown in Figures 8 and 9.

SUMMARY

Social skills assessment can be an important component of a comprehensive assessment. Social skill deficits may be accompanied by interfering behavior or the absence of social competence. Because of the wide array of social skills that can be taught, an ecological inventory can be used to identify the skills needed for a person's current and future environments.

The objective of assessing social skills and interfering behavior is to develop intervention to improve an individual's social relationships. If opportunities do not exist for developing friendships and enjoying a wide range of people, this assessment may be misguided. Environmental assessment is thus a prerequisite to the assessment of social skills and interfering behavior.

Because of the limited skill repertoires of people with severe disabilities, deceleration of interfering behavior alone is rarely an appropriate goal. Rather, the instructor considers the need for lifestyle enhancement and identifies the function of the interfering behavior to teach alternative skills. Identifying the function of problem behavior can be a time-intensive effort. This chapter offers a sequence of steps to follow from less intensive to more intensive assessment. Instructors need only use the assessment steps necessary to identify the function of interfering behavior (e.g., anecdotal records), and reserve more complex assessments for problems that are persistent or extremely serious.

STUDY QUESTIONS

1. What can a professional learn from environmental and social assessments, and why are these important prerequisites to the assessment of interfering behavior?
2. What are the steps to assessment of interfering behavior?
3. What type of data is important for ongoing assessment of interfering behavior?

FOR FURTHER THOUGHT

1. Why is it important to have an organized approach to assessing interfering behavior rather than just trying interventions to eliminate the problem?
2. For an individual with interfering behavior, consider the lifestyle questions and social skills given in this chapter. Is the interfering behavior indicative of the need for lifestyle and social skills enhancement?
3. Try the step-by-step approach to assess an interfering behavior and evaluate whether you agree with the author's sequence for obtaining information.

chapter 9

ASSESSMENT OF INTEGRATION AND GENERALIZATION

Christina L. Ager and Diane M. Browder

INTEGRATION AND GENERALIZATION are the most important outcomes for all assessment planning. In Chapter 2 and Chapter 5, the methodology of personal futures planning was described. Personal futures planning is a process that can be used to enhance the quality of life for individuals with severe disabilities. The process involves identifying new options for individuals to have more satisfying and enriching life experiences and providing the support needed to achieve these options.

Once new options have been identified, assessment for integration can be a form of support to enhance successful change. Initial assessment for integration can identify specifics about the integration environment that can confirm the match between person and setting and identify potential problems. This initial assessment can also identify skills for instruction to enhance the person's participation in the environment.

Skill generalization can further enhance an individual's options for a satisfying and enriching life. If the individual has learned to use skills across environments, for example, participation in a variety of settings or in new settings may be increased. Too often, instructors focus solely, or primarily, on assessment of skill acquisition. This chapter provides guidelines for initial and ongoing assessment of generalization. Guidelines for evaluation of generalization data are also included.

INTEGRATION ASSESSMENT

Initial Assessment for Integration

Many individuals with severe disabilities still spend a large portion of their day in segregated settings. These settings may be segregated schools, segregated classrooms, or residential environments. School integration is the focus of discussion in this chapter; ideas for home, community, and job integration assessment were offered in Chapters 5 and 6. Once a commitment is made to an individual to advocate and provide support for increased integration, several assessment strategies can enhance the planning for these efforts. The first step is to identify new options for integration. Identifying new options requires professionals to engage in creative thinking or in having a "dream" for what could exist for an individual. Once the vision for the integration ideal has been developed, assessment can provide important information for a successful transition. In some settings, "mergers" of special and regular services are occurring, with the student integrated for the entire school day in a regular class. In such instances, initial assessment for integration is not applicable and the reader is referred to ongoing assessment of integration in the section to follow. To some extent, temporal integration (e.g., moving to a regular school building) must be pursued as a first priority, whatever the student's skills may be, if social and curricular integration are to be enhanced. However, in many settings, once the building transition is made, integration into the school environment involves a transition time of increasing options for students. This section on initial assessment is for those teachers who are working toward increased school integration.

Two types of assessment can enhance this transition. The first is to consider the student's strengths and preferences in selecting opportunities within the school. The second is to use an ecological inventory to confirm the match between student and setting, and to identify potential problems so solutions can be tried at the onset of the integration.

Envisioning the Integration Options   In traditional special education assessment, the professional often began with a battery of tests for a student. Based on the student's performance on these tests, placement options were then considered. Placement options were often highly restricted for students with severe disabilities because they were viewed as "not ready" or as "functioning" too low for integrated settings.

To move beyond stereotypes about options for people with severe disabilities, professionals need a new assessment approach. An approach that has become increasingly popular is to envision options for a person and find ways to achieve these options *regardless of the person's disabilities*. Lifestyle planning (O'Brien, 1987) and personal futures planning (Mount & Zwernik, 1988) are used to refer to this process when applied to a person's home, work, and community options. An application to integration planning for school settings is called the McGill Action Planning System (MAPS) (Vandercook, York, & Forest, 1989). This planning process can then set the agenda for any further assessment of the student and his or her new environments. Also, MAPS becomes an ongoing process to continue brainstorming new options and problem solving when difficulties arise with integration.

MAPS (Vandercook et al., 1989) is a team process involving the student, family members, friends, and both special and regular education personnel.

Teachers who have worked in multidisciplinary or transdisciplinary programs with therapists will find the process similar—except that the circle of professionals is expanded to include regular class teachers, and the setting of focus is regular class and other school environments (e.g., cafeteria, playground). Another important difference is that classmates without disabilities who have begun to form friendships with the individual are also included. Together, the team addresses seven questions in a long meeting (e.g., planning retreat) or series of meetings:

1. What is the individual's history?
2. What is your dream for this individual?
3. What is your nightmare?
4. Who is the individual?
5. What are the individual's strengths, gifts, and abilities?
6. What are the individual's needs?
7. What would the individual's ideal day at school look like and what must be done to make it happen?

The reader is referred to Vandercook et al. (1985) for case studies of the MAPS process. Some of the information generated in the MAPS sessions for one student named Catherine is shown in Figure 1. The possibilities for change shown in Figure 1 became the agenda items for this team to continue to address until her plan for integration was achieved.

Assessment to Support the Transition   Once integration goals have been targeted, assessment can be conducted to support this transition. One type of assessment that can help confirm the match between person and setting is an ecological inventory. As described in Chapter 2, an ecological inventory is used to assess the environment to identify skills an individual may require in that environment or challenges that can be met through adaptations. Figure 2 provides an example of an ecological inventory used for integration planning for Eva. (This inventory was designed to be "generic": It has applicability for increasing job and community integration, as well as school integration.)

Eva's case study illustrates an application of this process for planning for integration. One of the activities identified as ideal for Eva was the middle school's needlepoint club. Eva enjoyed needlepoint, and this small club seemed to enhance close friendships between its members. To conduct the ecological inventory (see Figure 2), Mr. N. met with Ms. Taylor, the faculty advisor for the needlepoint club, to negotiate Eva's joining the club and to interview her about the specifics of the club (the numbers in parentheses that follow refer to the item number on the inventory in Figure 2).

The club was located in a hall adjacent to Eva's classroom, so it would be fairly easy for her to learn to go there without assistance (1,4). The primary activity of the club (2) was cross-stitch, and it met on Fridays at 2:00 P.M. (3). The five girls and two boys in this club were not into fashion trends, so Eva's

Catherine's priority needs identified by family, friends, and educators

Family	Friends	Educators
For others to know she is not helpless	More friends	More friends
Music and time to listen to it	Support to get more places and learn things there	Support to get more places and learn things there
Affection	A lot of opportunity to walk and use her hands	A lot of opportunity to walk and use her hands
To be with people	As an adult, to live in a small home with friends in a community where she is accepted	Opportunity to let people know what she wants and a way to communicate that with more people
To change environments and surroundings often	Teachers to accept her	To increase the opportunity and skill to make more choices
Healthy foods	To learn to hang onto the book when a friend is reading with her	Affection
		People to know how to: deal with her seizures, help her stand up, and accept and deal with her drooling

Tuesday morning schedule for Catherine: Moving toward the ideal school day

Time	Catherine's day (current)	3rd-grade day (current)	Possibilities for change (proposed)
9:00–9:30	Take off coat Use restroom Adaptive physical education	Pledge of Allegiance Seat work directions Spelling	Breakfast (could eat with nondisabled peers if school arrival coincided)

276

Time			
9:30–10:00	Breakfast Work on lip closure, holding the spoon, choosing objects she wants	Reading Group I Others do seat work, write stories, read silently	Switch center (in 3rd-grade reading) Transition to center, reaching, touching picture, activating tape player
10:00–10:45	Switch center Transition to center, reaching, touching picture, activating tape player using microswitch (leisure activity)	Physical education (10:00–10:20) Mousercize, Exercise Express, Use restroom Reading Group II (10:25–10:45)	Physical education (with 3rd grade) Skills related to maintaining ambulation and mobility (e.g., weight shifting, balance reactions, strength exercise) Cooperation with peer partner Rest time
10:45–11:10	Reading Group III (with 3rd grade) Make transition to floor, respond to greeting from peer, reach for peer's hand, hold onto book, look at book, close book, make transition to standing	Reading Group III	Maintain current activity with 3rd grade
11:10–11:30	Library (with 3rd grade) Return book, choose book, look at it, check it out, return to class	Library	Maintain current activity with 3rd grade

Figure 1. Examples of information generated in MAPS sessions. (From Vandercook, T., York, J., & Forest, M. [1989]. The McGill Action Planning System [MAPS]: A strategy for building the vision. *Journal of The Association for Persons with Severe Handicaps, 14,* 210; used with permission.)

Site Needlepoint Club	Interviewee Ms. Taylor
Date September 15th	Instructor Mr. N.
	Learner Eva

1. Travel/location (answer by traveling to site). What method of transportation will be needed for this site (e.g., van, pedestrian skills)?
   Meets in the school—no transportation needed.
   Is site accessible to wheelchairs?
   Not applicable for Eva.

2. What are the primary activities of the site (types of jobs, if vocational; activities, if leisure facility; services, if public facility; curriculum, if public classroom)?
   Cross-stitch and similar needlepoint.

3. What is the site's schedule (e.g., class time, hours open, work hours required)? What are the best times for integrated instruction (e.g., less busy times in public facilities, teacher's preferred times for regular class)?
   2:00 P.M. Friday.

4. To what extent are orientation/mobility required (e.g., sits in one place versus multiple rooms or stairs)?
   The club meets in "J" wing—close to Eva's classroom.

5. How important is a neatly groomed appearance? Other considerations regarding appearance?
   Girls and boys who attend are not into fashion trends.

6. What type of communication is required (e.g., placing orders, asking for help, asking for a locker)?
   Students converse while they sew.

7. What type of social interaction skills are required (e.g., working in groups versus being alone)?
   Students are close friends and talk about their experiences; no one works alone.

8. What type of help/assistance is available to individuals (e.g., peer instruction, information booths, job foreman)?
   Because of their friendship, students assist each other (e.g., to untangle thread).

9. How often does the site change routines or physical layout?
   Never—always just come and sew.

10. To what extent are other people in the site expected to be quiet/still versus tolerance for a range of behaviors (e.g., contrast theater and football game)?
    Students who come are generally quiet as they converse.

11. What natural reminders (cues) and rewards (contingencies) are available?
    Students are kind to each other; praise each other's work.

(continued)

Figure 2. Example of ecological inventory for integration planning.

Figure 2. *(continued)*

12. What is the interviewee's attitude toward the participation of individuals with disabilities in this site?
Cautious—wants to maintain the comfortable, friendly atmosphere of the club.

13. Will escorted assistance in restrooms or for eating or dressing be acceptable?
Not applicable for Eva—independent.

14. Are there any other special considerations for instruction for and in this site?
No.

clothes, though a bit juvenile for her age, would not be a problem (5). The club was run informally, allowing the students to talk while they sewed, so Eva's lack of conversational skills might be a challenge for adaptation (6,7). The students frequently helped each other when someone made a mistake, and the cross-stitch samplers had a wide range of difficulty. Eva would probably be able to perform the task with help from her peers (8). Because this club rarely changed its routine (i.e., sitting and sewing), it would be a good match for Eva's preference for consistency (9). However, it was a quiet group who rarely argued, so Eva's occasional outbursts would be another challenge for an adaptation, such as her requesting to leave when upset (10). However, the students also were kind, often praising each other's work, so Eva would have a rich supply for reinforcement for sticking with the task (11). The advisor's attitude toward having Eva join the group was cautious (12). Thus, it might be advisable to have Mr. N. accompany Eva for the first few club sessions to serve as her social "interpreter" until Ms. Taylor became familiar with Eva's subtle communication style. Eva would not need an escort in the restroom (13).

After this meeting with the needlepoint club advisor, Mr. N. thought this was an excellent match for Eva. He felt that by attending the first few sessions, to serve as Eva's interpreter, he could model how to converse with her, teach her to request leaving when distressed, and ease Ms. Taylor's apprehension about having a student with autism in the club.

A second type of initial assessment can provide accountability for IEP objectives being met in integrated settings. In this approach, the student's IEP objectives are listed on a matrix. Current and potential integration sites are also listed. The teacher can then determine how different sites might be conducive to meeting IEP objectives. A form for this planning is shown in Figure 3.

Eva's case study provides an example of this type of initial assessment. Eva's IEP objectives can be found in Chapter 2, Figure 13. Her school integration sites are physical education, home economics, homeroom, and needlepoint club. Mr. N. decided that the home economics class would be an excellent context for Eva to work on her sight words (e.g., recipe words), menstrual care, hanging up clothes, and age-appropriate dressing. These skills could be easily coordinated with the home economics units taught (e.g., personal grooming,

Student's name: Eva			Date: October 1		
	Settings				
Objectives	Community	P.E.	Home Ec.	Homeroom	Club
Sight words			+		
Purchase item	+				
Follow schedule				+	
Conversation		+			+
Group games		+			
Menstrual care			+		
Needlework					+
School mobility		+			
Clothing selection			+		
Order from menu	+				
Play basketball		+			

Figure 3. Example of matrix for planning IEP instruction in integrated settings. (+ = objective to be addressed in particular setting.)

foods and nutrition, clothing care). The physical education class would be an excellent context for working on her basketball skills, group games, social conversation, and school mobility. Homeroom would be a context for checking Eva's generalization of her conversation training; however, direct teacher instruction in this context would be intrusive. By contrast, peer tutoring on reading her daily schedule would be appropriate to the setting and would meet a skill need of Eva's. In the needlepoint club, specific needlework skills would be targeted, as well as social conversation. While Mr. N. planned to teach some of these skills in the special education classroom during natural opportunities for their use in the school-day routine, he had confidence that Eva's integration would also be directly related to meeting objectives of her IEP.

Ongoing Assessment of Integration

Once the instructor has identified the IEP objectives to be achieved in the integration settings, ongoing assessment can be developed to monitor progress. In Chapter 3, numerous recommendations were given for ongoing assessment; as noted, assessment of routines is most important. Additional task analytic or repeated opportunity assessment of specific skills can be used to supplement this routine assessment.

Figure 4 provides an example of a routine assessment for Eva's participation in the needlepoint club. As the figure shows, the variety of skills targeted for this setting are assessed by scoring the level of assistance and time variables associated with each. Mr. N. can use this routine assessment to evaluate Eva's

Instructional Data Sheet

Manager: **Mr. N.**

Name: **EVA**
Routine: **Needlepoint club (Passive Leisure)**
Date: **10-1**

Beginning natural cue: **Friday schedule; 2:00 p.m. bell**
Critical effect: **Sampler to take home**
Latency: **1 min.**   Duration of routine: **45-min. class**

Duration	Step	Assistance	Date	Date	Date	Assistance	Date	Date	Date
1'	1. Get materials	Verbal	ED	C	ED	Verbal + "hurry"			
3'	2. Go to activity area	Independent locate room	C+	C+	C+	Independent			
30"	3. Choose materials	Nonspecific verbal	C	ED	ED	Nonspecific verbal			
30'	4. Do activity (cross-stitch)	10 stitches with model	C	C	C	10 stitches with verbal			
5'	5. Request help	Nonspecific verbal	EL	C	EL	Nonspecific verbal			
5'	6. Interact with peers	Independent greeting	M	C+	C+	Independent greeting			
30"	7. End activity	Independent-bell rings	C+	C+	C+	Independent			
1'	8. Clean up materials	Verbal	M	C	C	Verbal			
3'	9. Return to room	Independent	ED	C	ED	Independent			

EL = Latency error
E = Response form error
ED = Duration error
C = Correct

Total duration: _____

© = Communication target

Program changes:
/ = Change in assistance
// = Change in consequence

Figure 4.   Example of form used for routine assessment. (+ = independent, NV = nonspecific verbal, G = gestures, V = verbal, M = model, PP = partial physical, P = physical, O = resists assistance.) (Blank form courtesy of Neel, R.S., & Billingsley, F.F. [1989]. *IMPACT: A functional curriculum handbook for students with moderate to severe disabilities* [p. 137]. Baltimore: Paul H. Brookes Publishing Co.; reprinted by permission.)

progress across time, as described in Chapter 4. It is important to note that Mr. N. would not conduct this assessment using a clipboard and stopwatch while trailing Eva down the hall of the school and into the needlepoint club, because of the stigma it would create for Eva. Rather, he would take data discreetly (e.g., by glancing at his watch to note times and making notes on a memo pad similar to that carried by most regular class teachers) and record the performance of each response on the clipboard kept in the classroom.

In addition to the routine, some high-priority skills for Eva might be monitored with specific skills assessment. For example, Mr. N. might conduct task analytic assessment of Eva's cross-stitch skills or repeated opportunity assessment of a social response. Due to Eva's limited conversational skills, he targeted teaching her age-appropriate greetings currently popular in the middle school as a starting point (e.g., "Hey," "Yo," "Que pasa"). He decided to do a repeated opportunity assessment of this specific skill in two ways. First, to be sure Eva had enough opportunities for practice, Mr. N. prompted the regular class peers who visited the room between periods to greet her so she could learn to be "cool." He scored her response to them using the data sheet shown in Figure 5. Also, as a generalization assessment, he counted the times she responded to or initiated greetings when changing classes. These generalization probes were "scored" by transferring pennies from one pocket to the other while casually walking down the hall near Eva as she went to physical education. Data were taken for generalization weekly and for classroom instruction daily. These specific skills data were evaluated on a biweekly basis to make instructional decisions, as described in Chapter 4. A decision made from the data is shown in Figure 5. As the figure indicates, transfer of stimulus control from the teacher's prompts to the natural cue of the peer's model was not occurring adequately (inadequate progress; mean increase was less than 5 %). Therefore, Mr. N. decided to delay his prompt by 10 seconds to encourage this transfer. This would result in more independent (+) responses, and thus, a higher mean increase in the next phase.

GENERALIZATION ASSESSMENT

Although skill acquisition occupies much of our instructional time, generalization may be the most important phase of the learning process. Generalization ensures true functionality by increasing the probability that the skill will be used across natural environments. Behaviors are generalized if they occur across settings, time, relevant objects, and/or people. In short, behaviors are generalized if they occur appropriately and spontaneously as needed. Behaviors that are to be considered functional are those that serve (or will serve) some extra instructional purpose valued by the individual and/or demanded by the community. Generalizing performance of target skills to nontraining environments is critical to both the success and the maintenance of skill acquisition and behavior change.

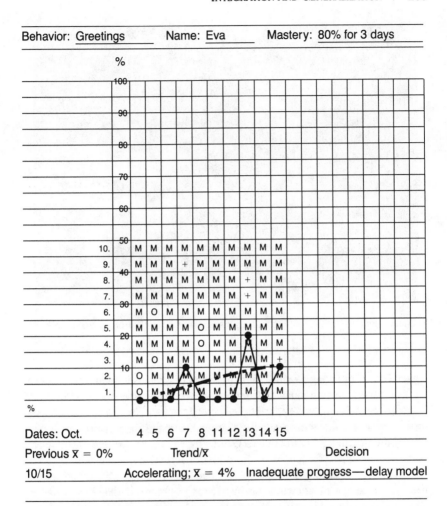

Figure 5. Example of specific skill assessment (repeated opportunity) for an integrated setting. (+ = independent, M = teacher model, O = no response.)

Initial Assessment of Generalization

Despite being of critical importance, generalization may be overlooked in educational planning for two reasons. First, instructors may fail either to assess generalization or to consider it as a component of skill acquisition. Second, after skills have been acquired, instructors may neglect to plan strategies to extend performance. The following methods are suggested for making generalization a part of initial assessment: 1) scatterplots, 2) decision rules, 3) general case assessment, and 4) assessment of pivotal behavior. Many of these strategies are also amenable to ongoing assessment of generalization, which is dis-

This instructor assesses this young man's generalization of handling stock. In this photo he is stocking produce in a job tryout in a food co-op.

cussed in the following section. Whichever strategy is used to assess generalization, instructors first must consider how to set up the assessment or "probe."

Format for Conducting Generalization Probes   Three basic formats may be utilized for conducting generalization probes: 1) direct observation by the instructor 2) direct observations by others, and 3) retrospective reports. Each of these formats is useful under different circumstances.

Directly observing learners' performance during generalization probes has the advantage of allowing the instructor to obtain firsthand information about the generalized performance. There are, however, a number of disadvantages associated with the instructor conducting these probes. One is that it may be hard for an instructor to interact with the learner in a natural manner. Having instructed the learner during acquisition, the instructor is more likely to provide cues or prompts unknowingly during the generalization probe. Another disadvantage is that the instructor's presence in the setting may act as a signal for the learner to perform the target skill.

To maximize the information gathered during a generalization probe, instructors should be as unobtrusive as possible. Covertly observing the individual from a distance while others in the environment (e.g., clerk) interact with him or her will result in better information being obtained than hovering close to the individual to record each discrete response.

Soliciting someone else to observe generalized use of a skill is a good strategy when opportunities to use the generalized skill are infrequent, when key features of the behavior are subtle, and when the behavior is easily overlooked or performed when the individual is alone. Skills to ask others to observe include saying "thank you" (which may be overlooked because it is expected) and playing alone with a hand-held video game. Also, as the use of certain communicative gestures may be subtle at first, it may be necessary to ask parents to look for their use.

Instructors would be wise to facilitate these direct observations by others and maximize the information gathered during these probes (White, 1988). Providing the observer with a small packet of materials may be helpful. This packet might include a description and examples of the targeted skill; suggestions for how and when to observe; acceptable cues, prompts, and assistance; and appropriate consequent events.

Retrospective reports provide the easiest and least expensive way to assess skill generalization. Retrospective reports involve asking someone in the natural environment, who is in the position to know, whether or not the individual performs the skill. For example, the instructor could ask parents whether their child can feed him- or herself with a spoon. Retrospective reports are also useful when natural opportunities for skill demonstration occur often enough for an accurate assessment to be made, and when the consequences of using or not using the skill are obvious or dramatic. When one or more people can be identified who are aware of whether a skill is being used, retrospective reports are an effective strategy.

Brief telephone interviews can be used to obtain accurate information from retrospective reports. Telephone interviews allow follow-up and clarification questions to be asked immediately, thus enabling the instructor to obtain the required information. White (1988) suggested five strategies to increase the accuracy of the information obtained during the interview. First, the instructor should prepare a list of questions prior to making the call, to help focus the questioning around critical information. Second, the instructor should describe the skill simply and ask the interviewee if she or he has seen the individual use it. Additional questions can then be asked to obtain more specific information. Initially, asking about broad skills may result in unexpected answers concerning what skills a learner is capable of performing within the natural environment (e.g., the instructor should inquire about the learner's independent dressing skills versus the skill of putting on socks). Third, the instructor should find out if there are sufficient opportunities for the behavior to occur. Parents may report that their child does not dress him- or herself. However, parents may dress the individual daily—not allowing an opportunity for independent dressing. If skill use is reported, it is still important to ascertain how many times skill performance has been observed and when. (Reports of skill use more than a few days prior to the call should be viewed with skepticism.) Fourth, the instructor should determine under what conditions the skill is being used. For example, does the individual independently initiate dressing or will he or she only get dressed after considerable prompting or nagging by the parents? Additionally, the instructor should ask if special prompts or assistance are given, and whether the consequences for the behavior are natural or artificial. The conditions under which the behavior is performed in the natural environment may provide valuable information for planning effective instructional programs. Finally, the instructor should ask for an overall evaluation of "satisfaction." It is important to determine whether the behavior is performed well enough that it will be maintained in the natural environment, or whether skill performance is so poor or slow that it is easier for the parents to do it themselves. If the latter is true, it is unlikely that sufficient opportunities will be provided to maintain the behavior within the natural setting.

After conducting the generalization probe, the instructor should record the information on a report. This report provides an organizational framework for the assessment information gathered during the probes. Figure 6 provides an example of the generalization probe report for Al.

Using Scatterplots to Assess Generalization   Scatterplots have been used to help identify patterns of responding in natural settings and to determine stimulus control of problem behaviors (Touchette et al., 1985; see also Chapter 8, this volume). Using a grid with time intervals along the ordinate and days along the abscissa, instructors can fill in the blocks of time contingent on occurrences of behavior.

In addition to being valuable assessment tools for discerning stimulus events that affect problem behaviors, scatterplots are also useful to assess skill use across the day. In Figure 7, Nat's use of verbal requests for assistance were plotted across 1 week (days 1–5). It was noted that during independent activities, Nat made requests for assistance. However, during small- or large-group activities Nat did not use this skill. Utilizing this information, Ms. S. began generalization training in group settings. Ms. S. continued plotting Nat's use of verbal requests (days 6–17). The scatterplot reflects increased use of verbal requesting across all settings. In this way, using scatterplots is an effective way to assess settings to which behavior needs to generalize as well as documenting generalization of targeted skills.

Scatterplots are generally easy to use and allow data collection to be conducted in a short amount of time. The benefit over simple graphs of behavior frequency is that scatterplots allow the visual assessment of patterns of responding. Being aware of patterns of responding enables instructors to target settings or activities where generalization needs to occur and choose target behaviors that are more likely to generalize to other behaviors. As an assessment tool, scatterplots provide valuable information to direct-care staff.

Decision Rules for Generalization   Discussions of decision rules thus far in this text have focused on skill acquisition. Recently, however, decision rules designed to improve instructional programming for generalization have been developed and tested (Liberty, White, Billingsley, & Haring, 1988).

Generalization Probe Report

Student: *Al*   Date: *4/1*

IEP Objective:[*] *Clean restrooms in job Setting to satisfaction of employer and in less than 20 minutes.*

Student Performance[*]

(1) Who provided the information on student performance?
Custodian in setting

(2) Was the skill directly observed for this probe?
yes

(3) How many opportunities did the student have to perform the skill?
2 restrooms

(4) When were the opportunities provided?
beginning of work day

(5) Did the student perform the target skill?
yes

(6) Did the student display inappropriate behavior or a previously learned skill instead of, or in addition to, the target skill?
no

(7) Did the student fail to respond?
yes

(8) Describe the student's performance: *Only cleaned one toilet — not all four. Did not fill towel on toilet paper dispensers*

Probe Situation

Reinforcers Accessed by Student[*]

(9)	( )	Were natural reinforcers for performance of the skill.
(10)	(✔)	Were not natural reinforcers for the skill.
(11)	( )	Included both natural and not natural reinforcers.
(12)	( )	Person reinforced inappropriate behavior, other behavior, or nonresponse, with reinforcer which should have been available for performance of skill.
(13)	( )	Student accessed natural reinforcer by doing something else.
(14)	( )	Person attended to other behavior.
(15)	(✔)	Person completed the skill task.
(16)	( )	Person physically assisted the student to complete the skill task.
(17)	( )	Person provided another reinforcer.
(18)	( )	Student did not access reinforcers.

Describe what happened: *Custodian praised what was done well and and then completed the job*

_____

(continued)

Figure 6.   Example of generalization probe report. (Asterisk note: see also Figure 8 for discussion of "Decision Rules.") (Blank form courtesy of Liberty, K.A. [1988]. Decision rules and procedures for generalization. In N.G. Haring [Ed.], *Generalization for students with severe handicaps: Strategies and solutions* [p. 181]. Seattle: University of Washington Press; reprinted by permission.)

Figure 6. *(continued)*

Stimuli Which Triggered the Opportunity to Perform the Skill*

(19) ( ) Were natural stimuli which occurred without need for intervention.
(20) (✓ Were naturally provided by persons in the generalization situation.
(21) ( ) Were not natural stimuli for the skill.
(22) ( ) Included both natural and not natural stimuli.
(23) ( ) Included training stimuli.
(24) ( ) Other:

Conditions Which Differed From Instruction (Check all that apply)*

(25) (✓ Materials or objects. Describe: *Different paper dispensers*

(26) (✓ Setting. Describe: *Trained in school restroom prior to job placement*

(27) (✓ Probe manager or persons who interacted with student.
(28) ( ) Person cued the student what to do.
(29) (✓ Person did not cue the student what to do.
(30) ( ) Person encouraged the student.
(31) ( ) Person did not encourage the student.
(32) ( ) Person physically assisted or physically prompted the student.
(33) ( ) Person did not physically assist or prompt the student.
(34) ( ) Person reinforced as often.
(35) ( ) Person reinforced less frequently.
(36) ( ) Student's performance criticized/corrected more frequently.
(37) ( ) Student's performance criticized/corrected less often.
      ( ) Person provided feedback on performance, especially errors or mistakes.
(38) (✓ Person did not provide feedback.
(39) ( ) Person praised the student during/after skill performance.
(40) ( ) Person did not praise the student.
(41) ( ) Other:

*Answers needed to apply Decision Rules.

These decision rules for generalization are an extension of decision rules for skill acquisition and fluency building into the area of skill performance in untrained situations (Liberty, 1985). Five major problem areas and corresponding remedial strategies are addressed by these rules. Use of these rules has been documented with results in 75%–80% of the instructional changes supporting the validity of the rules (Liberty, Haring, et al., 1988).

After completing a generalization probe, as described earlier (see Figure 6), the instructor can apply the decision rules for generalization (Figure 8), which are presented as a series of questions. (If being used as part of initial assessment, a current IEP/IHP objective can be targeted with conditions for generalization specified for this assessment.) Information about learner performance probe situations is used to answer each question in sequence. The answer to each question will determine whether to continue with the questioning, or to stop because the type of decision to be made has been identified. Figure 9 provides an example of the decision rules for generalization completed for Al's

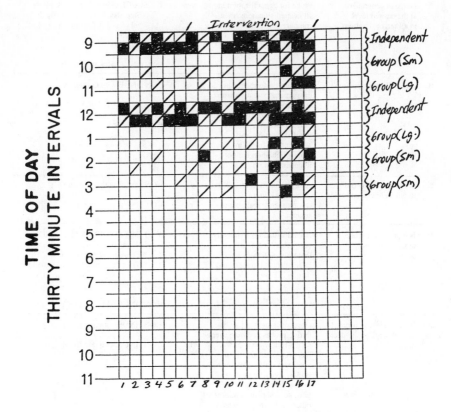

Figure 7.   Scatter plot grid used to assess generalization of Nat's verbal requests for assistance. (Blank grid courtesy of Touchette, P.E., MacDonald, R.F., & Langer, S.N. [1985]. A scatter plot for identifying stimulus control of problem behavior. *Journal of Applied Behavior Analysis, 18*[4], p. 344; reprinted by permission.)

generalization probe. As the figure shows, Mr. A.'s decision stopped at question F, which identified a reinforcement problem. A modification was then made so that the alternate behavior was no longer providing access to the same reinforcer as the target behavior did. A second problem then developed. The rules were reimplemented and Mr. A.'s decision stopped at question I, which indicated an additional need for training.

Decision Rules for Generalization

QUESTION	PROCEDURES	ANSWER	NEXT STEP/DECISION
A. Has skill generalized at the desired level in all target situations?	Probe for generalization in all desired situations, then compare performance with criteria (IEP objective).	yes	**1 SUCCESSFUL INSTRUCTION** * Step ahead to a more difficult level of skill * Choose a new skill to teach EXIT sequence
		no	CONTINUE with question B.
B. Has skill been acquired?	Compare performance in instructional situation with criteria for acquisition or performance levels specified in IEP objective. Answer yes if student has met performance levels in training situation but not in generalization.	yes	CONTINUE with question C.
		no	**2 SKILL MASTERY PROBLEM** * Continue instruction EXIT sequence
C. Is generalization desired to only a few situations?	Analyze function of skill in current and future environments available to student.	yes	CONTINUE with question D.
		no	CONTINUE with question E.
D. Is it possible to train directly in those situations?	Are all situations frequently accessible for training so that training time is likely to be adequate to meet aim date in IEP objective?	yes	**3 LIMITED GENERALIZATION SITUATIONS** * Train in desired situation * Train sequentially in all situations (i.e., sequential modification) EXIT sequence
		no	CONTINUE with question E.
E. Is the student reinforced even though he/she does not do the target skill?	Observe student behavior during probes and note events which follow appropriate, inappropriate, target, and nontarget skills. Determine if those events which should follow the target skill, or have been shown to reinforce other skills, are presented to the student, or available even if he does not respond, or if he does the skill incorrectly, or if he misbehaves.	yes	CONTINUE with question F.
		no	CONTINUE with question H.
F. Does the student fail to respond and is reinforced?	Answer yes only if the student is reinforced for doing nothing (i.e., accesses reinforcers for "no response").	yes	**4 NONCONTINGENT REINFORCER PROBLEM** * Alter generalization contingencies
		no	CONTINUE with question G.

(continued)

Figure 8. Decision rules for generalization. (From Liberty, K.A. [1988]. Decision rules and procedures for generalization. In N.G. Haring [Ed.], *Generalization for students with severe handicaps: Strategies and solutions* [pp. 182–183]. Seattle: University of Washington Press; reprinted by permission.)

Figure 8. *(continued)*

QUESTION	PROCEDURES	ANSWER	NEXT STEP/DECISION
G. Is the behavior reinforced by the same reinforcers as the target skill?	If misbehavior or other behavior accesses same reinforcer available for target skill, answer yes.	yes	**5 COMPETING BEHAVIOR PROBLEM** * Increase proficiency * Amplify instructed behavior * Alter generalization contingencies EXIT sequence
		no	**6 COMPETING REINFORCER PROBLEM** * Alter generalization contingencies EXIT sequence
H. Did the student generalize once at or close to criterion performance levels and then not as well on other opportunities?	Consider performance in current and past probes. Compare student performance for each response opportunity with performance level specified in objective. If near criterion performance occurred on the first response opportunity, and performance was poor or nonexistent after that, answer yes.	yes	**7 REINFORCING FUNCTION PROBLEM** * Program natural reinforcers * Eliminate training reinforcers * Use natural schedules * Use natural consequences * Teach self-reinforcement * Teach to solicit reinforcement * Reinforce generalized behavior * Alter generalization contingencies EXIT sequence
		no	CONTINUE with question I.
I. Did the student respond partially correctly during at least one response opportunity?	Analyze anecdotal data and observation notes from probe.	yes	**8 DISCRIMINATION FUNCTION PROBLEM** Vary stimuli: * Use all stimuli * Use frequent stimuli * Use multiple exemplars * Use general case exemplars EXIT sequence
		no	CONTINUE with question J.
J. Did the student fail to perform any part of the target skill?	Analyze student performance during probe situation.	yes	**9 GENERALIZATION TRAINING FORMAT** * Increase proficiency * Program natural reinforcers * Use natural schedules * Use appropriate natural stimuli * Eliminate training stimuli EXIT sequence
		no	*STOP.* You have made an error in the sequence. Begin again at Question A.

General Case Assessment One strategy used in programs designed to increase generalization across various situations has been to program for the general case. General case programming includes identification of the group of situations across which generalization is desired (the instructional universe) and the range of stimulus and response variation. Instruction is then conducted on the minimum number of examples that sample the complete range of stimulus and response variation. As the full technology of general case instruction is beyond the scope of this chapter, the reader is referred to Horner et al. (1982).

Generalization Decision Report

Student **Al**   Skill **Clean restrooms.**

Decision-Maker **Mr. A.**   Date **4/5**

QUESTION	ANSWER	DECISION	COMMENTS
A. Has skill generalized at the desired level in all target situations?	yes	**1 SUCCESSFUL INSTRUCTION** ( ) Step ahead to a more difficult level of skill ( ) Choose a new skill to teach	
	(no)	CONTINUE with question B.	
B. Has skill been acquired?	(yes)	CONTINUE with question C.	
	no	**2 SKILL MASTERY PROBLEM** ( ) Continue instruction	
C. Is generalization desired to only a few situations?	(yes)	CONTINUE with question D.	
	no	CONTINUE with question E.	
D. Is it possible to train directly in those situations?	yes	**3 LIMITED GENERALIZATION SITUATIONS** ( ) Train in desired situation ( ) Train sequentially in all situations [i.e., sequential modification]	*Al's ongoing job*
	(no)	CONTINUE with question E.	*placement is tentative.*
E. Is the student reinforced even though he/she does not do the target skill?	(yes) no	CONTINUE with question F. CONTINUE with question H.	*Custodian completes job.*
F. Does the student fail to respond and is reinforced?	(yes)	**4 NONCONTINGENT REINFORCER PROBLEM** (✓) Alter generalization contingencies	*No praise for known tasks; ask Custodian to praise filling dispensers.*
	no	CONTINUE with question G.	
G. Is the behavior reinforced by the same reinforcers as the target skill?	yes	**5 COMPETING BEHAVIOR PROBLEM** ( ) Increase proficiency ( ) Amplify instructed behavior ( ) Alter generalization contingencies	*Not applicable*
	no	**6 COMPETING REINFORCER PROBLEM** ( ) Alter generalization contingencies	
H. Did the student generalize once at or close to criterion performance levels and then not as well on other opportunities?	yes	**7 REINFORCING FUNCTION PROBLEM** ( ) Program natural reinforcers ( ) Eliminate training reinforcers ( ) Use natural schedules ( ) Use natural consequences	

(continued)

Figure 9. Example of generalization decision report. (Blank report courtesy of Liberty, K.A. [1988]. Decision rules and procedures for generalization. In N.G. Haring [Ed.], *Generalization for students with severe handicaps: Strategies and solutions* [pp. 184–185]. Seattle: University of Washington Press; reprinted by permission.)

Figure 9. *(continued)*

QUESTION	ANSWER	DECISION	COMMENTS
		( ) Teach self-reinforcement ( ) Teach to solicit reinforcement ( ) Reinforce generalized behavior ( ) Alter generalization contingencies	
	(no)	CONTINUE with question I.	
I. Did the student respond partially correctly during at least one response opportunity?	(yes)	8 DISCRIMINATION FUNCTION PROBLEM Vary stimuli: ( ) Use all stimuli ( ) Use frequent stimuli ( ) Use multiple exemplars ( ) Use general case exemplars	*Can do dispensers at school – use multiple exemplars of dispensers & restrooms with variation in number of stalls*
	no	CONTINUE with question J.	
J. Did the student fail to perform any part of the target skill?	yes	9 GENERALIZATION TRAINING FORMAT ( ) Increase proficiency ( ) Program natural reinforcers ( ) Use natural schedules ( ) Use appropriate natural stimuli ( ) Eliminate training stimuli	
	no	*STOP*. You have made an error in the sequence. Begin again at Question A.	

Figure 10 provides an example of how general case analysis can be used for assessment. The individual was assessed at four convenience stores: Penn Supreme, Nick's, 7-11, and Kate's. Generalization deficits were found for all steps except step 5, "Wait in line." The specific generalization deficits are shown in the last column. The assessment shows that this individual needs instruction across variations of doors, item displays, cashier counters, and cashier styles (e.g., stating price only, not bagging items). Concurrent instruction across Penn Supreme, Nick's, and 7-11 would be appropriate since these three stores provide the variation needed for the generalization deficit training.

Assessment of Generalized Responsivity and Pivotal Behaviors Often, people with severe disabilities who are allowed little control over their environment learn to be unresponsive. This failure to respond to environmental stimuli may further seriously inhibit behavioral and educational development. Although generalization is usually thought of in terms of specific skills or behaviors, generalized responding is a prerequisite for an individual's ability to generalize specific behaviors.

Research has begun to analyze the role of responsivity as a pivotal behavior (R.L. Koegel & Koegel, 1988). Responsivity involves making frequent discriminatory responses to complex environmental stimuli. It is important to assess whether the learner is responsive to his or her environment, and, if not, to program for increasing responsivity. This assessment can be done easily by considering the following questions:

GENERAL CASE ASSESSMENT FOR ONE-ITEM PURCHASE

Instructional Universe: Convenience stores in Lehigh Valley, PA

Generic responses: task analysis (TA)	Assessment Data: Sites to sample stimulus/response (SR) variation (parentheses show S/R variation for that TA step in that site)				Assessment Summary: generalization deficits
	Penn Supreme	Nick's	7-11	Kate's	
1. Enter store	+ (electric door)	− (push)	− (pull)	− (push)	Push/pull door
2. Locate item	− (multiple aisles)	− (display case)	− (aisles)	+ (behind clerk)	Scan aisles and cases
3. Pick out item	+ (bottom shelf)	− (open case)	− (top shelf)	+ (clerk selects)	Shelf location and opening case
4. Take item to counter	+ (large counter)	− (small counter)	− (small counter)	N/A	Size/location of counter
5. Wait in line	+	+	+	N/A	Mastered
6. Pay cashier	− (clerk states price)	+ (clerk extends hand)	− (clerk states price)	− (clerk states price)	Verbal cue
7. Take change/item	− (change with no bag)	− (no bag)	− (change and bag)	+ (bag)	Unbagged item Change cups
8. Leave store	+ (electric door)	− (pull)	− (push)	− (pull)	Push/pull
Number Correct/ Total Responses:	5/8	2/8	1/8	3/6	
Date of Probe:	Nov. 3	Nov. 10	Nov. 12	Nov. 15	

Figure 10. Example of general case assessment for one-item purchase, based on Horner, McDonnell, and Bellamy (1986). Prior to this assessment, the teacher defined the range of stimulus and response variation (not shown). The results of assessing purchasing skills at four convenience stores (Penn Supreme, Nick's, 7-11, Kate's) that sample this variation are shown. (+ = independent correct, − = incorrect or needed prompting, NA = not applicable to that site.) (From Gaylord-Ross, R., & Browder, D. [1990]. Functional assessment: Dynamic and domain properties. In L.H. Meyer, C.A. Peck, & L. Brown [Eds.], *Critical issues in the lives of people with severe disabilities* [p. 58]. Baltimore: Paul H. Brookes Publishing Co.; reprinted by permission.)

1. Does the individual make frequent responses to environmental stimuli?
2. Does the individual switch responding from one stimulus to another relatively frequently?
3. Does the individual make more responses to complex (multicomponent) stimuli than to simple stimuli?
4. Does the individual make frequent responses that relate stimuli to one another?

It is important to note that a person may be responsive in one environment, but not in another. When considering generalization of behaviors to untrained situations, assessing the individual's responsivity in the natural environment may aid the instructor in developing sound generalization strategies. For example, the instructor may find that a learner's responsivity is particularly low during recess on the playground because playmates may perform the activity for him or her.

If the learner is not typically responsive to his or her environment, two ways to increase responsivity are: targeting learners' motivation to respond to their environment, and teaching learners to self-monitor their responsivity. To assess ways to increase responsivity, the instructor may try: 1) prompting responding even when responses are incorrect (R.L. Koegel, O'Dell, & Koegel, 1987); 2) arranging learning tasks to increase the probability of success; or 3) interspersing maintenance tasks with new learning trials (Dunlap, 1984; L.K. Koegel & Koegel, 1986).

In each case, keeping a frequency count of the number of responses the individual makes under varying conditions will allow for the assessment of increased responsivity. For example, if the number of responses when maintenance tasks are interspersed with acquisition tasks is greater than when only new learning trials are presented, the instructor may want to modify subsequent instructional plans so that responsivity is maximized for that individual.

Writing Objectives Based on Generalization Assessment

At the end of initial assessment, IEP/IHP objectives should be written for generalization. The basic components of sound educational objectives have traditionally included specification of: 1) the learner, 2) the behavior to be exhibited, 3) the conditions under which the behavior should occur, 4) the criteria and aim date, and 5) the persons responsible for determining success. In addition to these basic components, generalized outcomes should be specified within the instructional objective. The value of objectives learned within instructional settings is reduced if target behaviors fail to be performed within the natural environment. Inclusion of generalized outcomes within the instructional objective will increase the likelihood that generalized responding is both planned for and assessed. Regrettably, research has found that a large percentage of objectives written for individuals in special education classes specify the performance of targeted behaviors in only one training situation (Billingsley, 1984; Kayser, Rallo, Rockwell, Aillaud, & Hu, 1986). A generalized outcome is specified if an objective requires the individual to perform the behavior in a situation or situations other than the training situation. These new situations might include new people, different times, alternate materials, or new settings. Non-training situations specified in the objective should reflect the range of situations the learner will encounter outside of training. Table 1 presents examples of objectives that specify a generalized outcome.

The criteria for successful performance may differ within training and generalization situations. There are three reasons why these differences may be appropriate. First, the criteria selected for training may be dictated by the con-

Table 1. Objectives that specify a generalized outcome

Example 1

By the end of the school year, Eva will demonstrate the ability to shop for 10 specific brand-name grocery items, using picture cards, at three different food markets, on three occasions each: Linden Street Market (455 Linden Street), Food Mart (532 Broad Street), and Barnum's Foods (892 Chester Avenue). Performance includes transportation to and from the store, selecting the items, and paying for the purchases, and must be completed within 60 minutes from leaving school, with no errors. Success will be determined by the instructor.

Example 2

By December, Nat will complete lunch at home within the amount of time deemed appropriate by his mother. Lunch completion includes eating lunch at the kitchen table, putting the dishes in the sink, and wiping the table, within the same time as the rest of the family (about 40 minutes). Success will be determined by his mother.

straints of the instructional environment (Billingsley, 1988). For instance, Nat (see Table 1, Example 2) may be required to finish lunch during training in school within 25 minutes (instead of 40 minutes, as at home) because this is the time allotted for lunch within the school schedule.

Second, the criteria for skill mastery may need to surpass natural demands to increase the likelihood that the target behavior will be performed in novel situations (White, 1985). Generalization criteria may be either less stringent or less precise. Example 2 in Table 1 illustrates the use of a less precise criterion by stating that the duration is that "deemed appropriate by his mother." This criterion may also be less stringent than the 25 minutes allotted for lunch at school.

Third, generalization data may have to be collected by individuals other than the instructor, such as parents or shopkeepers. For instance, in Example 1 in Table 1, the instructor might want to determine success by interviewing the three shopkeepers to see if Eva's performance falls within the norm of others shopping in the stores. Thus, these data will often be secondhand, and not as precise as data taken in the instructional setting. As such, the criteria for appropriate generalized performance may often be stated in terms of the satisfaction of another person in the natural environment.

It is not necessary that every objective include a generalized outcome. Initial objectives that target a level of functioning requiring large amounts of caregiver assistance may not include a generalization criterion. However, it is important to note that these types of objectives should be followed by more useful objectives targeting use of the acquired skill that would contain a generalized outcome.

Ongoing Assessment of Generalization

Instructors have at least two options for ongoing assessment of generalization. The first is to use the decision rules for generalization presented in Figure 8.

This method relies on a more qualitative appraisal of performance. At the least, generalization probes are scheduled prior to and following instruction. Probes may also be scheduled during the course of instruction if desired. As described earlier, significant others in the learner's environment (e.g., employer, parent) may be involved in this appraisal.

A second option is to utilize a data-based approach to assessing generalization. For a data-based approach, the types of assessment described in Chapter 3 can be utilized. Methods to apply this assessment to generalization are now described for fluency, maintenance, and generalization across tasks or settings.

Fluency Liberty (1985) noted that there are two phases of learning: acquisition and fluency. While acquisition is measured by accuracy, fluency is usually evaluated using a time-based measure. If an acquired skill is not fluent, it probably will not be used by the individual or encouraged by caregivers. The skill of putting on a shirt can serve as an example. While a learner might perform all of the steps in the task analysis to put on the shirt, this might take 10 minutes. The caregiver probably will not be able to allow 10 minutes in a busy morning routine for the individual to put on his or her shirt. Also, the individual may engage in an alternative response (e.g., whining until helped) that results in faster access to reinforcement (having the shirt on) even though he or she has "learned" to put on the shirt alone. Thus, instructors need to consider fluency objectives after acquisition of a response has occurred.

Fluency assessment may measure one or more dimensions of time: latency, duration, or rate. The choice of dimension depends on the skill to be evaluated. For example, in the dressing example given above, the important time dimension is the duration of dressing (i.e., the total time to put on the shirt). In a communication response, latency can be critical. For example, if an individual does not locate an appropriate response in a picture communication wallet within a socially acceptable time period, the listener may lose interest in the conversation (especially if the listener is another child). Rate is important for vocational assembly tasks, especially if pay is based on rate. Other skills may require more than one time dimension assessment to meet normalized criteria for fluency. For example, to master crossing streets with a light, the individual needs to respond in a short latency to the green light, and cross in the duration of time before the light turns red.

To set the time-based criteria for fluency, the instructor can use social validation procedures (see Chapter 2). For example, the instructor might measure the latency of communicative responses for several peers without disabilities. Or, the criteria for rate of vocational assembly can be identified through an interview with the employer. Naturally occurring consequences (e.g., the traffic-light example above) also may dictate the time dimension for normalized use of the skill.

Once the instructor has made the transition from acquisition instruction to fluency instruction, he or she may still need to decide when to change instruction if the fluency objective is not being achieved. To evaluate acquisition of fluency once a criterion has been set, the instructor should use a time-based measure (e.g., stopwatch) and graph performance accordingly. Figure 11 is a graph indicating deceleration of duration of loading a dishwasher. To evaluate

Behavior: Unload dishwasher   Name: Al   Mastery: 5 min./2 days
"Beat the clock"

Total number of minutes to load dishwasher (full load)

	20 20 20 20 20 20 20 20	20 20 20 20 20 20 20 20 20 20 20 20
	19 19 19 19 19 19 19 19	19 19 19 19 19 19 19 19 19 19 19 19
	18 18 18 18 18 18 18 18	18 18 18 18 18 18 18 18 18 18 18 18
	17 17 17 17 17 17 17 17	17 17 17 17 17 17 17 17 17 17 17 17
standard	16 16 16 16 16 16 16 16	16 16 16 16 16 16 16 16 16 16 16 16
quarter	15 15 15 15 15 15	15 15 15 15 15 15 15 15 15 15 15 15
intersect ♦	14 14 14 14 14 14	14 14 14 14 14 14 14 14 14 14 14
line of progress	13 13 13 13 13 13	13 13 13 13 13 13 13 13 13 13 13 13
	12 12 12 12 12 12 12	12 12 12 12 12 12 12 12 12 12 12
	11 11 11 11 11 11 11 11	11 11 11 11 11 11 11 11 11 11 11
	10 10 10 10 10 10 10 10	10 10 10 10 10 10 10 10 10 10 10 10
	9 9 9 9 9 9 9 9	9 9 9 9 9 9 9 9 9 9 9 9
	8 8 8 8 8 8 8 8	8 8 8 8 8 8 8 8 8 8 8 8
	7 7 7 7 7 7 7 7	7 7 7 7 7 7 7 7 7 7 7
	6 6 6 6 6 6 6 6	6 6 6 6 6 6 6 6 6 6 6 6
	5 5 5 5 5 5 5 5	5 5 5 5 5 5 5 5 5 5 5 5
	4 4 4 4 4 4 4 4	4 4 4 4 4 4 4 4 4 4 4 4
	3 3 3 3 3 3 3 3	3 3 3 3 3 3 3 3 3 3 3 3
	2 2 2 2 2 2 2 2	2 2 2 2 2 2 2 2 2 2 2 2
	1 1 1 1 1 1 1 1	1 1 1 1 1 1 1 1 1 1 1 1
***********	0 0 0 0 0 0 0 0	0 0 0 0 0 0 0 0 0 0 0 0

♦ Prediction line

Dates:
Oct./Nov.   7 8 9 10 11 14 15 16 17 18 21 22 23 24 25 28 29 30 31 1

Reviews		
Date	Trend	Decision
10/16/85	Flat	Change consequences. "Beat the clock"
10/26/85	Deceleration	Predict mastery 11/1.
		No change in instruction.

Figure 11.   Example of trend estimation for a fluency graph.

progress during the regularly scheduled review for each objective, the instructor can draw a line of progress to see if progress in performance is occurring. The instructor may also want to extend this as a prediction line to see if this rate of progress is acceptable. That is, will the individual reach the criterion in a reasonable period of time (see prediction line in Figure 11)? If not, the instructional decision most pertinent for fluency building (i.e., *what to change*) is to improve consequences for fluent performance (e.g., set a timer and allow the individual access to a preferred activity if he or she can "beat the clock"), or to teach more efficient ways to perform a task.

Maintenance Another extended performance objective that should be set is maintenance of the skill when instructor assistance and artificial consequences have been withdrawn. The instructor may want to set fluency objectives first, then, once these criteria have been met, measure maintenance. As stated previously, performance that does not meet normalized time criteria probably will not be maintained by naturally occurring consequences. To measure maintenance, the instructor can periodically probe performance once instruction has ended. If performance regresses below the established criteria for fluent performance, an instructional decision is needed for maintenance training. Maintenance training might involve reintroducing and fading more gradually the artificial consequences used to teach the skill. Or, the learner might be taught to self-manage the skill. This data collection and evaluation should be continued until the individual meets preset criteria for maintenance (e.g., across a month without instruction, or across a summer).

Sometimes, maintenance is naturally required by breaks in school programs. When a learner has not yet achieved a level of performance that will maintain without instructor assistance, such breaks can have a devastating effect on progress across years of instruction. The courts have tended to support extended school years (i.e., summer programs) for individuals who demonstrate skill regression during program breaks (*Armstrong v. Kline*, 1979; *Battle v. Commonwealth*, 1980; *Georgia Association of Retarded Citizens v. McDaniel*, 1979; *Mahoney v. Administrative School District No. 1*, 1979). Unfortunately, few guidelines exist for the evaluation of skill regression to determine extended school year eligibility (Browder & Lentz, 1985; Browder, Lentz, Knoster, & Wilansky, 1988).

Evaluation of skill regression is feasible if the instructor is maintaining graphs of ongoing assessment. Shorter breaks, such as winter vacation, may indicate regression. If the break had continued for 3 months (i.e., summer break duration), and a prediction line were drawn for the anticipated regression, then a case could be made for the substantial regression that would be predicted to occur. When evidence to justify an extended school year is inadequate, maintenance data can be compared and evaluated for all objectives from the spring to fall if the same graphs are used in September as were used in June. The time required by the individual to recoup the skill after the summer can also show the impact of the summer break on his or her long-term progress. Figure 12

Criteria	Source of information (secure written copies, attach to this form, and return to student's file)	Date of source	Supports ESY (yes or no)
Maintenance data			
Prior summer regression/poor recoupment (based on a summer when ESY was not offered; may apply to one or more IEP objectives).	1. Parent correspondence 2. Teacher report 3. Testing: pre/post summer 4. Ongoing data on IEP: spring to fall comparisons[a]	___	___
Current predictors of regression (during short winter breaks).	1. Parent correspondence 2. Teacher report 3. Testing: pre/post break 4. Ongoing data on IEP[a]	___	___
Current strategies are too complex and time consuming to be transferred to family full time for summer.	1. Parent correspondence 2. Teacher report 3. Written plans 4. Data on teacher behavior[a] 5. Other ___	___	___
"Maintenance" strategies have had inadequate success with student.	1. Parent correspondence 2. Teacher report 3. Ongoing data on IEP[a] 4. Other ___	___	___
Other considerations			
Family is highly stressed by student's care needs or behavior problems.	1. Parent correspondence 2. Teacher report 3. Other ___	___	___
Recent behavioral/medical problems may cause severe regression if a break in program occurs.	1. Parent correspondence 2. Teacher report 3. Ongoing data on IEP[a] 4. Medical report 5. Other ___	___	___

Figure 12. Checklist for assessment of extended school year (ESY) eligibility. ([a]Utilize for data-based eligibility decision.) (From Browder, D., Lentz, F.E., Knoster, T., & Wilansky, C. [1988]. Determining extended school year eligibility: From esoteric to explicit criteria. *Journal of The Association for Persons with Severe Handicaps, 13*[4], 241; reprinted with permission.)

provides an evaluation checklist to use in considering extended school year eligibility.

Generalization Another type of extended performance that is necessary to achieve normalized use of a skill is generalization, which may be taught during acquisition. For example, in teaching the manual sign for "more," the instructor may introduce use of this sign across activities and materials from the beginning of instruction. However, further generalization might be targeted for extended performance evaluation (e.g., across people, across settings). In other cases, generalization may not have been addressed in acquisition training, and multiple generalization goals may be targeted for extended performance.

The evaluation of generalization might be scheduled at several phases: 1) during acquisition, 2) before fluency, 3) concurrently with instruction in fluency, 4) after fluency training, or 5) concurrently with maintenance evaluation. The example shown in Figure 13 included a phase to assess generalization during and after acquisition, but before fluency training was begun.

The evaluation in Figure 13 provides an illustration of ongoing assessment from Nat's case study. The skill shown is washing hands. Acquisition training was conducted in the classroom and school restroom. Weekly probes of generalization to a nontraining site were conducted at the fast-food restaurant where Nat was learning to order lunch. After mastery of handwashing, Nat had not generalized this skill to the untrained site. Thus, the instructor, Ms. S., implemented instruction in this site and assessed another site for generalization (use of restroom while shopping).

While this training for generalization across sites was begun, Ms. S. also implemented fluency training in the school sites. If Nat "beat the clock" to get his hands washed, he could listen to music until the rest of the class was ready for the next activity (e.g., lunch). Once criteria for fluency were achieved, Ms. S. implemented a maintenance evaluation phase in which she no longer set the clock or told Nat that he could listen to music if he finished on time. Nat had free access to a tape player after use of the restroom. Nat's fluency regressed. Then, Ms. S. taught Nat to self-evaluate whether or not he should use the tape player by prompting him to sign "fast" when he finished quickly and "no" when he dawdled. She then faded her prompting and Nat maintained his fluent handwashing across the next month. Ms. S. also probed fluency in the community sites on a few occasions and found that even though the tape player was not present, Nat was finishing quickly and signing "fast." Ms. S. then discontinued data collection for this skill because she had evidence that it was acquired and extended to normalized use.

SUMMARY

Supporting integration and identifying generalization deficits are crucial components of initial and ongoing assessment. For integration planning, an instructor should begin with an outline or design for a learner's integration, verify the

Behavior: __Wash hands__   Name: __Nat__   Mastery: __100% for C, S, R__

Step																					
	20	20	20	20	20	20	20	20	20	20	20	20	20	20	20	20	20	20	20	20
	19	19	19	19	19	19	19	19	19	19	19	19	19	19	19	19	19	19	19	19
	18	18	18	18	18	18	18	18	18	18	18	18	18	18	18	18	18	18	18	18
	17	17	17	17	17	17	17	17	17	17	17	17	17	17	17	17	17	17	17	17
	16	16	16	16	16	16	16	16	16	16	16	16	16	16	16	16	16	16	16	16
	15	15	15	15	15	15	15	15	15	15	15	15	15	15	15	15	15	15	15	15
13. Discard towel.	14	14	14	14	14	14	14	14	14	14	14	14	14	14	14	14	14	14	14	14
12. Dry hands.	13	13	13	13	13	13	13	13	13	13	13	13	13	13	13	13	13	13	13	13
11. Get towel or push blowers.	12	12	12	12	12	12	12	12	12	12	12	12	12	12	12	12	12	12	12	12
10. Turn off cold water.	11	11	11	11	11	11	11	11	11	11	11	11	11	11	11	11	11	11	11	11
9. Turn off hot water.	10	10	10	10	10	10	10	10	10	10	10	10	10	10	10	10	10	10	10	10
8. Rinse hands.	9	9	9	9	9	9	9	9	9	9	9	9	9	9	9	9	9	9	9	9
7. Put soap on back of hands.	8	8	8	8	8	8	8	8	8	8	8	8	8	8	8	8	8	8	8	8
6. Rub soap on palms.	7	7	7	7	7	7	7	7	7	7	7	7	7	7	7	7	7	7	7	7
5. Get soap from dispenser.	6	6	6	6	6	6	6	6	6	6	6	6	6	6	6	6	6	6	6	6
4. Rinse hands.	5	5	5	5	5	5	5	5	5	5	5	5	5	5	5	5	5	5	5	5
3. Turn on hot water.	4	4	4	4	4	4	4	4	4	4	4	4	4	4	4	4	4	4	4	4
2. Turn on cold water.	3	3	3	3	3	3	3	3	3	3	3	3	3	3	3	3	3	3	3	3
1. Walk to sink.	2	2	2	2	2	2	2	2	2	2	2	2	2	2	2	2	2	2	2	2
	1	1	1	1	1	1	1	1	1	1	1	1	1	1	1	1	1	1	1	1
%	0	0	0	0	0	0	0	0	0	0	0	0	0	0	0	0	0	0	0	0

Dates: Nov. 4 5 6 7 8 11 12 13 14 15 18 19 20 21 22
Settings: C S C S R* C S C S R R R C S R

Reviews

Date	Trend/mean	Decision
11-14-85	Mastery C, S, Not R.	Train R (restaurant).
11-22-85	Mastery C, S, R.	Train fluency
		(Begin duration data graph.)

Figure 13.   Example of a graph showing generalization data during and after acquisition. (* = untrained site, C = classroom sink with paper towels and turn-knob soap dispenser, S = school restroom with paper towels and push-knob soap dispenser, R = restaurant with blow dryer and push-knob soap dispenser.)

match to settings with ecological inventories, and use a matrix to identify where IEP/IHP objectives will be addressed. Ongoing assessment of integration can provide information on progress in both routines and specific skills.

In assessing generalization, an instructor should observe performance in novel situations or collect information from significant others. The strategy for the generalization assessment might be a scatterplot, decision rules, general case, or assessment of responsivity. Ongoing assessment of generalization may rely on the decision rules or specific data summaries.

Further, the assessment of integration and generalization applies to all of the topics discussed in this book. The reader is encouraged to consider how the information presented in this chapter applies to assessment for the home and community and to assessment of related skills.

STUDY QUESTIONS

1. What is MAPS and how is it used for integration planning?
2. What are some examples of the assessment of integration?
3. What are some issues in assessing generalization?
4. Name and describe four types of generalization assessment.

FOR FURTHER THOUGHT

1. To what extent has integration been achieved in your program?
2. What is your goal for the integration of the individuals with whom you work?
3. What are some steps to achieving this goal?
4. How might you use the MAPS process to facilitate this goal attainment for individuals in your program?
5. Have you encountered instances of a failure to generalize?
6. Try using the decision rules in this chapter to identify why the failure occurred and how it might be resolved.

chapter 10

AN ASSESSMENT PLAN FOR SUPERVISORS

Diane M. Browder and MaryAnn Demchak

THROUGHOUT THIS BOOK, guidelines have been offered for instructors to develop an assessment plan for comprehensive educational evaluation. Through this careful planning, instructors identify priorities for instruction and evaluate progress toward these priorities. Similarly, supervisors who work with instructors in programs for individuals with severe disabilities need to set and evaluate priorities for overall program quality. This chapter offers suggestions for supervisors to plan program evaluation and to provide training through data-based supervision. These suggestions are also applicable to instructor goal setting and self-evaluation.

Program evaluation is a tool to determine if a program is meeting its stated goals. Thus, the first step in program evaluation is to identify a program's priorities. Once these priorities are established, the supervisor can develop a method of evaluation for each goal. If instructors assume the primary role in the assessment of these priorities through self- and peer evaluation, the supervisor's role may become that of quality enhancement. The supervisor may enhance quality by: 1) encouraging instructors' self- and peer appraisal, 2) providing periodic reliability assessment for instructors, 3) offering feedback on this assessment, and 4) helping instructors reach their goals through problem solving and resource procurement. Additionally, the supervisor may train new instructors in the components of excellence identified for a program. The following sections offer guidelines for select program priorities and for providing data-based supervision to support excellence in teaching. Also, suggestions are given for establishing ground rules with instructors about the use of supervisory data so that the most favorable results are accomplished.

SELECTING PRIORITIES FOR PROGRAM EVALUATION

Before evaluation begins, a program needs a clear mission statement and goals. In conducting program evaluation, professionals ask themselves, "Are we meeting the goals that we have set as steps toward achieving our mission?" To set program goals, it can be helpful for the organization or school district to establish a task force of administrators, instructors, and parents for this purpose. The task force may begin by conducting a self-assessment based on the components of best practice for programs for individuals with severe disabilities. Some consensus can be found in the literature (i.e., expert opinions) for the following best practices: 1) integration (e.g., regular schools, real jobs); 2) instruction in, as well as for, community settings; 3) a curriculum that focuses on age-appropriate, functional activities; 4) educative, positive procedures for problem behavior; 5) utilization of applied behavior analysis and normalization strategies (e.g., lifestyle planning) (e.g., Falvey, 1989; Gaylord-Ross & Holvoet, 1985; Goetz, Guess, & Stremel-Campbell, 1987; Horner, Meyer, & Fredericks, 1986; Snell, 1987; Wilcox & Bellamy, 1987b). Empirical support (i.e., data-based research) for the appropriateness of these priorities can also be found in the literature. For example, numerous studies exist in which individuals with severe disabilities acquired age-appropriate life skills through instruction that utilized applied behavior analysis procedures (for examples of this research, see Snell & Browder, 1986). Support for these priorities can also be developed logically. Donnellan (1984) described this logic as the "criterion of the least dangerous assumption." That is, it is probably less dangerous to assume that direct instruction of life skills in real settings will enhance community independence than to assume that individuals will generalize from artificial activities and settings to achieve this goal.

Meyer, Eichinger, and Park-Lee (1987) validated similar indicators of program quality by polling experts in severe disabilities, mental retardation, sensory impairments, and behavior therapy; state directors of special education; and parents. The Meyer et al. (1987) categories for program indicators are: 1) integration, 2) professional practices and home-school collaboration, 3) staff development, 4) data-based instruction, and 5) the criterion of ultimate functioning. (For definitions of these indicators, see Meyer et al., 1987.) A task force on program evaluation may want to begin by rating the program on each of these indicators and using this diagnosis of strengths and weaknesses to begin setting goals.

For example, the Urban Training Model of the Philadelphia School District interpreted the priorities of community-integrated instruction into program policy for a large, urban school district (McGregor, Janssen, Larsen, & Tillery, 1986). Philadelphia's priorities were explicitly stated as criteria for the program (see Figure 1). These criteria were selected after considerable collaboration among professionals from across the nation. They reflect not only the trends mentioned above, but operationalize these trends so that program evaluation can measure the degree to which each has been achieved.

Once program goals have been established, the supervisor needs to define the evaluation procedures for each and begin to conduct measurement. This

Program area	Components	Program area	Components
Assessment	Assessment tools and procedures are appropriate for the characteristics of the student and lead to the identification of functional skill needs.		are structured, consistent, and occurring throughout the school day in every instructional environment.
	The student's current performance and educational needs for increased independence and participation in the home, school, and community are specified.	Program implementation	Responsibilities of all paraprofessionals and student teachers providing instruction to the student are defined.
	Comprehensive assessments are completed for each student twice a year.		Instructional cues are effectively used and faded.
IEP	Annual student goals on IEPs reflect functional life skills leading to increased independence in the home, school, and local community.		Student-specific therapeutic techniques that are required for obtaining optimal performance in educational activities are used.
	Student objectives on IEPs are behavioral, measurable, and include the conditions required for successful performance.		Teaching techniques specific to student learning needs and current level of performance are effectively used.
	All students have complete and current IEPs with plans for providing related services, interactions with peers who are not handicapped, special therapeutic or adaptive equipment, and evidence of parent involvement.		Reinforcers which are effective and natural are systematically provided.
			Attention to student behavior is given when that behavior is appropriate rather than when it is inappropriate.
Parent involvement	Parent input on the student programs is solicited and feedback to parents on student progress is provided.		Generalization and maintenance of acquired skills is promoted by providing training in more than one activity, in more than one setting, and with more than one staff member.
	Regular communication is maintained with parents.		Each student's method of communication, as indicated on the IEP, is consistently used in all routine and structured activities.
	Parent involvement in student programs is facilitated.	Program evaluation	Data are collected on all objectives for all students.
Program organization and management	Instructional environments include classroom, school, and nonschool (community) settings.		Data are graphically plotted to evaluate the effectiveness of the instruction.
	The classroom is arranged to promote the learning of age-appropriate, functional skills in areas that simulate natural environments.	Integration	The class participates in the normal school routine.
	The materials are those naturally used in the performance of the activity.		An activity to promote interaction with nonhandicapped peers is planned and conducted.
	A master schedule which includes instructional activities, responsible staff members, and learning environments is designed and posted.		Information, attitudes, and appropriate interaction methods are modeled to regular education staff and students.
	Written instructional and emergency procedures are posted in the areas where they are used.	Transdisciplinary services	For students receiving related services, collaboration occurs between the teacher and specialist for planning and evaluating programs.
	Opportunities for student learning		For students with therapeutic goals, techniques are carried over into educational activities with input from the therapist.

Figure 1. Quality program checklist components. (From McGregor, G., Janssen, C.M., Larsen, L.A., & Tillery, W.L. (1986). Philadelphia's urban model project: A system-wide effort to integrate students with severe handicaps. *Journal of The Association for Persons with Severe Handicaps, 11,* 65; reprinted by permission.)

evaluation may include measures of: 1) staff performance, 2) learner skill acquisition or deceleration of problem behavior, 3) service delivery (e.g., hours of training), 4) program management (e.g., balanced budget, procurement of new resources), and 5) lifestyle measures (e.g., new jobs, social contacts). Newton et al. (1987) described applications of these types of measurement to supported living arrangements. For example, Figure 2 shows how lifestyle measures can be summarized on an ongoing basis. In this figure, the first set of line graphs shows the number of activities per week in which Mary has participated at home and in the community. The second set of graphs indicates the

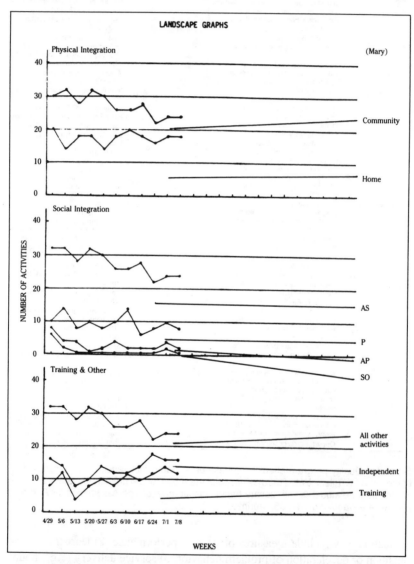

Figure 2. Lifestyle graphs. (From Newton, J.S., Bellamy, G.T., Horner, R.H., Boles, S.M., LeBaron, N.M., & Bennett, A. [1987]. Using *The activities catalog* in residential programs for individuals with severe disabilities. In B. Wilcox & G.T. Bellamy, A comprehensive guide to *The activities catalog: An alternative curriculum for youth and adults with severe disabilities* [p. 142]. Baltimore: Paul H. Brookes Publishing Co.; reprinted by permission.)

number of Mary's social activities in which she was accompanied by staff, peers, or significant others. The bottom set shows the number of Mary's activities that involved training, activities performed independently, and all other activities.

From such trends, instructors, support staff, and program directors can quickly see if a program is making progress toward increased integration. Similarly, data-based summaries of service delivery and staff performance can guide program evaluation for program improvement. The remainder of this chapter focuses on evaluation measures for staff performance. Learner progress summaries were described in Chapter 4.

SUPERVISION TO SUPPORT
EXCELLENCE IN TEACHING: DATA-BASED SUPERVISION

This chapter presents a method of program evaluation that is formative rather than summative. (The reader may refer to the introductory paragraph in Chapter 3 for definitions of formative and summative evaluation.) Professionals collect data on an ongoing basis to review progress toward annual program goals and make necessary changes when progress is inadequate (e.g., community activities are too infrequent). At the end of the year, a program director may provide a summative evaluation report for a board of directors or superintendent of schools. This report is more likely to reflect achievement of the year's goals if formative evaluation has also taken place.

Similarly, supervisors often provide summative evaluation to instructors and other direct service staff in compliance with personnel policy. However, if formative evaluation is also used, with the instructor as the primary evaluator of his or her own progress, the supervisor's summative evaluation can become an opportunity for praise, instructor recognition, and goal setting for the coming year. When instructors or staff are new to a program or to the profession, the supervisor may need to take a larger role in the formative evaluation to teach the staff member the competencies expected. However, since few programs have enough supervisors to maintain an intensive formative evaluation role for all staff, part of this training must be in self-evaluation so that the supervisor can fade his or her intensive involvement. Data-based supervision can be especially useful for this initial training and can be adapted for self-evaluation, as described at the end of this chapter.

DATA-BASED SUPERVISION PROCEDURES

To utilize data-based supervision, it is essential that the supervisor establish with staff the competencies that will be evaluated. Table 1 provides examples of instructor competencies used at Lehigh University for individuals entering the field of severe disabilities or beginning employment in the model programs.

Substantial literature on staff training supports the use of a data-based ap-

Table 1. Competencies for instructors of individuals with severe disabilities (used at Lehigh University to guide program evaluation)

Priority	Competency	Type of evaluation
1. Age-appropriate community-relevant plans.	At least six objectives based on ecological inventories across each domain and related skill; comprehensive assessment at least every 5 years.	Checklist for IEP. Checklist for comprehensive assessment.
2. Objectives and instruction operationally defined for each target behavior.	Every lesson has a written plan that meets checklist criteria.	Checklist for written plan.
3. Instruction matches operational definitions on plans.	90% of the observed teaching behaviors match definitions for three lessons.	Data-based observation of instruction.
4. Community-based and group instruction well planned and taught.	Same as #2 and #3 across one group lesson and one lesson in the community.	Same as #2 and #3. Supervisor goes with group in community to observe instruction.
5. Instructors interact with all learners positively, and encourage adaptive behaviors both in and between lessons.	Instructors use praise and attention as consequences for adaptive behaviors. For maladaptive behaviors, they give instruction, ignore, or reprimand (or use defined contingency).	Data-based observation of general behavior management.
6. Plans for problem behaviors follow an educative plan.	Plans written for each problem behavior meet checklist criteria.	Checklist for problem behavior plans.
7. Instructional plans revised to improve learner progress.	a. Data collection for each objective at least 3 times a week. b. Data collection 80% reliable. c. Graph meets checklist criteria. d. Data evaluation 90% reliable. e. Changes implemented within 1 week.	a. Graph. b. Reliability observation. c. Graph checklist. d. Data-based decision review. e. Change line on graph.

proach (see Demchak, 1987, for a review). Unfortunately, instructor supervision in special education has not kept pace with the precision of instruction expected of instructors (Markel, 1982). In particular, behavioral assessment of teaching that relates to learner behavior change has been rare (Csapo, 1981). For instructors of individuals with severe disabilities, instructor trainers have advocated and empirically supported using data to make instructional decisions about learners (Holvoet et al., 1983). Ironically, these same instructor trainers and supervisors often neglect to base instructor evaluations on observational data.

Collecting precise data on instructor performance has clear advantages over anecdotal strategies. First, and most important, observational data can help to validate the relationship between instructor behaviors and learner behavior change (Fredericks, Anderson, & Baldwin, 1979; Koegel, Russo, & Rincover, 1977). Second, ongoing data on instructor performance can document specific teaching behaviors or techniques that are acquired and maintained. Third, the data can form an objective basis of information provided to staff concerning their work behavior.

This feedback, in isolation or in conjunction with reinforcers (e.g., supervisor praise), may be provided through a variety of methods. Verbal feedback, comprising a verbal description of the observed behavior and verbal praise regarding specific staff behavior, has been demonstrated to be effective in improving staff behavior (e.g., K.M. Brown, Willis, & Reid, 1981; Realon, Lewallen, & Wheeler, 1983). A second type of feedback involves written messages concerning performance provided privately to individual staff members (e.g., Repp & Deitz, 1979; Shoemaker & Reid, 1980). A combination of written and verbal feedback may be most effective in communicating with staff (Alavosius & Sulzer-Azaroff, 1986; Dyer, Schwartz, & Luce, 1984). Another method of feedback, public posting, has been demonstrated to be effective (Greene, Willis, Levy, & Bailey, 1978; Hutchison, Jarman, & Bailey, 1980; Whyte, Van Houten, & Hunter, 1983), but may violate staff's right to confidentiality and may elicit negative staff reactions (Whyte et al., 1983). Public posting may be most appropriate for group efforts, such as increasing the amount of regular class integration within a school.

Even though it has been demonstrated that feedback can improve instructor behavior, the technology of data-based supervision is not well developed. While translating instructor behavior research into supervision practice can be difficult, the need for objective appraisals requires that supervisors do so. Resources to guide this practice have begun to emerge. For example, Stowitschek, Stowitschek, Hendrickson, and Day (1984) described procedures for supervisory observing of direct instruction. Page, Iwata, and Reid (1982) used validated instructor behaviors (i.e., procedures that facilitate learning) in their research on supervisors' use of an observational system. Their results support the feasibility of implementing data-based supervision with a staff of supervisors.

In a data-based approach, the supervisor reviews the teachers' written plans and also observes and evaluates instruction related to these plans.

The data-based supervision procedures that are presented in the remainder of this chapter were developed through review of the research on instruction and behavioral supervision, and were field tested at Lehigh University in the model programs for individuals with severe disabilities (Demchak & Browder, 1987). The competencies assessed by these procedures are listed in Table 1. These competencies can be generally divided into the areas of: 1) written plans for curriculum and instruction, 2) instruction that matches the written plan, 3) techniques for general management of behavior and problem behaviors, 4) community-based instruction, 5) ongoing evaluation of learner performance (i.e., data-based instructional decisions), and 6) annual evaluations of progress.

At Lehigh University, data-based supervision is preceded by an observation and consultation to ensure that the instructor has: 1) a well-balanced teaching schedule oriented toward functional life routines (not isolated skills) and that includes integration (e.g., community, school, job), and 2) rapport with the individuals with severe disabilities who are being taught (e.g., respectful, age-appropriate interactions). In this preliminary observation, the supervisor may use videotape or verbatim written recording to have a record for review with the instructor to discuss how to improve teaching routines and interactions. This preliminary observation is an important prerequisite to the data-based supervision to follow—it ensures that the instructor does not demonstrate a few "pockets" of excellence in a nonfunctional program that is not oriented to the learner as an individual.

Written Plans for Curriculum and Instruction

The first area to assess is instructors' written planning. Unclear written plans or plans not based on the program's overall goals for community-integrated instruction, will also be evident during subsequent observations of instruction or data evaluation. (That is, an instructor probably will not teach well with a poorly written or conceived plan.) A preliminary review of written planning increases the likelihood that instructors will perform well in subsequent observations of their teaching. The three levels of plans that can be reviewed include: the comprehensive assessment plan conducted to write a curriculum chart, the 1-year individualized plan, and the instructional plan for each lesson.

Comprehensive Assessment Plan Throughout this book, recommendations have been given for planning and implementing a comprehensive assessment to develop a 3–5-year curriculum chart. This assessment is critical to longitudinal planning for individuals to achieve the skills that are top priorities for each of their environments. Given the effort this assessment requires and its impact on the learners' education for several years, it may be worthwhile for supervisors to evaluate this assessment. In Figure 3, a checklist is provided to guide supervisors' evaluation of this assessment. The criteria in the checklist are based on the model for comprehensive assessment described in Chapter 2 and illustrated in Chapters 5 through 8. Supervisors will probably want to revise these criteria to reflect the expectations of a specific program's assessment approach (e.g., the instructors might be expected to utilize an existing life skills curriculum or school district–developed skills checklist at an early phase of the assessment planning).

Individualized Education Program or Habilitation Plan For school-age children, the IEP is developed annually as a guide for instruction. An IHP is also typically required in adult services. Hunt, Goetz, and Anderson (1986) provided an evaluation instrument to use when reviewing IEPs written for individuals with severe disabilities (see Figure 4). Hunt et al. recommended analyzing each IEP according to seven components identified as indicators of best practices.

In addition to the necessity that IEPs/IHPs reflect best practices, it is important that the objectives provided with the IEP/IHP be specific for both mea-

Instructor: ———————————— Supervisor: ————————————
Date: ———————————— Learner: ————————————

I. **Evidence of a well-planned assessment**
———— 1. Relevant records are summarized briefly.
———— 2. Parents have been contacted for initial information on learner, parental preferences, and relevant environments.
———— 3. Ecological inventories have been conducted.
———— 4. An adaptive behavior scale or alternative skill checklist has been used (e.g., curriculum-based assessment).
———— 5. Priorities and supporting rationale are stated.

II. **Assessment of the learner**
———— 1. Instructor-made assessments include clear directions and scoring.
———— 2. Testing is related to priorities stated.
———— 3. Testing supplements skill checklists used in screening so that information is available on skills in:
Related skills
———— communication
———— motor skills
———— academics (optional)
Home skills
———— housekeeping
———— personal maintenance
———— recreation/socialization
———— community preparation
Community skills
———— vocational skills
———— community recreation
———— other

III. **Preparation of a 3–5-year curriculum plan**
———— 1. Skills are listed for each area above (see II-3).
———— 2. Chart is organized so that skill areas and subskills are easily read.
———— 3. Skills chosen reflect assessment results and priorities.

Figure 3. Evaluation checklist for comprehensive assessment.

surement and life skills planning. In a review of IEPs for individuals with severe disabilities across Pennsylvania, Browder et al. (1988) found that most contained vague objectives. Annual goals were broadly written and were applicable to almost any individual (e.g., "improve communication"); short-term objectives also lacked behavioral terms, conditions for performance, and criteria for mastery. If Pennsylvania IEPs are typical of others across the nation, instructors obviously need guidance and feedback in writing behavioral objectives with a life skills orientation. Figure 5 provides guidance for evaluating whether IEPs/IHPs contain complete behavioral objectives.

Written Lesson Plans Another important part of planning is writing instructional plans for each lesson. (Because this book focuses on assessment, guidelines for writing instructional plans are not described. However, other re-

IEP ANALYSIS

Student _____

Birthdate _____

Teacher _____

INDICATORS OF BEST PRACTICES	DEFINITION		OBJECTIVE				CURRICULUM AREA(S)									TOTAL #	%
			1	2	3	4	5	6	7	8	9	10	11	12			
AGE-APPROPRIATE																	
1) Materials	It would be appropriate for a ND peer of the same chronological age to use the materials.	1)															
2) Task	It would be appropriate for a ND peer of the same chronological age to perform the task.	2)															
FUNCTIONAL																	
3) Basic Skill	The skill is based on needs identified in 1 of 5 areas: communication, social, behavior, motor, and pre-academic/academic.	3)															
4) Critical Activity	The task must be performed for the S if she can't do it for herself.	4)															
5) Interaction Activity	The activity necessitates the mutual participation of a ND and a SD person.	5)															
WILL GENERALIZE TO A VARIETY OF ENVIRONMENTS																	
6) Taught across settings and materials	The skill facilitates the S's ability to function in a variety of environments; specifically, a basic skill taught within and across critical activities, or a critical activity trained across settings and materials.	6)															
7) Taught in the natural setting	The skill is taught in a way that reflects the manner in which the skill will be used in the natural environment.	7)															
TOTAL POINTS PER OBJECTIVE																	

SUMMARY

	#	%
# of objectives		
% points obtained from total points possible		
average # of points per objective		
#/% use age-appropriate materials		
#/% use age-appropriate tasks		
#/% are Basic Skills		
#/% are Critical Activities		
#/% are Interaction Activities		
#/% will generalize to a variety of environments		
#/% occur in the natural setting		

DIRECTIONS

1) Next to the objective #, indicate the curriculum area(s) with the appropriate letter(s): Communication (C); Social (S); Behavior (B); Motor (M); Domestic (D); Vocational (V); Community (CM); Recreation/Leisure (L); Preacademic (Pre); Academic (A).

2) Score 1 point for each Indicator included in an objective; 7 points are possible for each objective.

Figure 4. Rating sheet for IEP analysis. (S = student, SD = severely disabled, ND = nondisabled.) (From Hunt, P., Goetz, L., & Anderson, J. [1986]. The quality of IEP objectives associated with placement on integrated versus segregated school sites. *Journal of The Association for Persons with Severe Handicaps, 11,* 128; reprinted by permission.)

Instructor: _____   Supervisor: _____
Date: _____   Learner: _____

Evaluation of complete behavioral objectives
Code each objective if it meets each of the following:

"A" (Antecedent)—The objective states the environmental stimuli that should set the occasion for the behavior to be performed. The setting is assumed to be the classroom unless stated otherwise.

> *Examples:*   "When escorted by the instructor or parents to McDonalds"
> "When given leisure time and a selection of toys"
>
> *Nonexamples:*   "John will brush his teeth." (no condition)
> "When given the cue" (nonspecific condition)

"B" (Behavior)—The objective states a measurable, observable response or responses. These reponses cannot be vague across time trends (e.g., "Improve").

> *Examples:*   "Point." "Grasp." "Say."
> *Nonexamples:*   "Experience." "Develop."

"C" (Criteria)—The objective states the degree to which the behavior should be performed for mastery.

> *Examples:*   "By performing all steps of the task analysis independently for two out of two observations"
> "Within 5 seconds on five out of six observations across 2 days"
>
> *Nonexamples:*   "Tie his shoes with 90% accuracy" (impossible to tie shoes with 90% accuracy; 90% of what?)
> "With physical guidance" (not a learner criterion—relies on instructor behavior)

Figure 5.   Evaluation of complete behavioral objectives for individualized plan.

sources on the education of people with severe disabilities have provided information and examples for writing these plans [e.g., Snell & Grigg, 1987].) The written plan is not only critical to evaluating whether or not lessons meet the criteria designated in the curriculum plan and IEP/IHP, but also provides the focus of supervisor observations. Therefore, it is important that the plan operationalize the procedures to be followed in teaching the specified lesson.

Typically, the written plan is reviewed prior to conducting an observation. Supervisors notify instructors about the upcoming observation and either ask for an instructional plan to observe at a specified time or ask for a time to observe a specified procedure. One purpose of reviewing the written instructional plan is to assess the instructor's planning skills. If the supervisor observes an instructional plan, the instructor submits that plan in a preobservation conference so the supervisor can evaluate it as well as obtain the necessary information for the observation. The instructional plan is completed on a form such as that shown in Figure 6. Figure 7 provides a checklist to evaluate this written plan.

SYSTEMATIC INSTRUCTIONAL PLAN

Name: _____ Date: _____

Routine: _____

Specific skill(s): _____

Instructional objective

Antecedent: _____

Response: _____

Criteria for mastery: _____

Setting and schedule for instruction:

Natural discriminative stimulus (S^D) to occasion response:

Instructor's initial S^D if no response to natural S^D:

Prompting and prompt fading to natural S^D:

Critical effect for response:
Instructor feedback for correct and for error:

Instructor-delivered reinforcing stimulus (S^R) (other than verbal praise):

How and when instructor-delivered S^R will be faded:

Generalization and maintenance plan:

Figure 6. Form for preparing and submitting an instructional plan.

Another reason for inspecting written instructional plans is to complete the preobservation form (Figure 8). Supervisors use this form to clarify the exact discriminative stimuli, prompts, reinforcements, and error correction procedures to be used. The form also permits instructors to identify particular questions or areas of concern for which they would like specific feedback.

Observation of Instruction

As outlined above, a complete review of the written plan is necessary to define the teaching behaviors to be observed. The current research on instruction of

		Yes	No
Instructor: _____ Date: _____			
Supervisor: _____ Plan: _____			

A. General information
  1. Is the activity identified? ____ ____
  2. Are the learner's first and last names given? ____ ____
B. Instructional objective
  1. Is the objective functional? ____ ____
  2. Is the antecedent defined? ____ ____
  3. Is the response in observable and measurable terms? ____ ____
  4. Are the criteria for mastery specified? ____ ____
C. Materials/equipment
  1. Are the needed materials/equipment listed? ____ ____
  2. Are the materials appropriate for the objective? ____ ____
  3. Are the materials functional? ____ ____
  4. Are the materials age appropriate? ____ ____
D. Assessment of progress
  1. Is the method of assessment listed? ____ ____
  2. Is the schedule for assessment provided? ____ ____
E. Instructional plan
  1. Is the skill task analyzed? ____ ____
  2. Is the natural cue listed? ____ ____
  3. Is the prompt procedure identified? ____ ____
  4. Is each prompt defined? ____ ____
  5. Is the response latency specified? ____ ____
  6. Is the type of reinforcement identified? ____ ____
  7. Are the criteria given for receiving reinforcement? ____ ____
  8. Is the reinforcement schedule provided? ____ ____
  9. Is an error correction procedure specified? ____ ____
  10. Is an error defined? ____ ____
  11. Are the codes for recording independent responses, prompts, and errors provided? ____ ____
  12. Is a maintenance plan identified? ____ ____
  13. Is a generalization plan identified? ____ ____

Figure 7. Evaluation checklist for instructional plan.

individuals with severe disabilities does not suggest one specific way to design this instruction, but rather provides demonstrations of various procedures that can be effective. In reviewing research on community-integrated instruction, Snell and Browder (1986) noted various prompting procedures, trial presentations, and locations for instruction that have proven effective (e.g., prompt hierarchies, time delay of a single prompt, whole task instruction, chaining, in vivo instruction, simulated instruction). Given the current diversity in research, it follows that educators will also vary their instructional plans. While it is beyond the scope of this chapter to describe observation assessment pro-

1. Skill: Buying and drinking a soda
2. Write task analysis on observation form.
3. Observation date: January 30 Time: 2:00 Place: Lounge
4. Materials: _____
5. Trial components:
   Discriminative stimulus: Escort to vending machine
   Response latency: 3 seconds
   Code for unprompted correct: +
   Prompts (in order): Gesture   (G)
                       Verbal direction   (V)

                       Verbal and model   (M)

   Reinforcement: Type: Praise
                  Criteria: Perform steps without prompt
                  Schedule: All steps
                  Error correction: Example: Does not imitate model
                                             prompt (learner has
                                             good imitation skills)
                                    Type: "No, that's not how you buy a
                                          soda." (physically guide)
6. Instructor's concerns/questions: _____
   _____
   _____
   _____

1. Skill: Cleaning a toilet
2. Write task analysis on observation form.
3. Observation date: February 1 Time: 10:00 Place: Bathroom
4. Materials: Brush, sponge, cleaner
5. Trial components:
   Discriminative stimulus: Picture job card
   Response latency: 3 seconds
   Code for unprompted correct: +
   Prompts (in order): Gesture   (G)
                       Verbal direction   (V)

                       Verbal and model   (M)

   Reinforcement: Type: Praise
                  Criteria: Performs starred steps without errors
                  Schedule: Starred steps
                  Error correction: Example: Does not imitate
                                             model prompt
                                    Type: "No, that's not how you clean
                                          a toilet." (physically guide)
6. Instructor's concerns/questions: _____
   _____
   _____

Figure 8. Examples of preobservation forms for task analytic instruction.

cedures for the many instructional plans that might be utilized, an example is provided for task analytic instruction.

Observing task analytic instruction is emphasized for two reasons. First, many skills required for daily living are taught and used as chains of behavior (Snell & Browder, 1986). Second, although task analyses are widely used, supervision of task analytic instruction is rarely presented in the literature.

Description of Task Analytic Instruction   Much of the research in which individuals with severe disabilities have acquired new skills has utilized a discrete trial format (e.g., Matson, DiLorenzo, & Esveldt-Dawson, 1981). The discrete trial format has been applied to task analytic instruction by treating each step of the task analysis as the discriminative stimulus of the next step and by providing prompts and consequences as necessary for each step of the task (Cronin & Cuvo, 1979; van den Pol et al., 1981). One prompt system that has been successfully replicated in several studies is a prompt hierarchy that provides progressive assistance from a verbal direction, to a model, to physical guidance—depending on the help an individual requires to perform each step of the task analysis (for reviews on prompting see Demchak, 1990, and Schoen, 1986). Based on this kind of research, the components of instruction of a task-analyzed skill are: 1) using a task analysis, 2) presenting the trial (i.e., waiting for the natural cue), 3) prompting, 4) fading prompts by using a prompt hierarchy, 5) specifying reinforcement procedures, and 6) specifying error correction procedures.

Definitions of Components of Task Analytic Instruction   In order to determine instructor competency in task analytic instruction, the above listed components must be defined. These definitions can be obtained from the instructor's written plan, or in an interview to clarify the plan. This clarification can be obtained by asking the following questions and noting the answers on the preobservation form (see Figure 8):

1.   Is the instructor training the entire task analysis or training some specific steps? Can the individual perform the steps out of order and receive credit for being correct? (Supervisor should make notes as necessary on the task analysis on the data sheet.)
2.   How long does the instructor wait for the individual to respond to the natural cue to begin the activity? (Supervisor should note on form as "Response latency.") How does the instructor prompt task initiation if the individual fails to respond? (Supervisor should note on form as "Discriminative stimulus.")
3.   What are the exact prompts to be used and what is the latency between prompts? (Supervisor should note on form as "Prompts.")
4.   If the instructor is using reinforcement in addition to the critical effect for the activity, what reinforcement will be used and when will it be delivered? (Supervisor should note on form as "Reinforcement.") How will errors be treated? (Supervisor should note on form as "Error correction.")

5. Does the instructor have any specific concerns with this lesson? (Supervisor should note on form as "Instructor's concerns/questions.")

Collecting Data on Task Analytic Instruction To assess individuals on the chain of behaviors, instructors score the learners' behavior on each step of the chain. When prompting is used, the type of prompt required for each step of the chain may be recorded. To develop this data collection system for instructor observation further, instructor behaviors (i.e., providing the discriminative stimulus, prompting, reinforcing, correcting errors) can be scored as correct or incorrect according to the instructor's written instructional plan and the definitions in the previous section. After the instructor provides the discriminative stimuli to begin the chain, he or she may provide from zero to several prompts and may also provide reinforcement or error correction on each step of the chain. The supervisor should record all of the defined instructor and learner behaviors for each step immediately after its occurrence. Figures 9 and 10 provide examples of data collection sheets for scoring instruction on a task-analyzed skill. The observation instrument in Figure 9 is designed specifically for supervisor use; the form in Figure 10 is one that an instructor would use to record learner data, but it is shown adapted for supervisor use.

Observation of Task Analytic Instruction Figures 9 and 10 show sample data for task analytic instruction of two different skills (i.e., buying and drinking a soda, and cleaning the bathroom, respectively). The preobservation forms in Figure 8 contain the information (e.g., the prompting system) the supervisor needs before the observation. Figure 9 shows the data for an instructor teaching an individual to select and drink a soda. Susan, the instructor, accompanied Sam to the vending machine; within 3 seconds, Sam, the learner, selected a soda. Susan correctly praised Sam (step 1 in Figure 9). Sam did not pick up the soda within 3 seconds. Susan correctly gestured and waited 3 seconds. When Sam did not respond, Susan gave him verbal directions. However, when he still did not respond, Susan did not model the response and mistakenly implemented the error correction procedure (step 2). The third step was one Susan performed for Sam in this phase of instruction. On the fourth step, Susan used the three prompts correctly and Sam performed the step. Susan then waited 3 seconds, and when Sam did not independently raise the can to his mouth, she mistakenly gave a verbal prompt. Susan mistakenly praised Sam for a prompted correct step (step 5). Sam performed the sixth step independently and Susan correctly praised him. On the final step, Sam again performed independently, but Susan did not praise him.

In the second example, in Figure 10, Jane, the instructor, correctly presented the picture job card to clean the toilet, and John, the learner, performed the first five steps independently. Jane mistakenly praised the second step (reinforcement was only to be delivered on the starred steps according to Jane's plan) but correctly praised step 5. On step 6, John did not respond within 3 seconds and Jane correctly provided a gestural prompt. On step 7, John did not respond

Teacher: Susan
Student: Sam
Skill: Buying and drinking a soda

Observer: Diane
Date: January 30
Time: 2:00

Discriminative stimulus: Vending machine   S^D correct: X   S^D incorrect: __

Task analysis	Teaching							Total trial correct?	Comments
1. Press selection panel.	+	1	2	3	4	R	E	Yes	
2. Pick up soda.	+	1	2	③	4	R	X	No	
3. (Instructor opens can.)	+	1	2	3	4	R	E		
4. Grasp can with thumb below drink hole.	+	1	2	3	4	R	E	Yes	
5. Raise can to mouth.	+	①	X	3	4	R	E	No	
6. Take sip of soda.	+	1	2	3	4	R	E	Yes	
7. Put can down.	+	1	2	3	4	⑧	E	No	
8.	+	1	2	3	4	R	E		
9.	+	1	2	3	4	R	E		
10.	+	1	2	3	4	R	E		

Key: + Student's independent response or initial response latency
   1 = Gesture
   2 = Verbal
   3 = Verbal and model
   4 = (only three prompts in this system)
   R = Reinforcement
   E = Error correction

Figure 9. Example of an observation form for task analytic instruction designed for the supervisor's use. (Slash [/] = correct response, circle [○] = omitted response, X = incorrect response.)

within 3 seconds and Jane omitted the gestural prompt and incorrectly gave him a verbal direction. John independently completed steps 8 to 10. On step 11, John did not respond within 3 seconds and Jane correctly provided a gestural and then a verbal prompt and praised John when he completed the step. John independently completed step 12, but did not continue to step 13; Jane provided three prompts correctly. The next two steps were completed independently and followed by step 16, which required a gestural prompt; Jane correctly praised John for completing the step. John completed steps 17 and 18 independently,

Teacher: __Jane__   Student: __John__   Date: __1/30__   Environment: __Bathroom__
Discriminative stimulus: __Picture job card__   Correct: __yes__   Incorrect: __——__

Task analysis

Task components																						
1. Obtain supplies.	+																					
2. Go to toilet.	+ Ⓡ																					
3. Lift seat.	+																					
4. Flush.	+																					
5. Put cleaner in bowl (one squirt).*	+ R																					
6. Scrub bowl with brush.	G																					
7. Flush.	Ⓞ Ⓥ																					
8. Rinse brush.	+																					
9. Put brush away.	+																					
10. Pick up sponge.	+																					
11. Put cleaner on sponge (one squirt).*	G V R																					
12. Wipe around lip of bowl.	+																					
13. Wipe under seat.	G V M																					
14. Put seat down.	+																					
15. Wipe seat.	+																					
16. Wipe back and sides.*	G R																					
17. Wipe top.	+																					
18. Wipe base.	+																					
19. Return supplies.*	G R																					

Key: + = correct without help   M = verbal and model
     G = gesture   R = reinforcement
     V = verbal prompt   * = step designated for reinforcement

Figure 10.   Example of an observation form for task analytic instruction that adapts the teacher's data collection form for the supervisor's use. (Circle [O] = omitted response, circled letter = incorrect response.)

but required a gestural prompt to complete the final step of the task. Again, Jane correctly praised John for completion of the step.

Providing Feedback to the Instructor   After the observation is completed, the instructor and supervisor should meet in a postobservation conference to discuss the observation. Since the supervisor completes a written postobservation summary (see Figure 11) as well as meets with the instructor, the instructor receives both written and verbal feedback. In order to have a maximum effect on instructor behavior, this feedback is paired with praise or approval for appropriate teaching behaviors (K.M. Brown et al., 1981; Cossairt, Hall, & Hopkins, 1973; Realon et al., 1983). Any particular concerns or questions instructors have regarding the observation are addressed. Before terminating the postobservation conference, the supervisor and instructor work together to establish goals for the instructor's ongoing training and to schedule

---

Instructor: _____   Date: _____

Supervisor: _____   Time of observation: _____

Lesson observed: _____

1. Observation purpose:

2. Summary of observation
   a. Discriminative stimulus correct: ____
   b. Use of task analysis correct: ____
   c. Number of prompts given: ____
      Number correct: ____
      Percent correct: ____
   d. Number of reinforcers given: ____
      Number correct: ____
      Percent correct: ____
   e. Number of error corrections used: ____
      Number correct: ____
      Percent correct: ____
   f. Percent total trials correct: ____
   g. Percent learner independent correct responses: ____

3. Questions/comments:

4. Instructor's goals for next observation (completed by supervisor and instructor):

5. Date/time of next observation: _____

Figure 11.   Postobservation summary form.

a date and time for a follow-up observation. (Throughout the observation process, it is essential that supervisors remember that instructor data are confidential—to be shared *only* with the instructor who was observed.)

Additionally, the supervisor works with the instructor to identify effective teaching techniques and apply them to a particular lesson. This assistance can be offered in several different forms. Supervisors might provide instructions, either verbally or in writing, regarding a specific technique. A technique might be modeled for the instructor, or the instructor and supervisor may engage in role-playing situations. Thus, data-based supervision is directly related to on-the-job training.

Observing Behavior Management Techniques

Behavior management consists of general management techniques as well as procedures for specific problem behaviors. This section discusses methods for evaluating both aspects of behavior management. One of the best ways to assess an instructor's general management is to evaluate how he or she utilizes differential reinforcement during leisure periods for individuals with severe disabilities.

Differential Reinforcement of Leisure Activities   Individuals with severe disabilities sometimes lack a repertoire of adaptive leisure skills; instead, they may engage in socially stigmatizing stereotypes or self-abuse. Leisure periods provide an excellent opportunity for supervisors to observe how instructors utilize differential reinforcement to encourage adaptive, rather than maladaptive, responses. Demchak and Koury (1990) provided a format for this observation, which is shown in Figure 12. In this observation, the supervisor employs a partial interval recording system to observe an instructor or other direct staff person interacting with up to six individuals with severe disabilities during a leisure activity with several choices of materials (e.g., playing music, painting, tabletop game). Within each 1-minute interval, the supervisor scores the response if it occurs at any time during the interval. The letters in each box in Figure 12 are the types of instructor responses that may occur (see figure for definitions). The supervisor slashes correct responses and circles errors during the interval observation.

At the end of the 20-minute observation, the supervisor summarizes the data using the grid included at the end of Figure 12. The summary includes the number of intervals in which each type of interaction occurred, an overall rate of instructor interactions with each learner, and an overall rate of learners' active involvement with leisure activities. During the follow-up conference, the supervisor praises specific examples of differential reinforcement and notes any errors. An example of an error that may occur is that the instructor may ignore one or more individuals for most of the observation time. Also, the instructor may present leisure materials without offering an opportunity for choice. Differential reinforcement errors may occur if the instructor praises and attends to

Instructor Melissa Jones Date 5/24/88 Time 10 A.M.

Observer Sue Smith Reliability Observer Jacob Brown

Clients' Names	Cory	Tracy	Rob	Erin	John	
Minute 1	LA 1 SI I S R	LA 1 SI I S R	LA 1 SI I S R	LA 1 SI I S R	LA SI I S R	LA SI I S R
2	LA SI I S R	LA SI I S R	LA SI I L S R	LA SI I S R	LA 1 SI ✓ I S R	LA SI I S R
3	LA SI I S R	LA 2 SI I S R	LA SI I S R	LA SI I S R	LA SI I S R	LA SI I S R
18	LA SI I S R	LA SI I S R	LA SI I S R	LA SI I S R	LA SI I S R	LA SI I S R
19	LA SI I S R	LA SI I S R	LA SI I S R	LA SI I S R	LA SI I S R	LA SI I S R
20	LA SI I L S R	LA SI I S R	LA SI I S R	LA SI I S R	LA SI I S R	LA SI I S R

Figure 12. Observation form for differential reinforcement of leisure activities. (From Demchak, M.A., & Koury, M. [1990]. Differential reinforcement of leisure activities: An observation form for supervisors. *Teaching Exceptional Children, 22*[2], 15; reprinted by permission.)

the individual when engaged in undesirable behavior and fails to attend to interactions with the leisure material.

This observation format can also be adapted for instructor use in observing interactions between individuals with severe disabilities and those without disabilities, to assess whether individuals without disabilities are improving their skills to offer choice and encourage adaptive leisure activity. In this instance, the instructor may not share these data per se, but rather give verbal encouragement and tactful suggestions for future activities.

Observation of Specific Management of Problem Behavior Sometimes, through careful planning, specific contingencies have been planned for problem and alternative behaviors. For example, instructors may have planned to praise individuals for working on assigned tasks at a variable-interval schedule of once every 2 minutes. A contingency for the problem behavior might also be planned, such as blocking attempts to hit peers and ignoring a learner for 30 seconds after an attempt to hit. Since such specific plans often require instructors to invest extra planning and effort, and may lead to more intrusive plans if unsuccessful, supervisors may want to assess instructors' consistency in applying these defined contingencies. One of the methods for doing this is to count frequency within intervals for the occurrence of the problem behavior and for instructor use of the appropriate contingency. Frequency within intervals can also be used to assess instructors' adherence to a schedule for praise statements or other differential reinforcement. Figure 13 shows an assessment of an instructor's adherence to a specific management plan. The second half of the figure shows a method for assessing both teaching and management behaviors concurrently. This concurrent observation can provide useful information to instructors who typically must manage problem behavior while teaching.

Applications to Community-Based Instruction and Community Integration

Most instructors and support staff who work with individuals with severe disabilities will implement some instruction outside the classroom and home settings. For example, money use and shopping skills might be taught at a grocery store or shopping mall. Also, students in regular schools may receive instruction in classes with nondisabled peers. Supervision to support excellence in teaching also needs to occur in these settings, without intruding on the ideals of integration. (In Chapter 6, ideas were given for making learner assessment portable and manageable in community settings, and Chapter 9 provided ideas for assessing integration.) Supervisors will need to adapt data collection for community and regular class settings so that it does not intrude on instruction and does not draw negative public attention to individuals with severe disabilities. Supervisors often can position themselves so that instruction and management can be observed at a distance. In public settings, the supervisor may

Problem behavior: Attempting to hit

Definition of problem behavior: Hand extended or raised toward another person. (*Exceptions:* Hand extended as for handshake or to offer toy or other material.)

Defined contingency: Block actual striking of another person by putting one's hands or arm between the raised hand and the other person, and, if necessary, assisting the other person to move. Provide no eye contact or verbalization to the learner for 30 seconds after the attempt to hit. During this 30 seconds, give positive attention (e.g., smile and praise or conversation) to at least one other learner who is sitting or working appropriately.

Alternative behaviors: 1) Appropriate appeal for attention from peers or instructor, 2) "other" behavior.

Definition of alternative behaviors: 1) Raising the hand in the air, vocalizing while looking at a peer or instructor, tapping the instructor's arm, signing "help" while vocalizing; 2) absence of attempts to hit.

Defined contingency: Use specific, labeled praise for the defined appropriate appeals for attention. Use specific, labeled praise for whatever adaptive behavior the learner is exhibiting, and converse with the learner after each 15 minutes without hitting. (Set a kitchen timer to cue use of the 15-minute fixed-interval DRO.)

Scoring: / = hitting
  ⊘ = Correct consequence for hitting
  A = Appropriate appeal for attention
  Ⓐ = Correct consequence for appeal
  P = Praise and conversation after 15 minutes of not hitting
  * = Errors

Optional scoring (instructional behaviors): I = action verb statement to begin a task
  G = gesture prompt
  V = verbal prompt
  M = model prompt
  P = physical guidance
  R = reinforcement for correct response _____

(*continued*)

Figure 13. Example of observation form for implementation of specific behavior management contingencies. (Form would be continued for 15–30 minutes of intervals.) (DRO = differential reinforcement of other behavior.)

purchase an item, for example, to blend with the other shoppers. Figures 14 and 15 provide checklists for the evaluation of community- and school-integrated instruction. The supervisor completes these checklists after the observation, in a more private, office or classroom setting.

Appraisal of Instructor
Implementation of Ongoing Evaluation

Another important planning activity is the periodic review of learner progress to make decisions about instructional changes. To make these decisions, in-

Figure 13. *(continued)*

Scoring for management	Scoring management and instruction

Minute 1
Intervals (10-second intervals; record each occurrence within intervals)

Interval	Management	Instruction
1	⊘	
2		(No interaction—ignoring)
3		
4		
5		I G V
6		M P R

Minute 2

Interval	Management	Instruction
1	Ⓐ	
2		
3		I G V M
4		P R
5	* /	I G V
6		M P R

Minute 3

Interval	Management	Instruction
1	⊘	
2		(No interaction—ignoring)
3		
4		
5		I
6		G V M P

Minute 4

Interval	Management	Instruction
1		R
2	* A	
3		I G V M
4		P R
5		
6		I G V M R

Minute 5

Interval	Management	Instruction
1	Ⓐ	
2		
3		I G
4		V M R
5		
6		

Summary: Number of hits: 3
Number of correct use of contingency for hitting: 2
Number of appropriate appeals: 3
Number of correct use of contingency for appeals: 2
Total errors/opportunities to use contingencies: 2/6

Learner's name: _____ Date: _____

Staff: _____ Setting: _____

I. Written plan includes:		
1. Priority skill for instruction	YES	NO
2. Additional skills for:		
Incidental teaching	YES	NO
Generalization	YES	NO
3. Assistance to be provided for:		
Managing money	YES	NO
Putting on coat/hat, etc.	YES	NO
Using transportation	YES	NO
Street crossing	YES	NO
Other individual needs	YES	NO
4. Social interaction for:		
Peers/friends	YES	NO
General public	YES	NO
Problem behavior	YES	NO
5. Emergency management for:		
Medical crises	YES	NO
Behavioral crises	YES	NO

SUMMARY AND COMMENTS:

II. Community-based instruction observation: The staff—		
1. Provided planned instruction	YES	NO
2. Provided assistance as planned for money, dressing, transportation, street crossing, other needs	YES	NO
3. Fostered social interaction for:		
Peers/friends	YES	NO
General public	YES	NO
Problem behavior	YES	NO
4. Managed any crises appropriately	YES	NO
5. "Blended" instruction/assistance so as to be undetectable	YES	NO
6. Collected assessment data discreetly	YES	NO

SUMMARY AND COMMENTS:

Figure 14. Checklist for evaluation of community-based instruction.

structors must collect reliable data on learners' behaviors and summarize these data with a graph.

Reliability of Data Collection Applied behavior analysis in teaching settings typically is carried out by one staff person, who may or may not have an aide trained in its use. Thus, interobserver reliability checks are more

Student's name: _____ Date: _____

Teacher: _____ Setting: _____

I. Written plan for integration includes:
1. IEP objective to be targeted   YES NO
2. Primary contact person   YES NO
3. Activities in the setting   YES NO
4. Assistance to be provided:
    Type of assistance needed   YES NO
    Who provides assistance   YES NO
    Plan to fade assistance (if appropriate)   YES NO
5. Method to assess progress   YES NO

SUMMARY AND COMMENTS:

II. Observation of integration (Check all of the items below that require more teacher planning and comment on each):
____ 1. Student arrives/departs at same time as peers.
____ 2. Student locates own seat and belongings.
____ 3. Student initiates activity when given natural cue to begin.
____ 4. Student interacts with peers during informal socialization.
____ 5. Student works with peers during class projects.
____ 6. Student's behavior is appropriate for age and setting.
____ 7. Student's appearance blends with peers.
____ 8. Student's IEP objective was clearly addressed in context of integration activities.

SUMMARY AND COMMENTS:

Figure 15. Checklist for evaluation of school integration.

difficult to attain than in research. Nevertheless, it is vital to conduct inter-observer checks so that instructors are not faced with the dilemma of having data with uncertain reliability. One solution is for the supervisor to observe data on the learner to check reliability, while simultaneously evaluating instructor performance. If reliability is poor during evaluation observations, further observations may need to be scheduled. The instructor definitions for the target responses may also need to be reviewed to make sure they are sufficiently explicit to obtain agreement across observers. In Figure 10, an example was given of a supervisor observation of task analytic instruction. In this case, the instructor recorded the highest level of prompt used for each step. Reliability was evaluated by comparing the last prompt recorded by the supervisor with each prompt recorded by the instructor. Reliability can then be calculated by dividing agreements by agreements plus disagreements and multiplying by 100. Similar procedures can be developed for incorporating reliability checks in observations of other forms of instruction.

Reviewing Graphs In addition to checking reliability during the observation, supervisors may ask to examine the ongoing data for the programs observed. This examination serves two purposes: It allows supervisors to evaluate both learner progress and the construction of the graph. Data collected on learner behavior should indicate improvement concurrent with, or subsequent to, instructor improvement. For example, in R. Koegel et al. (1977), several learners showed task improvement prior to instructor mastery of the targeted teaching behaviors. However, after the instructors mastered the skills, improvements in learner behavior were more rapid and resulted in more correct responses. Similarly, supervisors and instructors may find that learner behavior improves before instructors master the teaching techniques. However, learner performance after instructor mastery should reflect greater teaching efficiency (i.e., learner mastery with fewer teaching trials).

As stated earlier, reviewing learner graphs permits supervisors to evaluate the construction of the graph. The form in Figure 16 can be used to evaluate several graphs pertaining to one individual or for several individuals receiving instruction on the same program. If the graph is poorly constructed, it may not convey an accurate picture of the learner's progress. If instructors do not include all the necessary information on the graph (e.g., labels on both axes) or if the information is incomplete (e.g., a label reads number of steps versus number of steps independently completed), the graph will be difficult to interpret. Therefore, periodic reviews of instructors' graphs are important.

Review of Data-Based Instructional Decisions Chapter 4 described a method for systematic evaluation of data patterns to make instructional decisions that was based on the research of N. Haring et al. (1979) and a subsequent replication by Browder, Liberty, et al. (1986). Browder, Liberty, et al. found that instructors' evaluation of the data pattern and choice of instructional decisions disagreed with the supervisor's review prior to the implementation of self-monitoring. While self-monitoring is described in detail in the next section, it is worth noting here that instructors often make inaccurate judgments about data patterns. This inaccuracy for data evaluation has been observed in other research with instructors (Liberty, 1972), graduate students (Wampold & Furlong, 1981), and experts (DeProspero & Cohen, 1979). By contrast, accuracy typically improves when a standard method for data evaluation is used (Bailey, 1984; White, 1972). Thus, the supervisor's role in encouraging instructional decisions based on accurate data evaluation will probably be to teach a standard procedure, if instructors are unfamiliar with it (see Chapter 4), and to conduct reliability checks of the data evaluation and data-based decisions.

Instructor: _____ Supervisor: _____ Date: _____

Instructional program graph

Components of graph	Wash hands					
1. Label for student/activity/ mastery criteria	yes					
2. Vertical axis label	yes					
3. Horizontal axis label: Dates	yes					
4. Previous phase mean given	yes					
5. Vertical dashed lines for changes	yes					
6. Changes labeled	yes					
7. Daily data points plotted and connected	yes					
8. Trend line accurate	yes					
9. Phase mean accurate	yes					
10. Decision adheres to rule or rationale stated	yes					

Figure 16. Checklist for evaluation of learner graphs. Instructional program graph of "Wash hands" is offered as an example of how to complete the checklist.

GROUND RULES FOR DATA-BASED SUPERVISION

Data-based supervision can be misused and become a threat to instructors rather than a helpful guide for improvement. One of the first ground rules that should be established in its use is how these data will influence job evaluations, which are considered in promotions or job maintenance. It would be unfair to schedule only one observation to evaluate an instructor's performance since these data might not represent typical performance. Supervisors in the Lehigh University programs have found it useful to set criteria for instructor performance (i.e., those stated in Table 1) and a timeline for mastery of these criteria each year (e.g., over 2 to 3 months for new instructors). New instructors, and instructors in new classes, receive the most frequent observations to give them the opportunity to meet the criteria with frequent feedback during the timeline. Returning instructors receive less frequent maintenance observations. Additional observations are scheduled if instructors do not demonstrate maintenance. Instructors are encouraged to self-monitor and to share data so that they are better prepared for observations and so that supervisors and instructors can compare observations to the instructors' self-monitoring of typical daily performance. Thus, job evaluation is based on meeting criteria by a specified deadline. Each observation to help instructors meet these criteria is neither averaged nor summarized on their performance evaluation. Rather, the performance evaluation states criteria mastered or partially mastered by the specified deadline. Thus, instructors may perform poorly on some observations and still achieve the criteria by the deadline and receive an excellent evaluation.

A second ground rule that must be established is that these data, like any assessment, are subject to due process considerations. That is, instructors always have the right to review all data collected and notes written about their performance. Supervisors should not share these data or comments with anyone—except when the individual instructor's written permission has been obtained. Public posting of data would thus be a violation of confidentiality, unless written permission had been obtained. Such public posting is also a highly intrusive method of enhancing behavior change, in comparison to, for example, self-evaluation.

A third ground rule is that instructors have the same right to reliable and valid measurement as do learners. Supervisors should check reliability periodically, for example, by comparing data collected to instructors' self-monitoring during the same observation. Supervisors should also be prepared to give the rationale or references to relevant research to support the teaching competencies expected. However, learner progress is the ultimate criterion for the validity for any instructor activity assessed.

Finally, instructors, as professionals, should have considerable authority over the standards set for their classrooms and their own performance. As is mentioned in the next section, instructors' self-management should be a primary activity in program improvement. Supervisors may support this activity through data-based supervision. Supervisors' criteria for quality should be well known to instructors, and (ideally) derived from instructor and supervisor consultation. Supervisors should also solicit feedback from instructors to ascertain the helpfulness of the data-based supervision and for ideas for improvement.

INSTRUCTORS' SELF-EVALUATION

Throughout this chapter, suggestions have been given for supervisor appraisal of instructor performance. However, many of these suggestions can, and should, be implemented by instructors themselves once initial training has been completed. Additionally, instructors may perform best when they set their own standards for performance. For example, Csapo (1981) compared instructor effectiveness under self-imposed and externally imposed, stringent and lenient standards (e.g., number of work units learners should master in a given time period). Instructor effectiveness was greatest and most lasting in the self-imposed, stringent standard condition. Reinforcement for self-imposed standards was provided in the form of recognition at staff meetings for instructors who had set high standards. Other research has also supported self-management of teaching behavior, which can include self-monitoring (self-recording and self-evaluation), goal setting, or self-reinforcement (Kissel, Whitman, & Reid, 1983; Korabek, Reid, & Ivancic, 1981).

To self-manage improvement in data-based supervision, instructors might: 1) select the target lesson, 2) recommend a standard for their own and learners' behavior, 3) collect data on their own teaching (e.g., using Figure 10), and/or 4) self-praise in the postconference. The form in Figure 10 would easily permit instructors to monitor their own teaching behaviors. Instead of simply recording the level of prompt at which learners respond, instructors can record each prompt provided to learners as well as reinforcement given and error correction provided. When instruction is completed, instructors can review the data to determine the percentage of correct prompts, reinforcement, and error-correction procedures. Supervisors may periodically review these data and reinforce instructors for selection of difficult lessons, setting high standards, collecting data, and accurate self-praise.

In addition to self-evaluation of teaching excellence in systematic instruction, instructors may also want to conduct their own goal setting and program evaluation, as described earlier in this chapter. Instructors often feel overwhelmed with the abundance of new ideas proposed by experts and their own lack of time to try them all. Goal setting can help an instructor manage time the way a budget can help with money management. Since time, like money, is a limited resource, instructors can invest it better if they know their own priorities. A popular joke tells of a passenger who exclaims to the driver that they have taken a wrong turn and are lost. The driver glibly replies, "That's okay. We're making great time." Excellence sometimes requires slowing down to get focused on priorities.

SUMMARY

Data-based supervision can document the effectiveness of programs for individuals with severe disabilities. This supervision can be most useful if provided along with consultation to help instructors remediate deficiencies observed. Instructors should be encouraged to self-manage their improvement by setting standards and by self-monitoring performance. Through an annual evaluation of the learners' progress on IEP/IHP objectives, instructors and supervisors can note the impact of the program on this primary goal for high-quality service provision.

STUDY QUESTIONS

1. What are the components of best practice for programs for individuals with severe handicaps?
2. What are the types of data-based assessment a supervisor might utilize?
3. What are some precautions in using data-based supervision?

FOR FURTHER THOUGHT

1. Review the components of best practice and rate your program on each. What areas need further development?
2. What type of leadership is needed to achieve these goals?
3. How might data-based supervision be beneficial to you?
4. What procedures will you try?

appendix A

CURRICULUM CHARTS FOR CASE STUDIES

IN EACH CHART to follow, a brief description is given of the learner's current skills and deficits. Environments identified through the ecological inventory process are noted. For each learner, a list of skills follows the learner description. These skills will be the focus of instruction for 3–5 years. Priorities for the first year's plan are noted with asterisks. These charts are based on comprehensive assessments conducted of real learners by their instructors. Names and details have been changed to protect confidentiality. Further information on the comprehensive assessments can be found throughout the book.

Learner: <u>Nat</u>   Current age: <u>6</u>
Plan is for years: <u>1990–1995</u>   Instructor: <u>Ms. S.</u>

Brief learner description: Nat has received several classifications including severe mental retardation, autism, and severe emotional disturbance. Nat attended
a preschool program where he mastered basic self-care (e.g., feeds himself,
schedule trained for toileting) and acquired a vocabulary of 10 manual signs. Nat
uses his signs to label objects in the environment (e.g., point to toy car and sign
"car"). Nat has frequent severe tantrums and resists guidance during instruction.
Nat's parents and siblings are eager for him to learn daily living and social skills.
The family currently plans to provide Nat's ongoing home environment. Nat's family lives in a suburban community of a medium-size city.

Learner's strengths and capabilities: energetic, friendly, likes board games,
kind to animals, interested in community settings, tries to imitate other family
members on outings.

Environments used in planning: Nat's home, current school setting, middle
school setting, convenience store, shopping mall, fast-food restaurants, varied
streets, 1st-grade recess.

I. Skills for the home

A. Personal Maintenance
      Eliminate toilet accidents.*
      Wash hands.*
      Use restroom alone.
      Dress alone (simplified clothing).*
      Dress alone (zippers, snaps).
      Eat with spoon without spilling.*
      Drink without spilling.*
      Eat with a fork.

B. Housekeeping and food preparation
      Pour from pitcher or carton.*
      Prepare simple snacks.*
      Clean up after snack.*
      Open food packages.
      Prepare sandwiches.
      Pick up toys.*
      Put laundry in hamper.
      Dust furniture.
      Wipe tables.

C. Recreation/socialization
      Play "Cross 4" with sibling or school peers.*
      Play "Trouble."
      Play board games with counting moves (generalized).
      Play matching card games and board games (generalized).

Display a Matchbox/Hot Wheels car collection to peers, family.
Feed family's dog.

D. Community preparation
Put on coat alone.*
Gather belongings for school.
Communicate destination by pointing to picture.

II. Skills for the community

A. Vocational skills
Store belongings upon arrival.*
Food preparation (e.g., spreading, containers).
Work without instructor guidance or verbal instructions for 30 minutes
(first year, 10 minutes*).
Follow picture instructions.
Wipe tables.
Perform tabletop assembly and bagging tasks (simulation of high school
and adult program jobs).

B. Community recreation
Take leisure walks with friends or family.*
Attend spectator events with family.

C. Other community skills
Use a wallet.*
Communicate choice for purchase of snack.*
Purchase snack without help.
Accompany adult by walking close by.*
Stop at curbs while walking with adult in community.*
Order meal at fast-food restaurant.
Purchase one item in grocery store or clothing store.

III. Related skills

A. Communication
Greet familiar people.*
Communicate choice of display by pointing.*
Use existing signs as social replies.*
Ask "What is it?" with sign and pointing.
Communicate "yes" and "no" with headshakes.
Converse with family and friends about daily routine with signs and pic-
ture wallet.
Expand picture and sign vocabulary each year.*
Show identification card upon request.*

B. Motor skills
Throw a ball.*
Run to base or end of relay line.*

Catch ball.

Play kickball with peers without disabilities.

Play basketball (lowered basket) with peers without disabilities.

C. Academics

Perform action shown on picture (vocational assignment).

Select food versus nonfood packages during food preparation.

Discriminate quarters from other coins while using wallet.

Discriminate dollars from coins while using wallet.

D. Social and interfering behavior

Look at peer when name is called.*

Initiate and respond to social interactions during recess.

Problem: Running away in public. *Alternative:* Carry items, make choices, and walk with adult.*

Problem: Tantrums. *Alternative:* Signal "help" and "I'll do it alone" with signs and gestures; accept assistance.*

Learner: Dennis Current age: 8
Plan is for years: 1990–1995 Instructor: Ms. K.

Brief learner description: Dennis has been classified as having profound mental retardation with severe spastic quadriplegia. He has few observable, voluntary motoric responses. These few responses include lifting his head and moving one arm in a horizontal plane. Dennis must be properly positioned in his wheelchair or on other adaptive equipment to make these responses. To date, Dennis has made minimal progress in his school program. All personal care is provided for him. Dennis requires a mechanical soft diet due to oral-muscular problems. He wears diapers. He has no communication system. Dennis's parents are discouraged with his lack of progress to date, but are dedicated to keeping him at home. Dennis's family lives in a rural area, about 20 miles from a medium-size city.

Learner's strengths and capabilities: kind, quiet, smiles when greeted, responds to music, cooperative.

Environments used in planning: Dennis's home, respite care facility, city and state park, city indoor stadium, current school, middle school, shopping mall, family restaurant, family's church.

I. Skills for the home

A. Personal Maintenance

Communicate need for diaper to be changed by pressing buzzer, and touching side when asked, "What's wrong?"

Signal readiness to be dressed or fed by holding head up.*

Communicate food choice by lifting head when asked, "Do you want _____" and not lifting head for nonpreferred items.*

Communicate clothing choice as above by lifting head.

Communicate hunger and thirst by pressing buzzer and lifting head for "yes" when asked "Are you (hungry)?"

Communicate pain by pressing buzzer repeatedly.

Decrease time required to be fed.

Eat greater variety of food types, textures, temperatures.

B. Housekeeping and food preparation

Operate blender by using adaptive switch.*

Wipe tray after meals.*

Dust furniture using same motion as tray wiping.

Release dirty clothes into laundry hamper.

C. Recreation/socialization

Operate tape recorder using adaptive switch.*

Select tape choice by lifting head for yes when asked, "Do you want _____?"

Operate page turner with family photo album and other books.

Operate page turner to initiate or respond to family conversation.

D. Community preparation
Lift head to signal readiness to leave.*

II. Skills for the community

A. Vocational skills
None identified at this time. Expand recreation for increased experiences in the community and potential recreational placement as an adult. Continue to explore technological adaptations for existing jobs.

B. Community recreation
Hold head up while pushed during family walks in community or park.*
Lift head and look up at destination upon arrival.*
Communicate "yes" by lifting head when asked about preferences in outdoor recreation (e.g., sit in shade, go in water).
Communicate choice about attending spectator events.
Play tape recorder for peers in mainstream setting.*

C. Other community skills
Decrease time to be fed in community settings* (first year, small snack only).
Hold head up while pushed in shopping mall.*
Indicate choice during shopping.
Release item into cart during shopping.

III. Related skills

A. Communication
Greet familiar people by lifting head and smiling.*
Communicate "yes" by lifting head, "no" by lowering head.*
Push buzzer on chair or beside mat with hand to signal need for assistance.
Converse with peers and family by operating page turner for picture album.
Expand questions used for "yes/no" communication yearly.*

B. Motor skills
Remove food from spoon and swallow during eating (improve fluency).*
Increase time with head erect.*
Increase range of motion in arm in context of daily activities.*
Increase distance can be pushed in chair before tires.*
(Improvement targeted for each of the above areas annually.)

C. Academics
Not applicable.

D. Social skills and interfering behavior
(see social responses listed for communication)
Increase generalization across people for each social response.

Learner: Al
Current age: 18
Plan is for years: 1989–1991 (graduates)
Instructor: Mr. A.

Brief learner description: Al has been classified as having multiple handicaps, including severe behavior disorders, moderate mental retardation, and brain injury. Al was recommended for the "life skills" special education program because of his socially intolerable behaviors (e.g., hitting, destroying materials, profanity) and his poor academic progress. In his 3 years in the life skills program, Al acquired new social skills and stopped engaging in his problem behaviors. He also learned to apply his academic skills to daily living situations. For example, Al can read simple recipes, write a grocery list, and perform computation with a calculator. Al's parents have been extremely pleased with his progress in the life skills program. They are eager to help the instructor secure a job for Al upon graduation. Al also will be applying for placement in a group home that provides transitional training for supervised apartment living.

Learner's strengths and capabilities: outgoing, attractive smile, wide repertoire of skills for using community settings, many skills needed to be successful in an apartment, personal leisure interests (e.g., video games).

Environments used for planning: Al's home, group home for adults, bowling alley (vocational placement), city bus routes, street routes, shopping mall with grocery store, medical facility, YMCA.

I. Skills for the home

A. Personal maintenance
Shave.*
Maintain neat appearance throughout the day.*

B. Housekeeping and food preparation
Do all laundry (e.g., clothes, sheets).*
Operate dishwasher.
Prepare balanced meals: increase meal repertoire annually.*
Store food safely.*
Respond correctly to simulated emergencies for injuries, fire, or break-in.*

C. Recreation/socialization
Not a priority; has a repertoire of skills that he uses at home during his leisure time.

D. Community preparation
Use telephone to call for bus information.*
Use telephone to call to make plans with friends.
Plan purchases within budget.*
Keep appointment calender.*

II. Skills for the community

A. Vocational Skills (highest priority area)
Increase duration of work time without interaction or prompts to continue annually.*

Clean restrooms (generalization).*
Prepare short-order meals.*
Operate industrial dishwasher.*
Operate soda fountain.*
Clean lunch counter and food preparation area.*
Manage time using checklist and watch.*
Replicate above skills in bowling alley or similar facility in second- and third-year job placement; fade instructor supervision across these 2 years.

B. Community recreation
Increase fitness through use of YMCA facility.*
Interact appropriately with others at YMCA.*

C. Other community skills
Purchase groceries or other items from list alone.*
Use city bus across varied and changing routes.*
Demonstrate skill to go to medical appointment alone.*

III. Related skills

A. Communication
Use personal pronoun "I."
Use social links in conversation.
Respond with more information when asked for clarification.
(Teach above skills incidentally, in context of other activities.)

B. Motor skills
Improve fitness (see Community recreation).

C. Academics
Maintain use of calculator in shopping, budgeting.*
Read times, words, pictures to follow work schedule.*
Read and respond to signs found in employment setting.

D. Social skills and interfering behavior
Shop or travel alone.*
Refuse invitations to accompany people who do not know a code word.*
Refuse to stop working when given directions by people other than the designated boss.*
Ignore unwanted attention by moving away and continuing to work or perform activity.*
Problem: Inappropriate social comments. *Alternative:* No comments initiated to strangers; respond to appropriate requests from strangers with social amenities; initiate discussion about daily activities or give compliments to familiar people.

Learner: <u>Ann</u>   Current age: <u>32</u>
Plan is for years: <u>1990–1995</u>   Instructor: <u>Ms. P.</u>

Brief learner description: Ann has only lived in the community for a little over 1 year. Ann was placed in an institution as an infant, and left to enter a group home as a result of deinstitutionalization litigation at the age of 31. Ann has been classified as having profound mental retardation. She is able to walk alone, but has always been escorted. Thus, she currently does not walk across a room without assistance. Ann feeds herself with her fingers with considerable spilling and oversized bites. If unsupervised, she will choke while feeding herself because she does not judge mouth-size portions. Ann is partially schedule trained for toileting but has several accidents per week. Ann speaks occasionally, but the context is similar to delayed echolalia and not relevant to the context. She also shouts profanity when sick or distressed. She has no other communication. Ann does smile and laugh appropriately when other adults are laughing. Ann lives in a home with two other adult women from her previous placement. The home has 24-hour supervision and some instruction in home skills. Ann's assessment was designed primarily for her adult education placement, which is developing supported employment for her and currently provides her with continuing education, recreation, and community integration.

Learner's strengths and capabilities: happy, friendly, gentle with animals, flexible and likes to try new activities, attractive.

Environments used for planning: Home where Ann lives, continuing education center, job sites, senior citizen recreational center (future), indoor city stadium, shopping center near home, fast-food restaurant, family restaurant, convenience store, bus station.

I. Skills for the home

A.   Personal maintenance

Eliminate toilet accidents through schedule training* (generalize continence across changes in daily settings).

Push pants down/pull pants up in toilet stall.*

Use towel when washing hands (discard paper towel in public restroom).*

Use restroom without help (5-year goal).

Communicate need to use restroom (5-year goal).

Feed self finger foods without stuffing mouth.*

Feed self with spoon without spilling.

Feed self with fork.

Drink from glass without spilling.*

Brush teeth.

B.   Housekeeping and food preparation

Discard trash after lunch at work.*

Carry dishes to sink at home; lunchbox to shelf at work.*

Wipe table after meals.*

Push in chairs after cleaning.

Open containers (e.g., lunch containers, food packages).

C. Recreation/socialization (taught during breaks between work sessions)

Play electric self-playing piano.*

Operate volume control on radio that is on.*

Operate radio alone.

Operate cassette tape player.

Turn pages in photo album.

Select and use leisure materials without prompts.

D. Community preparation

Put on coat.*

Get lunch from kitchen (or lunchbox from shelf).*

Carry belongings to van.

Pack tote bag with change of clothes.

II. Skills for the community

A. Vocational skills (based on paid jobs at center and routines observed in business mailroom)

Put paper in self-feeding copier.*

Staple paper using electric stapler.

Use photocopier without help.

Put supplies on shelves.

B. Community recreation

Walk several blocks with escort.

Drink soda from can.*

Use vending machine.*

Walk up/down steps alone.*

Attend adult spectator events (e.g., music program).

C. Other community skills

Stop at curb and wait for escort's signal to cross.*

Walk without being physically guided for 3–4 blocks (goal for next 5 years; increase distance each year)

Take wallet from pocket.*

Use wallet alone.

Select choice of snack purchase by pointing.*

Walk with shopping cart.

Grasp/release item into shopping cart.

Order food in restaurant by using pictures.

III. Related skills

A. Communication

Point to make choice from display.*

Nod "yes" and "no" when asked, "Do you want _____?" when no display.

Converse by turning to page in photo album that companion discusses.

Communicate hunger, thirst, need to toilet, pain by using picture wallet.

Initiate communication by touching companion's arm.

Imitate social comments verbally (e.g., "Hello," "How are you?").

Show identification card upon request.

B. Motor skills

Use thumb in opposition to fingers to grasp glass or soda can, or to carry objects in activities listed for home or community.

Increase speed of ambulation (annually).*

Walk to nearby destination (e.g., restroom) without prompts (first year, walk across room with instructor in sight).*

Increase strength by carrying work supplies, tote bag.

Open doors without help (increase types each year).*

C. Academics

Not relevant for Ann.

D. Social skills and interfering behavior

Initiate social interaction by sitting near, walking to person during break.*

Respond to social comment with smile and eye contact.

Share picture photo album with new acquaintances.

Problem: Loud cursing and delayed echolalia in public settings. *Alternative:* Communicate desire to leave by pointing to door.

Learner: John   Current age: 53
Plan is for years: 1985–1990   Instructor: Ms. M.

Brief learner description: John left the institution where he spent most of his life about 3 years prior to this assessment. Since John left the institution, he lost his sight and most of his hearing ability. At one time, John was classified as having moderate mental retardation. However, as a young man, John rode his bicycle to leave the institution to visit his relatives in a nearby town. He also received subscriptions to magazines and newspapers in the institution. John has not yet acquired the skills to cope with his sensory losses. Instead, he has become sedentary with resultant deterioration in overall fitness and has developed behaviors that create disruptions in his home life and community integration (e.g., screaming, grabbing people). Although this curriculum was designed for John's adult education program, it was developed in consultation with the staff of the home where he resides.

Learner's strengths and capabilities: sense of humor, interest in baseball, cares for his personal needs, remembers events about family and friends.

Environments used for planning: John's group home, John's brother's home where he visits, continuing education center, business mail room, retirement club, shopping mall, city streets, city bus, restaurant, convenience store.

I. Skills for the home

A. Personal maintenance
    Pour from thermos (lunch at work).*
    Adjust pants in restroom only.*

B. Housekeeping and food preparation
    Wipe table.*
    Sweep floor.
    Clean windows.
    Make coffee.*

C. Recreation/socialization (teach during work breaks)
    Operate tape recorder.*
    Select own tapes.*
    Insert new batteries in tape recorder.

D. Community preparation
    State his daily schedule.*
    Keep appointment calendar.
    Use telephone with amplification to call brother.

II. Skills for the community

A. Vocational skills (based on paid jobs in the center and routine observed in business mailroom)
    Complete one insert and label job at half rate of worker without disabilities.*

Complete multiple-insert job.*

Fold letter and card style.*

Increase rate of multiple-insert job with folding to half rate of worker without disabilities.

Operate self-feeding photocopier alone.

Complete, collate, staple multiple-page photocopy job.

Work without standing or screaming until break (about 90 minutes) (first-year goal is 30 minutes).*

B.   Community recreation

Plan and participate in senior citizen bus tour (see communication, social, and motor skills needed).

C.   Other community skills

Walk to familiar room in center or home by trailing wall.*

Walk with escort, using cane to negotiate curbs.*

Take city bus with escort.

Take long bus tour with escort.

Use wallet.*

Select quarters from coins.*

Select dollars.

Organize wallet by type of money.

Count dollars to make purchase.

State order in restaurant or at convenience store.*

III.   Related skills

A.   Communication

Respond with factual answer when asked about schedule.*

Respond to most social comments or questions directed to him* (generalization to new acquaintances).

Ask for supplies when needed during work sessions.*

Ask questions for clarification about his schedule or activities.

State identification (e.g., name, address, phone number).

B.   Motor skills

Walk 4 city blocks without stopping to rest.*

Increase speed of walking with sighted guide.*

C.   Academics

Write signature on checks or forms using guide.*

Apply counting skills to job assignments.

D.   Social skills and interfering behaviors

Use social amenities (e.g., "please," "thank you").*

Initiate topics appropriate to adult conversation.

Problem: Attempts to kiss and hug all women when they say "goodbye."

Alternative: Express parting greeting with handshake and polite comment.

Problem: When unsure of schedule, wanders, screams, and grabs strangers. *Alternative:* Time management skills, appropriate waiting, and asking questions about schedule when uncertain.

Learner: <u>Lester</u>   Current age: <u>69</u>
Plan is for years: <u>1990–1993</u>   Instructor: Home—<u>Ms. K.</u>
                                                Community—<u>Ms. C.</u>

Brief learner description: <u>Lester has been classified as having severe mental
retardation. Lester resided in a large institution for individuals with mental retardation since he was a young child, and received a community placement in 1989.
Lester communicates socially with smiles and gestures. He also speaks using
one word, to request or to label objects. If confused or crowded, Lester sometimes aggresses against whomever is closest to him. Lester resides in a home
with four other adults with mental retardation. His natural family visits and maintains some contact with Lester by attending IHP meetings and inviting him home
for holidays.</u>

Learner's strengths and capabilities: <u>friendly, social, humorous, a good dancer,
fun-loving.</u>

Environments used in planning: <u>Lester's home, area restaurants, YMCA, craft
center stores.</u>

I. Skills for the home

A.   Personal maintenance
      Eliminate daytime toilet accidents.*
      Use toilet without assistance.
      Dress independently.*
      Shower independently.
      Participate in shaving.*
      Shave himself.
      Apply powder and ointments.*
      Brush hair.
      Self-medicate.
      Brush teeth.*
      Use deodorant.
      Shampoo hair.

B.   Housekeeping and food preparation
      Dust his bedroom furniture.*
      Dust rest of household.
      Put his clothes in hamper.*
      Participate in doing laundry.
      Use dishwasher.
      Make drink from mix.*
      Make simple snack.
      Participate in mealtime routines.*

C.   Recreation/socialization
      Use TV independently.*
      Use radio independently.*

Water his plants.*
Paint.
Prepare for parties.
Start a collection.

II. Skills for the community

A. Vocational skills
Not applicable (retired).

B. Community recreation (integrated retirement)
Operate tape player.*
Participate in square and folk dancing.*
Plant a community garden.
Participate in arts-and-crafts classes.*
Use paint brush.*
Use glue gun.
Use adapted scissors.
Play golf.
Play frying pan for senior citizen kitchen band.
Distribute songsheets for Men of Retirement Age Club.*

C. Other community skills
Enter/exit van.*
Purchase snack with 1 dollar.
Run errands.
Indicate food choice in restaurant.*
Indicate food choice while grocery shopping.
Participate in personal shopping.*
Prepare mailings as volunteer for Red Cross.*

III. Related skills

A. Communication
Express choice between array of items.*
Indicate choice of activity using pictures.
Show identification card upon request.*
State name to others.
Introduce self in clubs and classes.

B. Motor skills
Unscrew cap of tube.
Walk 4 city blocks without stopping to rest.

C. Academics
Not applicable.

D. Social and interfering behavior
Eliminate hitting.*

Request that others give him space.
Ask for help when confused.
Eliminate socially offensive language.
Teach socially appropriate ways to get a laugh.

Learner: <u>Eva</u>   Current age: <u>13</u>
Plan is for years: <u>1990–1993</u>   Instructor: <u>Mr. N.</u>

Brief learner description: Eva has received various classifications including autism, moderate mental retardation, and severe emotional disturbance. Although
she is able to converse, Eva does not initiate conversation and her replies are
often echolalic. Eva's family is bilingual, and speaks both Spanish and English
fluently. Eva is also bilingual, but has more English than Spanish vocabulary. Eva
attends a regular middle school and recently began receiving some regular class
integration.

Learner's strengths and capabilities: kind, quiet, attractive, good at handwork
such as crafts or needlework, has some reading skills, can add and subtract, can
use a fast-food restaurant with minimal help.

Environments used in planning: Eva's home, integrated school, job training
sites, local restaurants, local stores.

I. Skills for the home

A.   Personal maintenance
    Use napkin when eating.*
    Eat at acceptable rates.*
    Follow schedule to maintain appearance.*
    Take care of menstrual needs.*
    Shave legs and underarms.
    Select own clothes (age-appropriate clothes).
    Use makeup and perfume.

B.   Housekeeping and food preparation
    Wash and wipe dishes.
    Hang up clothes.*
    Prepare simple foods using stove.
    Plan simple meals.

C.   Recreation/socialization
    Do needlepoint.*
    Play board games.
    Play tapes with friends.

II. Skills for the community

A.   Vocational skills
    Follow schedule.*
    Dust and vacuum.
    Stock shelves.
    Sign in for work.
    Engage in social conversation.*
    Sign name.*

B. Community recreation
    Extend restaurant skills to going with friends alone.
    Order from menu.*
    Make small grocery purchases.
    Participate in community aerobics class.
    Remain with escort when in community.*
    Learn sight words related to shopping.*
    Keep personal calendar.*

C. Other community skills
    Cross streets with escort.*
    Cross streets independently.
    Match coins for vending machine use.
    Use public transportation.

III. Related skills

A. Communication
    Raise hand to get attention in regular class.*
    Converse with peers without disabilities.
    Greet peers in hall.*
    Use language courtesies.
    Ask for help (generalization).

B. Motor skills
    Increase hand strength.*
    Increase fitness by learning aerobics.

C. Academics
    Read menu words to place order.*
    Read words on physical education board to identify activity.*
    Read television guide to select show.
    Write and read language experience stories about community outings.
    Read work schedule.
    Read calendar words and numbers and keep personal calendar.*
    Read calendar posted at work site.
    Compute money needed for purchases up to $10.*
    Compute money with calculator to keep checkbook.

D. Social and interfering behaviors
    Play group games.*
    Request help, without screaming, in unfamiliar settings.*
    Participate in middle school activities and classes.

Learner: <u>Liz</u>   Current age: <u>6</u>

Plan is for years: <u>1989–1992</u>   Instructor: <u>Ms. G.</u>

Brief learner description: <u>Liz is a 6-year-old girl who has been classified as having cerebral palsy (ataxia) and severe mental retardation. Liz walks alone, and climbs stairs with a railing. She nods "yes" to express preferences and signs "eat." She feeds herself with supervision and is schedule trained for toileting.</u>

Learner's strengths and capabilities: <u>attractive, usually smiles, happy, sense of humor, social.</u>

Environments used in planning: <u>Liz's family home, visits to extended-family homes, school, convenience store, restaurants, church, playground, camp.</u>

Key: T = teacher, OT = occupational therapist, PT = physical therapist, SP = speech-language pathologist; 1st = first year, 2nd = second year, 3rd = third year.

I. Skills for the home

A. Personal maintenance

  Tolerate hair grooming (1st) (T, OT).
  Participate in hair grooming (2nd) (T, OT).
  Match clothes by color (3rd) (T).

B. Toileting

  Generalize use of toilet, no accidents across settings (1st) (T).
  Stay seated on toilet (1st) (T).
  Walk to the toilet when told (1st) (SP, T).
  Communicate need to toilet (1st) (SP, T).
  Push pants down (2nd) (PT, T).
  Wash own hands (2nd) (T).
  Wipe herself (3rd) (T).

C. Eating

  Stay seated at table (1st) (T).
  Eat variety of foods without assistance (1st) (T, OT).
  Communicate food choice (1st) (T, SP).
  Improve pointing response for communicating food choice (2nd) (T, SP).
  Make choices from picture booklet (3rd) (T, SP).
  Not grab food (1st) (T).
  Improve oral-muscular skills (e.g., tongue thrust) (1st) (OT).
  Master fork use (3rd) (T).
  Use a napkin (3rd) (T).

D. Housekeeping

  Put her toys away (1st) (T).
  Hang up her coat, bag (1st) (T).
  Put clothes in hamper (2nd) (T).

E. Home recreation/leisure
    Increase toy play skills (1st) (T).
    Increase tactile exploration in play (1st) (T, OT).
    Increase unsupervised play (2nd, 3rd) (T).
    Increase vocalizations (1st, 2nd, 3rd) (T, SP).

F. Community preparation
    Get into/out of car or bus (1st) (T, PT).
    Communicate where she is going (1st) (T, SP).
    Put hands in lap upon entering car (1st) (T, PT).

II. Skills for the community

A. Vocational
    Position items (1st) (T).
    Identify colors (1st) (T).
    Follow picture schedule (1st) (T, SP).
    Increase pictures in schedule, point to pictures, and use booklet to communicate (2nd, 3rd) (T, SP).
    Imitate job directions (3rd) (T).

B. Social integration
    Get others' attention by tapping or calling (1st) (T, SP).
    Choose activity (1st) (T, SP).
    Protest by nodding "no" (no screaming) (1st) (T, SP).
    Greet other children with wave (1st) (T, SP).
    Use pictures to converse with other children (1st) (T, SP).
    Increase pictures used to converse, point and use booklet to communicate (2nd, 3rd) (T, SP).
    Increase cooperative play (2nd) (T).
    Participate partially in age-appropriate group learning (e.g., art, crafts, music) (1st, 2nd, 3rd) (T).

C. Restaurants/stores
    Select snack in store (1st) (T, SP).
    Quietly accompany adult who is shopping, for 5 minutes (1st) (T).
    Increase shopping time (2nd, 3rd) (T).
    Not grab food (1st) (T).
    Eat neatly in restaurants (2nd, 3rd) (T, OT).
    Step up/down curbs without assistance (1st) (T, PT).

D. Community recreation
    Increase skills for use of playground equipment (1st, 2nd, 3rd) (T, PT).
    Step up/down curbs and raised surfaces without assistance (1st) (T, PT).
    Increase cooperative play at recess (2nd) (T).
    Look down to avoid extension (1st) (T, OT, PT).

Note: Communication, fine motor, gross motor, sensory integration, academics, and social skills/interfering behavior have been targeted within the functional activities listed in this curriculum as shown rather than listed as separate curricular areas.

appendix B

EXAMPLES OF A WRITTEN REPORT FOR A COMPREHENSIVE EDUCATIONAL ASSESSMENT

EDUCATIONAL EVALUATION

Student: Dennis Smith
Age: 8 yrs. 4 mos.   DOB: 6-3-79
Placement: Elementary SPMR
School: Lehigh Elementary

Date of report: October 12
Initial or reevaluation: Reevaluation
Evaluator: Ms. Dana Kay
Position: Teacher

BACKGROUND INFORMATION

Brief Student Description

Dennis Smith has received the medical diagnosis of severe spastic quadriplegia, and the educational classification of profound mental retardation with an accompanying severe physical disability. Dennis has a few observable, voluntary motoric responses. These responses include lifting his head and moving one arm in a horizontal plane. Dennis must be positioned properly in a wheelchair or on other adaptive equipment to make these responses.

Educational History

Dennis was first evaluated for educational services by United Cerebral Palsy in 1980. Dennis and his mother participated in an infant stimulation program at United Cerebral Palsy 1 day per week from January 1980 to May 1982. According to Mrs. Smith, this program included physical therapy and parent training in infant stimulation. Mrs. Smith shared a written evaluation from United Cerebral Palsy dated February 4, 1980, that summarized the use of the Koontz Developmental Assessment (Koontz, 1974). The summary identified no existing skills on the scale, and stated that Dennis's level was "below 1 month."

On August 1, 1982, Dennis was evaluated for the school district's preschool program. This evaluation utilized the Denver Developmental Screening

Test (Frankenburg, Dodds, & Frandal, 1968–70). Again, the evaluation concluded that Dennis's developmental level was "below 1 month." Dennis's preschool IEP included objectives in visual tracking, head control, swallowing food, swallowing liquid, and "sensory stimulation." These objectives remained the same from 1982 until 1984.

In September 1984, Dennis was placed in the elementary class for students with severe and profound mental retardation. On September 15, 1984, his teacher completed a school district–designed developmental checklist. On this checklist, the teacher noted that Dennis could swallow liquids and mechanical soft solids (e.g., foods prepared with a blender). He had begun to life his head for a few seconds at a time, and occasionally made eye contact and smiled. Dennis's IEP for 1984–1985 and 1985–1986 contained objectives in visual tracking, head control, removing food from a spoon with his lips, drinking liquids with minimal spilling, and "sensory stimulation." On the 1985–1986 IEP, Dennis's mother wrote, "While I approve this IEP because I know of no other alternatives for Dennis, I am discouraged that his IEP has been virtually the same since he entered the preschool program in 1982."

The current evaluation was conducted in response to Mrs. Smith's note on the 1985–1986 IEP to identify new objectives for Dennis's IEP for 1986–1987. Also, Dennis's educational program until 1985 had been based on infant development. This evaluation was conducted to develop a chronological age–appropriate life skills curriculum for Dennis.

Prior Educational Evaluations

The only educational evaluations conducted for Dennis up to this report were the developmental assessments mentioned earlier. Dennis's previous teachers did not conduct direct ongoing assessment, but rather kept anecdotal notes on Dennis. These notes were not available in Dennis's records. Mrs. Smith shared copies of several of these reports that typically summarized the teaching activities in which Dennis had participated. Mrs. Smith could not recollect any written reports of progress except the speech-language pathologist's evaluations of Dennis's improved eating skills in the reevaluation in September, 1985.

Other Evaluations

This report is one component of a multidisciplinary evaluation of Dennis that includes medical, physical therapy, occupational therapy, speech therapy, and educational evaluations. The family physician's report noted the need for Dennis to improve his overall health and stamina. Dennis currently tires easily and frequently is ill with viruses and other infections. The physical therapist recommended new equipment to accommodate Dennis's growth since his current equipment was purchased. Specifically, a large-size wedge and wheelchair were recommended. The physical therapist also noted that Dennis's improved head control should be encouraged. The occupational therapist noted that Dennis had some range of motion in one arm that might be usable to operate adaptive switches if it became stronger and more consistent. The speech-language pathologist targeted improved eating skills in removing food from the spoon and swallowing. The speech-language pathologist concluded that speech development was improbable for Dennis and that a "yes/no" communication system should be developed.

CURRENT ASSESSMENT

Identification of Skills for Assessment

Adaptive Behavior Screening An adaptive behavior assessment was used as a general screening of Dennis's current skills. *The Comprehensive Test of Adaptive Behavior* (Adams, 1984) was completed by using the Parent Survey form and observations of Dennis in the classroom. At the time of this assessment, Dennis had no self-care, daily living, or recognizable communicative responses.

Family Contact An ecological inventory was conducted through a teacher-made survey that was sent to the parents on September 2, 1986. This inventory revealed that Dennis shows some preference for bright lights and sweets, and dislike for applesauce and being cold. The parents would like for Dennis's progress in eating to be maintained in his ongoing curriculum plan. They would like to see "new goals" and "skills that will make him a more active member of the family" added to his plan. The mother noted that she provides most of Dennis's care and would be interested in implementing some daily instruction with Dennis. This survey was also used to identify the environments for further inventories. The parents identified these environments as ones that the family uses or would like to use: a respite care facility, city and state parks, an indoor stadium, a shopping mall, a family restaurant, and the family's church.

Ecological Inventories Ecological inventories were conducted for the identified environments through observations and interviews with significant people in each environment listed by the parents, and the student's current and future school environments. In each inventory, activities of other young elementary-age children were noted to identify possible skills to adapt for Dennis. From these various inventories, several general skills were noted: peer interaction, communication of preferences to parents and others in the environments, general conversation with family members and peers, making small purchases of toys or snacks, eating, and watching events or looking for a destination.

Priorities for Further Assessment From these inventories, it was concluded that Dennis would need to learn to use his few motoric responses in ways that would make him an active participant in various routines. For the next few years, the goal of partial participation in a variety of home and community activities was viewed as most important and feasible. Communication of preference was targeted as the highest priority because it would provide the quickest way for Dennis to become active in his daily routines. The parents' priority of maintenance of eating skills was also noted for further assessment and planning.

Direct Assessment

To address the priorities, assessment was planned and conducted over the period of 2 weeks in the classroom or the community environment noted. The results of this assessment follow.

Home Observation The adaptive behavior assessment provided minimal direction for planning home skills for Dennis because he had no skills listed on the survey. An observation was made of Dennis's mother performing Dennis's caregiving routine to identify responses that might be targeted for Dennis's participation. Feeding, diaper changing, and dressing were observed. From this observation, it was concluded that Dennis might learn to communicate preferences for food or clothes, and might communicate the need to be changed. It was apparent that Dennis's eating skills would need to become more fluent in order for the family to take him to a restaurant, since feeding him required over an hour.

Assessment of Head Control A teacher-made assessment was also used for head control. This response was considered a possible one for use in a "yes/no" communication system, and also was important for Dennis to observe events in his environments. The teacher presented repeated trials distributed across activities in which some object involved in the activity was shown to Dennis. Using a stopwatch, the number of seconds that Dennis held his head up was timed.

Communication Assessment A checklist was used to note any idiosyncratic responses that Dennis used to communicate, and the function of these responses over a 2-week period. Although Dennis typically sat passively and made no responses, five responses were observed over the 2-week period that could be considered communicative. On the first occasion, Dennis cried when his diaper was soiled and the teacher was preoccupied with another student. On the next occasion, Dennis looked at the teacher and smiled when she said, "Good morning, Dennis." During one day's lunch, Dennis was given spinach. He grimaced and spit it out. The fourth event occurred when his mother visited the class. When she left, Dennis cried and hit his arm against the side of the chair. In the fifth event observed, the teacher was conducting assessment to identify leisure skills. Dennis smiled and laughed when the teacher played a tape with upbeat music. A second checklist was used in consultation with the speech, occupational, and physical therapists to identify a response that might be used for "yes/no." These professionals concurred that lifting his head for "yes" would be the simplest to train since he could already lift his head. This response would also be portable across settings and activities.

Home Leisure A teacher-made observation was used to identify both Dennis's preferences for leisure materials and skills to use them. Task analytic assessment of pressing a flipper switch to activate a toy bus was used. Dennis made some effort to depress the switch, but could not do so alone. This switch could be used to adapt many battery-activated toys for Dennis. Preference was observed by noting whether or not Dennis made any response of pleasure in repeated trial presentations of items (e.g., smiling, laughing, watching as the teacher activated the material). Dennis showed the strongest preference for upbeat music. He showed no interest in electronic games, and some interest for colorful pictures. Dennis could not operate a switch-activated page turner when a task analytic assessment on this skill was used.

Community-Based Observation Dennis was taken to a shopping mall to observe his skills in that environmemnt. A teacher-made checklist was used to summarize skills that Dennis might acquire for community environments. It was observed that Dennis rarely lifted his head to see the environment. He did not look at a peer who talked with him during the outing. He also fell asleep after the first 10 minutes in the mall, and slept for most of the rest of the day (about 2 hours). A phone call to Mrs. Smith indicated that Dennis frequently tired during outings, and slept for several hours after being taken somewhere.

Assessment of Use of Arm and Hand in Daily Living Activities Task analytic assessment was used to assess Dennis's use of his horizontal arm movement and grasp for daily activities. He was assessed in wiping his tray, and in releasing clothes into a hamper. Dennis made slight voluntary movements in each of these assessments. For example, he moved his arm slightly to the right when a sponge was placed in his hand on his tray. He slightly uncurled his fingers when clothes were placed in his hand and his hand was placed on the edge of the hamper. These movements could be targeted for training across activities (e.g., dusting, releasing objects into a shopping cart).

Assessment of Eating Skills Repeated trial assessment was used to assess removing food from a spoon, and drinking from a glass when fed. The first 10 bites or sips were assessed for each new food or liquid. Dennis consistently removed food for some foods (pudding, potatoes, peaches), but did so inconsistently (two to six trials) for other foods (meat, green beans, beets). He drank from a cup consistently. Dennis's lunches were also timed for 2 weeks. Dennis's feeding time ranged from 30 to 55 minutes, depending on the amount of food. Although not timed, Dennis seemed to eat meat and vegetables more slowly than sweets and fruits.

TRANSDISCIPLINARY EDUCATIONAL EVALUATION

Student: Liz Brown

Age: 6 yrs. 8. mos. DOB: 10-18-82

Placement: Elementary SPH

School: Mallory Elementary School
Hampton, Virginia

Date of report: 6-21-89

Evaluators: Hampton School District Staff: Renee L. Barnes, speech-language pathologist; Alice M. Enault, occupational therapist; Bertina D. Giles, teacher; Robert F. Richardson, supervisor; Lisa T. Sawyer, physical therapist.

Consultant: Diane M. Browder.

BACKGROUND INFORMATION

Brief Student Description

Liz Brown's classifications are cerebral palsy with an accompanying seizure disorder and severe mental retardation. Liz is an attractive girl with light blonde hair. She frequently smiles and enjoys social contact. Liz can stand and walk alone, and use stairs with railings. She feeds herself with supervision and is schedule trained for toileting. Liz uses a modified form of the manual sign "eat," nods "yes" to indicate some preferences, and is beginning to use pictures to request food and drink.

Educational History

Liz's developmental delay was diagnosed medically at the age of 9 months and she received homebound early intervention educational and therapeutic services in Strasburg, Virginia. Beginning at the age of 2 years, Liz attended a special preschool program with therapeutic services provided in consultation with the classroom teacher. Liz's father's employment requires periodic relocation and thus, she continued her preschool and kindergarten education in a center-based program in Richmond, Virginia. After her move to the Hampton School District, Liz began to attend an SPH class in a regular school and to receive direct speech, physical, and occupational therapy.

Recent Evaluation

On May 25, 1989, Liz's teacher, Bertina Giles, completed the Woodcock-Johnson Scales of Independent Behavior (Bruininks et al., 1984) and the Comprehensive Test of Adaptive Behavior (CTAB) (Adams, 1984). On the

---

The name of the student in this example has been changed for reasons of confidentiality. Actual names of all professionals are used, with their permission.

Woodcock-Johnson, Liz received the functional level of severe deficit in all areas, with age scores from 0-8 to 1-6. On the CTAB, Liz's performance compared to other individuals her age with mental retardation was low average for self-help and language/academics; average for home living, independent living skills, and social skills; and high average for sensory motor skills.

Bertina Giles also summarized Liz's IEP progress on her final report card and noted the following skills acquired in 1988–1989. In the area of *domestic* skills: Liz touches a picture to request a drink and has improved her tolerance of food textures. She has also improved her tolerance for hairbrushing and tries to comb her own hair. Liz has achieved partial mastery for hanging up her coat. She places her cup on the table to request more milk as an alternative to loud outbursts. In the area of *community* skills: Liz has mastered standing from a floor-sitting position and made progress on using stairs, walking on the right side of the hall, and walking from the bus to the breezeway alone. She has mastered discrimination of the universal symbols for women's and men's restrooms and made progress in following simple directions (e.g., "Come here"). In the *vocational* skill area: Liz has improved her skills for working alone at a task, identifying objects receptively, and placing objects on a top or bottom shelf. For *leisure/recreation* skills: Liz has received instruction in group turn taking and age-appropriate play materials, but has not yet demonstrated mastery.

Renee Barnes's summary of Liz's 1988–1989 progress in speech therapy indicated that Liz still requires a physical prompt to point to pictures to indicate her preferences. She does follow several one-step directions consistently. Alice Enault noted in her occupational therapy summary that Liz has ataxic upper extremity movements, seeks tactile input, has good eye scanning movements without disassociation of head and neck, and is hyperflexive to startling sounds and physical prompts. Liz has improved maintaining a grasp while pulling up her pants or pulling off her coat sleeve. She also has improved her balance for small curbs while holding an object, and has increased her visual attention to an activity to 30 seconds. Liz has mastered protective extension. Lisa Sawyer noted in Liz's physical therapy annual summary that gaining rapport with Liz for therapy took nearly 6 months. In the final months of school, Liz mastered standing from a floor-sit, which was a difficult skill for her. Her ambulation has also improved, with infrequent falls.

Evaluation Purpose

The purpose of the current assessment was to develop a 3-year curriculum plan for Liz using a transdisciplinary model of service delivery in an integrated school setting. The parents' appraisal of Liz's strengths and skill needs was selected as the foundation for this curriculum development, given Liz's age and the extent of her family's involvement with her educational program.

CURRENT ASSESSMENT

Identification of Skills for Assessment

Since Liz had recent, descriptive evaluations of her educational progress—including adaptive behavior scales, data summaries for IEP objectives, and therapy reports—an ecological inventory in the form of a parent interview was used to identify skills for further assessment. Diane Browder interviewed the parents on June 18, 1989, and asked them to summarize Liz's current skills and skill needs in several home and community-related categories. The parents' preferences for Liz's skill development were also noted in this initial interview.

The parents noted some skills that were not reflected in the professional annual summaries. In skills for the *home, personal maintenance:* Liz participates in handwashing by putting her hands in the water. She also uses a spoon consistently when eating. For *community preparation:* Liz will go get her bathing suit to indicate a desire to swim, and walks to the car alone. In the *vocational* area: Liz loves to assemble toys shaped like eggs and nuts and bolts, which might be developed toward a vocational preference. For *other community activities:* Liz has good skills for eating in restaurants and going to the movies. She also loves to swim and can tread water with "Water Wings."

For *future skill needs:* The parents noted a strong preference for Liz to eliminate toilet accidents and to stay in bed at night. Further tolerance for having her hair groomed was noted as important because of Liz's hair type and the family's church participation. Her parents considered housekeeping to be unimportant for Liz at this time compared to her other skill needs, but saw value in teaching her to put toys away as an alternative to "cluttering" her room. For home recreation, unsupervised play skills were identified as very important. For community preparation, getting into and out of a car alone and not putting her fingers in the door frame were selected as most crucial now. For using public settings, Liz does not use stores because she grabs food items. However, having Liz grocery shop was a low priority for the parents. Social integration with people without disabilities was discussed, with consideration given to Liz's church contacts with nondisabled peers. The family identified the need for Liz to improve her skills for group learning settings (e.g., Sunday School), but did not see "mainstreaming" as a top priority. Some concern was noted for Liz's behavior of pulling the hair of younger children.

From the parents' interview and the professionals' year of work with Liz, a draft of a 3-year curriculum was initiated. To complete this plan, more information was needed in several areas. These included: 1) an assessment of Liz's response to a brief food-shopping trip, to observe adaptive/maladaptive behavior in public; 2) an assessment of the generalization of her skills to a summer camp and of social interaction with both disabled and nondisabled peers in that setting; 3) consideration of integration options; 4) clarification of the type of symbols and symbol format for Liz's communication; 5) clarification of Liz's tactile defensiveness, and ideas of how unsupervised play might be linked to improving her tactile exploration; 6) clarification of Liz's oral-muscular difficulties and fine motor skills; 7) a task analytic assessment of her entry into/exit from a car; and 8) Liz's generalization of her gross motor skills to a home environment with high motivation (i.e., playground), since Liz sometimes resists physical therapy.

Direct Assessment

Community Observation   Bertina Giles, Liz's teacher, and Diane Browder accompanied Liz to a convenience store to observe her use of picture cards to indicate a preference, and her general behavior. Upon entering the car and again at the store, Liz clearly selected a Photo Cue Card picture of potato chips from a three-choice array. At the end of the shopping time, she picked one bag of chips from the shelf shown to her. Liz shopped with Diane Browder who told her, "I'll do my shopping first and then you can shop." Using a stopwatch, Liz's shopping duration was 4 minutes and 32 seconds from the time she entered the store until the purchases were made. During this time, she sat down three times and had five verbal outbursts. However, she was able to be quickly redirected to shop by Diane Browder after each outburst.

Generalization to Camp   Bertina Giles interviewed the camp staff to review Liz's generalization of skills on the first day of camp. Liz was attending a therapeutic camp for children with special needs that was integrated in a day camp for children without disabilities. According to the camp staff, on the way to camp on the bus (unescorted), Liz had befriended a peer without disabilities who helped her off the bus. She generally socialized with the other campers (with and without disabilities) and at one point left her special needs group to join a group of children without disabilities who were playing a video game. However, she stayed to herself during most of the playground activities. The staff found Liz's behavior to be either appropriate or easily manageable. No hair pulling was observed. During lunch, Liz threw her food on the ground, but later ate with assistance. Liz's eating skills were of some concern to the staff, who asked for more information on her abilities and preferences. In general, Liz had generalized her school skills (e.g., walking, standing, joining a group) to a novel setting with no known adults or peers, and had blended well in this setting.

Integration Checklist   To consider further how Liz's social strengths might be enhanced in group activities, Bertina Giles completed an integration checklist of activities that could foster contact with children without disabilities. In her special class, Liz participated in small-group projects (e.g., cooking), shared books, had art and music lessons, went outside for recess, and had a group socialization lesson (circle time). She showed a high interest in all of these activities and had some skills for each. She had the least skills for music, circle time, and eating with others. From this checklist, recess and art or music classes seemed to be potential areas for integration planning that matched Liz's preferences and skills.

Communication Picture Use   Renee Barnes observed Liz's use of several types of pictures to indicate preferences. Liz's preferences were counted to note both her interests and her ability to discriminate between the pictures. Liz's touching/patting response was consistent and voluntary, and could be shaped to a pointing response. She was interested in a small photo album and turned some pages, which indicated that a small book format could be a future goal for her picture system. However, her attention span was short and she tore pages after turning a few.

Liz's preferences for various play items (e.g., puzzles, Play-Doh, doll, bubbles, swing, sliding board) was evaluated with the object present. When Liz vocalized and extended her arm toward the object, she was given a picture display to indicate her choice. Liz's discrimination was best with commercially available Photo Cue Cards that depict one item with a high-contrast background, which increases the picture's visual clarity. She was less successful with Polaroid pictures and least successful with line drawings. Some consideration was given to using small objects for her communication system, but Liz showed skill in the Photo Cue Card use and thus, did not need objects for communication. During the assessment, Liz vocalized frequently, indicating an ongoing potential for speech acquisition.

Fine Motor/Tactile Response Observations   Alice Enault observed Liz when she ate the snack she bought at the store and when she played at the family playground. During these times, Liz had no upper extremity spasticity and was able to bring her hands to midline. She had a persistent startle reflex and exhibited an extension reflex when items or activities were presented above eye level. While eating, Liz showed swallowing, elevation of the tongue, and lip extension within normal limits. However, her lip closure was poor and a primitive tongue thrust was observed. Her platal reflex (sucking) was weak and drooling, and though inconsistent, was evident. Liz showed a clear preference for use of her left hand in eating and play. Her fine motor tone was decreased at midline when she grasped or held objects. Her ulnar reflex, stimulated by contact to the lower edge of the palm, was strongly evident. Her toy play skills were similar to that of an 18–24-month-old, in that her primary motivation was pleasure seeking (not symbolic play). She did have near age-appropriate social skills for parallel play, but sharing and turn taking were not yet evident. Liz generally sought tactile stimulation that was wet, slippery, and sandy to the touch; and crunchy, crispy foods. She avoided light touch to her face and scalp, hot surfaces, very cold liquids, and chunky foods (e.g., meat).

Task Analytic Assessment for Car Entry/Exit   Liz was assessed on entering/exiting the car to run an errand with her mother. In this highly motivating circumstance, Liz negotiated some aspects of getting out of the car and positioned herself correctly to sit upon getting into the car. She could not step into or out of the car, and needed assistance for safe car entry. She also needed assistance to place her hands on her lap to avoid getting them caught in the door when it closed.

Playground Observation Lisa Sawyer observed Liz at a playground near her home with her brother and cousin present to note her motor skills in a motivating setting, since Liz had shown displeasure with traditional physical therapy. On previous occasions, Liz had been observed to climb up and down a traditional slide. However, this playground equipment consisted of a rough wood platform without stairs and the slide was too hot, so she did not use the slide during the observation. On the playground, she showed strength in ambulation, and in standing from a sitting position when she fell to the ground while walking over rough, grassy terrain. During play, skill deficits observed for further therapy were her need for hip and trunk stability, the need for stability in stepping up and down curbs, and unilateral weight shifting.

SUMMARY AND RECOMMENDATIONS

A curriculum chart was developed from this transdisciplinary evaluation that was derived from prioritization of each skill area by Liz's mother, who gave her own and Liz's rankings, the teacher, and the therapists (see Appendix A.) In a group meeting, priorities were selected for the 3-year plan from these rankings. In addition, several general recommendations were made for enhancing Liz's skill development for use of her home and community environments, including:

1. Liz demonstrated excellent generalization and social skills in her camp setting. Opportunities to learn and play with peers without disabilities could capitalize on her social strengths and offer role models to motivate her performance.
2. Liz needs continued instruction to use public settings (i.e., convenience stores) with appropriate social behavior. School instruction may improve her skills so that she can accompany her parents without their having to "work with Liz" whenever making a small purchase. Teaching Liz to select small items of preference can make these outings more meaningful to her and motivate her to be patient while others shop.
3. Toilet training has been mastered at school but has not generalized fully to home. Liz may be relying on certain setting cues to wait to be toileted that are less likely to be consistent in a normal, relaxed home environment as compared to a school day routine. Further instruction should focus on Liz's generalization of this skill to less structured times and settings, and on teaching her to communicate the need to toilet.
4. Liz's oral-muscular difficulties make eating neatly unfeasible at this time. Therapy should be provided to increase her oral skills. Desensitization of the mouth area prior to eating (i.e., by giving Liz a Popsicle or ice, brushing

her teeth thoroughly) may improve her tolerance for varying food textures. Liz can be taught to clean up food spillage and can have her mouth wiped with firm pressure. Her own use of a napkin should be delayed for a year or two.

5. Liz should be taught to point to pictures. Instruction should begin with high-contrast Photo Cue Cards. Over the 3 years, the number of pictures should be increased and the pictures should be faded to a smaller size. By the 3rd year, instruction in use of the pictures in a booklet may be feasible. Liz should use the same set of pictures across therapy, the classroom, and home, and should carry her pictures with her (e.g., in a purse or hanging from a belt loop). To increase Liz's communication options, both her speech and "yes/no" responses should continue to be encouraged. Liz should use the pictures not only to state her preferences, but also to follow a schedule (prevocational) and to converse with friends.

6. Materials and instructions should be presented to Liz so she does not have to look up; this avoids extension, which can cause her to fall backward. To optimize Liz's use of her trunk, arms, and hands while sitting, her tabletop should be at chest level. Toys and activities that require finger flexion are recommended to improve her fine motor skills. Finally, Liz's left-handedness should be considered in writing task analyses or in presenting tasks that require hand dominance.

FORMS FOR ANNUAL ASSESSMENT FOR IEP/IHP PLANNING

FORMAT FOR ANNUAL ASSESSMENT FOR IEP/IHP PLANNING

Learner: _____ Date: _____

Instructor: _____ Placement: _____

I. **Annual Progress:** (Summarize increment of progress, current mean, and state whether mastery, partial mastery, regression, or no progress on Skill Selection Chart. Summarize key points about previous year's progress here.)

II. **Learner's Preferences:** (To determine preferences, consider how the learner has responded to past instruction. Or, if learner is able to converse, interview the learner. Summarize the learner's preferences here.)

III. **Caregivers' Preferences:** (Interview the primary caregiver to review annual progress. Rate caregivers' priorities for continuing previous objectives on Skill Selection Chart. List new skills on chart and summarize caregivers' requests for new instruction here.)

IV. **Integration Priority:** (Complete the Ecological Inventory for Integration Planning for the site that will be the highest priority for the coming IEP/IHP period. List ongoing integration and new priority on Skill Selection Chart and use these to rate each skill and add new skills. Briefly summarize results of ecological inventory here and comment on any special considerations regarding integration to be maintained.)

V. **Longitudinal Planning:** (Review comprehensive assessment, if available. If not, review most recent curriculum-based assessment and/or adaptive behavior assessment. Also, consider learner's future placements. List longitudinal resources on Skill Selection Chart and use these to rank each skill and add new skills. Summarize most recent comprehensive assessment results briefly and comment on longitudinal priorities here.)

VI. **Instructor Preferences:** (Review Skill Selection Chart and rate each skill based on your own preferences and other considerations such as safety, normalization, and skill utility. Comment on your priorities here.)

VII. **Skill Selection:** (Select skills for the IEP/IHP with comments on Skill Selection Chart. Use this space for selection decisions that require more information than chart allows.)

ECOLOGICAL INVENTORY FOR INTEGRATION PLANNING

Site: Interviewee:

Date: Instructor:

                                    Learner:

1. Travel/location (answer by traveling to site). What method of transportation will be needed for this site (e.g., van, pedestrian skills)? Is site accessible to wheelchairs?

2. What are the primary activities of the site (types of jobs, if vocational; activities, if leisure facility; services, if public facility; curriculum, if public classroom)?

3. What is the site's schedule (e.g., class time, hours open, work hours required)? What are the best times for integrated instruction (e.g., less busy times in public facilities, teacher's preferred times for regular class)?

4. To what extent are orientation/mobility required (e.g., sits in one place versus multiple rooms or stairs)?

5. How important is a neatly groomed appearance? Other considerations regarding appearance?

6. What type of communication is required (e.g., placing orders, asking for help, asking for a locker)?

7. What type of social interaction skills are required (e.g., working in groups versus being alone)?

8. What type of help/assistance is available to individuals (e.g., peer instruction, information booths, job foreman)?

9. How often does the site change routines or physical layout?

10. To what extent are other people in the site expected to be quiet/still versus tolerance for a range of behaviors (e.g., contrast theater and football game)?

11. What natural reminders (cues) and rewards (contingencies) are available?

12. What is the interviewee's attitude toward the participation of individuals with disabilities in this site?

13. Will escorted assistance in restrooms or for eating or dressing be acceptable?

14. Are there any other special considerations for instruction for and in this site?

ANNUAL ASSESSMENT FOR IEP/IHP
PLANNING SKILL SELECTION CHART

Instructor: _____   Placement: _____

Date: _____   Learner: _____

Caregiver: _____   New integration priority: _____

Ongoing integration: _____

Resources for longitudinal planning: _____

| Annual progress for current objectives | Current objectives/ new skills | Priority source | | | | | Selected for IEP/IHP | Comments |
		Caregiver prefer-ences	Learner prefer-ences	Integration	Longitudinal planning	Instructor prefer-ences		

(continued)

Annual progress for current objectives	Current objectives/ new skills	Priority source					Selected for IEP/IHP	Comments
		Caregiver prefer-ences	Learner prefer-ences	Integration	Longitudinal planning	Instructor prefer-ences		

(continued)

Annual progress for current objectives	Current objectives/ new skills	Priority source					Selected for IEP/IHP	Comments
		Caregiver prefer- ences	Learner prefer- ences	Integration	Longitudinal planning	Instructor prefer- ences		

(Use duplicate pages as needed to list all skills.)

SCORING GUIDE FOR SKILL SELECTION CHART

The codes HP, MP, I, X, and XM are applied to each source of the prioritization process as described below.

HP Highest Priority

Caregiver wants objective to continue—no change.
Learner shows obvious interest in activity.
Integration inventory indicates clear need for skill.
Longitudinal planning indicates clear need for skill.
Instructor considers this skill to be high priority for learner.

MP Medium Priority

Caregiver considers skill important—objective may change.
Learner shows some interest or inconsistent interest in activity.
Integration inventory suggests need for the skill.
Longitudinal planning suggests need for the skill.
Instructor considers this skill to be important—but not one of learner's highest priorities.

I Impartial

Caregiver has no preference regarding this skill; or skill is not especially important to caregiver, but continuation is acceptable.
Learner shows indifference or neutral response to this activity.
Integration inventory provides no information to prioritize this skill.
Longitudinal planning provides no information to prioritize this skill.
Instructor is undecided about importance of this skill until other priorities are considered.

X Discontinue Objective

Caregiver requests objective be discontinued (rationale should be discussed).
Learner shows clear dislike of this activity (resistant; aberrant responses when skill taught.)
Integration inventory suggests that this skill is not functional or appropriate for future settings.
Longitudinal planning suggests that this skill is not the most efficient or most functional for learner's ongoing skill development.
Instructor prefers to discontinue objective (state rationale for discussion with caregivers).

XM Discontinue Because Mastered Objective

Instructor discontinues objective because no further formal instruction needed at this time.

appendix D

STANDARD FORMS FOR GRAPHS

STANDARD SLASH-NUMBER
DATA COLLECTION/GRAPH FORM

Behavior: _____ Name: _____ Mastery: _____

	100																				
		20	20	20	20	20	20	20	20	20	20	20	20	20	20	20	20	20	20	20	20
		19	19	19	19	19	19	19	19	19	19	19	19	19	19	19	19	19	19	19	19
	90	18	18	18	18	18	18	18	18	18	18	18	18	18	18	18	18	18	18	18	18
		17	17	17	17	17	17	17	17	17	17	17	17	17	17	17	17	17	17	17	17
	80	16	16	16	16	16	16	16	16	16	16	16	16	16	16	16	16	16	16	16	16
		15	15	15	15	15	15	15	15	15	15	15	15	15	15	15	15	15	15	15	15
	70	14	14	14	14	14	14	14	14	14	14	14	14	14	14	14	14	14	14	14	14
		13	13	13	13	13	13	13	13	13	13	13	13	13	13	13	13	13	13	13	13
	60	12	12	12	12	12	12	12	12	12	12	12	12	12	12	12	12	12	12	12	12
		11	11	11	11	11	11	11	11	11	11	11	11	11	11	11	11	11	11	11	11
	50	10	10	10	10	10	10	10	10	10	10	10	10	10	10	10	10	10	10	10	10
		9	9	9	9	9	9	9	9	9	9	9	9	9	9	9	9	9	9	9	9
	40	8	8	8	8	8	8	8	8	8	8	8	8	8	8	8	8	8	8	8	8
		7	7	7	7	7	7	7	7	7	7	7	7	7	7	7	7	7	7	7	7
	30	6	6	6	6	6	6	6	6	6	6	6	6	6	6	6	6	6	6	6	6
		5	5	5	5	5	5	5	5	5	5	5	5	5	5	5	5	5	5	5	5
	20	4	4	4	4	4	4	4	4	4	4	4	4	4	4	4	4	4	4	4	4
		3	3	3	3	3	3	3	3	3	3	3	3	3	3	3	3	3	3	3	3
	10	2	2	2	2	2	2	2	2	2	2	2	2	2	2	2	2	2	2	2	2
		1	1	1	1	1	1	1	1	1	1	1	1	1	1	1	1	1	1	1	1
**********	0 %	0	0	0	0	0	0	0	0	0	0	0	0	0	0	0	0	0	0	0	0

Dates: _____

Reviews

Date   Trend/mean   Decision

_____

_____

_____

_____

STANDARD FILL-IN
DATA COLLECTION/GRAPH FORM

Behavior: _____   Name: _____   Mastery: _____

```
100
 90
 80
 70
 60
 50
 40
 30
 20
 10
  0
  %
```

Dates: _____

Date   Trend/mean   Decision
_____
_____
_____
_____
_____
_____

STANDARD EQUAL
INTERVAL GRAPH

Behavior: _____ Student: _____ Mastery: _____

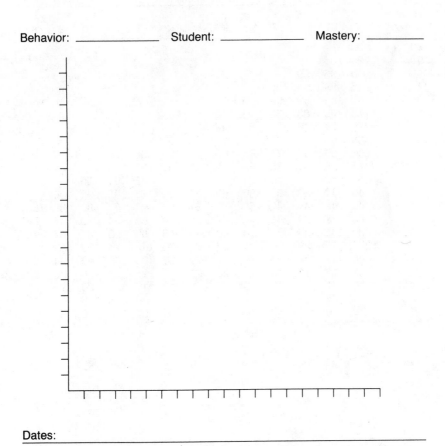

Dates: _____

PERCENTAGE TABLE

Number Total

Number correct	20	19	18	17	16	15	14	13	12	11	10	9	8
20	100												
19	95	100											
18	90	95	100										
17	85	89	94	100									
16	80	84	89	94	100								
15	75	79	83	88	94	100							
14	70	74	78	82	88	93	100						
13	65	68	72	76	81	87	93	100					
12	60	63	67	71	75	80	86	92	100				
11	55	58	61	65	69	73	79	85	92	100			
10	50	53	56	59	63	67	71	77	83	91	100		
9	45	47	50	53	56	60	64	69	75	82	90	100	
8	40	42	44	47	50	53	57	62	67	73	80	89	100
7	35	37	39	41	44	47	50	54	58	64	70	78	88
6	30	32	33	35	38	40	43	46	50	55	60	67	75
5	25	26	28	29	31	33	36	38	42	45	50	56	63
4	20	21	22	24	25	27	29	31	33	36	40	44	50
3	15	16	17	18	19	20	21	23	25	27	30	33	38
2	10	11	11	12	13	13	14	15	17	18	20	22	25
1	5	5	6	6	6	7	7	7	8	9	10	11	13
0	0	0	0	0	0	0	0	0	0	0	0	0	0

REFERENCES

Alavosius, M.P., & Sulzer-Azaroff, B. (1986). The effects of performance feedback on the safety of client lifting and transfer. *Journal of Applied Behavior Analysis, 19*, 261–267.

Adams, G.L. (1984). *Comprehensive Test of Adaptive Behavior.* Columbus, OH: Charles E. Merrill.

Armstrong v. Kline, 476 F. Supp. 583 (E.D. Pa. 1979).

Ayres, A.J. (1981). *Sensory integration and the child.* Los Angeles: Western Psychological Services.

Bailey, D.B. (1984). Effects on lines of progress and semi-logarithmic charts on ratings of charted data. *Journal of Applied Behavior Analysis, 17*, 359–365.

Balthazar, E.E. (1976). *Balthazar Scales of Adaptive Behavior.* Palo Alto, CA: Consulting Psychologist Press.

Bates, P. (1989). Vocational training for persons with profound disabilities. In F. Brown & D.H. Lehr (Eds.), *Persons with profound disabilities: Issues and practices* (pp. 265–293). Baltimore: Paul H. Brookes Publishing Co.

Battle v. Commonwealth, 79-2158, 79-2188-90, 79-2568-70 (3rd Cir., July 18, 1980).

Becker, H., Schur, S., Pavletti-Schelp, M., & Hammer, E. (1986). *Functional Skills Screening Inventory.* Austin, TX: Functional Resources Enterprises.

Bellamy, G.T., Horner, R.H., & Inman, D.P. (1979). *Vocational habilitation of severely retarded adults.* Baltimore: University Park Press.

Bellamy, G.T., Rhodes, L.E., Wilcox, B., Albin, J.M., Mank, D.M., Boles, S.M., Horner, R.H., Collins, M., & Turner, J. (1984). Quality and equality in employment services for adults with severe disabilities. *Journal of The Association for Persons with Severe Handicaps, 9*, 270–277.

Benson, H.A., & Turnbull, A.P. (1986). Approach families from an individualized perspective. In R.H. Horner, L.H. Meyer, & H.D.B. Fredericks (Eds.), *Education of learners with severe handicaps: Exemplary service strategies* (pp. 127–157). Baltimore: Paul H. Brookes Publishing Co.

Bigge, J.L. (1982). *Teaching individuals with physical and multiple disabilities* (2nd ed.). Columbus, OH: Charles E. Merrill.

Bijou, S.W., & Baer, D.M. (1961). *Child development: Vol. II. Universal states of infancy.* New York: Appleton-Century-Crofts.

Billingsley, F.F. (1984). Where are the generalized outcomes? *Journal of The Association for Persons with Severe Handicaps, 9*(3), 186–192.

Billingsley, F.F. (1988). Writing objectives for generalization. In N.G. Haring (Ed.), *Generalization for students with severe handicaps: Strategies and solutions* (pp. 123–128). Seattle: University of Washington Press.

Blankenship, C.S. (1985). Using curriculum-based assessment data to make instructional decisions. *Exceptional Children, 52*(3), 233–238.

Blau, A., Lahey, M., & Oleksiuk-Velez, A. (1984). Planning goals for intervention: Can a language test serve as an alternative to a language sample? *Journal of Childhood Communication Disorders, 7*, 27–37.

Bleck, E.E., & Nagel, D.A. (Eds.). (1975). *Physically handicapped children: A medical atlas for teachers.* New York: Grune & Stratton.

Bloom, L. (1970). *Language development: Form and function in emerging grammars.* Cambridge, MA: MIT Press.

Browder, D. (1987). *Assessment of individuals with severe handicaps: An applied behavior approach to life skills assessment.* Baltimore: Paul H. Brookes Publishing Co.

Browder, D. (1989). Functional skills screening inventory. In J.C. Conoley & J.J. Kramer (Eds.), *Tenth mental measurements yearbook* (pp. 315–317). Lincoln: University of Nebraska Press.

Browder, D., Demchak, M., Heller, M., & King, D. (1989). An in vivo evaluation of the use of data-based rules to guide instructional decisions. *Journal of The Association for Persons with Severe Handicaps, 14,* 234–240.

Browder, D., Hines, C., McCarthy, L.J., & Fees, J. (1984). A treatment package for increasing sight word recognition for use in daily living skills. *Education and Training of the Mentally Retarded, 19,* 191–200.

Browder, D., & Lentz, F.E. (1985). Extended school year services: From litigation to assessment and evaluation. *School Psychology Review, 14,* 188–195.

Browder, D., Lentz, F.E., Knoster, T., & Wilansky, C. (1988). Determining extended school year eligibility: From esoteric to explicit criteria. *Journal of The Association for Persons with Severe Handicaps, 13*(4), 235–243.

Browder, D., Liberty, K., Heller, M., & D'Huyvetters, K. (1986). Self-management by teachers: Improving instructional decision-making. *Professional School Psychology, 1,* 165–175.

Browder, D.M., Morris, W.W., & Snell, M.E. (1981). Using time delay to teach manual signs to a severely retarded student. *Education and Training of the Mentally Retarded, 4,* 252–257.

Browder, D., Shapiro, E., & Ambrogio, B. (1986). Movement training: When self delivered reinforcement is not enough. *International Journal of Rehabilitation Research, 4,* 363–372.

Browder, D., & Snell, M.E. (1987). Functional academics. In M.E. Snell (Ed.), *Systematic instruction of students with moderate and severe handicaps* (pp. 436–438). Columbus, OH: Charles E. Merrill.

Browder, D.M., & Stewart, K.L. (1982). Curriculum development for the severely handicapped student. *Journal of Special Education Technology, 5*(3), 43–52.

Brown, F., Evans, I.M., Weed, K.A., & Owen, V. (1987). Delineating functional compentencies: A component model. *Journal of The Association for Persons with Severe Handicaps, 12,* 117–124.

Brown, K.M., Willis, B.S., & Reid, D.H. (1981). Differential effects of supervisor verbal feedback and feedback plus approval on institutional staff performance. *Journal of Organizational Behavior Management, 3,* 57–68.

Brown, L., Branston, M.B., Hamre-Nietupski, S., Pumpian, I., Certo, N., & Gruenewald, L. (1979). A strategy for developing age appropriate and functional curricular content for severely handicapped adolescents and young adults. *Journal of Special Education, 13,* 81–90.

Brown, L., Branston-McLean, M.B., Baumgart, D., Vincent, L., Falvey, M., & Schroeder, J. (1979). Using the characteristics of current and subsequent least restrictive environments as factors in the development of curricular content for severely handicapped students. *AAESPH Review, 4,* 407–424.

Brown, L., & Leigh, J.E. (1987). *Adaptive Behavior Inventory.* Austin, TX: PRO-ED.

Brown, L., Nietupski, J., & Hamre-Nietupski, S. (1976). Criterion of ultimate functioning. In M.A. Thomas (Ed.), *Hey, don't forget about me!* (pp. 2–15). Reston, VA: Council for Exceptional Children.

Brown, L., Shiraga, B., York, J., Kessler, K., Strohm, B., Rogan, P., Sweet, M., Zanella, K., VanDeventer, P., & Loomis, R. (1984). Integrated work opportunities for adults with severe handicaps: The extended training option. *Journal of The Association for Persons with Severe Handicaps, 9,* 262–269.

Brown, R., Fraser, C., & Bellugi, U. (1964). Explorations in grammar evaluation. In